GEORGE ORWELL

GEORGE ORWELL
INTO THE TWENTY-FIRST CENTURY

EDITED BY

THOMAS CUSHMAN AND JOHN RODDEN

Paradigm Publishers

BOULDER • LONDON

Copyright © 2004 by Paradigm Publishers

Chapter 3, "Hope against Hope: Orwell's Posthumous Novel," copyright © 2004 by Morris Dickstein

Published in the United States by Paradigm Publishers, 3360 Mitchell Lane, Suite E, Boulder, Colorado 80301 USA.

Paradigm Publishers is the trade name of Birkenkamp & Company, LLC, Dean Birkenkamp, President and Publisher.

Library of Congress Cataloging-in-Publication Data

George Orwell : into the twenty-first century / edited by Thomas Cushman and John Rodden.

p. cm.

ISBN 1-59451-002-4 (hardcover : alk. paper) — ISBN 1-59451-003-2 (pbk : alk. paper)

1. Orwell, George, 1903–1950—Criticism and interpretation.   I. Cushman, Thomas, 1959–   II. Rodden, John.

PR6029.R8Z6397 2004

828'.91209—dc22   2004014919

Printed and bound in the United States of America on acid-free paper that meets the standards of the American National Standard for Permanence of Paper for Printed Library Materials.

Designed and Typeset by Straight Creek Bookmakers.

10   09   08   07   06   05
5   4   3   2

Contents

Acknowledgments ix

Introduction: George Orwell into the Twenty-first Century 1
THOMAS CUSHMAN

I. THE USE AND ABUSE OF *NINETEEN EIGHTY-FOUR*

Chapter 1
Abolishing the Orgasm: Orwell and the Politics of Sexual Persecution 23
JONATHAN ROSE

Chapter 2
In Defense of Comrade Psmith: The Orwellian Treatment of Orwell 45
IAN WILLIAMS

Chapter 3
Hope against Hope: Orwell's Posthumous Novel 63
MORRIS DICKSTEIN

II. IDEAS, IDEOLOGIES, AND INTELLECTUALS

Chapter 4
George Orwell and the Liberal Experience of Totalitarianism 77
CHRISTOPHER HITCHENS

Chapter 5
On the Ethics of Admiration—and Detraction 86
JOHN RODDEN

Chapter 6
The Public Intellectual as Connected Critic: George Orwell and Religion 96
RONALD F. THIEMANN

Chapter 7
Orwell, Pacifism, Pacifists   111
LAWRENCE ROSENWALD

Chapter 8
Varieties of Patriotic Experience   126
TODD GITLIN

Chapter 9
Vulgar Nationalism and Insulting Nicknames:
George Orwell's Progressive Reflections on Race   145
ANTHONY STEWART

Chapter 10
Orwell's "Smelly Little Orthodoxies"—and Ours   160
JIM SLEEPER

Chapter 11
Orwell in an Age of Celebrity   178
JONATHAN B. IMBER

III. OF BIOGRAPHY AND AUTOBIOGRAPHY

Chapter 12
Writing about Orwell: A Personal Account   187
PETER STANSKY

Chapter 13
Orwell: Unmasker of Underlying Realities   194
DENNIS WRONG

Chapter 14
Third Thoughts about Orwell?   200
DAPHNE PATAI

IV. LITERARY AND STYLISTIC ISSUES

Chapter 15
Orwell's Perversity: An Approach to the Collected Essays   215
WILLIAM E. CAIN

Chapter 16
Prescience and Resilience in George Orwell's Political Aesthetics   229
LYNETTE HUNTER

Chapter 17
Outside/Inside: Searching for Wigan Pier   243
MARGERY SABIN

Chapter 18
Orwell's Satirical Vision on the Screen: The Film Versions of
Animal Farm *and* Nineteen Eighty-Four   252

ERIKA GOTTLIEB

V. ORWELL ABROAD

Chapter 19
George Orwell: Russia's Tocqueville   267
VLADIMIR SHLAPENTOKH

Chapter 20
May Days in Barcelona: Orwell, Langdon-Davies,
and the Cultural Memory of War   286
MIQUEL BERGA

Chapter 21
From Ingsoc to Capsoc: Perceptions of Orwell in France   295
GILBERT BONIFAS

About the Contributors   312

Acknowledgments

Thomas Cushman wishes to thank Wellesley College, and several of its academic departments, for its enthusiastic financial and technical support for the George Orwell Centenary Conference, which was held May 1–3, 2003. A particular note of thanks is due to the Committee on Lectures and Cultural Events for providing most of the resources for the conference and to the director of special events, Mary Morris. Beyond that, a number of offices and individuals at Wellesley were instrumental in helping to make the conference, and therefore this volume, a success. The broad support of many departments and colleagues at Wellesley is testament to the college's intellectual environment. Special mention and praise is due to Jennifer Redfearn, who helped to organize and execute all of the details of the conference. Also due special thanks is William Cain of the Department of English at Wellesley College who was a persistent and knowledgeable collaborator and supporter. Kevin Alexander assisted in assembling and editing the final drafts of all of the essays and communicating with authors. Finally, I would like to thank John Rodden, who is my intellectual guide on things related to Orwell and much else. As the co-organizer of the Orwell Centenary Conference and coeditor of the volume, John worked closely with all of the authors whose essays appear in this volume, and editorial improvements to the essays are due primarily to his efforts.

The editors enjoy a special and serendipitous intellectual and personal relationship that generated and incubated the idea for the George Orwell Centenary Conference, brought it to realization, and made it possible to produce the present volume. Both of us would concur with Horace: *"Quia natura mutari non potest idcirco verae amicitiae sempiternae sunt"*—Since nature cannot change, true friendships are eternal.

John Rodden expresses his gratitude first to Thomas Cushman, whose intellectual acumen has made our dialogues about Orwell always stimulating—and whose practical expertise in conference organizing made the Orwell symposium the academic highlight of the Orwell centennial year. I consider it my good fate and fortune both to have met Tom in the year 1984 and to count him today as my intellectual (big) brother. Mitch Baranowksi, a former student and longtime friend, also deserves my deep thanks for his brilliant work in directing *Does Orwell Matter?* (the documentary film that emerged from the conference). I am also grateful to Lynn Hayden, a special friend and an inspiring presence throughout the Orwell conference. Lynn helped make the interviews for the film run smoothly in countless small ways. Finally, I too would like to acknowledge William Cain, whose outstanding intellectual contributions and personal generosity played a significant role behind the scenes to assure the success of the Orwell conference.

Introduction

George Orwell into the Twenty-first Century

Thomas Cushman

On May 1 through 3, 2003, Wellesley College hosted the George Orwell Centenary Conference, which was the single largest world event commemorating Orwell's life and work on the hundredth anniversary of his birth. The event featured leading Orwell scholars, writers, and public intellectuals who have been influenced by Orwell's thinking and who engaged Orwell's work as a catalyst for their own thinking on a wide variety of issues. The essays assembled in this volume are a result of this conference and testify to the sustained interest in this most enigmatic of writers and to his enduring influence into the twenty-first century.

There is a curious irony in such a commemorative event. As is well known, Orwell willed that no biography of him should appear after his death, perhaps an entirely unreasonable expectation given his prominence in twentieth-century literary life. The event would probably have been disdained by Orwell himself. One imagines that his desire not to be the subject of a biography or centenary conference might be based on his suspicion of the possibilities of hagiography implicit in such enterprises. To be sure, as several authors in this volume point out, there has been much sanctification of Orwell since his death.

The object of this conference, however, was not to celebrate Orwell, let alone contribute to the ongoing hagiography of "St. George Orwell," although a certain degree of honor is inherent in the centennial celebration of a writer. One does not usually hold centenary conferences for people whom one disdains. The germ of any centenary event is usually a sense of esteem and common recognition of intellectual influence. Centenary events are, in some sense, rituals of solidarity with the dead. However, the intention of our conference, and of the present volume, was not to foster a spirit of uncritical admiration of Orwell. This is something that Orwell would have utterly scorned, since he was aware not only of his own shortcomings and limitations but also those of others. As a result, the essays here reflect a range of thinking about Orwell's life and work and its continuing relevance for understanding society and culture in the new millennium. Central to the volume is the belief that Orwell's observations about the politics and culture of the twentieth century remain as relevant as ever for interpreting the events and complexities of the twenty-first century.

The hundredth anniversary of Orwell's birth caused many people to imagine what Orwell might think about the events that have transpired since his death in 1950. What would Orwell have thought about the Vietnam war, the rise of the United Nations as a force in world politics, September 11, and the war in Iraq? Such imaginings are a normal part of intellectual history, part of which is to make arguments for why a particular thinker from the past remains relevant to the present. For instance, Marxist scholars have considered such phenomena as globalization and the rise of the American empire as events about which Karl Marx would have much to say. But beyond such speculation, we can only say: "Here are Marx's ideas and thoughts about the advent of modernity, *his* modernity, and they provide a very interesting frame of reference for understanding this period of *our* modernity." In Orwell's case, our answer has to be much the same. As Christopher Hitchens, author of *Why Orwell Matters,* noted in his keynote address at the conference, which appears as an essay in this volume, "A thing that I am no longer interested in is the question of whether or not George Orwell would take my view or anyone else's if he was still with us. In 1984, it was actually possible that Orwell could have lived that long. We are now at the point that we are as far from him as he was from Dickens. We have to say goodbye to him as a contemporary and ask why it is, therefore, that he remains so vivid and actual in our own lives."

Hitchens's observation provides the whence and the wherefore of this volume. We might say: "Here are Orwell's ideas. They were the product of a prodigious effort to understand *his* century. How do they continue to provide insights by which we can understand *our* century?" While biographers continue to explore the complexities of the man's life, we recognize that, quite apart from that task, Orwell's ideas have what John Rodden calls an "afterlife." Their pattern of influence cannot be known in any predictable way, nor should they, since Orwell's work is like a tool kit from which we can construct a plethora of interpretive projects. His influence can be detected in a variety of ways in all of the essays in this volume, even for those authors who engage Orwell in a highly critical and even polemical way. The editors of this volume hope that the essays assembled here will serve as examples of a number of pathways from Orwell's work in his own time to our work in our own time—not all possible pathways, of course, but a highly respectable and important sampling. All of the essays indicate that for a range of thinkers and writers, Orwell still matters.

The essays in this volume are grouped in five main sections: 1. The Use and Abuse of *Nineteen Eighty-Four;* 2. Ideas, Ideologies, and Intellectuals; 3. Of Biography and Autobiography; 4. Literary and Stylistic Issues; and 5. Orwell Abroad. There are any number of ways that one might group a collection of essays on Orwell's life and work. One might start by noting that there are a number of different Orwells, but at least three that are most important: the *biographical* Orwell, the *literary* Orwell, and the *sociological* Orwell. Each of these Orwells can be approached quite independently, but they also intersect with one another. The primary approach to Orwell has been biographical and it is this genre that continues to be a prominent one for interpreting his life. Indeed, on the one hundredth anniversary of his birth, three new biographies were issued. Secondary to this has been the focus on the literary Orwell, an approach that is natural given the imprint of his major work, *Nineteen Eighty-Four* (and, to a lesser extent, *Animal Farm*), on the literary imagination of the twentieth century. The third

Orwell, the "sociological Orwell," has received somewhat less attention, at least in a systematic way. By this we mean the Orwell whose work exemplifies the intersection of his own biography and history (what C. Wright Mills referred to as the "sociological imagination"). This is the Orwell who authored his own enduring brand of "sociological nonfiction."

THE USE AND ABUSE OF *NINETEEN EIGHTY-FOUR*

We open the volume with essays on the biographical Orwell by focusing attention on Orwell and his masterwork, *Nineteen Eighty-Four,* because popular consciousness has focused on that work, giving rise to the adjective "Orwellian," the metaphor of "Big Brother," the practice of "thoughtcrimes." Indeed, it is difficult to navigate through contemporary political discourse without encountering these terms. Nonetheless, these are often used with a certain lack of understanding that belies the historical specificity of the terms themselves. The adjective "Orwellian," for instance, is usually used to describe any practice of an opponent with whom one disagrees. Anyone exerting too much power is labeled with the epithet "Big Brother," and those who feel the sting of criticism for their controversial ideas find comfort in seeing their heresies as "thoughtcrimes." Such hyperbole is the inevitable fate of great ideas. In the essays in this section, however, we are reminded that *Nineteen Eighty-Four,* not only as a literary work but also as a sociological blueprint of totalitarianism, still has much to teach us in interpreting our present experience of modernity.

In Jonathan Rose's essay, "Abolishing the Orgasm: Orwell and the Politics of Sexual Persecution," we see how Orwell's work (ironically, given Orwell's own negative and Victorian disposition toward homosexuality) remains relevant for understanding the dynamics of sexual persecution and the various "micrototalitarianisms" that continue to inhabit the crevasses of contemporary cultural life. Rose points out that Orwell was particularly prescient, even before such philosophical gurus as Michel Foucault or Wilhelm Reich, in noting that "sexual repression was the foundation—and not merely a byproduct—of totalitarianism." In this sense, Orwell also anticipates several feminist dystopian writers such as Margaret Atwood, who link the sexual repression of women directly with the exercise of nightmarishly excessive power. Commenting on contemporary affairs, Rose notes that *Nineteen Eighty-Four* is instructive for understanding the "adolescent and tawdry sex scandals of the 1990s" and the more general moral panics regarding sex characteristic of modern times. In this sense, *Nineteen Eighty-Four* continues to be a model for the social analysis of that enduring human phenomenon of "witch hunting," which is still to be found in many quarters of contemporary culture.

Ian Williams's essay in this section follows up in a more specific and autobiographical sense the ways in which Orwell's work illuminated the often vicious authoritarian vicissitudes of British left politics. One of the more interesting facts of Orwell's afterlife is the way in which various groups across the political spectrum have appropriated his ideas for widely divergent causes. This is partially due to the fact that his own thought resisted orthodoxy and in doing so promoted heterodoxy across a wide spectrum of thought. Yet, in his own lifetime, Orwell was never forgiven for his exposures of the left intellectuals who betrayed the promise of democratic socialism by overtly going over to Stalin or remaining indifferent to his nightmarish regime. The response to Orwell is a critical moment in the history of the 1930s motto "No enemies on the left" when those who dared to criticize the left were branded as class traitors, marginalized as "conservatives," or branded as reactionaries. Among his critics at the time, Williams notes, "one finds a deep nostalgia for the Soviet Union and the Third International embedded in much of the criticism of Orwell, even when it is expressed on other, ancillary grounds, whether literary failings, sexism, sadism, homophobia, imperialism, anti-Semitism, and jingoism, all of which sins his enemies have variously found in him." The assault on Orwell has continued to the present day, carried on by various left intellectuals who engage in a process of "reputational entrepreneurship" that aims to discredit Orwell's life and work through ad hominem attacks and by focusing on Orwell's "questionable" political activity, in this case, his infamous "list" in which he noted the communist sympathies of various figures of the day.[1] Williams understands, like Orwell himself, that one can criticize the excesses of one's own side without being blind to other forms of power. One can not, for instance, turn a blind eye toward the gross violations of human rights in Castro's Cuba because one finds fault with George W. Bush's war in Iraq. In Williams's words: "Orwell's work gives us the intellectual tools to understand what is happening and to combat it—without becoming the unthinking, metaphysically minded enemy that polemics can and do make of people."

In "Hope against Hope: Orwell's Posthumous Novel," Morris Dickstein revisits Orwell's masterwork, noting that in Orwell, "the Cold War had found its authentic poet." His essay centers around three important questions: "Should we remember Orwell as a great writer, or simply a timely one? Was his work genuinely prophetic or merely an exaggeration of tendencies he lamented in his own time? What kind of book was *Nineteen Eighty-Four* that readers could connect to it at so many different levels?" Dickstein comes at these questions from a variety of Orwell's works, but he sees Orwell's crystalline vision of totalitarianism as "simple, stark, and unforgettable; this helps explain why Orwell's fable has struck a chord in millions of readers, including many who actually grew up under versions of the system he describes but never actually saw. That so much of the novel has become a permanent part of our thinking and terminology testifies to its power as myth and its cartoonish accuracy." The novel captures the essence of totalitarianism as Orwell perceived it. Dickstein notes that *"Nineteen Eighty-Four* is a flawed novel, but seminal as an act of witness to the most odious features of twentieth-century history, especially the barbarism of the Nazi and Soviet dictatorships, with their cult of personality, their scorn for ordinary standards of truth and decency, to say nothing of their intrinsic violence and contempt for human life." In this age of continuing human rights abuses and the persistence of various forms of fascism, the novel is more relevant than ever.

IDEAS, IDEOLOGIES, AND INTELLECTUALS

One of Orwell's most enduring legacies is his work on the intellectual currents and the intellectuals of his day. At first glance, his writings on the latter are particularly refreshing, especially in the American context in which stark and candid critique in the public sphere—especially within academe—has given way to self-censorship and the sacralization of sensitivity, both of which have severely disrupted the rough-and-tumble vigor of the marketplace of ideas. In this respect, Orwell's writings bring us back to an appreciation of an intellectual life that is not necessarily characterized as a Hobbesian state of "Warre, each-against-all," but of a cultural climate where we can, in Orwell's phrase, "tell people what they do not want to hear." In this, Orwell's perduring lesson is the possibility of promoting intellectual heterodoxy over and against intellectual orthodoxy. To be sure, if Orwell were operating in the present cultural environment, he would be much maligned by the guardians of various contemporary ideological orthodoxies. Christopher Hitchens, for instance, in his essay in this volume, displays a modern-day Orwell-like disposition in his willingness to criticize various leftist intellectuals for what he sees as their abdication of their responsibility to promote liberal internationalism, provide solidarity with the weak, and fight fascism.[2] As happened with Orwell, many of Hitchens's critics have gone into fits of apoplexy over Hitchens's supposed defection from the left in supporting the war in Iraq and have eerily adapted the same practices of vilification that were used on Orwell: ad hominem attacks, banishment from the leftist fold, and accusations of "conservatism," to name just a few. Like Orwell, Hitchens considers it to be quite the opposite case—that many left intellectuals, in opposing the war and the liberation of Iraq, have carved out a new, even conservative, orthodoxy that betrays the cause of liberal internationalism in favor of anti-American shibboleths and, more generally, anti-Western sentiments that have assumed the status of a secular religion among many intellectuals.[3]

In "On the Ethics of Admiration—and Detraction," John Rodden offers some further reflections and extensions on his earlier work on the sociology and politics of literary reputation. As Rodden has noted elsewhere, Orwell's reputation has been claimed by those who seek to use him for the legitimation and sanction of all kinds of divergent political and intellectual programs. Rodden has insistently pointed out in his work that this process has led to a sometimes blind and uncritical fetishism of Orwell and his work. Yet, at the same time, Rodden recognizes that there is a similar process in the cultural politics of reputation that focuses on discrediting Orwell. In either case, whether it be sanctification or vilification, Orwell's posthumous fate reminds us of Voltaire's dictum that "History is a trick we play on the dead." In his essay, Rodden reminds those who would sanctify or scourge Orwell that they ought to consider a number of ethical matters. His essay offers a template that might guide study of the reputation of not only Orwell but also any influential author. At the same time, Rodden, who has authored three books devoted to Orwell's legacy, offers us a poignant idea of what Orwell has meant to him: "The indebtedness is literary and political—but also existential and even spiritual. It has to do with clear writing and plain speaking, with a comradely insistence on holding one's own side to the highest standards. But more importantly, it owes to Orwell's repeated emphasis on—and inspiring enactment of—intellectual integrity. And it has also to do with his clear-sighted recognition of its complexity and its difficulty, of the manifold temptations to succumb to la trahison des clercs."

In his essay "The Public Intellectual as Connected Critic: George Orwell and Religion," theologian Ronald F. Thiemann addresses himself to Orwell and religious ideas. As Thiemann notes, Orwell's attitude toward religion was a mixture of cynicism and hostility. Yet, Orwell managed to understand the importance of a more general spirituality or faith to the secular project of democratic socialism. As Thiemann notes: "The 'religious attitude' that was crucial to the vitality of British culture could only be sustained, he believed, by a form of nonideological socialist practice that would be relevant to the working-class people of England." In this respect, Orwell was similar to other humanist intellectuals for whom modernity had precluded the possibility of traditional religious faith but enabled the possibility of new secular forms of the sacred. In Thiemann's words, Orwell . . . "rejected, once and for all, the belief system of Christianity, [but] he continued firm in the conviction that the most important values represented by Christianity, particularly human decency and a commitment to justice and equality, must be incorporated into the form of ethical socialism he so fervently advocated." Orwell's spiritual encounter with socialism not only explains the stark pathos of his works but also provides an explanation of Orwell's sometimes fierce critiques of his socialist comrades who seemed to him to be betraying socialism's higher principles. For Thiemann, Orwell represents a model of "the connected critic," who manages to resist the pulls and perils of politics through a constant mindfulness and reflection on higher, sacred, humanist ideals.

In "Orwell, Pacifism, Pacifists," Lawrence Rosenwald offers a comprehensive overview and critique of Orwell's views about pacifism and antiwar activism. Orwell was perhaps more cantankerous on this issue than any other. Orwell's relation to pacifism is somewhat complex. In his earlier stages, he was quite avowedly pacifist, thinking, like other leftists of his generation, that nation-states were the root of war and aggression and that democratic socialism had to resist these forces with all of their might. Orwell's "inversion" on the issue occurred during World War II, when Orwell subjected pacifists and pacifism to scathing and often demeaning attacks. For Orwell, war required one to choose between lesser evils. In his view, pacifists, in arguing against British involvement in the war, were appeasing fascism and, thus, in his view, were "objectively pro-fascist." He even went so far as to accuse certain British pacifists of secretly hoping for German victory and felt that they were treasonous in doing so. Rosenwald, who is a pacifist of a rather fundamental sort, provides what is perhaps the best extant elaboration and critique of Orwell's thinking on pacifism. Rosenwald reminds us that Orwell's view of pacifism was perhaps caricaturish and failed to capture the variety and complexity—and moral courage—of pacifism as a historical movement. More importantly, given the theme of the present volume, Rosenwald cautions against a reaction against pacifism in relation to the War on Terror, the war in Afghanistan, or the war in Iraq. It is all too simple, Rosenwald argues, to stop at the pragmatic assertion that pacifists were aiding and abetting Saddam Hussein by opposing the war. A more complex view would consider the vision of pacifism as a position of strong moral principle, which, ironically, articulates its own spiritual vision and commitment in terms that are just as strong as Orwell's own vision of and commitment to democratic socialism. Rosenwald's essay is a fine example of how one might approach Orwell's thinking from a rather critical standpoint to reflect on contemporary philosophical and political issues.

Todd Gitlin's essay, "Varieties of Patriotic Experience," offers a primary historical document which serves as an example of how Orwell's work has influenced the biography and views of the public intellectual, especially in light of the attack on America that occurred on September 11, 2001. In addition to providing a living model of what might be called a "left patriot" (in the sense of a radical who is also a patriot), Gitlin provides a model of what might be called "the flexible intellectual." The flexible intellectual is one who, like Orwell, remains connected to a core of central ideas and values but allows himself to reflect, rethink, and criticize in response to ongoing historical events. In the process, his transformations might lead him in a direction that his ideological compatriots might find reprehensible, but conscience, rather than conformity, is the flexible intellectual's guiding impulse. Some of the most prominent left intellectuals used the events of September 11 to hoist old battle flags and revivify firmly entrenched ideological canards about such things as the evils of Western and American imperialism and capitalism, the disasters of American foreign policy, and the like. Gitlin, an important figure in the history of leftist thought in America, has had a long history of articulating some of those critiques. But by virtue of his closeness to the events of 9/11, and his reflection on their significance, Gitlin reexamines his own sense of patriotism, or love of country, in light of his central identity as an activist and critic of the actions of various governments in U.S. history. Gitlin, like Orwell, finds a way to maintain a sense of patriotism as a form of dissent and critique, but also understands how the latter, as ends in and of themselves, can threaten the sense of commitment to a core set of liberal-democratic values that must be defended against intolerance and fundamentalism. Orwell became patriotic during World War II, understanding patriotism as a defensive stance against the threat of fascism. He did this without abandoning his critiques of British politics or conservative policies that threatened his view of democratic socialism. For Orwell, the practical consequences of history—in his case, the threat of fascism—had to be integrated with commitment to a set of loftier and abstract ideals. In the face of fascist threat, there was a necessity to choose sides against fascism. And, most importantly, this had to be done without turning toward blind support of governmental policies. Gitlin provides a model of how one can balance a legitimate sense of commitment to "constitutional patriotism" and to the values of liberal democracy without abdicating the responsibility of the intellectual to hold his or her own government to the highest standards of truth and democracy.

Anthony Stewart's essay, "Vulgar Nationalisms and Insulting Nicknames: George Orwell's Progressive Reflections on Race," explores Orwell's contributions to the enduring problems of race relations in the modern world. Over the past twenty years, race has become one of the most visible and conflict-producing issues, especially in North America. Stewart revisits Orwell's thinking on race without the usual dismissals of such thinking via references to some of Orwell's less progressive pronouncements on the subject (which are often cited to discredit him more generally). There is little value in ignoring or failing to criticize some of Orwell's obvious prejudices. In some sense, as with other matters, he exhibited a sort of reckless temerity about expressing views—on not only race but also many issues— that many people of the time surely thought but would not put to paper. More often than not, though, these thoughts have been part of the arsenal of ad hominem strategies used to discredit his thinking more generally. Yet, as Stewart shows, Orwell's writings reflect serious thinking about race and about imperialism more generally. Orwell's formative years in Burma left him with a lifelong disgust with imperialism and its program of racial domination, and he recognized with remarkable prescience that racism would continue to be an independent and volatile factor in world politics. Stewart notes the following passage from Orwell's 1939 essay "Marrakech": "But there is one thought which every white man (and in this connection it doesn't matter twopence if he calls himself a Socialist) thinks when he sees a black army marching past. 'How much longer can we go on kidding these people? How long before they turn their guns in the other direction?'" Stewart notes as well Orwell's critical views on British racial politics that were expressed in his 1939 essay "Not Counting Niggers," which, reflecting the current culture of political correctness, was republished in Peter Davison's masterful collection without the all-important title. Stewart's essay calls us to reconsider Orwell's reflections on race as an important contribution to ongoing discourse about race and racial conflict.

Jim Sleeper reflects on Orwell's struggles with ideological conformity, in general, and of editors, especially those on the left, who maintained a tense and often repressive relationship to him. Orwell was one of the most important English-language authors of the twentieth century, and his difficulties with literary gate-keepers is, indeed, ironic, if not immediately understandable, to the sociologist of ideology. One of the signature stories that crystallizes such struggles involves Orwell's relationship with his publisher Victor Gollancz, the founder of The Left Book Club, who was so affrighted by Orwell's honest exposé of sham socialist intellectuals in *The Road to Wigan Pier* that he felt compelled to write a rejoinder to it in the introduction to the book. Sleeper outlines in some detail the self-censorship that is characteristic of orthodox intellectual communities and extends some of his observations to the interpretation of his own literary career. Sleeper's own writings, including *The Closest of Strangers* and, perhaps more so, *Liberal Racism,* seem indebted to Orwell's example of "telling people things they don't want to hear" and challenge the conventional wisdoms of one's "own side." Sleeper offers some lucid observations based on a lifetime of observing failed liberal policies toward the disadvantaged, which he sees, ironically, as conservative. He writes: "Although racism and capitalist exploitation are real, some of what passes for antiracism and anticapitalism among otherwise-intelligent, progressive political chroniclers and activists is unreal because it is self-referential enough to do subtle but corrosive harm to the dignity of intended beneficiaries through the articulation of a common destiny." Sleeper's own biography and critical disposition offer a modern-day example of how Orwell's intellectual spirit might be maintained in the analysis of contemporary culture, albeit with some consequences for the author. Sleeper notes Ivan Turgenev's lament: "The honest man will end by having to live alone."

Finally in this section, Jonathan Imber, in his essay "Orwell in an Age of Celebrity," notes that Orwell remains salient for us today as a model of cultural criticism that has more or less been discredited in an age where infatuation with celebrity and form, rather than with substance, increasingly characterizes modern culture. Orwell was, if anything, an iconoclast and was always willing to attack and criticize famous and saintly figures. In his essay "Reflections on Gandhi," for instance, Orwell dared to challenge the uncritical veneration of the Mahatma, noting that "Saints must be judged guilty before being proved innocent." He was able in that essay, and in all his work, to provide balanced assessments of saintly figures, both acknowledging their virtues and pointing out their failings.

In this vein, Imber addresses Orwell's essay "Benefit of Clergy: Some Notes on Salvador Dali." Imber notes that, in addressing Dali as an artistic celebrity, Orwell "identified a dilemma of modernity in which the achievement of notice—or what today is called celebrity—is more important than who or what is noticed." He notes that Dali was a prototype of someone who manipulated the modern cult of celebrity to his distinct advantage, thus rendering artistic reputation more a matter of persona than consideration of material cultural products. Orwell's essay remains a perfect example of what would be nearly impossible to find in most contemporary art history: moral judgments about aesthetic creations. Orwell pulled no punches and declared that Dali was a "disgusting human being," but beyond that he wonders why Dali became so popular. In some ways, ironically, Orwell did to Dali what many have tried to do to Orwell himself, and that fact bears remembering. Ultimately, though, Orwell's essay offers an interesting sociological hypothesis about the course of artistic production and consumption in the modern age. In the last lines of his essay, Orwell writes

> One would still like to know why Dali's leaning was towards necrophilia (and not, say, homosexuality), and why the *rentiers* and the aristocrats would buy his pictures instead of hunting and making love like their grandfathers. Mere moral disapproval does not get one any further. But neither ought one to pretend, in the name of "detachment," that such pictures as "Mannequin rotting in a taxicab" are morally neutral. They are diseased and disgusting, and any investigation ought to start out from that fact.

This is hard-hitting criticism, but, as Imber notes, instructive for reminding us that cultural or artistic criticism does not have to sanitize itself against moral judgments. Indeed, in a culture which is systematically degraded by mindless and substance-free celebrity, Orwell provides a moral compass for navigation and the restoration of the respectability of considering art's relation to moral issues.

OF BIOGRAPHY AND AUTOBIOGRAPHY

Peter Stansky, Orwell's first biographer, takes the occasion of Orwell's Centenary to reflect not so much on Orwell himself but on the process and politics of writing biography. In his essay, "Writing about Orwell: A Personal Account," Stansky outlines his path to becoming an Orwell biographer and some of obstacles that he and his colleague, William Abrahams, encountered along the way. One of the most significant of these was Orwell's opportunistic widow, Sonia Orwell, who blocked Stansky and Abrahams from using the Orwell archive and quoting material from Orwell's unpublished writings. Nonetheless, Stansky believes that this was not ultimately a disadvantage, since it forced him and his colleague to analyze information instead of relying too much on quotes, which is often a problem among biographers. Stansky's essay reminds us that the outcome of any effort at biography is a highly contingent one and offers in his essay a fascinating "biography of biography."

In his essay, "Orwell: Unmasker of Underlying Realities," Dennis Wrong provides a different kind of reflection that tracks the ways in which Orwell's life and oeuvre intersected with his own. Wrong's essay suggests a close affiliation between Orwell's raison d'être and that of the sociologist. Wrong read many of Orwell's works when they were first published and testifies to their relevance in the context in which they were written. Wrong sees Orwell as a writer who "combined qualities of performance and of morality [that] account for the unique appeal that has instantly struck so many readers: the sense that here was a writer who, in the later idiom of the 1960s, was truly 'telling it like it is' without any hype, pretension, self-serving apologetics, or even literary adornment."

In the year 1984 (appropriately enough), Daphne Patai published *The Orwell Mystique: A Study in Male Ideology.* This book established Patai as a prominent critic of Orwell's work and was the first full-length feminist analysis of Orwell. In her essay for this volume, "Third Thoughts about Orwell?" Patai reflects on Orwell twenty years after the publication of her book, based on her experiences with "postmodernist rhetoric" and her "disillusionment with the role of feminism in teaching and research." In spite of her feminist critique of Orwell, Patai displays a remarkable Orwell-like sensibility in her willingness to challenge academic feminist orthodoxies that she sees as a fundamental threat to academic freedom. Her view that Orwell was basically a misogynist has not changed, and she also finds fault with Orwell's attraction to war and idealized masculinity, romanticization of working-class men, and repugnance toward homosexuality (among other things). She also sees Orwell as "self-righteous and judgmental. He had a marked preference for coercive discourse—that is to say, sweeping assertions and generalizations that tended to ward off criticisms by the sheer certainty with which they were declared. . . ." Yet Patai also recognizes, in light of her negative experiences with the stultifying realities of academic feminism, that her own book represented an indulgence "in a dogmatic or quasi-religious statement rather than one based on evidence. . . . I let my feminist politics dictate the results of my analysis." Her present essay also focuses on how Orwell "continues to be used for the sake of political slam dunks (or efforts at these), regardless of the inappropriateness of the particular cause in which his name is being invoked." In this respect, it is perhaps useful to read her critique in tandem with the more general work of John Rodden, who discussed these issues at length in his *Politics of Literary Reputation* and revisits them in his essay in the present volume. Patai's essay reminds us of the dangers of sacralization of reputation and calls us to "see the warts, the contradictions, as well as the strengths of this restless character." One imagines that this is quite how Orwell himself would have proceeded if he were, in 2003, writing about Orwell.

Yet, Patai's essay brings up the issue of how Orwell's personal imperfections ought to influence our appraisal of his work. Orwell suffered various types of personal attacks in his own lifetime, and these continued on after his death. One of the most prevalent attacks raises the issue of his notorious "List," in which he listed his observations, including personal and ad hominem comments about the political reliability of his opponents. Timothy Garton Ash has offered a most recent refutation of such attempts to discredit Orwell.[4] But the effort to discredit continues, in both sincere and disingenuous forms. One example of a tendentious account of Orwell can be seen in a recent examination of Orwell by Louis Menand in *The New Yorker.*[5]

Menand understands Orwell's contribution but seeks to paint him, ultimately, as a flawed thinker. It seems that Menand's real motive was to counter some of the trends in resacralization of reputation that always attend centennial years, but he also engages in a kind of reverse process of "reputational entrepreneurship" that is meant to diminish Orwell's reputation more generally. In order to paint Orwell in the worst possible light, he examines Orwell's supposed relation to Gandhi and Hitler as evidenced in Orwell's writings about these men. He takes a sacred figure like Gandhi and he insinuates that Orwell was trying to malign him. Menand notes that Orwell thought of Gandhi as something of a charlatan, but he leaves out key information from the essay. Orwell notes specifically that "[Gandhi's] character was an extraordinarily mixed one, where there is nothing in it that you can put your finger on and call bad and I believe that even Gandhi's worst enemies would admit that he was an interesting and unusual man who enriched the world by simply being alive." To write an essay on Orwell's views on Gandhi and not include this view can only be seen as a tendentious effort to malign Orwell.

Menand then pulls the "Hitler card," which is perhaps the ultimate tactic of intellectual discreditation. Of all Orwell's critical writings against Hitler—and these appear constantly in his work—Menand quotes only the following passage from Orwell's review of *Mein Kampf:* "I've never been able to dislike Hitler." The next line in the essay, however, a line of which Menand is surely aware but intentionally does not quote, is as follows: "Ever since he came to power—till then, like nearly everyone, I had been deceived into thinking he did not matter—I have reflected that I would certainly kill him if I could get within reach of him, but that I could feel no personal animosity."[6] One cannot possibly read, even in a shallow way, Orwell's writings and get a sense of anything other than the fact that Orwell loathed Hitler with all of his might.

Menand's article is just a recent example of ongoing attempts to selectively quote from Orwell in order to stress his flaws rather than his virtues. In her essay in this volume, as well as in her original book, Daphne Patai holds fast to the idea that Orwell was a misogynist. Patai's contribution to this volume is useful since she reminds us that it ought not to be an occasion for intellectuals to engage in what Orwell himself referred to as the "mutual arse licking" so prevalent among intellectuals. Yet at the same time, attaching a highly charged negative label to a thinker is perhaps not the best way to "desanctify" what has acquired an overly sanctified reputation. All of the participants in this volume are in agreement that Orwell had some serious flaws and some highly problematic views. Yet to focus only on these is to move too far in the other direction, the direction of demonization rather than sanctification, to say nothing of begging the important question: what is the relationship between an individual's personal faults and the quality or relevance of their work? As a teacher in the ideologically orthodox world of academia, I have become sensitized to the use of this strategy of ad hominem attack as a way of discrediting opponents or having to avoid rational engagement with their arguments. If you are a white person—no matter what your general political orientation—and you make a public criticism of a person of color, you can almost always expect to be called a racist. Jim Sleeper's experiences in this regard, noted at length in his contribution to the present volume, are confirming. Similarly, men who attack women, or specifically feminist arguments, can also expect to have their argument attributed to their gender or to some presumed sexist attitude rather than assessed in relation to some mutually shared canon of logic or criticism.

As a teacher at a college for women, I have often thought about what exactly the term "misogynist" means. For me, it simply means the hatred of women. There is a rather stark difference, though, between misogyny and sexism: the two might be fundamentally related, the one leading directly to the other. Or they may not be. There are such things as sexists who are not misogynists, and Orwell was an example of such a person. Thomas Jefferson was a racist, but not a hater of Africans. His practices in relation to them were based on a deeply flawed and essentialist idea—quite common at the time—that Africans were inferior to whites. This does not discredit his entire opus, but it does call on us to rethink the ways in which social and cultural conditions caused one of the most powerful thinkers in American history to make fundamental and perhaps tragic errors in considering matters of race. There is much evidence, both in his writings and in archival sources, that indicate that Orwell held some sexist views. In this regard, he was not too dissimilar to most people of his time. So why can we not acknowledge this sexism, ask ourselves how it might have limited his perspective, and keep these issues in mind as we consider his work, without tagging him with the label "hater of women"?

In light of these observations, it is important as well to consider how other various types of negative judgments circulate as symbolic frames of reference that people use in their interpretations of Orwell. Prior to the George Orwell Centenary Conference, John Rodden, co-organizer of the conference and coeditor of this volume, appeared on a local National Public Radio call-in radio talk show called "The Connection." I was in the studio during the program and sat next to the person who was fielding calls from the public. With some exasperation, the person asked me if I could assist her in determining the quality of the questions that were to be aired and addressed by Rodden and the host. From my perch as the unwillingly seconded guardian of the public airwaves, I was amazed to see the number of callers who wanted to challenge Orwell on his supposed personal views and characteristics rather than any specific points about his work. One caller wanted to ask why Orwell was so pro-Hitler during World War II. Of course, Orwell was vehemently anti-Hitler, but that had really no relevance to the genesis of the question, which was most likely based on a negative slogan grabbed from the universe of commentary on Orwell and that the caller had internalized as the "reality" of George Orwell. Further proposed questions came in through the teleprompter: what about Orwell's anti-Semitism, his racist views, his sexism, and so on? This was a fairly interesting "cultural moment" for me as a sociologist of modern culture, because I realized that a good deal of public perception of Orwell was based on ideological slogans that circulate through the cultural environment rather than close readings of his texts. I make this extended point mainly to stress that the ethics of literary reception, and what John Rodden calls in his essay in this volume "the ethics of admiration," are severely challenged by what might be called "argument by epithet," which seeks to reduce a complex figure to one character flaw and adjudicate the value of his or her entire oeuvre on that basis alone.

And what of the relation between the different Orwells? What bearing does the biographical Orwell, with all of his flaws, have on the literary or sociological Orwell? This is an important question for intellectual history. I attempt to answer it by thinking not about Orwell, but, strangely enough, about Socrates. Recently, while reading Plato, I came to wonder: what was Socrates like at home? One never gets even a glimpse of his home life, his relations with his children or his wife. One starts to suspect that, given his omnipresence in the agora, he was most likely a neglectful spouse and father, concerned more about ethereal issues than mundane ones. So, in dialogue with my own philosopher-friend Nicolas de Warren, I raised the question of Socrates' personal characteristics and their bearing on his work. My colleague answered, tersely, "well, it doesn't matter." The quality and importance of the text has very little to do with his private life, unless, of course, one wants to make the case that it does, and that is a difficult case to make. I raised the same query to my literary colleague Lawrence Rosenwald, whose essay on Orwell appears in this volume, and he noted, quite wisely (the quote is loose): "if you're modeling your life after someone, it is a good idea to know what he or she is like." He noted that it is good to know, for instance, that Thoreau ate at the Emersons' three nights a week. I take this to mean that it is good to know that Thoreau, as a result of this, was probably greatly inspired by the sage of Concord. This is a view you might take if you *like* Thoreau. But if you have an axe to grind with him, you could just as easily come to the conclusion that, by eating at the Emersons' three nights per week, he showed himself to be a freeloader. The label you choose will depend, more generally, on your own relation to those to whom you apply it.

Another interesting case would be Karl Marx. He was one of the most influential of modern thinkers, yet his biographers have pointed out a lot of negative things about him. He was a lousy father and husband, a terrible provider, and an adulterer. He was vicious and mean-spirited, and racist as well, as one can readily see by looking at his correspondence with Friedrich Engels. So how you relate to Marx's past depends fundamentally on what one is trying to *do* with or *to* Marx in the present. If you are a Marxist, your argument is probably going to run something like: "Well, it's the thought and influence that is important and which serves as a model for interpreting the problems of today." If you are a conservative or a defender of capitalism, you are likely to bring Marx's flaws into relief in order to discredit his ideas. And so it is with interpreters of Orwell: you can deduce a great deal about the politics of an intellectual by looking at how he or she chooses to talk about Orwell and his flaws. It would be interesting, incidentally, to compare the views on Marx and Orwell of those leftists who have sought to discredit Orwell based on personal aspects of his life. John Rodden's contribution to this volume outlines a series of ethical considerations that can serve as a template not only for the moral adjudication of Orwell, but of any writer whose life and work are being examined through the lens of the present.

The Literary Orwell

The literary Orwell is, perhaps one of the most prominent of Orwell's various personae. For the most part, there is a general recognition among literary scholars that Orwell's novels were not "great" novels, and even Orwell seems to have shared this view in his own judgments of his work. His reputation as an exemplary writer of English prose seems to come mainly from his creative nonfiction, first published in his *Collected Essays, Journalism, and Letters* (1968), edited by Sonia Orwell and Ian Angus. In his essay in this volume, literary scholar William E. Cain turns to Orwell's essays in order to reconsider the source of his power as a writer and our abiding interest in his work. Cain's answer is highly original: he sees in Orwell's writings a certain "perversity" that is characterized by a provocative and sharp ironical style that relies on a "bracing unexpectedness" and "persistently oppositional and contradictory turns of his thinking." Cain extracts from Orwell's works examples of this perversity that demonstrate Orwell's particular power as a writer. It is precisely this perverse style that was both a source of attraction to Orwell and a source of criticism from his detractors. Orwell's often deriding tone and caustic irony did not always play well in his time, especially to those who fell under his guns. Nor do they always play well to modern audiences, many of whom have let sensitivity and self-esteem replace the sharp critical edge that is so vital to the free-marketplace of ideas and perhaps to the definition of sublime writing itself. Cain's innovative concept of perversity might also be used to understand the styles of other provocative authors and their continuing attraction to those who understand that sublimity in writing often entails offering unexpected twists and turns.

In her essay, "Prescience and Resilience in George Orwell's Political Aesthetics," Lynette Hunter examines Orwell as a voice of the less fortunate. She notes that Orwell himself anticipated modern theoretical debates about the problem of how intellectuals speak about the lives and experiences of people who are situated outside of both the intellectual classes and other formal hierarchies of power and privilege. Hunter notes that Orwell was a prescient observer of what modern literary theorists refer to as "situated textuality," which understands the limitations of how writers can represent the experiences of others and otherness. Orwell was keenly aware of the ways in which modern culture excluded the voices of the dispossessed, and much of his work sought to give voice to the voiceless. Indeed, an enduring aspect of his work lies in its example of the intellectual as a class intermediary and a representation of the intellectual as a progressive voice for those who are part of yet outside of modernity.

In her essay on Orwell's *The Road to Wigan Pier,* Margery Sabin reexamines Orwell's famous reportage as an exemplum of Orwell's ability to "break through ordinary oblivion" and unearth the social unconscious. She notes Orwell's capacity to move inside social life and lay bare the stark realities of Depression-era England. His ability to "get inside" the life of the lower classes, however, was always affected by his own awareness that he was an outsider, in his own words, thoroughgoingly middle class. By calling attention to his outsider status, Orwell showed himself to be a master of reflexivity, constantly aware of his own presence as observer even while trying to offer an inside view of the subjectivities of the underclass. This self-awareness as observer shows Orwell to be something of an anthropologist: discussions of "insider-outsider" questions have dominated that field throughout its history. Sabin notes the "special power of Orwell's writing to move the reader outside his own preoccupations at the same time as he insists on the ways that full access into other worlds is inevitably limited by what you cannot help but bring to them." Her essay reminds us of the contemporary benefit of rereading Orwell's work, which, in her words, "teaches us to approach the 'ordinary' world equipped with never fewer than two minds." This is a lesson that has continuing relevance to the interpretation of modern culture.

In the last essay in this section, Erika Gottlieb provides an analysis of the transmutations of Orwell's masterworks, *Animal Farm* and *Nineteen Eighty-Four,* as they were adapted in successive film versions after his death. In the case of *Animal Farm,* she notes that the early animated version of the film, made in 1955, more or less captured the original context of Orwell's novel, while the 1999 film version failed to capture the original context of Orwell's novel, which was to provide a political allegory debunking the Soviet myth. In the later film, especially, the key element of satire—which was, in her opinion, the very essence of the novel—was lost. Gottlieb then examines successive film versions of *Nineteen Eighty-Four,* both in comparison to the novel and to each other. She raises some very important questions about verisimilitude, or the extent to which the films capture the "reality" of Orwell's works. She understands that in this "postmodern" world, both filmmakers and viewers may have little hope of bringing a sophisticated understanding of the historical context of Orwell's works to bear on their interpretation. This makes it all the more important (especially for teachers of Orwell's work) to provide an understanding of such context and to view the film versions of Orwell's work in relation to the works in their original literary forms.

ORWELL ABROAD

Orwell's reputation diffused not merely across the lines of political parties and ideologies but across geographical and linguistic lines as well. Riding the wave of the rapid developments and globalization of mass media in the last half of the twentieth century, Orwell's works have received worldwide attention. An adequate consideration of the global importance of Orwell's work would require several volumes. In this section, three cases are examined that show the important influence of Orwell's work in Russia, Spain, and France.

Orwell's relationship to the Soviet Union is central to understanding his entire oeuvre. Indeed, it is perhaps the driving force of his opus more generally, as is evident in *Nineteen Eighty-Four* and *Animal Farm* as well as in his collected essays. In his essay, "George Orwell: Russia's Tocqueville," noted Russian sociologist Vladimir Shlapentokh provides us with an indispensable overview of Orwell's "career" in the Soviet Union. He notes, quite accurately, that "Orwell's place in history is linked more to my native Russia than to any other country besides England." The experience with Orwell of those who lived under Soviet Communism is important, since it involved the transformation of Orwell from a mere observer of totalitarianism to a kind of "prophet" through which people living under Soviet totalitarianism could crystallize and understand their own experiences. If Orwell was revolutionary in any sense, it was in providing a model to the Soviet people of a cognitive awareness that was central to challenging Soviet domination, either collectively in the form of active political dissidence or in the more common practice of "internal emigration," the process of private subjective rebellion, à la Winston Smith, against the hand of Big Brother. Shlapentokh marvels, as others have, about Orwell's brilliant dissection of the nature of totalitarianism, made not by constant visits and ethnographic observation but from the inertia of his deathbed. Shlapentokh's account offers us some appreciation of the awe and wonder of Soviet citizens as they read *Nineteen Eighty-Four,* not as a literary allusion but as an anthropological account of their everyday lives. Shlapentokh notes his own engagement with Orwell as an intellectual in fascinating detail and with wry and sardonic insight. He describes his difficulties in securing copics of *Nineteen Eighty-Four* and *Animal Farm* from the "Spezkhran," the notorious special department of the library where the most dangerous books were kept:

"According to legend, had I been clever enough I might have gotten access to *Animal Farm* if I had asked for it from the agricultural section of Lenin's library, where it had supposedly been hidden until the censors discovered it." For Shlapentokh:

> Orwell not only was the first in the West who understood the essential elements of totalitarian society but also stands up today against the thousands of researchers of totalitarian society, now fifty years after his death, and still sounds like a fresh voice. This is especially true with respect to the legion of scholars, so-called revisionists, who with their open or hidden hatred of capitalism and their attempts to embellish the Soviet system, attacked the concept of totalitarianism in the 1970s and early 1980s under the specious pretext that this concept "simplifies" the complexity of the totalitarian society and ignores the social life within it.

While many commentators ignored Orwell's observations, perhaps intentionally and perhaps because they wrote it off as literature rather than sociology, Shlapentokh notes Orwell's prescience in describing what, for many, is an impossibility: the love of Big Brother in Soviet-type societies. In spite of the recognition of domination, many Soviet citizens not only capitulated but also participated in the maintenance of the system by rendering their affections toward their masters. This point is made quite clear in *Nineteen Eighty-Four,* and Shlapentokh confirms it with interesting autobiographical details of his own life under such a regime. Such love, the ultimate form of what Erich Fromm described as the "escape from freedom" characteristic of modernity, was underestimated not only by Western observers but also by Orwell himself.

Nowhere is Orwell more relevant than in Spain during the period of the Spanish Civil War. Orwell's engagement in the war is perhaps one of the most poignant periods of his life and is captured as such in the pages of *Homage to Catalonia.* For Orwell, engagement in the war was the apotheosis of his political practice, the event that proved, above all, that his beliefs and values were, at base, oriented toward *practice.* In reading *Homage to Catalonia,* one searches for a definitive explanation for why this sickly intellectual undertook the arduous task of becoming a soldier in the fight against fascism. The nearest we can get is one line in which he says: "At the time, I did not see what else one could do." This simplistic explanation is perhaps an anachronistic display of the older model of the intellectual, one that has been lost in the comfort of bourgeois modernity: that one's thought is inextricably tied to action. If you advocate a particular theoretical or political view of the world, you are obligated to engage in action toward realizing your view. One can hardly imagine intellectuals these days taking such positions, for instance, those who advocated the defense of Bosnian Muslims taking up arms against their Serbian oppressors or those who resist American imperialism (even from their enclaves in America) taking up arms against it.

In his essay, "May Days in Barcelona: Orwell, Langdon-Davies, and the Cultural Memory of War," Miquel Berga discusses Orwell and the cultural memory of the Spanish Civil War. For the Western historical consciousness, Orwell is central to understanding this event: without his English-language testimonial to the war, the Spanish Civil War quite likely would have disappeared, perhaps unknown and unappreciated, into the vortex of twentieth-century conflicts and proxy wars. As Berga notes, "If Orwell's capacities as a fighter had had a very minor impact on the outcome of the war, his abilities as a skilled writer played, in the long run, a most important role in shaping our cultural memory of that war." Berga offers a fascinating glimpse of how the drama of Western responses to the Spanish Civil War were played out, in situ, between Orwell and John Langdon-Davies, a communist sympathizer who was in Spain at the same time as Orwell. In Berga's view, Langdon-Davies represents the kind of intellectual who, despite fluency in Catalan and a bird's-eye view of events in Barcelona, nonetheless, came to disdain the anarcho-syndicalist forces in favor of the emergent Communist Party (PSUC) that took its marching orders from Stalin. Langdon-Davies came to see the former as chaotic and unorganized, representative of "anarchist disorder" and unable to to accept "communist discipline" (as dictated by Moscow). In keeping with this view, he also saw Orwell as an interloper who was a dangerous impediment to the success of the communist revolution in Spain. Berga notes Langdon-Davies's own words: "Orwell's *Homage to Catalonia* . . . gives an honest picture of the sort of mentality that toys with revolutionary romanticism but shies violently at revolutionary discipline. It should be read as a warning." Ultimately, the fascists triumphed over both the anarchists and the communists: Langdon-Davies was forgotten as a Stalinist lackey, and Orwell was celebrated, after the demise of Franco, as a hero to the Spanish people. In 1998, the mayor of Barcelona ceremoniously named a square "Plaza Orwell." Berga notes, in an ironic fashion that would have pleased Orwell, that the same plaza is also the site where inconspicuous cameras meant to provide surveillance of public activities were installed by municipal authorities. Politics is base, Orwell endures.

In the volume's last essay, Gilbert Bonifas outlines the history of Orwell's reception in France, with particular emphasis on Orwell's continuing relevance to French debates about modernity. Orwell's entrance into French intellectual life came relatively late and this probably had much to do with the hegemony of left-wing intellectuals, many of whom were attracted to the USSR and hostile to Western capitalism and, especially, the United States. It is perhaps the case that Orwell was shunned by French intellectuals for daring to expose the Stalinist political myths that were the basis of their very existence. Ultimately, the attraction to the USSR waned and Orwell's work received much favorable attention in France, especially in liberal circles. Bonifas notes the influence of Orwell on one thinker in particular: Jean-Claude Michéa, who has emerged as a stark critic of globalization and "overmodernity." For thinkers such as Michéa, Orwell provides a model for unpacking the perils not only of Soviet-style totalitarianism, which appears in *Nineteen Eighty-Four* as Ingsoc, but also of the destructive juggernaut of capitalist modernity, or what might be called Capsoc. Bonifas notes: "After the fall of the Berlin Wall and the demise of communism, liberalism began to behave like any other ideology. It, too, could now afford to claim that it embodied absolute principles and display a Manichean vision of the world, a messianic will to reshape society according to its dogmas." For many French critics of the march of neoliberalism, Orwell remains starkly relevant.

SOME FINAL THOUGHTS ON ORWELL

Since the orienting principle of this volume is that there are three Orwells—the biographical, the literary, and the sociological—and since I am a sociologist, it behooves me to say something about Orwell as a sociologist. I have found it useful to consider Orwell as a kind of "lay theorist" of modernity. What I mean by this is that I can induce from his writings a crystalline set of conceptual observations that help me to understand the structural contours of modernity as well as the general nature of subjectivity in modern industrial society. Margery Sabin's excellent essay in this volume looks at Orwell as a kind of ethnographic observer, an anthropologist of everyday life whose writings have the character of detailed ethnography and a heightened sense of reflexivity. I do not mean to insinuate that Orwell was a theorist of modernity in the sense that Karl Marx or Max Weber or Émile Durkheim were; indeed, it might be a kind of slight to label Orwell as any kind of theorist, since he was generally hostile to the jargon of theory and never saw himself as a part of any academic tradition. But like Marx, Weber, and Durkheim, his life was devoted to chronicling and interpreting modern industrial society, especially its underside.

By theorist, I mean it in the sense that we think of Marx as a theorist when he says "The history of all hitherto existing societies is the history of class struggle." By theory, I mean thought that crystallizes a number of empirical observations made across a span of time or space into a simple idea or concept. Orwell was a kind of "aphoristic" theoretician, whose insights are distilled from across a broad range of observations and his theoretical statements are made in poignant, or as William Cain terms it, perverse ways: "Intellectuals flock to the idea of progress like blue-bottles to a dead cat" or "Pacifism is objectively pro-fascist" are examples of Orwell's kind of aphoristic theorizing. Vladimir Shlapentokh's essay on Orwell shows that Orwell was able to offer an interpretive vision of Soviet society that made the lives of Soviets intelligible to themselves, and that is precisely what theorists ought to do. Margery Sabin shows us that Orwell's *The Road to Wigan Pier* is a kind of theory of the underclass. But more than that, *The Road to Wigan Pier* calls attention to the fact that modern civilization depends fundamentally on unseen labor that is purposely hidden as part of the price of bourgeois comfort. In that book we also see an extended critique of mechanization, which resonates remarkably with other more high-minded philosophical accounts of modernity rendered in more abstract terms by Martin Heidegger, Theodor Adorno, and others.

Of course Orwell did not engage with the latter, but he does offer a vision of modernity in which several classes of victims of modernity can see themselves. Consider, for instance, Orwell's passage from *The Road to Wigan Pier* in which he describes his encounter with a woman whom he encounters in an industrial slum and who is cleaning out a drainpipe. Orwell's description of his experience provides us with a model of what it means for an author to engage intersubjectively with social suffering. In this sense, Orwell was a master of comprehension of not only political realities but also the various subjectivities of modernity: the suffering but stoic worker, the bourgeois intellectual attracted to false ideology, and the victims of British imperialism, Nazi fascism, and Stalinist communism.

What does it mean to comprehend? Hannah Arendt notes that

> Comprehension does not mean denying the outrageous, to do something unprecedented from precedence or explaining phenomena by such analogies and generalities that the impact of reality and the shock of experience are no longer felt. It means rather examining and bearing consciously the burden, which our century has

placed on us. Neither denying its existence nor submitting meekly to its weight. Comprehension in short means the unpremeditated, attentive, facing up to and resisting of reality. Whatever it may be.[7]

By Arendt's definition, we can view Orwell as "a great comprehender." Not *the* "Great Comprehender." Not the "Big Comprehender." Just a great comprehender, whose insights remain valuable for understanding the modern world. Those who argue that invoking Orwell is an excuse for not thinking for oneself are wrong. Of course this may be true in some cases, but for me, invoking him as an intellectual guide is no different than invoking Marx, or Weber, or George Simmel to understand some complex aspect of social reality in a new light: we don't let them do the thinking for us, but we are guided by their thoughts, and we stand on their shoulders for a clearer view when we need to and step down when they are not necessary. When I read Orwell, I realize that he has uncovered structures of social life that exist across time and place and that is what sociologists look for. So something that Orwell observed and crystallized remains important for understanding something that I encounter fifty years later, long after he is gone. Consider this quote from Orwell: "To be anti-American now a days is to shout with the mob. Of course it is only a minor mob but it is a vocal one. Politico-literary intellectuals are not usually frightened of mass opinion. What they are frightened of is the prevailing opinion within their own group. At any given moment, there's always orthodoxy, a parrot-cry, which must be repeated. And in the more active section of the left, the orthodoxy of the moment is anti-Americanism."[8] You can read this quote today and it sounds like it was written *precisely* for the purpose of understanding the behavior of many modern intellectuals over the last few years, from the terror attacks on America on September 11 up through the present-day war in Iraq. This quote describes a good segment of the modern intellectual class, particularly on the left, which Christopher Hitchens discusses in his essay here and has discussed elsewhere, and it helps us to understand the persistence of anti-American orthodoxy and the ways in which that orthodoxy is connected more deeply to apologetics for and appeasement of Islamo-fascism. Orwell was a critic and a sociologist of ideology.

Orwell's great ability was to be able to capture the pathos and absurdity of the modern world. As with others who have done this, the experience made Orwell a profoundly sad man. During the centenary conference, Orwell biographer Michael Shelden mentioned that there are very few pictures of Orwell smiling. He could, of course, have been a nonsmiler who was happy. But there seems to be an essentially dour quality to the man. My sense is that Orwell was a tragic figure whose own soul was deeply inflected with the tragedies of modernity. In a philosophical or anthropological sense, he had a keen perception of the vulnerability of human beings. He was really perceptive about human vulnerability and frailty. When he writes about people, he seems to capture their frailty in ways that very few people in his time were able to do, especially bourgeois socialist intellectuals whose socialism was mainly self-serving rather than directed toward working people. Sometimes his perversity and bitter sardonic style keeps us from understanding his empathy, but there is no getting around the fact that it is there. The word *vulnerable* comes from the word *vulnerate,* which is a transitive verb. It takes a direct object. To vulnerate means to wound somebody. The word vulnerable means "able to be wounded." It seems to me that Orwell's life is a progression that shows him to be wounded in a profoundly existential way and, in response, wounding the world back. That cycle of vulnerability and attack, and its seeming indication of a mind in conflict, is something that perhaps Orwell is a model of, but one that is rather common in human beings who live enmeshed in the ambiguities of modernity.

There can be no last word on Orwell so long as people return to his thought for guidance in their own intellectual journeys, as the authors in this volume have. In this sense, Orwell has the last word. But in considering last words, I have often wondered what Orwell's last words were. He died, perhaps appropriately, alone, so we will never know. In the last volume of his *Collected Essays,* we find the last line that Orwell wrote in his notebooks. So perhaps, given that we have no extant recording of his voice, and since we only know him now from his writings, we can take these lines as his last words. Orwell wrote: "At fifty everyone has the face he deserves."

NOTES

1. The most recent and balanced discussion of this list and its significance (or lack thereof) can be found in Timothy Garton Ash, "Orwell's List," *New York Review of Books* 50, no. 14 (September 25, 2003).

2. For examples of this, and how Hitchens has dealt with it, see his essay in this volume as well as Christopher Hitchens, *Long Short War: The Postponed Liberation of Iraq* (New York: Plume, 2003).

3. For a further critique in this vein, see Ian Buruma, "Wielding the Moral Club," *Financial Times,* September 13, 2003, 26.

4. Ash, "Orwell's List."

5. Louis Menand, "Honest, Decent, Wrong: The Invention of George Orwell," *The New Yorker,* January 27, 2003, 84.

6. Review of *Mein Kampf, The Collected Essays, Journalism and Letters of George Orwell,* vol. 2, 1940–1943, ed. Sonia Orwell and Ian Angus (New York: Harcourt, Brace and Jovanovich, 1968), 13.

7. Hannah Arendt, *The Origins of Totalitarianism* (San Diego: Harcourt, Brace and Jovanovich, 1979), viii.

8. Quoted in Norman Podhoretz, "If Orwell Were Alive Today," in *The Norman Podhoretz Reader: A Selection of His Writings from the 1950s to the 1990s* (New York: Free Press, 2004).

I

The Use and Abuse of
Nineteen Eighty-Four

1

Abolishing the Orgasm: Orwell and the Politics of Sexual Persecution

Jonathan Rose

I remember the day at school when I looked up from my desk and was shocked to see my classmates verbally tormenting our teacher. It was the eighth grade, and they had decided that the teacher was a homosexual. The school was actually a highly progressive institution in Greenwich Village, and the faculty were exceptionally tolerant on this score. But the Stonewall affair was still a few years in the future, so our teacher was (in the eyes of his students) fair game.

If you ask, Did I defend him? the answer is yes, up to a point, ineffectually. But I was certainly not a premature activist for gay liberation. At that age, I had no clear idea what a heterosexual was, let alone a homosexual. I was appalled, yet utterly innocent of the issues involved. My classmates' behavior was incomprehensible and, therefore, all the more frightening. What I felt was the horror you feel when you see a mob tear a human being apart for no good reason. The term was not current at the time, but I had witnessed my first "outing"—and it's a filthy business, whoever does it.

This classroom drama took place around the time I first read *Nineteen Eighty-Four.* There is a connection between the two, though I didn't see it until I sat down to write this essay. Then it struck me that the novel might have been written as a subtle but devastating indictment of the persecution of homosexuals. Perhaps it was, like *Animal Farm,* an allegory—only this time, an allegory in which heterosexuals are hunted down just as homosexuals were in the 1940s. In *Nineteen Eighty-Four* the regime mercilessly and equally punishes both homosexuality and "normal intercourse practiced for its own sake" (*NEF* 251–52).[1] In fact there is no linguistic difference between the two in everyday Newspeak, no distinctive terms for homosexual and nonprocreative heterosexual intercourse: both are subsumed under the word *sexcrime.* Like homosexuals in 1949, Winston and Julia dare not indulge in any public displays of affection, and they are apprehended by entrapment.[2] The torture sessions in Room 101 resemble all too closely the electroshock treatments then used to "cure" homosexuals. Hilary Spurling recently suggested that Orwell found a model for the Winston-Julia affair in a review of Roger Peyrefitte's novel *Les Amitiés particulières,* published by Sonia Brownell in the

July 1946 issue of *Horizon*. The novel deals with a passionate friendship between two boys at a Catholic boarding school, and Sonia (who loathed her convent school) excoriated the priests who treated such liaisons as subversive. "Two children who love each other create a world they cannot enter," she bitterly wrote, "and their whole object is to control, utterly, every thought and feeling. Friendship must be healthy, i.e. boring, or it must be stamped out."[3]

At this point you may protest that Orwell was hardly a premature activist for gay rights. Wasn't he fond of sneering nastily at "nancy poets"? He certainly was, and those slurs do him no credit. Nor can we retreat to the excuse that he simply shared in the biases of his time. In fact, fairly liberal attitudes toward homosexuality prevailed in the leftist circles in which Orwell moved, as he once complained in a bit of doggerel:

> . . . where's the pink that would have thought it odd of me
> To write a shelf of books in praise of sodomy? (*CW* 15:143)

What can and should be said is that Orwell eloquently and perceptively defended homosexuals more often than he snorted at them. Surely we have come to realize that he was a complicated man who often contradicted himself, frequently changed his mind, and sometimes changed it back again. He had the soul of an anarchist trapped in the body of an imperial policeman. And as he once observed (in the context of anti-Semitism), bigotry can only be fully understood "by people who know that they are not immune to that kind of emotion" (*CW* 17:70). That is a recurring pattern in his ideological development: he began with a full complement of public-school prejudices, but once he saw the downtrodden of the earth as individual victims, his sympathies shifted radically. No agent of the British Empire ever wrote as effective an indictment of imperialism as "A Hanging," devastating in its simplicity. Orwell's early novels are sprinkled with anti-Jewish remarks, but once Hitler's persecutions gained momentum, he decisively repudiated anti-Semitism and publicized early reports of the Holocaust (*CW* 14:234, 245–46, 271). You can certainly find a barrack room misogyny in his writings, but Orwell also recommended *A Room of One's Own* to male readers (*CW* 17:238) and affirmed that "women are the equals of men in everything except physical strength" (*CW* 16:271). Rosemary of *Keep the Aspidistra Flying* is a feminist and the only wholly likeable character Orwell ever created (far more sympathetic than the feminists in Virginia Woolf's fiction). *A Clergyman's Daughter* exposed schools that kept girls sexually ignorant, the plight of female homelessness, and the oppression of housework (back when housework was really oppressive). It is, for all practical purposes, a feminist novel—and, as I will show later, not the only feminist novel that Orwell wrote.

Orwell himself had an answer for critics today who charge him with various forms of bigotry. "Of course all these nationalistic prejudices are ridiculous," he granted, but they only become inexcusable when they are directed against people who are truly victimized. Therefore it was unfair to label T. S. Eliot anti-Jewish:

> Of course you can find what would now [1948] be called antisemitic remarks in his early work, but who didn't say such things at that time? One has to draw a distinction between what was said before and what after 1934. . . . In the early twenties, Eliot's antisemitic remarks were about on a par with the automatic sneer one casts at Anglo-Indian colonels in boarding houses. On the other hand if they had been

written after the persecutions began they would have meant something quite different. Look for instance at the Anglophobia in the USA, which is shared even by
people like Edmund Wilson. It doesn't matter, because we are not being persecuted.
But if 6 million Englishmen had recently been killed in gas vans, I imagine I should
feel insecure if I even saw a joke in a French comic paper about Englishwomen's
teeth sticking out. (*CW* 19:461)

You may not accept that as an excuse, but it does explain Orwell's stance
toward homosexuality, which swung back and forth between contempt and genuine sympathy. In August 1937 he called Stephen Spender a "pansy" (*CW* 11:67),
but in short order he apologized ("I've often said rude things about him in print
etc") and invited Spender to his home at Aylesford (*CW* 11:100, 130–33, 146).
Orwell's hostility toward homosexuals surfaced when he saw them as members of
privileged literary cliques—but when they were arrested, he was on their side. You
see that ambivalence in a November 1943 radio talk on *Lady Windermere's Fan,*
where he first dismisses Oscar Wilde's "rather cheap witticisms" but then condemns the society that persecuted him (*CW* 15:337). While composing *Nineteen
Eighty-Four* he read with interest Hesketh Pearson's biography, "especially the
part about Wilde's time in prison. . . . I should like to read a more detailed account
of the two trials," he remarked. "I've always been very pro-Wilde," insisted Orwell
(*CW* 19:157–58), who, as a libertarian socialist, could not help but admire *The
Soul of Man under Socialism* (*CW* 19:333–34). His list of books read in 1949
included *De Profundis,* H. Montgomery Hyde's *Trials of Oscar Wilde,* and George
Woodcock's *The Paradox of Oscar Wilde* (*CW* 20:221–22). While awaiting the
publication of *Nineteen Eighty-Four* he observed: "In 1895, when Oscar Wilde was
jailed, it must have needed very considerable moral courage to defend homosexuality" (*CW* 20:75). Is it far-fetched to suggest that Wilde's ordeal was, to some
extent, the model for Winston Smith's?

How did Orwell come to be a foul-weather friend of homosexuals? Michael
Shelden suggests that he had a crush on at least one other boy at Eton.[4] Well, who
didn't? You could attend an English public school without passing through a homosexual phase, but you could not graduate without learning a lot about the
homosexual condition. Schoolboy romances and mutual masturbation sessions
periodically provoked severe disciplinary crackdowns: the original model for the
Anti-Sex League is crashingly obvious. Orwell grew up in a world where everyone, it seemed, was "systematically warping your sex life," regardless of your
orientation (*CW* 12:540). In 1940 he favorably reviewed Stephen Spender's *The
Backward Son,* an autobiographical novel that undoubtedly was a source of inspiration for "Such, Such Were the Joys." Trapped in a cheap boarding school that
strikingly resembles St. Cyprian's, Spender's protagonist "lies awake at night
worrying about . . . the sexual desires which he believes . . . to be peculiar to him
alone" (*CW* 12:163–64). By now Orwell was identifying closely with the man he
had once dismissed as a "pansy."

And with good reason. Orwell recognized that boarding school was the only
experience of a totalitarian society that the English middle classes ever knew, and
it hardly needs pointing out that St. Cyprian's offered a model for *Nineteen Eighty-
Four.* The headmaster's wife gave Orwell one of his first brushes with censorship,
when she punished him and Cyril Connolly for reading Compton Mackenzie's
Sinister Street—a novel that portrays, among other things, homosexuality at Oxford

(*CW* 11:254, 19:336–37). When he was about twelve a more general panic over homosexuality blew up at St. Cyprian's. "There were summonses, interrogations, confessions, flogging, repentances"—as in *Nineteen Eighty-Four.* There were even torture sessions: "One of the ringleaders, a boy named Cross, was flogged, according to eyewitnesses, for a quarter of an hour continuously before being expelled. His yells rang through the house. But we were all implicated, more or less, or felt ourselves to be implicated. Guilt seemed to hang in the air like a pall of smoke." An assistant master harangued the boys about abusing "the Temple of Body," specifically singling out young Eric Blair: "And you, whom I'd always believed to be quite a decent person after your fashion—you, I hear, are one of the very worst." In fact Eric had done nothing, nor was he ever cross-examined or punished. Nevertheless "a feeling of doom descended upon me. So I was guilty too. I too had done the dreadful thing, whatever it was, that wrecked you for life, body and soul, and ended in suicide or the lunatic asylum."

Some months later Blair saw Cross in the street, and remarkably the outcast "looked completely normal. He was a strongly-built, rather good-looking boy with black hair. I immediately noticed that he looked rather better than when I had last seen him—his complexion, previously rather pale, was pinker—and that he did not seem embarrassed at meeting us. Apparently he was not ashamed. . . ." And apparently one could commit homosexual acts in school and still be perfectly normal, though Orwell only drew that conclusion many years later. At the time he was still willing to report a suspected homosexual to one of the masters: "I did not know very well what homosexuality was, but I knew that it happened and was bad, and that this was one of the contexts in which it was proper to sneak." The master called him "a good fellow," which made Eric "feel horribly ashamed" (*CW* 19:372–75). Eric Blair, then, betrayed a schoolmate just as Winston Smith would betray Julia. There is a difference of sexual orientation here, but no moral difference. Though Orwell was not a homosexual, he had been treated as one. In *Nineteen Eighty-Four* he would work out the guilt, resentment, and anger he felt in connection with the condition of homosexuals, with whom he had a common bond. After all, at St. Cyprian's as in Oceania, homosexuals and heterosexuals are equally persecuted: Cross would have been flogged and expelled all the same if he had been caught with a girl.

Orwell significantly defended a homosexual in the very first work he published as a professional author. "La Censure en Angleterre" (Censorship in England) appeared in a French paper, *Le Monde,* on October 6, 1928 (*CW* 10:117–19). The article generally condemns "that strange English Puritanism, which has no objection to dirt, but which fears sexuality and detests beauty," and it calls for the complete abolition of moral censorship. But the immediate inspiration for this polemic was Radclyffe Hall, whose lesbian novel *The Well of Loneliness,* printed by a Paris-based publisher, had just been impounded by British customs on grounds of obscenity. (Orwell would again defend the novel in 1947, when he was writing *Nineteen Eighty-Four* [*CW* 19:47].)

In his 1928 article, Orwell made several critical points about puritanism. First, it was "illogical," wildly inconsistent, and anything but pure. Bernard Shaw's *Mrs. Warren's Profession,* a serious and unsensational play about a former prostitute, was banned by the Lord Chamberlain, but salacious comedies were permitted, while "prostitution is just as widespread in England as it is elsewhere." Orwell fully understood that sexual mores are socially constructed: "Why is the sense of decency so different at different times and with different people?" And he recognized that the history of sexuality, like the history of politics, was not an inexorable Whiggish advance toward ever greater freedom and enlightenment; both were always capable of reeling backward into repression. The lusty Elizabethans and Jacobeans had given way to a harsh but brief interval of Puritanism, followed by the coarse era of Sterne and Smollett. Then, in the nineteenth century, industrialization "brought the puritan merchants and factory-owners back into power" and, with them, a "sudden growth in prudery." By 1928 the intellectual classes at least had "returned spiritually to the eighteenth century; neither Smollett nor Rabelais shocks them any longer." But in *Nineteen Eighty-Four* the Ingsoc Revolution has put the puritans in the saddle once again. The Party apparently claims Oliver Cromwell as its ideological forefather: his statue stands off Victory Square (*NEF* 95). (The actual statue is of Charles I: it has been either replaced or renamed.) Orwell once compared Cromwell to Stalin (*CW* 17:342–43) and more broadly characterized the Lord Protector as the "prototype of all the modern dictators, who perpetrated massacres which make the German exploits at Lidice look like a schoolgirls' romp" (*CW* 16:168).

Still more revealing is an incident Orwell described in August 1931, when he was investigating tramping among hop-pickers. He recorded in his diary one tramp's account of what would now be called a gay bashing. Orwell devoted less than a paragraph to it, but in that short space he developed a persuasive theory of the anthropology of sexual persecution. That is, he answered the question that confronted me in the eighth grade: Why do people attack other people who engage in unconventional but harmless sexual activities? Orwell reported that a group of tramps in Trafalgar Square "had discovered one of their number to be a 'Poof', or Nancy Boy. Whereupon they had instantly fallen upon him, robbed him of 12/6d, which was all he had, and spent it on themselves. Evidently they thought it quite fair to rob him, as he was a Nancy Boy."

Orwell's sympathies here are obvious. He finds the tramps' behavior "revolting . . . disgusting." They are, he concludes, motivated first of all by economics (*CW* 10:218). Michel Foucault concluded that Marxism could not explain the persecution of homosexuals, since they were not an economically exploited class. But of course homosexuals can be exploited economically, either through blackmail or, in this case, a simple mugging. As Orwell later wrote, every form of Puritanism has "a clear though unconscious economic motive behind it." Nineteenth-century manufacturers knew that "if you could persuade the working man that every kind of recreation was sinful, you could get more work out of him for less money" (*CW* 16:207).

Thus we define homosexuals as perverts because we can then brutalize them and take away their property. The difficulty is that there are not enough homosexuals to make this a very profitable business. If we want to enjoy absolute power, we have to think in larger terms. We must find a way to persecute not just homosexuals but anyone we choose. In *Nineteen Eighty-Four,* the Party achieves that by extending the definition of sexual perversion beyond homosexuality to include all sexual activity whatsoever, with the exception of "normal intercourse between man and wife, for the sole purpose of begetting children, and without physical pleasure on the part of the woman" (*NEF* 252). Everything else is *sexcrime,* a label the

Party can stick on anyone it wishes to eliminate. In Oceania's periodic show trials, ideological deviationists are accused of all kinds of unbelievable crimes, but there is one common denominator throughout: without exception, all purge victims confess to sexcrime (*NEF* 57). Political repression is based on the same primitive instinct to persecute sexual heretics that Orwell observed among hop-pickers many years earlier. If a tramp is a Nancy Boy, other tramps have the right to rough him up and take his spare change. If you commit sexcrime, the Party has the right to send you to Room 101 and monopolize the means of production.

For Orwell, the connection between political and sexual repression gelled in a May 1940 review of *My Life: The Autobiography of Havelock Ellis* (*CW* 12:154–56). The pioneering sexologist, he noted, was married to a lesbian: "It was one of those queer marriages that were possible at a time when Socialism, vegetarianism, New Thought, feminism, homespun garments and the wearing of beads were all vaguely interconnected." You may detect an echo in that last sentence: it sounds like his famous sneer, in *The Road to Wigan Pier,* "that the mere words 'Socialism' and 'Communism' draw towards them with magnetic force every fruit-juice drinker, nudist, sandal-wearer, sex-maniac, Quaker, 'Nature Cure' quack, pacifist and feminist in England."[5] And now, four years later, you expect him to ridicule the Ellises in similar terms. But no, not this time: remarkably, Orwell has nothing but respect and admiration for them. "In every line that Havelock Ellis wrote . . . you can see what he was after: a sane, clean, friendly world, without fear and without injustice."

That may surprise us, because we are so used to picturing Orwell as a critic of the left intelligentsia. So he was, up to a point—but he was also very much a part of that intelligentsia, and he absorbed a host of radical political and sexual ideas from that milieu. He applauds Ellis's dispassionate and tolerant treatment of all forms of sexual expression, his "inability to regard anything as absurd or indecent. . . . This brings up the subject of abnormalities. But what is normality?—a question that would hardly trouble any commonplace mind." That question has been posed by every gay rights activist, and it should be double-underlined for the benefit of anyone who assumes that Orwell was unremittingly hostile to homosexuals. In fact he condemned the 1898 prosecution of Ellis's *Sexual Inversion,* which made the revolutionary argument that homosexuality should be treated not as a sin, crime, or disease but, rather, as a normally occurring variation in sexual behavior, which in some cases (Michelangelo, Marlowe, Wilde) could be a source of exceptional artistic talent.

Happily, Orwell concluded, today Ellis's works can be found on the shelves of public libraries: "So progress persists—or at any rate, it was persisting till recently." Orwell could not help noting that on the day Ellis died, "the Germans were in Prague." The contrast could not have been more stark. Ellis belonged to "a type now becoming extinct, the completely rational, completely civilised man." Precisely because he practiced sexual freedom, he was profoundly peaceful: "Probably it would be impossible for him to strike a blow, utter an insult, or even score a cheap repartee." And on the other hand, the Nazis were rampaging across Europe, making war not love. The conclusion was inescapable: far ahead of Foucault, without reading Wilhelm Reich, and well before he read Yevgeny Zamyatin, Orwell grasped that sexual repression was the foundation of totalitarianism, and sexual freedom the key to political liberation. Here was the germ of the theory that would be worked out in detail in *Nineteen Eighty-Four.*

Literally from the beginning to the end of his professional literary career, he consistently denounced moral censorship, whether the victim was Radclyffe Hall, James Joyce, Baudelaire (*CW* 10:320–21), Henry Miller (*CW* 10:404–5), Salvador Dali, or even rubbishy American horror comics (*CW* 18:523–54). He defended the right to print four-letter words (*CW* 18:511–12), he found a healthy irreverence in dirty jokes (see "The Art of Donald McGill"), and when he hired a nurse for his son Richard, his first order of the day was "You must let him play with his thingummy."[6]

Sexual freedom is no less fundamental to female emancipation. That point is boldly illustrated in *Nineteen Eighty-Four* by Julia, a woman with a fine disregard for gender boundaries. She enjoys doing a traditionally male job, servicing an industrial electrical motor. She is a living symbol of a woman's right to erotic gratification, her right to take the sexual initiative, her right to speak "the kind of words that you saw chalked up in dripping alleyways" (*NEF* 102), even her right to enjoy men as sexual objects. In the novel's only intentionally funny passage, Winston seeks reassurance that Julia is interested only in his somewhat decrepit body: "You like doing this? I don't mean simply me; I mean the thing in itself?" "I adore it" (*NEF* 105). When Erica Jong published *Fear of Flying* in 1973, Henry Miller and John Updike were impressed to no end that a woman could bonk men at random and write raunchy fiction, as if this were something shockingly new. But Orwell had been there twenty-four years earlier. He knew that if women put their minds to it, they were perfectly capable of writing pornography: the dirty book department at the Ministry of Truth has (except for a male boss) an all-female staff (*NEF* 109). Some radical feminist critics complain that male novelists are too fond of phallic imagery and demand equal time for vulvular imagery. But here again, Orwell was far ahead of Judy Chicago; he practically hits you over the head with the symbolism of that bit of pink coral embedded in glass. That's why I'm puzzled when I hear Margaret Atwood's *The Handmaid's Tale* described as "a feminist *Nineteen Eighty-Four*." *Nineteen Eighty-Four* is a feminist *Nineteen Eighty-Four*.

Granted, when I argue that *Nineteen Eighty-Four* is a kind of allegory for gay liberation, I am stretching a point to make a point. It would be more exact to say that the novel is a broad endorsement of erotic freedom and that its logic inevitably leads to toleration of homosexuals. Orwell seems to be pointing toward the conclusion that sex becomes a perversion only when it is used to harm another human being, and especially when it is used as a political weapon. That principle is as relevant today as it was in 1949—but to fully understand that relevance, we must retrace the historical steps that brought us from there to here.

Right on cue, just when *Nineteen Eighty-Four* was published, sex was deployed as a political weapon, with devastating effect. The McCarthyite witch hunts, then getting underway in the United States, targeted gays as well as communists, who were often conflated in the minds of red-baiters. "You can't hardly separate homosexuals from subversives," barked one senator, and the Reverend Billy Graham denounced "the pinks, the lavenders, and the reds who have sought refuge beneath the wings of the American Eagle." A 1953 executive order banned all homosexuals from the federal civil service.[7]

But a few years later, as the McCarthyite hysteria began to recede, there was a parallel revulsion against gay-baiting as well, which seemed to leave a rancid taste in everyone's mouth. When Walter Jenkins was arrested for homosexual conduct in the closing days of the 1964 presidential campaign, the incident did no real damage to his boss, Lyndon Johnson. It is significant that Barry Goldwater, no less anticommunist than Joe McCarthy, declined to use the Jenkins scandal against Johnson. In fact, until the 1990s, the use of any kind of sex scandal—gay or straight—as a political weapon was beyond the pale. Of course, if a Wilbur Mills went out of his way to make a conspicuous ass of himself over a woman, he had only himself to blame. The Gary Hart–Donna Rice affair of 1987 raised disturbing questions about the conduct of the media, who seemed to be going out of *their* way to dig up dirt, but to my knowledge no rival politician used this issue against Hart. In the 1988 presidential campaign Donna Brazile, a deputy field operator for Michael Dukakis, accused George Bush of adultery and was quite deservedly fired by Dukakis, one of those rare politicians endowed with what George Orwell called "decency." Though it was under some stress, the healthy taboo against political scandalmongering seemed to be holding.

And then the Anita Hill–Clarence Thomas scandal broke. Now, if you are sick of hearing about that sorry episode, good: that's a sign of mental health. Rest assured that I will not bore you with the question of whether Clarence Thomas did what he was accused of having done. But I will say something that is long overdue: *It doesn't matter.* No adult with a sane attitude toward sex would care either way. Any adult with a sane attitude toward sex would have dismissed Anita Hill's charges as absurdly trivial. She accused Thomas of nothing more than asking her out on dates, telling naughty jokes, and discussing dirty movies. As my wife told me, she didn't get it either: she had often asked me out on dates, told me naughty jokes, and discussed dirty movies with me. In the 1980s sophisticated single urban professionals spent quite a lot of company time asking each other out on dates, telling naughty jokes, and discussing dirty movies. Perhaps Justice Thomas is fond of pornography; at any rate, I hope he is. Every man ought to have a hobby, and as he must rule on questions of obscenity, we can't fault him for doing his homework. Moreover, we must repudiate any double standard regarding pornography: as Anaïs Nin, Erica Jong, and *The Story of O* should have taught us, girls like it too.

So even if Clarence Thomas did everything he was accused of doing, he clearly has no reason to be ashamed of that.[8] On the other hand, Anita Hill's conduct in this affair was disgraceful—even if she told the truth. If that is not immediately apparent, let me draw an analogy that should make the moral issues clear.

Imagine that I am a federal employee, working with a supervisor who is gay. He is, however, in the closet, because if his sex life became public knowledge, his career would be finished. But he befriends me, he trusts me, and when we are alone together in the office, he reveals that side of himself. He reveals it in the off-color jokes he tells and in his critical dissections of blue movies. I do gently suggest that I'm not entirely comfortable with this line of discussion, but with a devil-may-care, I-am-what-I-am attitude, he goes right on talking. He even suggests that we go out together. I decline those invitations, but there is no retaliation of any kind. Quite the contrary; when I leave government service for academia, my supervisor writes me a glowing letter of recommendation.

Some years later, my former supervisor is up for promotion to a very high government post. He is about to be confirmed when, at the eleventh hour, I go public. I expose him. I out him. I reveal things that were meant to be private. I don't lie: everything I say about him is true. But my motive is to destroy him—personally and professionally.

If I did that, what would you think of me? What if, on top of all this, I tried to elicit sympathy by portraying myself as the victim? You would consider my behavior beneath contempt. Well, I have just told you the story of Anita Hill, following her version of events.[9] Only one insignificant detail has been changed. In fact the Hill–Thomas affair exposed a glaring hypocrisy at the very heart of the concept of "sexual harassment." According to Thomas's attackers, if a man describes a smutty film to a grown woman in private, neither intending nor doing her any harm, that man is a monster who must be stopped at any cost. But if the woman then goes on national daytime television, when children are watching, and repeats that conversation, with all the salacious details, with the intent of ending the man's career, then that woman is a heroine and a model for emulation. It takes a special kind of doublethink to believe all that.

At the time, it was sickening to watch the Thomas–Hill hearings, where the high serious business of confirming a Supreme Court justice was transformed into a solemn pornographic farce. Surely, I thought, such a degrading spectacle was unprecedented. And then it gradually dawned on me that this was all too familiar. I had seen it all back in the eighth grade. Someone who might have indulged in some unconventional but harmless sexual behavior was now being exposed as a "deviant," and that was the signal to tear him to pieces. Back then, I learned that transgressing sexual norms can incite the most irrational hatreds, and now many feminists were openly proclaiming that Clarence Thomas had aroused in them profound feelings of hate (though they generally preferred the term "rage"). This was not about sexual harassment: even if Anita Hill told the truth, she had not been harassed in any meaningful sense of the term. This was an outing, the moral equivalent of the old McCarthyite gay-bashing. Since Senator McCarthy drank himself to death, politicians had generally been loathe to stoop to such tactics. But Anita Hill and her supporters once again legitimized the use of sex as a weapon of political destruction. And it's a filthy business, whoever does it.

The consequences for American politics were, as we now know, disastrous. Today, when we have to deal with real issues of war and terrorism, we can see how adolescent and tawdry the sex scandals of the 1990s were. Once one party launched these weapons, it was inevitable that the other party would retaliate in kind—and as a lifelong registered Democrat, I am ashamed to say that my party began this mudslinging contest. The individual responsibility is clear. No Anita Hill, no Paula Jones. No Nina Totenberg, no Monica Lewinsky. If you condemn Kenneth Starr, you must equally condemn Pat Schroeder, because he was playing the game according to her rules. As Jeffrey Rosen shows, "The subpoenas issued by Starr were perfectly legal," the inevitable outcome of the sexual harassment laws that feminists and Democrats had generally supported. The fault is not in Starr, but in ourselves.[10]

The sexual harassment hysteria was part of a larger moral panic that gripped the United States in the 1980s and 1990s, a panic that manifested itself in several related witch hunts. Fantastic charges of sexual abuse were lodged against daycare workers. Psychotherapists convinced thousands of suggestible patients that they had been sexually molested by their parents; if they remembered nothing of these incidents, then they were clearly victims of "Repressed Memory Syndrome." An astonishing number of Americans have persuaded themselves that they were sexually used by satanic cults or space aliens, and they can become indignant and abusive if you suggest that it was all a nightmare.[11]

This sexual hysteria is, in its paranoid psychology and its destructiveness, comparable to McCarthyism, Prohibition, and the "white slavery" panic of the early twentieth century. (The last of these involved the widespread belief that thousands of young women were being kidnapped and forced into prostitution. The alleged perpetrators somehow always turned out to be Chinese or Jewish.) As James Morone recently demonstrated in *Hellfire Nation,* these waves of puritanism have periodically swept through American society like hurricanes, starting with the Salem witch trials. They have originated on the political Left as often as on the Right. They usually grew out of fears that were not entirely unfounded. Clearly, some college professors interpreted the sexual revolution of the 1960s as a license to treat their female students as fringe benefits, and they deserved to be drummed out of the teaching profession. Clearly, some American communists spied for the Soviet Union in the 1940s, and they deserved to go to jail. Alcohol abuse has always been a major cause of crime, domestic violence, addiction, and premature death. Prostitution has always been a degrading, dangerous, and exploitive business. But in each of these cases, legitimate anxieties were absurdly exaggerated. The rational side of our minds shut down, and we began to see demons everywhere. We were told that we faced a conspiracy so immense that we could no longer afford to respect rights of privacy and due process. Legal and scientific safeguards designed to protect the innocent were dismantled and, as could have been predicted, vast numbers of innocent people were victimized. This, as Orwell understood, is the typical trajectory of puritanical scares. He conceded that the temperance movement began as "a well-meant reaction against the frightful drunkenness of the nineteenth century, product of slum conditions and cheap gin. But it was necessarily led by fanatics who regarded not merely drunkenness but even the moderate drinking of alcohol as sinful" (*CW* 16:207).

It is therefore no coincidence that the most devastating exposé of the "sexual harassment industry" was written by an Orwell scholar. Daphne Patai's book *Heterophobia* penetratingly analyzes the theory and practice of sexual McCarthyism and courageously defends its innocent victims, who often have no other defenders.[12] And precisely because George Orwell understood the politics of puritanism, he anticipated, with uncanny insight, how the sexual harassment hysteria would work. After all, Winston Smith's crime is having sex with a coworker.

To begin with, Orwell appreciated the economic motives behind puritanism. Not only may we punish deviants: we can also help ourselves to their property. If a tramp is a Nancy Boy, other tramps have the right to steal his change. If your professor cracks off-color jokes in class, you have the right to sue the university for much larger sums. Many Americans fervently want to believe that they are victims of sexual abuse even in the absence of monetary incentives, as we have seen in the case of alleged abductions by aliens. (You can't sue Vulcans for sexual harassment.) If, in that climate of paranoia, you offer people huge cash rewards to denounce their coworkers for sexual irregularities, then you will inevitably create a witch hunt fueled by greed. Employers know that they could lose millions if they respect the rights of the accused. Universities know that they could lose hundreds of millions in federal aid if they "don't take sexual harassment seriously." Nathan Pusey, president of Harvard University, famously stood up to Joseph McCarthy, but then McCarthy could not sue Harvard or deny it federal funds simply for employing communist professors. The coercive economic power behind the sexual harassment hysteria is vastly greater. No university president today would dare say "We will of course protect our students against any real victimization, but we cannot in good conscience enforce the sexual harassment guidelines laid down by the federal government, because they are frequently used to punish the innocent." If a university president said anything like that, he or she would place the institution at grave economic risk and would immediately be sacked by the trustees. The lifeblood of puritanism, then, is money.

Now you might want to stop me right there. Surely, you may object, this is not a matter of puritanism. After all, the same feminists who most vociferously denounce sexual harassment can be equally vehement in supporting gay rights, and some of them write about their own erotic adventures in excruciating detail. Surely, whatever their other faults, these women are not puritans.

But that reflects a serious misunderstanding of what puritanism is—a misunderstanding that Orwell perceptively corrects. We tend to equate puritanism with the moral codes that prevailed in colonial Massachusetts or Victorian England, but these are only particular types of puritanism. As a broad generic term, puritanism should properly be applied to any set of arbitrary rules banning harmless sexual activities.

We can illustrate this point by posing a simple question. Which of the following is a puritan: Gloria Steinem, Jerry Falwell, or Osama bin Laden? One's first impulse might be to strike Gloria Steinem off the list, if only because she champions gay rights, where the other two consider homosexuality to be an abomination. On the other hand, Miss Steinem and Mr. bin Laden consider the Miss America pageant an abomination, while Rev. Falwell seems to feel that if consenting adults wish to participate in a beauty contest, why can't the girls have a little innocent fun? On the third hand, what about alternative forms of marriage? Why must it always be between a man and a woman? Why not a man and two, three, or four women? On that issue, Osama is open-minded, tolerant, loathe to impose Eurocentric norms on non-Western societies; now it is Gloria's and Jerry's turn to recoil in pious horror. My point is that all three of them are puritans, though they embrace three different kinds of puritanism. All three are inconsistent and illogical, but that hardly matters. What matters is this: Who gets to make the rules and impose them on the rest of us? Who gets to judge the accused, set penalties, and (most importantly) pocket the fines? Sexual mores are socially constructed, and those who construct and enforce them enjoy enormous power. It sounds like Foucault, but Orwell had advanced a similar theory much earlier.

In *Nineteen Eighty-Four,* the Party makes the rules, which are as arbitrary and contradictory as feminist rules or evangelical rules or Muslim fundamentalist rules. In principle everything other than joyless procreative sex is sexcrime, but in practice enforcement is wildly irregular. The Party tolerates rampant prostitution and, to distract the proletariat, produces "films oozing with sex" (*NEF* 39) as well as outright pornography. Even homosexuality is allowed to flourish in the forced labor camps (*NEF* 187). Sex between Party members is ostensibly punishable by death, but Julia has had "scores" of lovers (i.e., at least forty) over ten years. That works out to one Party man every ninety days, at an absolute minimum. The women of *Sex and the City* would envy Julia's track record, and she has racked it up right under the noses of the telescreens. Julia has never had a fling with an

Inner Party member but, she assures Winston, "there's plenty that *would* if they got half a chance. They're not so holy as they make out." Obviously, as Winston concludes, "the Party was rotten under the surface, its cult of strenuousness and self-denial simply a sham concealing iniquity" (*NEF* 104).

The sexual hypocrisy described in *Nineteen Eighty-Four* is mirrored in our own contemporary American mores. Our movies, magazines, novels, and television programs are oozing with sex. We have hot and cold running pornography piped into our homes through the Internet. But if we discuss sex in the workplace, or even joke about it, we can be hit with a sexual harassment suit. It's madness, of course, but there is a method to it.

As I've noted, in Oceania all victims of Party purges are charged with sexcrime. You might conclude that these charges are trumped up, like the fantastic accusations in Stalin's show trials. But given that sexcrime is defined so broadly, it is entirely probable that every one of the accused is guilty. Winston and Julia certainly are. Likewise, federal guidelines state that "offensive" behavior or the creation of a "hostile work environment" constitutes sexual harassment, terms as vague and elastic as "sexcrime." They can be made to cover anything, including asking co-workers for dates, discussing blue movies, telling off-color jokes, complimenting a woman on her dress, or even looking at her for more than few seconds. If these are crimes then, once again, it is almost impossible to be innocent.

Thus *sexual harasser* has become a vague term of abuse that can be stuck on anyone, from a serial rapist to a reader of *Playboy*. Puritanical movements invent various smear words—*subversive, Trotskyite, bourgeois, sinner, Papist, heretic, Orientalist, Goldstein*—to use against anyone they wish to demonize. Orwell observed in 1944 that, "as used, the word 'Fascism' is almost entirely meaningless. . . . I have heard it applied to farmers, shopkeepers, Social Credit, corporal punishment, foxhunting, bullfighting, the 1922 Committee, the 1941 Committee, Kipling, Gandhi, Chiang Kai-Shek, homosexuality, Priestley's broadcasts, Youth Hostels, astrology, women, dogs and I do not know what else" (*CW* 16:133).

The word "offensive" serves the same function in sexual harassment cases. It is a purely subjective term that means nothing more than "I don't like it, and therefore I have a right to suppress it." Not very long ago, most Americans found homosexuality offensive; many still do. My eighth-grade classmates certainly did. The masters at St. Cyprian's were offended by masturbation sessions. O'Brien is offended by Winston and Julia. All are manifestations of essentially the same kind of hatred. If you give people a license to attack anyone who engages in "offensive" sexual behavior, then it is open season on "deviants"—however the attacker chooses to define deviance. And if you permit employees to sue employers who are at all lax in suppressing "offensive" sexual behavior, then you offer a huge cash bounty for the heads of those "deviants."

When we say that sexual taboos are socially constructed, we tend to assume that deconstructing them will bring about a more tolerant society. Often that is the case; in recent decades we have seen how social criticism, education, and legal reform have transformed attitudes toward homosexuality. But Orwell realized that the same process could be run in reverse, creating new taboos out of the whole cloth. In *Nineteen Eighty-Four* nonprocreative heterosexuality has been constructed as a crime, and contemporary American sexual harassment law allows complainants to construct almost anything as "offensive."

This brings us to a moral contradiction at the core of that law, which can be illustrated as follows. Suppose a female office worker complains to her supervisor that two male coworkers sat opposite her in the company cafeteria reading "offensive" magazines. She told them that she felt offended and asked them to put the magazines away, but they both ridiculed her and told her to mind her own business, so now she is formally filing a sexual harassment charge. The supervisor investigates and finds that in fact the two male coworkers were reading, respectively, *Out* magazine and *Penthouse.* Which (if any) of these men should be disciplined? Many feminists say that *Penthouse* is misogynistic—but people used to say that about male homosexuals, didn't they? Betty Friedan certainly did. She insisted that the "Feminine Mystique" was promoting "the homosexuality that is spreading like a murky smog over the American scene." (As evidence, she cited *Breakfast at Tiffany's* and the plays of Tennessee Williams.)[13] If we now laugh at her hysterics, why should we solemnly enforce Catharine MacKinnon's?

The important difference between Friedan's hysterics and MacKinnon's is that today the latter are more destructive and far more fashionable. In practice, where there are gay rights laws in force, the abovementioned supervisor could not (quite rightly) take any action against the *Out* reader, though he might have to discipline the woman who complained against him. But sexual harassment law would probably compel the company to fire the *Penthouse* reader. Nor is this a purely hypothetical case. In 2002 Harvard University discovered a secret disciplinary file from 1920 dealing with the expulsion of one teacher and eight students for being gay or associating with gays. Harvard President Lawrence H. Summers affirmed that "persecuting individuals on the basis of sexual orientation is abhorrent and an affront to the values of the university," and called the incident "part of a past that we have rightly left behind."[14] We would be right to leave it behind, but we have not. In 1998 Larry Summers's predecessor forced the dean of the Harvard Divinity School to resign for downloading pornography onto his home computer. The university cited rules banning "inappropriate, obscene, bigoted or abusive" materials in an educational environment.[15]

This double standard is as absurd as it is hypocritical. The expulsion of the divinity school dean in 1998, no less than the expulsion of gays in 1920, was inappropriate, obscene, bigoted, and abusive. Yet as Orwell recognized, people who fiercely defend one kind of sexual deviation may be fiercely intolerant of another: "Like all men addicted to whoring, he professed to be revolted by homosexuality" (*CW* 20:190). Today we defend homosexuality and while suppressing pornography, though there is no moral difference between the two. Both are unconventional but essentially harmless forms of sexual expression. For centuries both endured a shameful history of persecution, and both (around 1970) finally began to enjoy a long-overdue measure of toleration. But whereas homosexuals went on to win more rights, in the realm of pornography the authoritarian wing of the feminist movement succeeded in establishing a new reign of oppression. Indeed, the stereotypes which were once applied to homosexuals (that they are misogynists, sexual predators, child molesters, sadomasochists) were now transferred en bloc to readers of pornography by MacKinnon and other feminist "theorists." The same hatreds which became unfashionable after Stonewall simply found a new and more acceptable target. Orwell noted this psychological dynamic after the Second World War: when the liberation of the death camps made anti-

Semitism unacceptable, the prejudices once focused on Jews were refocused on another group, in this case the Poles (*CW* 19:23–25). The larger point here is that, in many if not most cases, sexual harassment charges amount to gay-bashing directed against heterosexuals. Hence the title of Daphne Patai's book.

Because the "sexual harasser" has replaced the homosexual as a target of hatred, childishly trivial accusations can have terribly destructive consequences. Daphne Patai cites the cases of two men—one a high school teacher, the other an AT&T employee—who were charged with telling mildly off-color jokes, suspended from their jobs, and ultimately driven to suicide. In the former case, a sensitive school spokeswoman expressed concern "that the suicide would have the effect of discouraging other students from filing complaints."[16] It may seem incredible that a joke could lead to suicide, but in the midst of a sexual witch hunt this is entirely unsurprising. If you take a harmless act and make it a crime, if you persecute people who commit these acts, make them objects of public shame and hatred, haul them before inquisitorial tribunals, and destroy their careers and reputations, then some of them will kill themselves. Ask any homosexual.

Daphne Patai relates another case that Orwell could cast a glaring light on. It concerns Ramdas Lamb, a religion professor at the University of Hawaii at Manoa, who discussed in class the fraught question of false rape accusations: how common are they? Three students dogmatically insisted that "women don't lie about rape" and charged Lamb with sexual harassment because he suggested that there might be another point of view on this issue.[17] When that accusation failed to stick, one student rapidly escalated the charges, accusing the professor of raping her in her own apartment ten to sixteen times in the space of a month. At the trial she could produce no evidence, and her testimony was a tissue of inconsistencies, so her lawyer fell back on the same dogma that began the witch hunt in the first place: "There is no motive to lie."[18]

Orwell would have identified three powerful motives. The first was O'Brien's motive: thoughtcrime. Lamb was guilty of ideological deviation and had to be punished. The second motive was economic, the same motive that drove those tramps to rob a Nancy Boy. Though Lamb was ultimately exonerated, the student who accused him was rewarded with $175,000 from the university as compensation for delays in dealing with her charges, which, of course, were lies. (Lamb received nothing, though the university's sexual harassment officers grossly violated his rights of due process.) The third motive was the motive of my eighth-grade classmates, the motive of the masters at St. Cyprian's when they thrashed and expelled boys for masturbating: some people derive a sadistic thrill from destroying other people, and they can feel righteous about it if they tag their victims as sexual criminals.

The witch hunt against Lamb was assisted by feminists who, with no special knowledge of the case, sent in letters of support arguing that Lamb fit the pattern of a typical sexual harasser. Of course he did: everyone fits the pattern. Billie Dziech and Linda Wiener concocted those patterns in *The Lecherous Professor,* a standard guidebook for identifying academic Lotharios, in which pretty much everyone is guilty. There's the "Public Harasser," who will either "dress up or down" and "seldom employs standard academic vocabulary." Then there's the "Private Harasser," who (just to throw you off guard) "dresses conservatively" and "often adheres to academic stereotypes." There's the "Intellectual Seducer" and the

"Counselor-Helper" (like Ramdas Lamb): if a teacher wins over students with his brilliance and generosity, then he is obviously out to bed them.[19] (You can use these last two labels to eliminate colleagues who are smarter or more popular than you are.) "In fact," Cristina Nehring comments, "the only professorial type conspicuously absent from this colorful gallery of closet criminals is the one we might call 'The Unpleasant Idiot.'"[20] In *Nineteen Eighty-Four* Parson's seven-year-old daughter employs this paranoid logic when she denounces an odd-looking gentleman as an enemy agent. As her father brags:

> "What do you think put her onto him in the first place? She spotted he was wearing a funny kind of shoes—said she'd never seen anyone wearing shoes like that before. So the chances were he was a foreigner. Pretty smart for a nipper of seven, eh?" "What happened to the man?" said Winston.
> "Ah, that I couldn't say, of course. But I wouldn't be altogether surprised if—" Parson made the motion of aiming a rifle, and clicked his tongue for the explosion. . . .
> "Of course we can't afford to take chances," agreed Winston dutifully. (*NEF* 50–51)

In the year 1984, when everyone was comparing the novel with present reality, it appeared that civil liberties were fairly secure in the United States. But soon thereafter, as Jeffrey Rosen has shown, two unforeseeable inventions combined to overwhelm privacy rights: a body of sweeping and ill-defined sexual harassment law, and a machine that kept a permanent record of messages sent, received, and read. Under those conditions, the personal computer became our telescreen. Given that "offensive" e-mail messages can spark a lawsuit, employers can only protect themselves by spying on their employees. In a 1998 dissent, Clarence Thomas warned that "sexual harassment is simply not something that employers can wholly prevent without taking extraordinary measures—constant video and audio surveillance, for example—that would revolutionize the workplace in a manner incompatible with a free society."[21] (Perhaps the one good thing to come out of the Hill–Thomas hearings is this: we have a justice on the Supreme Court who has a personal understanding of the destructiveness of sexual harassment law.)

The following year, as Justice Thomas had predicted, the *New York Times* fired twenty-two male and female employees in its Norfolk, Virginia, business office (10 percent of the work force) for sending naughty e-mails. One of them reproduced that Donald McGill archetype, the very large woman in a very small swimsuit. It is not clear that anyone actually felt harassed by all this, but employees were required to report e-mail messages that seemed "offensive" even if they were not personally offended. Office supervisors seem to have gone on a fishing expedition, trawling hard drives and dismissing anyone caught up in the sweep.[22] Employers have a right to ban annoying e-mails, but the *New York Times*'s panic resembled the masturbation scare at St. Cyprian's, or (if you prefer another literary allusion) Captain Queeg's demented search for a can of stolen strawberries in *The Caine Mutiny*.

The point is that the newspaper only resorted to such Orwellian surveillance because the definition of sexual harassment is constantly expanding. As it expands, it offers ever-greater opportunities for punishing the innocent and (not incidentally) ever-greater career opportunities for the campus counselors and lawyers who enforce and profit from sexual harassment accusations. Daphne Patai cites a standard textbook, Bernice R. Sandler and Robert J. Shoop's *Sexual Harassment on*

Campus: A Guide for Administrators, Faculty, and Students (Boston: Allyn & Bacon, 1997), which offers "a fifteen-point list of predictions of future developments on campus, and almost every item begins with the word 'increased': increased incidence of sexual harassment (yes, this is what they say), increased reporting, increased training, increased recognition of nonsexual but gender-related 'hostile environments,' increased charges by men against women, increased use of a systematic, comprehensive anti-sexual-harassment program."[23] Reading that sentence, you assume there must be a misprint somewhere: surely if we have more and stricter sexual harassment policies there will be *less* harassment. Otherwise, what are these policies accomplishing? But in a sense Sandler and Shoop are right: if you create more sexual harassment committees and give them ever-expanding powers, they will generate more accusations. Even if these accusations are mainly bogus, the apparent "incidence" of sexual harassment will continually rise until it includes nearly everyone. By counting any sexual joke or comment, the American Association of University Women was able to claim that 85 percent of schoolgirls and 76 percent of schoolboys had been harassed.[24] These figures are about as trustworthy as the production statistics for bootlaces in Oceania, but they have been used to justify ever more surveillance and more draconian policies. Very largely (though not entirely) sexual harassment is a demon manufactured by the feminist movement in order to recruit followers and attack anyone it chooses to attack. Therefore the demon can never be defeated; if it were eliminated, then what Patai calls the Sexual Harassment Industry would lose its raison d'être. Always there will be female dupes waiting to be seduced by lecherous males. In *Nineteen Eighty-Four* the Party has created a demon of its own to serve the same purpose:

> what was strange was that although Goldstein was hated and despised by everybody, although every day, and a thousand times a day, on platforms, on the telescreen, in newspapers, in books, his theories were refuted, smashed, ridiculed, held up to the general gaze for the pitiful rubbish that they were—in spite of all this, his influence never seemed to grow less. Always there were fresh dupes waiting to be seduced by him. . . . (*NEF* 15)

However, neither the Thought Police nor campus sexual harassment committees have any intention of enforcing their rules consistently. That would be impossible: they would have to arrest everyone. Instead they pursue an enforcement strategy common in totalitarian regimes, one that endows them with enormous arbitrary power. First, they define the crime so sweepingly that everyone feels guilty and apprehensive; then they prosecute that crime selectively. A Party official in Oceania may tolerate prostitution, and might even himself direct the office in charge of producing pornography, but if he wants to eliminate a political adversary, he can simply file a charge of sexcrime. Likewise, a sexual harassment suit can be a convenient means of getting rid of an office rival, shaking down a corporation with "deep pockets," or dealing with an uncooperative college professor. Not long ago, an instructor at Fairleigh Dickinson University gave a student a failing grade on a history exam because she wrote that the United States entered the First World War when the Japanese bombed Pearl Harbor and identified Frank Lloyd Wright as the inventor of the airplane. Her father was the president of a professional basketball team and a generous contributor to the university, and when the professor resisted pressure to change her grade, he was charged with sexual harassment. Specifically, he was accused of using the word "pussy" in the classroom (professional basket-ball managers can be terribly sensitive to foul language). In fact he said "pusillan-imous," but the episode illustrates why speech codes are a dangerous fraud: by twisting a single word, they can be and have been used to frame innocent people. The professor produced e-mails that showed that Fairleigh Dickinson administra-tors knew the charges were bogus, and won a defamation lawsuit against the university. It is encouraging that some of the victims of sexual McCarthyism are finally fighting back successfully. But when you are smeared by powerful inter-ests, the emotional toll can be devastating: this professor endured depression and attempted suicide.[25]

Orwell further recognized that sexual persecutions inevitably involve the aboli-tion of privacy. You cannot effectively police the bedroom unless you set up tele-screens over every bed. Alongside the three principles of Ingsoc—WAR IS PEACE, FREEDOM IS SLAVERY, IGNORANCE IS STRENGTH—there is a fourth dou-blethink slogan that is never directly stated, but unmistakably implied—THE PER-SONAL IS POLITICAL. That is one of the foundation dogmas of the contemporary feminist movement, but it could have been used just as easily to justify the McCar-thyite pursuit of "deviants." The implications are inescapable: if there is no person-al sphere into which political institutions may not intrude, then privacy has been abolished. There is no part of our lives that may not be outed, nothing we do that may not be policed—which is precisely Jeffrey Rosen's point.

Once you are charged with sexual harassment, all your private sexual peccadil-loes become "relevant" to the charge and may be exposed: this is the trap that ensnared both Clarence Thomas and Bill Clinton. In *Strange Justice,* Jane Mayer and Jill Abramson used the charges against Thomas as a pretext for publishing not-terribly-relevant allegations about his private life. "An interest in pornography might ordinarily be considered a private matter," they wrote, but privacy has been abolished. They proceeded to allege that Thomas had been fond of blue movies while a student at Yale Law School—though they were compelled to admit that many Yale law students watched blue movies in the 1970s, when pornography was considered hip.[26] They even charged, with a palpable frisson, that when he was between marriages, he decorated his bachelor pad with pictures of naked wom-en[27]—a revelation that must have outraged fans of Robert Mapplethorpe. Of course it's all hypocritical. Of course (as Mayer and Abramson admitted) none of this proves that Thomas harassed anyone. Their objective was to humiliate Thomas, to brand him as a sexual deviant (hence the title of their book), and thus arouse against him the kind of hostility we used to direct against homosexuals.

In a word, *Strange Justice* is an exercise in voyeurism. And as Orwell under-stood all too well, hatred of "deviant" sexuality is inevitably bound up with voy-eurism. Antipornography agitators from Anthony Comstock to Andrea Dworkin and Catharine MacKinnon have always been luridly fascinated by what they pro-fess to loathe, subconsciously or consciously enjoying what they publicly de-nounce. "No qualms need be felt," Orwell observed, "because these deeds are committed by the enemy, and the enjoyment that one gets out of them can be disguised as disapproval" (*CW* 17:19). Seventeenth-century clergymen produced salacious accounts of all the lewd things that accused witches were supposed to have done with the devil. The Clarence Thomas hearings descended to a new low, a national orgy of voyeurism, broadcast into millions of homes. And of course, the

ultimate fantasy of a voyeur is the telescreen. Once again Orwell was prophetic: he
foresaw live sex acts over the Internet. O'Brien has a direct video feed from the
bedroom where Winston and Julia make love. The Thought Police even show
Winston their collection of photos (*NEF* 228). One has to ask: if O'Brien is really
so keen on eradicating sex, why didn't he arrest Winston and Julia the moment
they jumped into bed? Why did he allow the affair to continue for a few months
before springing his trap? There can be only one explanation. Big Brother Is
Watching You—and that is what he likes to watch.

Can such an absurdly repressive regime endure for long? That question is posed
in both *Nineteen Eighty-Four* and *Heterophobia*. Orwell's answer is No; he understood that sexual witch hunts ultimately self-destruct. That much is made clear in
the appendix to *Nineteen Eighty-Four*, written from the vantage of a future time
when the regime no longer exists. The narrator speaks with a frankness possible
only in a free society. He discusses the Party in the past tense, and Newspeak is
treated as a dead language. When did the revolution happen? The final scene in the
Chestnut Tree Café takes place a few years after 1984. Discussing planned translations of classic literature into Newspeak, the appendix states that "it was not
expected that they would be finished before the first or second decade of the
twenty-first century" (*NEF* 256). Those benchmarks suggest that the collapse occurred sometime between the late 1980s and 2001—roughly when communism
collapsed, in fact.

The cause of the revolution is simply this: witch hunts inevitably run out of
control. At first they may be a useful tool for eliminating your enemies, but they
are very loose and highly destructive cannons, and eventually the paranoia turns
against the people who unleashed it in the first place. The Salem witch hunts first
targeted common people but then moved up the social scale, until even the governor's wife was accused: at that point the leading men of Massachusetts concluded
that there was "ground to suspect some mistake."[28] Stalin's henchmen made their
careers by carrying out his purges, but they realized that the NKVD could come
knocking on their doors no matter how high they rose in the party hierarchy, so
they prudently scaled down the terror as soon as the dictator was safely dead.
Republicans tolerated or encouraged Joseph McCarthy as long as he went after
lefties, but when he turned on George C. Marshall and the U.S. Army, he was
finally ostracized. Democrats tolerated or encouraged attacks on Clarence Thomas
until similar methods were used against Bill Clinton: then and only then did they
denounce "sexual McCarthyism." When sexual harassment charges are pressed
against women's studies professors, then even feminists come around to the conclusion that there is ground to suspect some mistake.[29]

Something similar will happen in Oceania. "We shall abolish the orgasm," raves
O'Brien. "Our neurologists are at work upon it now" (*NEF* 220). What if they
figure out how to do it, by putting something in the drinking water or snipping a
connection in the cerebral cortex? Will the proles, otherwise so passive, tolerate
that kind of mass castration? Many Party members, as Julia reveals, are enjoying
illicit sex. Rather than give that up, they may well join the revolution. Orwell
could not be more explicit about this: "The animal instinct, the simple undifferen-
tiated desire: that was the force that would tear the Party to pieces" (*NEF* 105).

Something similar is happening to us. To illustrate that, it is worth quoting at
length from a 2000 posting to a feminist electronic newsgroup:

I have long been a rather strong feminist, though admittedly not on the "cutting edge". I married a nice man, one who I have been with for more than 20 years. I know him extremely well. Not perfect, but a good guy who holds nearly as strong pro-women opinions as I. . . . He is absolutely among the least sexually "threatening" people I have ever known, and I am as confident about his restraint around other women as it is possible to be. He has helped many other women and has taken particular pride in doing so. He and I both believed that in general, women do not lie when they report such crimes as rape and sexual harassment. Last year, however, two women who worked for him, who had been presenting increasing disciplinary problems and who were openly expressing increasingly hateful thoughts about my husband and several other coworkers, charged him with sexual harassment. . . . Several dozen witnesses were brought in by the women in an internal investigation, and apparently not a one said anything to support the women's charges. Repeatedly women and men attested to the fact that my husband was the last person on earth who would do such things as the women alleged, and virtually all spontaneously voiced the opinion that the women were hateful and were acting out of malice. Everyone who was supposed to have witnessed my husband's offenses apparently completely denied that he had done any of the things he was charged with. Nevertheless, his self-confidence, self-opinion, and productivity suffered to the extreme, since he was totally floored and depressed by the false allegations. He has been so opposed to sexual harassment his entire life that these charges were extremely demoralizing to him. His depression is harming our home life and his every interaction with his peers and friends. The investigation has been in progress now for 10 months. He lives under a cloud, and his every action that relates to these women is considered as a possible "retaliation". He can do nothing at all to defend himself. I think this is the major reason for his depression, since his extremely positive position at work has turned to one in which his employer officially views him as a criminal monster of some sort. The women continue to be provided every benefit of the doubt, completely protected from negative consequences of any kind. His declining self-esteem has affected me greatly as well. I am a woman who is victimized by a recklessly pro-woman, uncritical law. I was so happy with the progress of women that I NEVER thought I would someday write something like this. I am wondering where we are going with feminism these days. At what point did we decide to elevate even the most malicious women to the level of untouchable victim at the expense of men? Isn't this sort of power that women hold something that will hurt us in the long run? When these false charges are allowed to relentlessly harm the reputation of men, while depriving them of any defense, doesn't this greatly harm all of our credibility when we are really subjected to sexual harassment, abuse, and rape?[30]

Orwell would have recognized a parallel here. Just as feminists in the 1990s insisted that "women don't lie," communists in the 1930s insisted that the accused in the Moscow show trials must have been guilty. Both cases involved a reversion to the lettre de cachet of Ancien Regime France, when an accusation was tantamount to conviction. In both cases, the presumption of guilt and gross biases in favor of the accuser encouraged liars and guaranteed that the innocent would be victimized. And in both cases, those who said "they're all guilty" fell into two categories. There were cynics, opportunists, and apparatchiks who knew perfectly well that the accusations were false but pursued them in order to eliminate rivals, advance their careers, or protect the company from lawsuits. However, there were also naïve idealists like this woman and her husband, who sincerely believed that the system was infallible. When the system turned on them, they could not defend themselves without repudiating their core ideological convictions. They also had to confront a painful truth about themselves: if some other innocent person had been purged, they would have supported the prosecutors. Reviewing Arthur Koestler's *Darkness at Noon,* Orwell grasped why the Old Bolshevik victimized in the Purges confessed. It was not simply a matter of torture: "Any right to protest against torture, secret prisons, organised lying and so forth he has long since forfeited. He recognizes that what is now happening is the consequence of his own acts" (*CW* 12:357–59).

Witch hunts move through stages, and this particular hysteria is now at the stage where we snap out of it and awaken to the damage that has been done. The fact that public opinion was not stampeded by very belated harassment charges lodged against Arnold Schwartzenegger, Harold Bloom, and V. Gene Robinson (the gay Episcopalian bishop) suggests that the worst may be over. In another promising sign of the times, Margaret Talbot recently proposed that sexual harassment be abolished as a legal category. A woman would still enjoy legal protection against anything that could reasonably be called harassment. If Bill Clinton in fact did what Paula Jones and Kathleen Willey said he did, they still could have charged him with sexual assault. Women would still have the option of resorting to defamation suits or tort law, which have long been effective weapons against men who were verbally abusive or sexually predatory.[31] In fact we had in place a reasonably good system for dealing with genuine sexual harassment long before the term was invented. The witch hunts only began when we made employers responsible for vaguely defined sexual misbehavior among their employees. Limit that responsibility to the actual harasser, and employers would no longer feel pressured to fire people for telling the kind of jokes one might find on a Donald McGill postcard.[32] If you ask my opinion of this modest proposal, I say we should decide to be sane.

NOTES

I must thank my colleagues at Drew University, Frances Bernstein and John Lenz, for helping me thrash out some of the ideas in this essay.
    1. The following abbreviations are used in this essay: *CW—The Complete Works of George Orwell,* 20 vols., ed. Peter Davison (London: Secker and Warburg, 1998); and *NEF*—George Orwell, *Nineteen Eighty-Four* (New York: New American Library, 1961).
    2. Orwell was familiar with police entrapment of homosexuals as early as 1931. That is the meaning of the couplet he then saw scrawled on the wall of a patrol wagon: "Detective Smith knows how to gee;/Tell him he's a cunt from me" (*CW* 10:256).
    3. Hilary Spurling, *The Girl from the Fiction Department: A Portrait of Sonia Orwell* (London: Hamish Hamilton, 2002), 67–69.
    4. Michael Shelden, *Orwell: The Authorized Biography* (New York: HarperCollins, 1991), 69–71.
    5. George Orwell, *The Road to Wigan Pier* (New York: Harcourt Brace Jovanovich, 1958), 174.
    6. Bernard Crick, *George Orwell: A Life* (Boston: Little, Brown, 1980), 347.
    7. James A. Morone, *Hellfire Nation: The Politics of Sin in American History* (New Haven, Conn.: Yale University Press, 2003), 391–92.
    8. Of course, if you argue that Thomas should not have been confirmed because he was inexperienced or too conservative, then you are raising reasonable issues that reasonable people can debate. The Thomas confirmation hearings began by focusing on these legiti-

mate questions, but they were quickly forgotten amid a welter of sexual smears. I am not necessarily saying that Thomas should have been confirmed, but anyone with a moral compass would object strenuously to some of the tactics used against him.

9. Specifically, I follow the account given by her supporters, Jane Mayer and Jill Abramson, *Strange Justice: The Selling of Clarence Thomas* (Boston: Houghton Mifflin, 1994).

10. Jeffrey Rosen, *The Unwanted Gaze: The Destruction of Privacy in America* (New York: Random House, 2000), esp. 27, 53.

11. Psychologist Susan Clancy constructed an experiment that indicated that "victims" of Repressed Memory Syndrome and "victims" of abuse by aliens were equally prone to remember things that had never happened. When she published her results, she received a torrent of hate mail from both camps. See Bruce Grierson, "A Bad Trip Down Memory Lane," *New York Times Magazine* (July 27, 2003): 36–39. For general accounts of sexual hysteria in the late twentieth century, see Richard Ofshe and Ethan Waters, *Making Monsters: False Memories, Psychotherapy, and Sexual Hysteria* (New York: Charles Scribner's Sons, 1994); Elizabeth Loftus and Katherine Ketcham, *The Myth of Repressed Memory: False Memories and Allegations of Sexual Abuse* (New York: St. Martin's, 1994); Joan Acocella, *Creating Hysteria: Women and Multiple Personality Disorder* (San Francisco: Jossey-Bass, 1999); and Dorothy Rabinowitz, *No Crueler Tyrannies: Accusation, False Witness, and Other Terrors of Our Times* (New York: Free Press, 2003).

12. Daphne Patai, *Heterophobia: Sexual Harassment and the Future of Feminism* (Lanham, Md.: Rowman & Littlefield, 1998). See also Cathy Young, *Ceasefire! Why Women and Men Must Join Forces to Achieve True Equality* (New York: Free Press, 1999), esp. ch. 7.

13. Betty Friedan, *The Feminine Mystique* (New York: Dell, 1984), 273–76.

14. "In Harvard Papers, a Dark Corner of the College's Past," *New York Times,* November 30, 2002, p. A13.

15. Rosen, *Unwanted Gaze,* 159–60.

16. Patai, *Heterophobia,* xiii, 215. For the case of the AT&T employee, see Christopher Byron, "The Joke That Killed," *Esquire* (January 1995): 84.

17. Prosecutors and police estimate that between one in eight and one in five rape accusations are false. One study, by sociologist Eugene Kanin, found that 41 percent of rape charges were eventually recanted by the accuser. Young, *Ceasefire,* 150–52.

18. Patai, *Heterophobia,* 81–87.

19. Billie Dziech and Linda Wiener, *The Lecherous Professor,* 2nd ed. (Urbana and Chicago: University of Illinois Press, 1990), ch. 5.

20. Cristina Nehring, "The Higher Yearning," *Harper's* (September 2001): 65–66.

21. Rosen, *Unwanted Gaze,* ch. 2.

22. Ann Carrns, "Prying Times: Those Bawdy E-Mails Were Good for a Laugh—Until the Ax Fell," *Wall Street Journal* (Eastern Edition), February 4, 2000, p. A1.

23. Patai, *Heterophobia,* 62.

24. *Hostile Hallways: The AAUW Survey on Sexual Harassment in America's Schools* (Washington, D.C.: American Association of University Women, 1993).

25. Richard Monastersky, "Former Professor Wins $5.3–Million in Lawsuit Against Fairleigh Dickinson U.," *Chronicle of Higher Education,* 1 June 2001, p. 10.

26. Mayer and Abramson, *Strange Justice,* 55–57.

27. Mayer and Abramson, *Strange Justice,* 108–9.

28. Morone, *Hellfire Nation,* 92.

29. For examples, see Philip Weiss, "Don't Even Think About It. (The Cupid Cops Are Watching.)" *New York Times Magazine* (May 3, 1998): 43ff.

30. Posting by "Colleen," Subject: Sexual harassment charges, Newsgroup soc.feminism, March 18, 2000.

31. Take Melvil Dewey, for example. Best known as the inventor of the Dewey Decimal System, he was also the founder of the American Library Association, and he created the academic discipline now known as library and information science. In short, he was the

most powerful man in his profession. He also had a habit of fondling women without their express permission. In 1929 his stenographer sued him. Dewey's lawyer warned him that juries almost always side with the woman in such cases, and he settled for $2147.66—a fair sum of money then, roughly comparable (allowing for inflation) to what President Clinton would have paid Paula Jones if he had chosen not to contest her charges. See Wayne A. Wiegand, *Irrepressible Reformer: A Biography of Melvil Dewey* (Chicago: American Library Association, 1996), 353–55. There is no denying that universities sometimes try to protect professors who are guilty of real harassment. But in that case the victim has an alternative: she can haul the offender into court, where (as Dewey discovered) his academic cronies cannot rescue him.

32. Margaret Talbot, "Men Behaving Badly," *New York Times Magazine,* October 12, 2002, pp. 52ff.

2

In Defense of Comrade Psmith: The Orwellian Treatment of Orwell

IAN WILLIAMS

Nothing vindicates Orwell so much as his critics—except perhaps the usurpers who have posthumously enlisted his name in support of causes that he would have detested. He has become a literary Rorschach test, an intellectual inkblot onto which critics and followers alike project all their fears and hopes. This is made much easier, of course, in these days of deconstruction, postmodernism, and post-structuralism, when it is almost respectable in academia to ignore what a writer says or wanted to say and parse the "text" in the way you want.

Orwell's own clearly stated political and moral positions have been chucked down the memory hole so that he can be rewritten as a free-market conservative or, for example, enlisted by Christopher Hitchens as somehow simultaneously a Trotsky-ist and a retrospective "neo-neoconservative" supporter of current American impe-rial ambitions. For different reasons, those who hanker for the great days of the Third International tend to unite with the conservatives in denying Orwell's own often declared socialism.

Ironically, in view of recent scandals over its journalistic flops, the *New York Times* obituary for Orwell in 1949 set the record straight: "Although many reviewers read into Mr. Orwell's novel a wholesale condemnation of left wing politics, he considered himself a Marxist and a member of the non-Communist wing of the British Labor Party." In fact, I doubt whether there was a Jura branch of the party for him to join, and certainly there was no overt communist wing of the Labour Party, but right up to his death, Orwell had indeed proclaimed his support for the antitotalitarian democratic socialism that he saw the Labour government of 1945 trying to implement.

It is safe to say, if only from the ubiquity of his books on library shelves today and his coinages that have passed into the common language, that Orwell has the support of a majority, which, if not silent, is perhaps less vociferous than his critics. Indeed as liberal supporters of human rights who are "decent," his support-ers attract the scorn of some of the latter who regard "decency" as a pejorative term (see, for example, the bitter ending of *Orwell* by Scott Lucas).[1]

Even his political critics usually allow that Orwell had a lucid and easily com-prehensible prose style, which makes it stranger that so many commentators, even supporters, ignore what the man himself so plainly wrote. In the United States in particular, relative ignorance of the social, political, and economic context of Britain helps Orwell's critics to look at his work with a partisan squint.

That is not to say that Orwell was a parochial writer; the frequent translations and continual publication of his work show that readers all over the world recognize the validity of what he described. However, understanding Orwell's roots is important to understanding and appreciating him, especially for those in the United States for whom, for example, the connotations of the word "socialism" are different from those of the rest of the world, even when qualified as "democratic socialism," and who may also be unfamiliar with the linked comforts and oppression of the British class system.

That U.S.-colored perception could be seen in the reaction of many American liberals to the issue of the "List" that Orwell provided to the British government of people whom he thought unsuitable to do writing assignments. For Americans, this conjures up HUAC hearings, McCarthyite purges, and dismissals. But that was not what happened in Britain. Not one of those on the "List" lost their jobs, were imprisoned, or can provably be said to have had any resulting impediments to their chosen careers, except missing freelance assignments from a government department that they presumably disagreed with anyway!

It is best to use the Orwellian method on Orwell: to look at the context without the dubious benefit of a ready-made, off-the-peg line. For the purposes of this essay, I will use *Orwellian* in a benign sense, which gives what I consider to be due credit to the author, rather than in its usual derivative and derogatory sense, which somewhat unfairly attaches his name to the concepts that he was actually attacking.

That confusion, which also reflects some of the lack of context just referred to, is apparent in a recent *Wall Street Journal* review by David Henderson of Robert Schiller's book *The New Financial Order,* in which Henderson described as "Orwellian" Schiller's statement that "We will want to arrest any possible tendency for the fruits of our economy to be distributed much more unequally between rich and poor in the future."

Henderson ironically thought he was using the word in the sense that most of us use, the derivative, malign meaning referring to the tyranny of *Nineteen Eighty-Four,* but in fact he was, unwittingly, using it in a proper positive sense, since Orwell the socialist would very much have wanted to arrest, and indeed to reverse, any such tendency toward inequality. Later, more in accordance with current usage, Henderson used the word again to describe the government's collection of data on its citizens—which he called Orwellian, but perhaps correctly this time in the full, Big Brother, sense. The *Journal* notwithstanding, and although the Oxford English Dictionary gives both definitions of "Orwellian" ("Characteristic or suggestive of the writings of 'George Orwell', esp, in his satirical novel *1984* which portrays a form of totalitarian state seen by him as arising naturally out of the political circumstances of his time. Hence as *n.,* an admirer of the ideas of Orwell."). Its negative sense has clearly overtaken the positive sense, so I am aware that my effort to turn back the tide of language is a quixotic tourney.

But it reinforces the point that far from simply being an inventive fantasy and science fiction writer—which is another aspect of Orwell's work not usually given sufficient weight—there is a distinctively "Orwellian" analysis, a way of looking at the world, that merits the benign use of the adjective.

That worldview derived from his own personal experiences of totalitarianism, but above all from his observation of how people of conscience will, as Lewis Carroll said, believe three impossible things before breakfast in a good cause. Orwell saw otherwise moral and good people, hoping to improve the world, support unspeakable atrocities and try to silence those who did not support them.

I hope you will excuse some autobiographical details intruding to explain how my path intersects with Orwell's, even though he had died just before I was born in the North of England that he wrote about in *The Road to Wigan Pier.* Indeed, I was one of the first beneficiaries of the National Health Service under the postwar Labour government that did so much to ameliorate the horrors that Orwell described.

It has now become a truism that writers, particularly journalists, who write about Orwell are angling for some reflected glory. The accusation often comes from writers who do not like him at all, so it is a backhanded compliment to all concerned in its implication that there is indeed glory to reflect. Certainly, any such comparisons would flatter me greatly, but that is not my purpose, which is to rescue George Orwell from many of his admirers and his critics, by placing him in an accurate social and political context: and that context is very, very British.

Indeed, if anything, my background would strongly prejudice me against old-Etonians like Orwell, with ready-made networks of patronage and influence. My view of the British social system was bottom up, not top down!

I first read *Nineteen Eighty-Four* when Orwell was nine years dead. It was a battered, unadorned Penguin paperback, which I still have, given to me by an old Scot exiled to Liverpool who was a founding member of the Independent Labour Party. In fact, since he was blind, I used to read to him and one of the things I read out loud every week was *Tribune,* of which he was a founder subscriber (hence in part my precocity in reading material). I acquired more in politics from him than I did from my father, a communist carpenter shop steward and former unemployed organizer, whose Stalinist political views tended to be mirrored by his aloof patriarchal approach.

In my early teens, I joined the Labour Party Young Socialists, flirted with the Young Communist League, became a teenage Maoist, and even visited China during the tail end of the Cultural Revolution. It may seem that my early reading of *Nineteen Eighty-Four* had missed its mark on this young comrade but, in fact, in an odd way, it hadn't. I became a Maoist *because* of it.

Some of you may remember the books by people like Felix Green and others who followed in Edgar Snow's footsteps and cast the Chinese revolution as a sort of libertarian antithesis to the bureaucracy of the Soviet Union. The Cultural Revolution looked like a liberating experiment, in its own weird oriental way, and slogans such as "Bombard the Headquarters" and "It is right to rebel" had a certain refreshing appeal to us rebellious youth. However, unsurprisingly, I subsequently discovered that they were only kidding.

In the course of a New Year's Eve drinking competition with Chou En-lai, I became embroiled in an argument with Mme Mao, Chiang Ching, who asserted that there were only two great English proletarian novels, *Jane Eyre* and *Hard Times.* I knew enough of her life not to tread on the first—clearly a case of identification—but I had to point out that the hero of *Hard Times* was a strike-breaker. The rest of the Gang of Four and their comrades looked distinctly worried. But I was not reeducated on the spot. She hissed, "You have long hair. You look like a girl!" In retrospect, it is pretty much the same critical method used by many who attack Orwell. When faced with the irrefutable, go for the ad hominem and inconsequential details.

Certainly, the British "Marxist-Leninist" groupuscule that I was in was no more tolerant of dissent than the Chinese Communist Party. The members stood on their heads whenever there was an inner party coup in China. My favorite was the veteran Indian communist at a meeting in London who was asked why the Chinese government was providing weapons to Sri Lanka to fight the Maoist guerrillas. Without pausing for breath, in a stunning example of both doublethink and duck-speak, she explained that the cunning revolutionary purpose of the Chinese comrades was that the guerrillas would then steal the weapons from the government. I was expelled, and left, eventually to rejoin the Labour Party back in 1978, inoculated against the doctrine of democratic centralism, which personal example and historical study had demonstrated was all about centralism and had little to do with any recognizable form of democracy.

Twenty years ago I closed the circle and began to write for *Tribune,* to which Orwell contributed so many of his best essays. The paper's position has no real equivalent in the United States. Its circulation is relatively small but highly influential. Its columnists have always included many of the major union leaders and cabinet ministers. Its editorial line is on the left of the Labour Party but staunchly non-Leninist in its approach, and its columns are open to all Labour Party members, including "New Labour" ministers excoriated in the editorials.

It is, in fact, without being a fossil, in pretty much the same political position it had when Orwell wrote for it. American students of Orwell, without direct acquaintance with Britain and British politics, often seem to fail to appreciate the difference in approach entailed by having a mass socialist, noncommunist, non-Leninist movement that actually runs cities and the country on a normal basis.

Equally, they often miss the "caste" aspect of the British class system, which is indeed difficult to appreciate unless you have experienced it personally. As a working-class child who reached university, was expelled, and became a railroad worker and union official before becoming a writer, my experience lets me appreciate Orwell's efforts at social amphibiousness and the difficulties involved, and it also allows me to see his appreciation, indeed on occasions, envy, of the social world of the proles that he could never quite penetrate.

In the late 1970s and early 1980s the Liverpool Labour Party was in the process of being infiltrated and taken over by a secret entrist organization, the Revolutionary Socialist League (RSL), which for those of who you are interested in the obscure taxonomy of the Trotskyist movement was part of the Pabloite Fourth International, a faction that sought to burrow into other parties. It was to some extent competing with and filling the ecological niche formerly held by the now waning Communist Party and its fellow travelers, who had, for example, managed to make Liverpool a twin city with the East German port of Rostock.

I take some modest pride in having played a part in defeating the attempts of the RSL, partly on ideological grounds and partly by exposing some of its more corrupt leading members for adding Al Capone to the canon of Leon Trotsky. The RSL had in fact tried to recruit me and then later stood up at meetings and denounced me as both a liar and a red-baiter for mentioning their existence. They never seemed to notice the contradiction.

While members of the RSL were not averse to offering physical violence, what they were really adept at was pulling the inner strings of party loyalty and faith in their various "left" litmus tests, which worked even on Labour Party members to inculcate a feeling of thoughtcrime. The party was under siege, and anyone who broke ranks was, objectively, an ally of Margaret Thatcher.

One of my more enduring memories of the power of thoughtcrime as a working concept was of members of parliament from Liverpool, under siege from Trotskyists in their constituency Labour Parties, who privately encouraged me and fed me information while publicly distancing themselves and even denouncing us dissidents. Orwell was my guide during these trying Orwellian times. He had described their genuine doublethink so well.

As George Orwell had in the more trying circumstances of Catalonia, I realized that democratic socialism was not a neutral position between two poles; it was a belief and a cause to be vigorously defended and advanced in its own right, against totalitarianism in whatever guise it came. Indeed, democratic socialism should actually be something of a tautology. If a society does not have political and civil rights, then it cannot be truly socialist. Far from maintaining "unity of the left," any socialist who made concessions to the totalitarianism of the various post-Leninist groups, parties, or governments was actually, in the language that they themselves were much more likely to use, "betraying" socialism.

In April 2003, as the war in Iraq raged, I was one of the drafters of a letter signed by a group of democratic socialists in the United States and elsewhere who castigated Cuba for the savage sentences meted out against dissidents under cover of the war. Needless to say the usual suspects accused us of providing political cover for a U.S. attack on Cuba, even though in reality our statement opposed the U.S. embargo on Cuba while Castro's behavior provided aid and comfort to his enemies in the United States who wanted to maintain it.

Some of the American Castro supporters were more honest, in their own peculiar way. Even as they castigated Attorney General Ashcroft for his encroachment on American civil liberties, they sought to prove that dissidents in Cuba "deserved" twenty-eight-year sentences after brief kangaroo courts.

These events called to mind Orwell's essay "Prevention of Literature." "When one sees highly educated men looking on indifferently at oppression and persecution, one wonders which to despise more, their cynicism or their shortsightedness."[2] Orwell would, of course, have recognized the dishonest and illogical metaphysics of Castro's American defenders, their belief that it is not the perpetrator of outrages—the purges, the gulags, or the show trials—who is at fault but the messengers who draw attention to it, and their belief that ethical principles are expedient, to be used and abused on an *ad patriam* basis. In the case of Cuba, "one star flag good, fifty, bad" becomes a universal principle.

It may be sweeping and unjustified generalization, but one rather suspects that those who opposed criticism of Saddam Hussein or Fidel Castro would not be fans of George Orwell and his works. Indeed, all too often one finds a deep nostalgia for the Soviet Union and the Third International embedded in much of the criticism of Orwell, even when it is expressed on other, ancillary grounds, whether literary failings, sexism, sadism, homophobia, imperialism, anti-Semitism, or jingoism, all of which sins his enemies have variously found him to be guilty.

This approach is indeed *Orwellian,* since Orwell's critics know that they cannot criticize him for his basic opposition to totalitarianism and the Soviets, because this would deprive them of an audience outside a few Leninoid sects. But they still feel he must be punished for his thoughtcrime, so they look for other cudgels with which to attack him.

To be fair, it is equally disturbing that many of those on the right who stay silent about the continuing affront to human rights and international law in Guantanamo Bay claim to be supporters of Orwell. We have seen so-called human rights lawyers urbanely discussing the advantages of torture in the modern age. We have seen far too many intellectuals silent about the assault on civil liberties under this administration. And we have seen media people conspire with presidential power to cover up the deficiencies in his arguments for war.

Orwell was rather prolific, and as I said earlier, many of his critics and mistaken admirers alike seem not to have taken the elementary step of checking his works. In particular the "Conservative" claims to Orwell's legacy are usually based either on ignoring his own explicit and frequently repeated declarations, right up the end of his life, that he was a democratic socialist. Ironically, some of them adopt the same arguments as his Leninist critics, that Orwell's career, if he had lived would have been extrapolated inevitably to some future proto-NeoCon position.

This ignores the very real strength of the British non-Leninist Left, either from American unfamiliarity with British politics and history or from the retrospective attempts to claim Orwell as a Trotskyist. Neither Aneurin Bevan, nor Michael Foot, to name but two of his colleagues on *Tribune,* drifted rightwards, and they and the newspaper, as mentioned earlier, still maintained a clear line of separation from the Bolshevik tendencies.

Indeed, had Orwell actually been a Trotskyist, it is not unlikely that he would have polemicized himself into a neoconservative position. But he was *not,* and so I suspect he would not have gone that path. Indeed, one of the characteristics that I would claim to be *Orwellian* in the most positive sense is that, perhaps paradoxically in view of his argumentative propensities, he was never a vicious polemicist in the traditions of the Third and Fourth Internationals, which have traditionally punished unwary thought-criminals to a comprehensive calumniation. In the Leninist tradition, defiance leads to demonization, and in the old Soviet Union, possibly to death. Just look at the fate of anyone, no matter how fine a comrade, who suggested that Mendel had a better grasp of biology than Lysenko. The Trotskyist branch tended more to splits and expulsions but probably gained in the vocabulary of its mutual denunciations what it could not use in brute force. This certainly appears to be one of the Trotskyist methodologies that survived the extinction of the former ideology of the NeoCons.

Trotsky was wittier about it. He wrote of Stalin, "Every word he wrote was a mistake—and some were two." As a sharp jibe it works, but sadly, it reveals a mind-set. In contrast, Orwell tried to be fair, albeit robust of phrase with opponents. He wrote to his editor to change *Animal Farm* because he noted that Stalin had stayed in Moscow during the war, and thus his depiction of Napoleon as cowardly when the windmill is blown up was thus unfair (3:407). Perhaps in conscious reaction to these traits, Orwell, never short of strong opinions, often seems to be straining to hold back his own polemical tendencies and trying to be fair: to hate the sin while being open-minded about the sinned.

So Orwell is prepared to countenance that Churchill may have some attractions and even, as we saw, to try to be "fair" to Stalin, without going the whole hog of both the communists and Conservatives, whose hagiographers each promptly converted their mutual demons into saints for the duration of the war. Indeed the more rabid contemporary critics of Orwell epitomize the polemical excommunications of that era—*Nation* columnist Alex Cockburn, who described Orwell as "a whiner . . . a snitch, and informer to the secret police, Animal Farm's resident weasel"[3] springs to mind. Orwell, as so often, has the last word about such inquisitional language when he says of the totalitarian mindset, "To admit that an opponent might be both honest and intelligent is felt to be intolerable. It is more immediately satisfying to shout that he is a fool or a scoundrel, or both, than to find out what he is really like" (3:331).

ORWELLIAN METHOD

It is this generosity of spirit Orwell displayed, even when it is wrapped in crusty Tory curmudgeonliness, that leads to my title for this essay, invoking Comrade Psmith (where the P is silent), one of P. G. Wodehouse's characters. Wodehouse was a brilliant comic writer who faced persecution for making some ill-considered, frivolous radio programs in Berlin during the Second World War, after he had been interned there as an enemy alien.

Many of those who wanted him punished were also those who protested at the release from preventive detention of Oswald Mosley, the British fascist leader during the war. As Orwell pointed out, these included many communists who had themselves earlier opposed the war for more than two years while the Hitler-Stalin Pact lasted. Orwell decried Mosley's internment once the threat of invasion had gone—albeit with the somewhat devastatingly pragmatic aside that if an invasion had been mounted then he should have been shot quickly to head off the threat of a quisling administration.

Consistently, Orwell even opposed the banning of the Communist Party's *Daily Worker* because it represented a restriction of free speech, although, with a sharpened sense of irony, he pointed out that the *Daily Worker*'s eagerness to ban the fascists had prepared the ground for restrictions on communists—and tactfully did not mention the paper's frequent attacks on him and his work.

Despite Wodehouse's manifest failures in the field of socialist realism, or indeed his failure to make much of an attempt to deal with contemporary politics or society at all, Orwell, with the open mindedness that characterizes many of his assessments, was a strong public admirer of his literary skills.

That aspect of Orwell's writings becomes even more noticeable when it is contrasted with the work of his critics. In fact, his essays have much of Anglo-American empiricism about them. They do not start with a line, into which the facts have to be squeezed. Instead, he looks at each issue in its own context, with the motives of the parties and the practical implications of their decisions providing the material on which to base any action. As he said, "to accept an orthodoxy is always to inherit unresolved contradictions" ("Writers and Leviathan," 4:467). Much of Orwell's work is an attempt to tease out those contradictions and resolve them in a practical way so that any calls for action should be informed by some thought about the likely outcomes. For example, while regarding Stalin's country as a threat to peace and democracy in Europe, he tried to restrain philosopher (and ex-pacifist!) Lord Bertrand Russell's attempts to rouse support for a preemptive nuclear strike on the USSR.

The refusal to take binary positions may seem like common sense, but looking at political debate on the Left in general, particularly the Leninist Left, and even in the partisan world of American politics, it is surprising how uncommon common sense is. Orwell applied "fuzzy logic" before it was invented, and he tended to see the world—and people—in shades of gray rather than black or white. However, there is nothing in this "Orwellian" method of the archetypal soggy liberal, so balanced that they teeter in the middle, unable to take sides. When Orwell came to a conclusion, it was usually incisive and vigorously expressed. More often than not, to defeat a great evil, we will find ourselves with flawed allies. The important thing for Orwell was not to forget the flaws. Because Churchill and Stalin acted together against Hitler did not mean that they had become democratic socialists.

I was stricken by how uncommon this commonsensical empirical approach is during the contemporary debates over "humanitarian intervention" in which support for intervention in, say, Kosovo was assumed to mean that one must necessarily support war on Afghanistan and Iraq, because those who opposed intervention did so completely regardless of the particular circumstances. For them, it was a metaphysical idea, the *concept* of intervention, that they opposed rather than any particular application. One always suspects that much of the hard Left regard such questions as catechismal litmus tests for political purity rather than as a guide to action.

Orwell was well aware of the dangers to those who anchor their moral principles to nation-states. Those of us who will not stoop to say "My country right or wrong" will surely still have the courage to admit that occasionally our country may be right, even if only on the principle of a stopped clock being right twice a day. On the other hand, it is surely dangerous to support someone else's country, right or wrong, whether it be the Soviet Union, Cuba, China, or North Korea, and indeed certainly not Ba'athist Iraq or, for that matter, Likudnik Israel.

Principles come first and then can be used to judge countries, and that consistency of method worked often and well in Orwell's work. Those of us who remember that just over a decade ago Saddam Hussein was the frontline friend and ally of the United States and United Kingdom against the Islamic hordes of Iran, visited and feted by the Donald Rumsfelds of this world, will surely recognize Orwell's odious but telling comparison of Radio Moscow's denunciation of the British naval blockade of Germany as an inhuman measure starving German women and children with the same service's denunciation as pro-Nazi of critics of the Soviets' ethnic cleansing of some ten million German peasants from the east of Germany.

Reading *Nineteen Eighty-Four* itself, one could say that it anticipates Hannah Arendt on the "banality of evil." One of the essential "Orwellian" features is an appreciation that seemingly pleasant and urbane people can perpetrate great evils. O'Brien is not demonized or caricatured any more than Charrington, the Thought Police landlord of Smith's love nest. And it is worth remembering that for the cause of Goldstein's underground opposition, Winston and Julia, our hero and heroine, pledge themselves to commit brutalities, in fact terrorism. They promise O'Brien that they are prepared to throw sulfuric acid in a child's face or commit sabotage causing the deaths of hundreds of people. And these are the nice people in the novel!

Orwell's essay "Revenge Is Sour" (4:19), in which he describes how a Jewish prison guard mistreated a club-footed German SS officer, is typical of his depiction of the complexity and the banality of evil and the futility of revenge. "It is absurd to blame any German or Austrian Jew for getting his own back on the Nazis," he says, but his experiences taught him that "the whole idea of revenge and punishment is a childish day dream." And then he points to the intelligentsia's acquiescence in "crimes like the expulsion of all Germans from East Prussia" (4:19). However, Orwell forgivingly maintained that "it is possible to meet thinking people who have remained Communists for as much as ten years before resigning or being expelled, and who have not been intellectually crippled by the experience" (4:366). Indulgently, he also felt about the "cryptos," the undercover members and fellow travelers whom he so often denounced as a type, that "one ought not to hurriedly assume that they are all equally dishonest or even that they all hold the same opinions. Probably some of them are actuated by nothing more than stupidity" (4:368).

ORWELL THE SOCIALIST

Both conservatives and Stalinoids agree: Orwell was not a socialist. They treat Orwell as Procrustes used to treat his guests—by stretching them or truncating them to fit his bed. Theseus killed the legendary Procrustes, but his methods live on in literary and political criticism.

Even more neutral critics such as Louis Menand in the *New Yorker* seem to have difficulty actually *reading* Orwell's work. It must be common in literature departments nowadays. Menand claims that Orwell "spent much of his time criticizing professional Socialists, particularly the leaders of the British Labour Party, because, apart from the commitment to equality, there was not much about Socialism that was important to him. His economics were rudimentary, and he had little patience for the temporizing that ordinary politics requires."[4]

In fact, exactly the opposite is true; if Menand had actually read the readily available work, he would have seen that Orwell's essays are models of balance and understanding of the practical problems facing a Labour government in a country that had just bankrupted itself in a world war—and was actually carrying out much of what Orwell thought that it would not be able to deliver. Indeed anyone who knows the period and Orwell's own history may find remarkable his *lack* of criticism for the government on rereading those essays. Even on his death bed when he repudiated the suggestion that *Nineteen Eighty-Four* was antisocialist, Orwell was stressing his support for the Labour government. Maybe Menand just knows very little about British politics.

On the other hand, the secret of this particular cutting to size may be that Orwell did not share Menand's inflated views of Gandhi (Orwell referred to Gandhi as a "bit of a charlatan"); Menand complains that Orwell's appreciation of the Indian leader was "a grudging piece of writing." "'I have never been able to feel much liking for Gandhi, but I do not feel sure that as a political thinker he was wrong in the main, nor do I believe that his life was a failure,' was the most that

[Orwell] could bring himself to say," Menand says, seemingly in mild shock at the sacrilege.[5] In fact, Orwell's essay was a well-balanced appreciation, certainly more so than one would expect from him on a sandal-wearing vegetarian in a dhoti who carried his chamber pot around on his head and slept with young female disciples so that he could test his celibacy!

Returning to Orwell's actual political position: ironically, Orwell also needs defending against one of his most vociferous supporters. Christopher Hitchens, whose style is still imbued with the polemical ghosts of Fourth Internationals past even if he has now abandoned their ideology, persisted in his recent book in treating Orwell as a Trotskyist at heart.[6] In the peculiar dualism of Orwell studies, he probably shares this prejudice with the communists, who would not necessarily see this as a positive attribute, and many American academic socialists, who come from a shrinking tradition but one in which Trotsky, the former Bolshevik leader, had reframed himself as a democratic socialist in his exile.

There is a conflict here between Hitchens's intellectual honesty and his nostalgia for Trotsky, whose record while in power in the Soviet Union showed no signs of overly deep attachment to democracy or human rights. Hitchens's introduction claims that Orwell dealt with the three great subjects of the twentieth century, which he asserts are fascism, imperialism, and "Stalinism." In fact, looking at Orwell's work, the subjects are totalitarianism, which encompasses clogged rivers in Rwanda and death squads in Central America; Leninism in all its forms; and, indeed, imperialism, with all its baggage of racism. Hitchens himself admits that "Orwell in his essays was fond of saying that both Lenin and Trotsky bore some responsibility for Stalinism" (133). In fact, Orwell made it very plain, over and over again, that far beyond "some responsibility," there was little or no difference between the three. Indeed, Orwell's criticism of Arthur Koestler, with whom he maintained cordial relations, could be a prescient comment on Hitchens himself— at least until recently. Orwell took Koestler to task for the residual loyalty to the party "and a resulting tendency to make all bad developments date from the rise of Stalin," whereas Orwell maintained that "all the seeds of the evil were there from the start, and that things would not have been substantially different if Lenin or Trotsky had remained in control" ("Catastrophic Gradualism," 4:35).

Had Lenin lived "it is probable that he would either have been thrown out, like Trotsky, or would have kept himself in power by methods as barbarous, or nearly as barbarous as those of Stalin," (4:200) Orwell later added, which puts him closer to Robert Conquest than Hitchens, even though *Why Orwell Matters* is dedicated to Conquest.

But why go on about Trotskyism in fifty-seven varieties? There are two reasons. One is that Hitchens's residual adherence to one branch of it has distorted some of his analysis of where Orwell stands in the socialist tradition. While he establishes firmly that Orwell is indeed in that tradition, and remained there until he died, Hitchens and, I suspect for similar reasons, many Americans, even more so, underestimate the homegrown democratic socialist influences on Orwell.

In the United States, following the Dewey Commission and with the general weakness of the American Left, the Trotskyists often seem to have been able to pass themselves off as cozy social democrats, not least on the age-old principle of "my enemy's enemy is my friend." There could be no more vitriolic opponents of the Soviet Union than the Trotskyists, which tended to make them moderately more respectable in the United States during the cold war, even if the FBI could not always tell one red from another. Indeed they became so respectable that their descendant neocons in their current avatars as Pentagon advisors are currently directing the most aggressive foreign policy ever for the United States. This is truly "Orwellian" in the sense I pledged not to use.

With the disappearance of a mass socialist tradition with any political leverage in the American governmental system, socialism as a concept in the United States has been dominated by academy and ideology in a way that excludes the pragmatism of the British Labour tradition and that perhaps occludes its significance in considering Orwell's work.

Orwell's political epiphany came when he went to Spain as a member of the Independent Labour Party (ILP) and not by the usual route, through the Communist Party, which fed recruits to the International Brigade. The ILP was a Marxist-leaning but non-Leninist body with its own traditions of activism and militancy and of parliamentary activity, although the latter diminished rapidly after it split from the Labour Party itself in 1931. The ILP was Orwell's political home until it effectively dissolved away during the war. Most of its members rejoined the Labour Party, which Orwell certainly publicly supported even after it took office. They tended to cluster around *Tribune,* the paper that he eventually joined as columnist and literary editor.

Most of the American Left, and even many in Britain, pay lip service to some forms of the popular frontism of the late 1930s, in which slogans like "No enemies on the left" or calls for "Left Unity" even now all too often inhibit democratic socialists from distinguishing themselves from the assorted Leninists, who in return remember all too well Lenin's call to support the social democrats "like rope supports a hanged man."

For all such, Orwell invites us to the ultimate in thoughtcrime. As befits one who fought against both, he came to "the old, true and unpalatable conclusion that a Communist and a Fascist are somewhat nearer to one another than either is to a democrat" (1946, 4:192).Although this was the constant theme of Orwell's well-argued work for the last decade of his life, this is still a shocking concept to many on the left. Of course he infuriates his overt opponents because, as he says, "one defeats the fanatic by not being fanatic oneself, but on the contrary by using one's intelligence" (1949, 4:539). The intelligence of his criticism, its effectiveness, is what reduces so many of his attackers to paroxysms of ad hominemism. They tend to look at what he was *against,* rather than what he was *for,* because their dialectic does not grasp alternatives. "Every line of serious work that I have written since 1936 has been written, directly or indirectly, *against* totalitarianism and *for* democratic Socialism, as I understand it" ("Why I Write," 3:28).

Those brought up in the binary and polemical tradition of politics have difficulty in interpreting all those lines of serious work.. As mentioned earlier, there is an ironic convergence between some on the Left and the Right who unite in concluding that since Orwell was anti-Soviet, he must be antisocialist. But as he said just before he died, *Nineteen Eighty-Four* "is NOT intended as an attack on Socialism or on the British Labour Party (of which I am a supporter) but as a show up of the perversions to which a centralized economy is liable" (4:564).

Perhaps some of the flavor can be seen in the tirades masquerading as criticism from the Left in the work of Scott Lucas, who is professor of American studies at

Birmingham University (United Kingdom) as well as author of the most intemperately anti-Orwell biography. Lucas is not one to let mere repeated declarations by Orwell, right up to his death, interfere with the bilious flow of his vitriol. According to Lucas, Orwell's "socialism consisted primarily of bashing other socialists" (*The New Statesman,* May 29, 2000). Scott Lucas's biography of Orwell is effectively a sustained polemic against its subject, and his revulsion for his subject oozes through in almost every chapter. Lucas is an odd choice for the publishers, almost as if they had commissioned a biography of Shakespeare from someone who thought that the Earl of Oxford had actually written the plays. Orwell's contempt for alleged left intellectuals seems amply justified when reading this bad-tempered biography, which seeks to "rescue ourselves from 'Orwell.'"

Orwell described totalitarian literary language as having "a curious mouthing sort of quality, as of someone who is choking with rage & can never quite hit on the words he wanted," and it is a prescient description of Lucas's treatment of his subject, which sneers its way along with epithets like "Orwell, the armchair general," and in which "Orwell's crusade against socialism," is proved by Orwell's observation that the Conservative Council in Liverpool was engaged in slum clearance and building decent council homes. In fact the Conservative Council did clear slums and build houses, and I was brought up in one of those inconveniently really existing council houses that Lucas tries to shove down a memory hole. Most of the tenantry managed to vote Labour even as they lived in the politically incorrect Conservative-Council-built houses.

Lucas repeatedly accuses Orwell of "animosity towards the Left." But this is true only if you accept a peculiar definition of "Left," one that can love concentration camps, show trials, and the Hitler–Stalin pact and which can stay silent while Spanish socialists and British ILP members are pursued, imprisoned and executed by KGB agents. Sometimes the sound of silence is deafening. Lucas's essay, while impugning Orwell's claims to socialism, is completely silent on the nature of the alternative—what Orwell was "bashing." This is a significant a gap in his argument, since Lucas does not say what *he* considers to be socialism. From its boundaries, the gap appears to occupy the same space-time continuum as the Soviet Union of the 1940s. We can only conclude that socialism equals gulags plus electrification. However, we must assume that Lucas knows that an overt argument for this case would lose conviction with most of the readers of the *New Statesman,* not to mention his students and colleagues at Birmingham. It is a remarkable application of the dialectic, all antithesis and no thesis.

So Lucas denies Orwell's own clear statements, the views of the British Labour Party, and those of the Socialist International, and he declares that "Orwell found his true calling as an anti-communist liberal." Now in the context of the purges, gulags, and ethnic cleansing it may be surprising that someone would consider that a pejorative title. But these things happen. Ironically, Comrade Lucas's views converge with those of the Conservatives: socialism means concentration camps and thought police. However, the inference to be drawn from his work is that Lucas thinks they were good things, and the intellectuals who defended them were victims of red-baiting and, of course, socialists.

Indeed, critics from the Leninist Left attack Orwell for being a "Tory" without realizing what an honorable position this has been in the British tradition. From the time of the Civil War, when rebels claimed to be overthrowing the Norman

Yoke, British radicalism has had a strong Tory streak. They are usurped *ancient* liberties that British radicals have often tried to reclaim and that were indeed invoked during the American Revolution. From William Cobbett, the heir of Tom Paine, to the modern satirical magazine *Private Eye,* the *persona* of a crusty curmudgeonly Tory has been an effective position to snipe at authority. It is certainly not inconsistent with socialism allied with the decency that Orwell wanted.

Orwell himself certainly had his own definitions of socialism, which even if they do not have the false clarity of "gulags plus electrification" are reasonable and humanitarian expositions of democratic socialism, of a pragmatic kind that could easily infuriate Leninist academics. "Socialism until recently was supposed to connote political democracy, social equality and internationalism" (4:197). Orwell said after the war, and he added that, to the masses everywhere, "'Socialism' means, or at least is associated with, higher wages, shorter hours, better houses, all round social insurance" (4:427). These may be humble, liberal, and even anticommunist goals. But they were real ones for the working people of Britain who elected the party Orwell supported in 1945. And that party, for all its faults, overfulfilled the plan. Critics accuse Orwell of being a false prophet, because Ingsoc never happened. But in fact he did at the end of his life suggest that "The only area in which it (Democratic Socialism) could conceivably be made to work, in any near future, is western Europe" (4:425). In reality, the western European form of social democracy, so sneered at by Marxisant professors, has delivered the highest standards of human, civil, and economic rights and security in the world to hundreds of millions of people.

However, Orwell knew that, in the real world, there was no yellow brick road to socialism. There were potholes and diversions to be watched for. In an essay on James Burnham, Orwell states "it has always been obvious that planned and centralized society is liable to turn into an oligarchy or dictatorship," and likewise that the "notion that monopoly must imply tyranny, is not a startling one" (4:195). This fairly obvious point has not always been self-evident to some academic socialists whose attraction to tidy planning tended to exclude messy popular participation. It does not necessarily negate public ownership per se, as any comparison of the recent output of the state-owned but not government-controlled British Broadcasting Corporation with the private media monopsonies would indicate.

In his review of Friedrich von Hayek's "Road to Serfdom," which dealt with the dangers of centralized state power, Orwell agreed that "collectivism is not inherently democratic, but on the contrary gives a tyrannical minority such powers as the Spanish Inquisition never dreamed of" (3:143). But he was not original in saying so. Throughout the 1930s in Britain the large cooperative movement and even some of the syndicalist-influenced unions were well aware of the dangers of state control and centralization before von Hayek. They were concerned that simple nationalization and state control of industries would be far from liberating for workers and customers alike.

In short, Orwell was not a lone voice, although he was an outstanding voice. He was part of a large, well-established British tradition that, far from being marginalized like the Trotskyist sects worldwide or the American Left, became the governing party of one of the world's major nations. It was the clarity and strength of his voice that set him apart. Interestingly, it was, indeed, the intellectuals who were less eager than the organized "proles" to agree with his points.

The List

For both extremes of the political spectrum, Orwell's revulsion for the Soviet Union makes him a cold warrior, and to the communists, and indeed some of the Trotskyists, a traitor. But if one takes into account his factually correct view of the essential identity of totalitarianism, then it was inevitable that a British Labour government had hard choices to make. Even before the 1945 election he warned, "There is the impending showdown with Russia which people at the top of the Labour Party no doubt realize to be unavoidable" (3:432). He left no doubt which side he would put himself on. "In case of war breaking out, if one were compelled to choose between Russia and America, I would always choose America," he told his former publisher Victor Gollancz (4:355). "In international politics . . . you must be prepared to practice appeasement indefinitely, or at some point you must be ready to fight," he warned. However, it is worth remembering his attempts to curb Bertrand Russell's enthusiasm for a preemptive nuclear strike against Russia. Of course, to self-hating American leftists, Orwell's restraint on Russell notwithstanding, this is grotesque red-baiting. So when the famous list that Orwell sent to Celia Kirwan not so much surfaced as was rediscovered, it allowed lots of people who were still in shock from the fall of the Soviet Union to get a second lease on life as they went frothing about on what Alexander Cockburn called "snitching."[7] For Americans who are not fully aware of what Cockburn meant by "snitching," it is actually an entirely appropriate term. In the privileged public (in the United Kingdom that means "private" of course) school that Comrade Cockburn's communist father sent his sons to, boys, even if buggered and bullied near to death by others, were not supposed to tell. That was "snitching."

One cannot help but suspect that Orwell's critics were really looking desperately for something that could detract from *Animal Farm* and *Nineteen Eighty-Four,* since they had little factual grounds for doing so, at least since the 20th Congress of the Soviet Communist Party in 1956 when Nikita Khrushchev first revealed the crimes of Stalin. But, any truncheon in a rage, and Orwell is fair game.

Recently, at the New York Socialist Scholars Conference, Andrew Rubin used another term to repeat, admittedly in more measured tones, the gist of Lucas's polemic. He sought to prove at length that Orwell had "collaborated" with the British Government. This is an accusation with, well, Orwellian overtones. The Oxford English Dictionary gives two definitions of collaborator, the second of which ironically cites Orwell. The first, "One who works in conjunction with another or others, esp. in literary, artistic or scientific work," is clearly not the one that Rubin is using. No, it is the second, pejorative sense, "One who collaborates with the enemy," for which usage the OED actually cites Orwell ("1946, 'G. Orwell' Critical ess. 137. At this moment with France newly liberated and the witch-hunt for collaborators in full swing") that is undoubtedly the pejorative sense that Rubin intended.

So let us consider the inferences we can draw from this choice of words. First, it implies that the postwar British Labour government was "the enemy" with whom the accused collaborated. It is reminiscent of the pamphlet by U.S. communist leader Earl Browder that tickled Dwight Macdonald so much, "How the People Can Win the Election." In those far-off days before Florida 2000, it was difficult for a rational person to think of how "the people" could lose!

Never mind that the Labour Party was elected by a landslide majority, and in the course of its term introduced a welfare state of which many American so-called socialists could only dream six decades later. The Labour Party introduced free health care and free education up to and including university. It nationalized coal, steel, transport, and electricity. It began dismantling the British Empire, beginning with India and Burma. And it did all of this without threatening dissidents, let alone transporting them to prison camps and shooting them.

What is more, George Orwell was an active supporter of the government in its policies and wrote for *Tribune,* a Labour newspaper. So in what way was he "collaborating"? Who was the enemy? In fact, of course, the Labour Party was the "enemy" of the Soviet Union and its totalitarian system. The Soviet communists were rounding up members of Labour's social democratic counterparts in Eastern Europe and shooting them. Orwell had watched the Soviets and their comrades in operation in Spain, where he narrowly escaped with his own life from the purges and show trials they were staging in Barcelona and elsewhere. "We were lucky to get out of Spain alive and not even to have been arrested once. Many of our friends were shot and others spent a long time in prison or simply disappeared" (3:456). Orwell had watched the Soviets ally with Nazi Germany and British communists decide that the war in which Britain barely survived was an "imperialist" war and that the British Royal Navy was starving German workers by blockading European ports. He had deplored the ethnic cleansing of the former German lands by the advancing Russians and their allies.

So the use of the term "collaborator" for Orwell implies that his accuser does not regard an elected social-democratic government as in any way legitimate. In some topsy-turvy metaphysical way, Orwell should have accepted that the Soviets represented the sweep of history, and so his opposition to them was a form of thoughtcrime even if in the real world he was supporting the party he supported and the government that he had helped elect against a totalitarian enemy.

These accusations, of course, are part of the ad hominem barrage of the Leninist polemic. In the United States, discussion of this issue has often been colored by memories of the McCarthy era, without perhaps appreciating the differences between the two situations. Orwell's list was not of people to be shot, as it would have been in the worker's fatherland, nor even of people to be imprisoned. In fact, he did not even want them dismissed from their present positions. He simply felt that they were unfit to represent a social-democratic Britain in world affairs. As stated earlier, Britain did not undergo McCarthyite purges, which is why many persecuted artists like Charlie Chaplin fled to London to escape.

In fact, in 1948, Orwell had written to George Woodcock suggesting that their organization, the Freedom Defence Association, consider action against blacklisting (4:471). He explained, "It's not easy to have a clear position, because, if one admits the right of governments to govern, one must admit their right to choose suitable agents, & I think *any* organization has the right to protect itself against infiltration methods. But at the same time, the *way* in which the government seems to be going to work is vaguely disquieting." Indeed, he goes on point out that the communists were victims of the type of measures that they had themselves been calling for against fascists, while he himself more consistently lamented a general public indifference to freedom of speech. So, ironically, one has to read Orwell and use the analytical tools he developed in order to be able to understand his critics. The Orwell quotation that the *OED* cites is also highly relevant. Orwell, after a long war against fascism that had begun for him in Spain years before the Second World War began, was arguing for tolerance against the witch hunts of alleged "collaborators" in France by people more often than not, he suspected, covering up their own history of collaboration.

Tangential Criticisms

When I was young in Liverpool, the old Communist Party members used to dismiss Orwell because "he said the working class smelt." Actually, Orwell didn't say this, but, in fact, the working class did smell. When in most working-class homes there was no hot water except what could be heated on the stove—and it took a lot of that to fill up the galvanized iron tub—it would have been difficult for them not to! When I was a kid, even in the relatively sophisticated homes built by Liverpool's Conservative Council, we had baths once a week, whether we needed it or not, and the bath water would be reused for all the kids. We considered ourselves respectable working class, and we had hot running water, when we could afford the coal. Woolen clothes with no dry-cleaning would not help too much either. It is perhaps typical that Orwell should be condemned for something he did not say—but that would have been true in any case.

Similarly Beatrix Campbell, a British author, berated Orwell for not being a protofeminist and suggests that his choice to study miners in *The Road to Wigan Pier* proved that he was a misogynist because there were no women miners (I simplify, I admit!). In fact, one cannot help suspecting that it is much more relevant that Comrade Campbell was a longtime Communist Party member, writing for the *Daily Worker*'s successor paper, the *Morning Star*, for many years. We see here existing antipathy looking for an excuse.

Christopher Hitchens has analyzed Raymond Williams's critiques of Orwell and is correct about the origins of this amazing continuing antipathy. In general one suspects that being prematurely correct is an unforgivable sin to some people. After Nikita Khrushchev's speech to the 20th Congress denouncing Stalin, the main British Communist Party theoretician R. Palme Dutt was asked why he had been silent after these years and he reportedly said, "I never said that there were no spots on the sun." Few if any of the Communist Party supporters and those in their orbit can ever forgive Orwell for his prescience in pointing out that the whole Soviet solar system was blighted. Unable to defend gulags, Orwell's denouncers pick on the picayune to damn him, such as his failure to have a precocious 1970s sensibility toward women, his alleged olfactory sensitivity to unwashed workers, or his eagerness to defend democracy and socialism in the face of totalitarianism. They find these sins to be unforgivable and unforgettable. But it is remarkable that they can dismiss wholesale massacres and deportations in the Soviet Union as "mistakes." Lucas and others have also tried to infer Orwell's rightist perfidy because Edgar Hoover liked one or two of his books or because the CIA and British agencies used his work to advance their arguments about communism in Russia. Orwell was of course dead by that time, and his widow protested at the changes made to the film versions of his novels. However, it is a measure of their frustration that, despite half a century of disputing his significance, Orwell's left critics have never made him an unperson.

CONCLUSION

At the George Orwell Centenary Conference at Wellesley College in May 2003, I had a sort of epiphany. Scholars were analyzing Orwell's deep pessimism, and I had to go to the rostrum to share a brainstorm: in fact, Orwell was a hopeless *optimist.* In *Nineteen Eighty-Four* he thought that rulers would *care* enough about history to want to rewrite it! Does George W. Bush know or care?

Soaked in twenty-four-hour context-free cable TV driveling amnesia over them, a huge percentage of American voters not only were unaware that WMDs have not been found in Iraq but also thought that they were actually *used* during the war. Even higher percentages still think Saddam Hussein was behind the September 11, 2001, attack on the World Trade Center. On the other hand, a small but noisy percentage, including many self-professed intellectuals, portrayed the bloodstained Saddam Hussein (just as they had canonized Slobodan Milosevic) as a freedom fighter in the front line against globalization. It has been a truly Orwellian prospect in the bad sense.

In *Nineteen Eighty-Four,* the heretical Goldstein text that O'Brien lent to Winston looked back: "In the general hardening of outlook that set in round about 1930, practices which had been long abandoned, in some cases for hundreds of years—imprisonment without trial, the use of war prisoners as slaves, public executions, torture to extract confessions, the use of hostages, and deportation of whole populations—not only became common again, but tolerated and even defended by people who considered themselves enlightened and progressive." Orwell wrote this in the aftermath of Spain, World War II, the gulags and the concentration camps, and while Stalin continued to use the techniques he had perfected at home to seize control of Eastern Europe. The horrifying thing about the turn of the millennium is that there are still apologists for all these practices and more. As Kurt Vonnegut says about the consistency of human barbarity, "so it goes."

These totalitarians span the whole traditional political spectrum. On the establishment side, there has been toleration for death squads in Central and Latin America; on the left, apologetics for ethnic cleansing in the Balkans and users of poison gas in Iraq. The Khmer Rouge found support from both the Left and the Right as a stick to beat the Soviets and Vietnamese, while recently both right isolationists and alleged left anti-imperialists found common cause in defending Slobodan Milosevic. More currently, the case of the shifting excuses for the war on Iraq, the manipulation of facts to mold public opinion, the twenty-four-hour hate of the cable networks that has replaced *Nineteen Eighty-Four*'s more modest Two Minutes Hate all combine to ensure the continuing relevance of Orwell.

The good news, even in these gloomy times, is that the concept of human rights, as principles that apply *universally,* to all regimes, whatever their claimed political orientation, is gaining ground. It is a war of attrition, in which each gain has to be hard fought for, and massacres and ethnic cleansing still occur. But I cannot help thinking that it is a victory for decency, the concept that Orwell's critics have used almost as a slur, that in the twenty-first century, people like

Henry Kissinger, Ariel Sharon, Saddam Hussein, and General Pinochet all have to consult their lawyers before they go to their travel agents.

To understand the twentieth century, I regularly reread *Animal Farm, Nineteen Eighty-Four, Alice in Wonderland, Alice Through the Looking Glass,* and *Darkness at Noon.* The canon has not changed significantly for the twenty-first century, but it has shifted. Now, the main purpose of reading *Darkness at Noon* is to understand why Leninist critics of Orwell can believe so many impossible things before breakfast. The others still stand as guides to the abuses of language and thought that are possible in defense of tyranny and atrocity.

Orwell's work gives us the intellectual tools to understand what is happening and to combat it—without becoming the unthinking, metaphysically minded enemy that polemics can and do make of people. He offers an outstanding example of a writer and thinker who fights rough and tough, but fairly, for decency. Because Orwell realized that when you stop being fair, you have lost the very cause you are fighting for.

NOTES

1. Scott Lucas, *Orwell* (London: Haus Publishing, 2003).

2. *The Collected Essays, Journalism and Letters of George Orwell,* ed. Sonia Orwell and Ian Angus (Harmondsworth, UK: Penguin Books, 1970), 4:94. Sources for subsequent quotations from this edition will be given by parenthetical citations in the chapter.

3. Alexander Cockburn, "Foreword," in John Reed, *Snowball's Chance* (New York: Roof Books, 2002), 7.

4. Menand, "Honest, Decent, Wrong: The Invention of George Orwell," *The New Yorker,* January 27, 2003.

5. Menand, "Honest, Decent, Wrong."

6. Christopher Hitchens, *Why Orwell Matters* (New York: Basic Books, 2002).

7. Cockburn, "Foreword," 7.

3

Hope against Hope:
Orwell's Posthumous Novel

MORRIS DICKSTEIN

Very few books published in the twentieth century had the impact of *Nineteen Eighty-Four*. It crossed the line between the popular and the literary audience and intrigued students of politics as much as readers of futuristic fiction. It mirrored contemporary history but also influenced history by making the case against totalitarianism—especially Soviet-style communism—accessible and unforgettable. It turned the long-standing themes of Orwell's journalism into a fable and the utopian claims for the workers' paradise into a nightmare. When I first read it in high school I was most taken with Orwell's ingenious phrasemaking: *Newspeak, Big Brother Is Watching You,* the *Anti-Sex League,* the *memory hole, unperson, doublethink.* Though I was no great fan of science fiction, I knew that the cold war had found its authentic poet.

Rereading the book in 1984, I marveled at how the ubiquitous surveillance in Orwell's future state anticipated later advances in the technology of snooping. I was struck too by Orwell's geopolitical vision, borrowed in part from the work of a well-known social critic, James Burnham, as he portrayed three large blocs in perpetual but limited war against each other—the cold war and the "nonaligned group" in a nutshell. The early 1980s saw Orwell writ large as we witnessed the last intense flare-up of the cold war. In the aftermath of the Soviet takeover in Afghanistan, an American president revved up the arms race, campaigned against the "Evil Empire," and helped undo the conservative, geriatric leadership in the Kremlin. New long-range missiles were to be installed in Europe, provoking large-scale peace protests. There was still a dynamic, anti-American third world bloc, spearheaded by the religious revolutionaries who had only recently humiliated the United States in Iran. Since Orwell's future had formally arrived, discussions of the novel turned narrowly on his political forecasting, which was hardly the main purpose of *Nineteen Eighty-Four*.

Should we remember Orwell as a great writer, or simply a timely one? Was his work genuinely prophetic or merely an exaggeration of tendencies he lamented in

This essay first appeared in *The American Scholar* (Spring 2004) and is reprinted by permission of the author.

his own time? What kind of book was *Nineteen Eighty-Four* that readers could connect to it at so many different levels? If we raised these questions about his nonfiction work, it would be easy to demonstrate that he was one of the great essayists of the century. The social reportage of the first half of *The Road to Wigan Pier* and the lonely moral witness of *Homage to Catalonia* stamp them as extraordinary documents that illuminate yet also transcend their age. The first is a pioneering work on the culture of poverty, the second a testament to the duplicities of Stalinism. Early essays like "A Hanging" and "Shooting an Elephant" help us understand the workings of empire at ground level, while Orwell's essays on popular culture prefigure the whole field of cultural studies. Apart from Orwell's insight as an observer and critic, his essays can be singled out for their rhetorical effects alone: their deceptively straightforward yet memorable prose, their arresting openings and endings, their seductive way of anchoring the subject in Orwell's own quirky personality and experiences—from Burma to Spain to the industrial north of England. A slight but perfect autobiographical essay like "Bookshop Memories," based on Orwell's months of working in a bookstore, stands out as a gallery of recognizable English types, a lethal Swiftian comedy of humors deftly exposing some of the foibles of English eccentricity.

Despite his direct manner, Orwell was anything but a simple writer. In his signature piece "Why I Write" (1946), which Sonia Orwell and Ian Angus used to introduce his collected essays, the famous declaration that "good prose is like a window pane" is followed by a striking summary of his own work: "I see that it is invariably where I lacked a *political* purpose that I wrote lifeless books and was betrayed into purple passages, sentences without meaning, decorative adjectives and humbug generally."[1] This is one of those memorable sentences so easy to misread. Orwell's credo becomes clearer if we recall his definition of "political purpose" a few pages earlier: he was, as he said, "using the word 'political' in the widest possible sense. Desire to push the world in a certain direction, to alter other people's idea of the kind of society they should strive after."[2] Described this way, political purpose can be seen as essential to all serious writing: Orwell soon declares that "no book is genuinely free from political bias." This follows hard upon his account of three other literary purposes, egoistic, aesthetic, and historical. He was determined, he tells us, "to make political writing into an art," crossing it with goals that had no clear connection to politics. "So long as I remain alive and well I shall continue to feel strongly about prose style, to love the surface of the earth, and to take pleasure in solid objects and scraps of useless information. It is no use trying to suppress that side of myself."[3] Orwell's essays are the fruit of his mixed motives, the sum of his contradictions. Orwell's view of himself as a political writer seems a good deal more nuanced when we read it in context.

When we turn to his last and most celebrated novel, the questions of how good a writer Orwell is and what kind of writer he is become more challenging. In *Animal Farm* he had projected the details of Soviet history into a barnyard fable, beautifully simple and consistent, written in a bemused childlike tone full of loving details of real farm life that make the tale so concrete. *Nineteen Eighty-Four* would prove to be a more haphazard and ambitious work. Few serious Orwell readers think of it as their favorite among his books. He himself was aware of the novel's flaws, which were partly the result of his desperate effort to get it finished in the face of grave illness. ("I ballsed it up rather," he told Julian Symons, "partly owing to being so ill while I was writing it."[4]) But *Nineteen Eighty-Four* also lies outside the mainstream of modern literature, which tends to be either realistic or formally inventive—focused either on creating a lifelike, credible, self-contained world, like most classic novels, or on refining new techniques for exploring individual consciousness, as in the works of Proust or Joyce. In different ways both stress verisimilitude. The dystopian political novel, with its projection into the future, its anxious fascination with technology, and broad use of satire, allegory, and symbolism, is at best an interesting minor current, though it included books Orwell admired and imitated, such as Jack London's *The Iron Heel* and Yevgeny Zamyatin's *We*. When, in another letter to Symons, Orwell acknowledged the "vulgarity of the 'Room 101' business,"[5] he was partly conceding the limits of the pulpy symbolism endemic to the genre. "I didn't know another way of getting somewhere near the effect I wanted."

If Winston Smith's horror of the rats in Room 101 is too crude and melodramatic, the torment he endures after his arrest is a weak echo of prison literature from Dostoevsky to Arthur Koestler's *Darkness at Noon*. While there is something impressive about Winston's mental disintegration, I doubt that I'm alone in finding his interrogator, O'Brien, a ludicrous and unconvincing figure. He is cast as a mouthpiece of the system, at once an intellectual and an executioner. Yet he merely repeats the rationale for thought control that has already been explained by Winston himself and developed in the arch-enemy Goldstein's subversive manuscript, which reads like an Orwell essay interpolated into the novel. Do we really need the diabolical O'Brien to tell us yet again about doublethink, about killing the sex instinct and abolishing the orgasm, about doctoring reality, abolishing memory, and consigning opponents to utter oblivion? It was one thing for Winston or the fictitious "Goldstein" to dissect these features of the Nazi or Soviet system. It's quite another for an actual character to use Kafkaesque logic to boast about these ingenious forms of subjugation, which he is sure will last forever. O'Brien may embody the system but he cannot plausibly speak for it. O'Brien is no Grand Inquisitor, whose arguments he tries to match; he is not even in a class with the icy, relentless interrogator Gletkin in *Darkness at Noon,* a type Koestler knew at first hand.

We could salvage O'Brien, perhaps, by casting him not as an articulate sadist or spokesman but as a lunatic who manages to impose his sense of reality through mental and physical torture. But Orwell, whose fatalism was intensified by his own fatal illness, is determined to see these fiendish excesses not as an aberration, ghastly yet not necessarily permanent, but as the way history is actually heading. Though we hear of O'Brien's "exaltation," his "lunatic enthusiasm,"[6] and though Winston questions his own sanity for being out of step, the book offers little support for seeing this thuggish creature simply as a madman who plays mind games with his victims while he happens to have his hand on the dial. When O'Brien tells Winston that the system's only goal is self-perpetuation—power for its own sake, torture for its own sake, dictatorship for its own sake—he becomes little more than an ideological construct. In the course of a suggestive analysis of O'Brien in *Contingency, Irony, and Solidarity,* the philosopher Richard Rorty argues that "he is as terrifying a character as we are likely to meet in a book,"[7] but to me he seems more a concept than a character. This is a major pitfall of this kind of allegory.

Nineteen Eighty-Four has several minor characters who also serve as emblems of Orwell's argument—including Syme, the ideological zealot, and Parsons, the slovenly, stupid true believer who is turned in by his own children—but they have a Dickensian vividness that makes them immediately credible. The most ingeniously conceived of these characters, Comrade Oglivy, that exemplary hero of the Revolution, never existed at all; he is simply the product of Winston Smith's talent for Orwellian fiction. His invented biography begins: "At the age of three Comrade Oglivy had refused all toys except a drum, a submachine gun, and a model helicopter. At six—a year early, by a special relaxation of the rules—he had joined the Spies; at nine he had been a troop leader. At eleven he had denounced his uncle to the Thought Police after overhearing a conversation which appeared to him to have criminal tendencies."[8] Though Christopher Hitchens says that *Nineteen Eighty-Four* "contains absolutely no jokes,"[9] Orwell, for a change, is having some serious fun here. But as his own vitality waned, he allowed his bleak outlook to take over the novel, especially after Winston and Julia are apprehended.

Winston's fate is determined from the moment he buys a diary and begins writing, falls in love, and rents a room of his own, but Orwell allows him a small pinhole of hope that makes all the difference, for it energizes the first three-quarters of the novel. While a fear of the future, especially the inhuman effects of technology, links *Nineteen Eighty-Four* to the mainstream of science fiction, Orwell softens his foreboding by giving Winston not only moments of respite, pleasure, and rebellion but also a curious faith in the future, not for himself but for what he personifies—a knotty residue of individuality, a stubborn resistance to regimentation. Orwell's appeal to posterity brings to mind poems like Whitman's "Crossing Brooklyn Ferry" or Brecht's "An die Nachgeborenen" (To Posterity), which begins, "Truly, I live in the dark ages," and ends with an appeal for understanding: "Think back on us/ With kindness." Winston scribbles in his diary, as Orwell writes the novel, "for the future, for the unborn," though he wonders if communication is really possible under a system that claims it can wipe out any trace of him. In "Why I Write," Orwell describes the writer's historical purpose as a "desire to see things as they are, to find out true facts and store them up for the use of posterity."[10] If Winston (like Orwell himself) already feels like a dead man, a corpse waiting to be interred, the book throws out a lifeline to some future time, a message in a bottle. Writing what he knows will be a posthumous novel, Orwell lends Winston his own sense of mission and purpose.

What is the basis for Winston's secret hope, the flicker of optimism that lights up Orwell's novel? The Party tells him that "who controls the past controls the future: who controls the present controls the past."[11] O'Brien makes him strip naked to see how puny and emaciated he has become. But Winston has put his trust in the proles, whose ordinary lives, still grounded in the past, lived outside of history, somehow preserve the continuity, the fellow feeling, that the Party has tried to stamp out. "They were not loyal to a party or a country or an idea, they were loyal to one another. . . . The proles had stayed human. They had not become hardened inside. They had held onto the primitive emotions which he himself had to relearn by conscious effort."[12] Orwell always believed that ordinary people had more sense than most intellectuals, for at least they trusted the evidence of their senses. Yet he describes their popular culture as trashy and mechanical, and when Winston tries to learn about earlier times from one old man, he gets a mass of irrelevant details. Orwell idealizes the proles but denies them any capacity for reflection or agency, for connecting the dots.

Winston also puts his faith in the biology of sex and desire that brought him and Julia to this room, where day after day they can hear a woman below, as ample of girth as he feels wan and wasted, as fertile as he feels sterile, singing contentedly as she hangs out her wash. *Nineteen Eighty-Four* offers many such touches that resonate against the book's ultimate gloom. The room itself is more than a love nest and refuge. Like the small crystal paperweight that Winston cherishes, it stands for the private life that resists being leveled and mobilized into any system. Though the room is finally a trap, set up and bugged by the Thought Police, and the paperweight is shattered when the police come to arrest them, they evoke traces of longing, tiny bits of individual happiness that no system can fully efface. "The room was a world, a pocket of the past where extinct animals could walk."[13] Gazing at the paperweight, he feels that "it was as though the surface of the glass had been the arch of the sky, enclosing a tiny world with its atmosphere complete. He had the feeling that he could get inside it, and that in fact he was inside it. . . . The paperweight was the room he was in, and the coral was Julia's life and his own, fixed in a sort of eternity at the heart of the crystal."[14]

All this comes to a head in a stirring passage in which Winston imagines what it might be like to be in the hands of the police, which he knows will happen soon enough:

> Facts, at any rate, could not be kept hidden. They could be tracked down by inquiry, they could be squeezed out of you by torture. But if the object was not to stay alive but to stay human, what difference did it ultimately make? They could not alter your feelings; for that matter you could not alter them yourself, even if you wanted to. They could lay bare in the utmost detail everything you had done or said or thought; but the inner heart, whose workings were mysterious even to yourself, remained impregnable.[15]

Sartre, during his existentialist period, also argued that the willingness to die was the ultimate basis of freedom. But the last part of Orwell's book, the O'Brien part, is designed—unconvincingly, I think—to refute this faith, to show that the "inner heart," the feelings, were anything but impregnable. But in passages like the ones I've quoted, Orwell gives us poignant images that counter the barbarous bureaucratic poetry of Newspeak and Ingsoc, images of a private world of desire and enclosure that survives from a dimly remembered past. They are linked to the book's positive values—truth, decency, loyalty, family feeling—but also to the memory of ordinary things that suddenly seem valuable when they can no longer be taken them for granted, as one might feel in wartime or grave illness. Hearing a snatch of an old tune about church bells, Winston "had the illusion of actually hearing bells, the bells of a lost London that still existed somewhere or other, disguised and forgotten."[16] In bed with Julia, listening to the woman singing in the courtyard and the distant shouts of children, "he wondered vaguely whether in the abolished past it had been a normal experience to lie in bed like this, in the cool of a summer evening, a man and a woman with no clothes on, making love when they chose, talking of what they chose, not feeling any compulsion to get up, simply lying there and listening to peaceful sounds outside. Surely there could never have been a time when that seemed ordinary."[17]

This lyrical strain complicates *Nineteen Eighty-Four* and helps make it a great book, but it is rarely noticed by readers who focus on Orwell's grim picture of the future or his parable of totalitarianism. The very syntax of that sinuous sentence about lying in bed evokes the languid condition it describes. But moments like this also undercut the widely accepted view that Orwell was blind to the potential for resistance, the enduring strength of human values even under the most crushing tyranny. Though he is strangely proud of his work for the system, simply because it is well done, Winston feels an irresistible pressure to shout out obscenities, to step across the line. But by describing totalitarianism as a self-perpetuating monolith, virtually impossible to overthrow from within, Orwell did not anticipate how totalitarian systems could decay and evolve. Yet Orwell the essayist made exactly this point about the huge slave states described by James Burnham, even arguing that "the Russian regime will either democratize itself, or it will perish."[18] The year after 1984, Mikhail Gorbachev came to power in the Soviet Union, and within six years the Soviet Union itself no longer existed. But Orwell in *Nineteen Eighty-Four* was not so much predicting what would happen in four decades as extrapolating from the world he actually saw around him.

Many futuristic novels are welded together from conceptual abstractions, often labored, occasionally ingenious; their setting is mechanical, their characters lack flesh and blood. Orwell's novel is a more hybrid work. It has often been noted that the world of *Nineteen Eighty-Four* resembles nothing so much as the England of the 1940s: the austerity of wartime and postwar rationing, the dreadful food and decaying, scruffy countryside, the shabby environs of the new welfare state. Orwell has a positive gift for Graham Greene–ish descriptions of gray, threadbare, rubble-strewn settings, reminiscent of London in the blitz, that induce a chronic feeling of sensory deprivation. Orwell infused this monochromatic late-Dickensian world with something that couldn't be more different: the new technology of mass destruction, surveillance, and indoctrination. His sources were as close as Chaplin's *Modern Times,* in which a barking forerunner of Big Brother uses a telescreen to oversee workers on an assembly line that has reduced them to cogs in the industrial machine. Orwell was also one of the first to describe a new kind of terror state since 1930, in which older forms of resistance, including what we today call civil society, could no longer function. Active opposition was wiped out by the secret police but mental opposition was leveled just as effectively by new tools for lying, spying, and propaganda.

The germ of Orwell's account of the new order can be found in *Homage to Catalonia* and in many essays and reviews, most explicitly in "Looking Back on the Spanish War" (1943), "Arthur Koestler" (1944), and "The Prevention of Literature" (1946). "Since about 1930 the world has given no reason for optimism whatever," he writes in the Koestler essay. "Nothing is in sight except a welter of lies, hatred, cruelty and ignorance, and beyond our present troubles loom vaster ones that are only now entering into the European consciousness."[19] In the essay on the Spanish war he asks himself whether it is "perhaps childish or morbid to terrify oneself with visions of a totalitarian future." Yet he ends the essay with a poem about fortitude that evokes the inner heart as a "crystal spirit" that can never be broken ("No bomb that ever burst/ Shatters the crystal spirit"), which prefigures the significance of the crystal paperweight of *Nineteen Eighty-Four.* Surely, this tension between Orwell's fear of the future and his obstinate faith in some innate power of resistance is the kernel from which the novel grew.

In the essay he notes, "before writing off the totalitarian world as a nightmare that can't come true, just remember that in 1925 the world of today [1943] would have seemed a nightmare that couldn't come true." Orwell observes that the literature of ideological disillusionment barely exists in English; it is a Central European phenomenon. He speaks to the civilized English distaste for extreme visions of any kind: "We in England underrate the danger of this kind of thing, because our traditions and our past security have given us a sentimental belief that it all comes right in the end and the thing you most fear never really happens. Nourished for hundreds of years on a literature in which Right invariably triumphs in the last chapter, we believe half-instinctively that evil always defeats itself in the long run."[20] In *Nineteen Eighty-Four,* as in this essay, Orwell insists that it *could* happen here. He grafts features of the Soviet police state, the Nazi terror, the Holocaust, and the cold war onto a contemporary English setting. Alarmed and disgusted by the sympathy of English intellectuals for both fascism and communism, Orwell tries to show that even England, complacent in its poky traditions of liberal individualism, is not immune to the specious appeal of totalitarianism.

Those who argue that Orwell was a dying man who projected his own illness into a deeply pessimistic world picture are not completely off the mark. At thirty-nine, Winston Smith feels like a sick man, ashamed to reveal his gaunt body to a young woman but drawing vitality from her youth, health, and sensual abandon. Yet he also connects sex with death and, even as he grasps at life, has "the sensation of stepping into the dampness of a grave."[21] Repeatedly he thinks of himself as an ambulatory corpse, like the three spectral Party leaders when they were temporarily reprieved before being arrested again and executed. But Orwell, perhaps feeling hopeless for himself, turns his hopes to posterity instead. Winston tries to convince Julia, who lives for the moment, "that the only victory lay far in the future, long after you were dead, that from the moment of declaring war on the Party it was better to think of yourself as a corpse."[22] "We are the dead," he says, in his frequent refrain, ironically echoing a tribute the gladiators paid to the Roman emperor before fighting in the arena.

Commentators go astray in assuming that Orwell's dark personal feelings somehow distort the picture he draws of the larger system. This may be true of the garish horrors of the last part of the book, fueled by a well-documented streak of sadomasochism in Orwell's own makeup, but not of *Nineteen Eighty-Four* as a whole. His personal stake in this story is mostly a source of strength. In his indispensable essay on the withering effects of totalitarianism on writing, "The Prevention of Literature," Orwell compares what censorship does to the journalist to its effects on the imaginative writer.

> The journalist is unfree, and is conscious of unfreedom, when he is forced to write lies or suppress what seems to him important news: the imaginative writer is unfree when he has to falsify his subjective feelings, which from his point of view are facts. He may distort and caricature reality to make his meaning clearer, but he cannot misrepresent the scenery of his own mind: he cannot say with any conviction that he likes what he dislikes, or believes what he disbelieves. If he is forced to do so, the only result is that his creative faculties dry up.[23]

Orwell insisted that his best writing always had a political purpose, yet he also believed that creative writing is ineluctably personal, whatever its subject. As he says here, the novelist writes from his "subjective feelings, which from his point of view are facts." The "facts" of the case are to be found in the subjective landscape of his own mind. By investing his own feelings in Winston Smith's fate, and by making the setting an England he had experienced, one that his readers would recognize, Orwell rescues *Nineteen Eighty-Four* from the merely speculative horizon of most futuristic writing; he lends an emotional unity, an authentic immediacy, to an otherwise eclectic and occasionally contradictory work.

Orwell adds that "even a single taboo can have an all-round crippling effect upon the mind, because there is always the danger that any thought which is freely followed up may lead to the forbidden thought. It follows that the atmosphere of totalitarianism is deadly to any kind of prose writer." As Orwell makes clear, any *political* taboo quickly becomes a mental one; political repression translates into repression as the psychoanalyst understands it. The kind of censorship that would guarantee the failure of an analysis also ensures a failure of imagination. Orwell's emphasis on the psychological effects of totalitarianism points to powerful elements in *Nineteen Eighty-Four* that go beyond H. G. Wells, London, Zamyatin, Aldous Huxley, and Orwell's other literary models. Orwell's treatment of language, truth, and history, a main concern of his essays over the previous decade, makes for the most original feature of the novel. Winston instinctively recoils from a regime that unhinges language from reality, history from memory, and he finally breaks down when his own sense of reality has been undermined.

In his essay on the Spanish Civil War—the conflict that was the testing ground for both the weaponry and the propaganda of the great war that followed—Orwell looks back at how the war was reported and distorted. He voices the fear that its true history would never be written, that under the pressure of ideology "the very concept of objective truth is fading out of the world." All governments lie, he says, and "history is for the most part inaccurate and biased, but what is peculiar to our own age is the abandonment of the idea that history *could* be truthfully written." Anticipating a key theme of *Nineteen Eighty-Four,* he worries about the coming of "a nightmare world in which the Leader, or some ruling clique, controls not only the future but *the past.* If the Leader says of such and such an event, 'It never happened'—well, it never happened. If he says two and two are five—well, two and two are five. This prospect frightens me more than bombs."[24]

Repeated in *Nineteen Eighty-Four,* this numerical example is not perhaps the best illustration of totalitarian control, and it is even less effective as an argument against the postmodern skepticism and relativism that Orwell so clearly anticipated. But like so much in *Nineteen Eighty-Four,* it is simple, stark and unforgettable; this helps explain why Orwell's fable has struck a chord in millions of readers, including many who actually grew up under versions of the system he describes but never actually saw. That so much of the novel has become a permanent part of our thinking and ready terminology testifies to its power as myth and its cartoonish accuracy. We almost never think of insidious modern techniques of surveillance and persuasion—some of which invade our own lives, from the workplace to the bureaucracy—without using terms like *Big Brother* and *Newspeak* that Orwell invented. They are all summed up in that elastic and overused adjective, "Orwellian," which we apply promiscuously not only to the worst dictatorships but to sundry forms of political lying, techno-jargon, public relations, electronic spying, and mass indoctrination—in short, everywhere language is used to obscure and falsify (or simply to "spin") what is actually happening. In that respect, Orwell's celebrated essay "Politics and the English Language," which analyzes the political effects of this linguistic smokescreen, is the perfect discursive pendant to the novel.

Orwell's position on language and truth, history and fact, is a moral one, rooted in his faith in common sense, including the intuitive savvy of ordinary people. He prided himself on holding to a notion of fact as straightforward as his firmest values, among them decency and candor. Orwell's no-nonsense views of objective truth can be traced to a bluff British empiricism, which puts all its stress on first-hand experience and direct perception. Yet this limitation also contributes to Orwell's strength as a reporter, an intellectual, and a political man. Whatever Orwell's efforts to declass himself, to expiate his sense of social guilt for growing up middle class, going to St. Cyprian's and Eton, and serving the Empire, the net result of his downward mobility was a determination to see things with his own eyes, whether in Wigan Pier or in Spain, and to describe precisely what he saw. His calling as a journalist, along with his fundamental honesty, entailed a descent into the particular. He was appalled by journalists and intellectuals who indulged their high-minded idealism; as he saw it, they put the idea, the theory, before the plain fact, the long-range political goal before the immediate human reality.

As he saw it, the responsible journalist, like the novelist, would surely emerge with a point of view, but it had to begin from what he actually saw—the facts on the ground, the words on the page. From early on Orwell knew that he "had a facility with words and a power of facing unpleasant facts."[25] But Orwell did not carefully distinguish between fact and interpretation. Historians typically differ less on the facts than on what they mean. By drawing attention to the most extreme, even transient, features of the totalitarian system—the wholesale rewriting of the past, the constantly shifting political line, the outright doctoring of texts and pictures, the deification or demonization or wholesale elimination of historical figures, even the outright denial of simple fact (two plus two is four)—Orwell anticipates the postmodern debate about truth and language yet falls short of contributing to it.

He had an exaggerated faith in objectivity, which his own polemical writing—confident, opinionated, sometimes blatantly unfair—did not always exemplify. Orwell is nothing if not definite, whatever the issue, even when he himself has changed his mind. But he gives an indelible picture of what happens when truth, memory, and history are made to serve political ends. His nightmare was the system that aims to control not only public but also private behavior, not only action but also thinking and feeling, including memory, the sense of the past. He indicts the complicity of intellectuals whose bien-pensant ideals override common sense and allow them to excuse heinous deeds with a clear conscience.

Nineteen Eighty-Four is a flawed novel but seminal as an act of witness to the most odious features of twentieth-century history, especially the barbarism of the Nazi and Soviet dictatorships, with their cult of personality, their scorn for ordinary standards of truth and decency, to say nothing of their intrinsic violence and contempt for human life. Orwell's propaganda work for the BBC, his observations of England in the 1940s, the state of mind induced by his illness, his experience in Spain, the scars of his battles with the fellow-traveling Left, his continuing faith in the working class and hopes for English socialism, his horror of the cold war and fears of impending atomic war—all these give his monitory tale an emotional weight, a density of experience unusual in books of this kind. Orwell understood that genre writing, for all its drawbacks, could be a more effective tool for portraying the daily grit of a totalitarian world than any straightforward realism. The unprecedented impact and enduring popularity of the novel have borne this out. His famous image of the future as "a boot stamping on a human face—forever"[26] is less a forecast than a warning, by way of a grim, perhaps sadistic, metaphor that no one would ever forget. On the other hand, his terminal illness lent a lyrical glow to the fugitive pleasures of ordinary life.

The bleak side of Orwell's novel, its punishing sense of entrapment, is closely linked to popular film genres of the same period, including film noir, horror, and science fiction, which responded to the same postwar traumas, including anxieties about nuclear war, permanent stalemate, and the loss of individuality. They too were grounded in the fear that the individual could somehow be "vaporised," effaced. Though reviewers stressed the anticommunism of *Nineteen Eighty-Four,* the book found an echo in works that sounded the alarm against conformity and intimidation during the McCarthy era, which began not long after Orwell died in 1950. The new science fiction, spun off from Orwell, included Ray Bradbury's 1953 novel *Fahrenheit 451,* where the Thought Police become the firemen who burn objectionable books, and Don Siegel's 1956 movie *Invasion of the Body Snatchers,* in which ordinary citizens become happy zombies, mere physical replicas of themselves, bereft of individual thought and emotion, and only one couple, much like Winston and Julia, hold out desperately against the collective tide. Such works lack the political reach of Orwell's novel, whose original title was "The Last Man in Europe," but they demonstrate the power of his fable about those who hold out precariously in a world where the rudiments of human freedom and difference have virtually been stamped out.

NOTES

1. George Orwell, *The Collected Essays, Journalism, and Letters,* 4 vols., ed. Sonia Orwell and Ian Angus (Harmondsworth: Penguin Books, 1970), 1:30. (From here on referred to as *CEJL.*)
2. *CEJL,* 1:26.
3. *CEJL,* 1:30.
4. *CEJL,* 4:536.
5. *CEJL,* 4:565.
6. George Orwell, *Nineteen Eighty-Four* (New York: Harcourt, Brace, 1949), 259.
7. Richard Rorty, *Contingency, Irony, and Solidarity* (Cambridge: Cambridge University Press, 1989), 182.
8. Orwell, *Nineteen Eighty-Four,* 47.
9. Christopher Hitchens, *Why Orwell Matters* (New York: Basic Books, 2002), 190.
10. *CEJL,* 1:26.
11. Orwell, *Nineteen Eighty-Four,* 35.
12. Orwell, *Nineteen Eighty-Four,* 166.
13. Orwell, *Nineteen Eighty-Four,* 151.
14. Orwell, *Nineteen Eighty-Four,* 148.
15. Orwell, *Nineteen Eighty-Four,* 168.

16. Orwell, *Nineteen Eighty-Four* , 99.

17. Orwell, *Nineteen Eighty-Four,* 144–45.

18. *CEJL,* 4:214.

19. George Orwell, *Collected Essays* (London: Mercury Books, 1961), 231. (From here on referred to as *CE.*)

20. *CE,* 198.

21. Orwell, *Nineteen Eighty-Four,* 160.

22. Orwell, *Nineteen Eighty-Four,* 137.

23. *CEJL,* 4:88.

24. *CE,* 196–97.

25. Orwell, "Why I Write," *CEJL,* 1:25.

26. Orwell, *Nineteen Eighty-Four,* 271.

II

Ideas, Ideologies, and Intellectuals

4

George Orwell and the Liberal Experience of Totalitarianism

CHRISTOPHER HITCHENS

George Orwell didn't make it into 1950 before expiring. Nonetheless, his identity thereafter has been subject to theft and appropriation. His essay on Dickens begins by saying, "Dickens is a writer worth stealing." Orwell is closer in time and in some ways in life to Dickens than we are to Orwell. And Orwell died, in a sense, a Dickensian death. He died partly of poverty, ill health, neglect, and the unavailability of drugs that he could have had if he had been better informed. He lived to be forty-six in the twentieth century and yet as we enter the twenty-first century there must be a good answer as to why we are so preoccupied with him.

I am going to give this conundrum my very best shot and I am going to start by reading a short extract from Saul Bellow's novel *Mr. Sammler's Planet.* Mr. Sammler describes himself, exiled as he is in New York, lucky to be alive, very conscious of his luck, as a Polish Oxonian. He makes the mistake of accepting an invitation to speak at Columbia University and I would say from the date, timing, and context that this was in the late 1960s. He decides to speak about what he knows best, the utopian theories that governed Europe in the interwar period. He associates these with the names of R. H. Tawney, Harold Laski, John Strachey, George Orwell, and H. G. Wells. He gives his best shot at telling the students what they missed and what they don't yet know. This is as far as he gets. I am quoting now from Saul Bellow.

> Telling this into the lighted, restless hole of the amphitheater with the soiled dome and caged electric fixtures until he was interrupted by a clear loud voice. He was being questioned. He was being shouted at.
>
> "Hey."
>
> He tried to continue. "Such attempts to draw intellectuals away from Marxism met with small success. . . ."
>
> A man in Levis, thick bearded but possibly young, a figure of compact distortion was standing shouting at him.

Portions of this chapter have previously appeared in *Why Orwell Matters* (New York: Basic Books, 2002); reprinted by permission of the author.

"Hey! Old Man!"

In the silence, Mr. Sammler drew down his tinted spectacles, seeing this person with his one effective eye.

"Old Man! You quoted Orwell before."

"Yes."

"You quoted him to say the British radicals were all protected by the Royal Navy. Did Orwell say that? British radicals were protected by the Royal Navy."

"Yes I believe he did say that."

"That's a lot of shit."

Sammler could not speak.

"Orwell was a fink. He was a sick counterrevolutionary. It's good he died when he did and what you're saying is shit." Turning to the audience, extending violent arms and raising his palms like a Greek dancer he said, "Why did you listen to this effete old shit? What has he got to tell you? His balls are dry. He's dead. He can't come."

Sammler later thought that some voices had been raised on his side. Someone had said, "Shame. Exhibitionist."

But no one really tried to defend him. Most of the young people seemed to be against him. The shouting sounded hostile. Feffer was gone. . . .

And he was not so much personally offended by the event but struck by the will to offend. What a passion to be *real*. But *real* [Bellow's italics] was also brutal and the acceptance of excrement as a standard. How extraordinary? Youth? Together with the idea of sexual potency? All this confused sex excrement militancy, explosiveness, abusiveness, tooth showing, Barbary ape howling. Or like the spider monkeys in the trees, as Sammler had once read, defecating into their hands and shrieking, pelting the explorers below.[1]

Now, I know that Saul Bellow had had some bad experiences in the academy, as had his friend Allan Bloom, and I know that Bellow has written well about them. I have often quarreled with him about his tendency to exaggerate or to be self-pitying about that kind of intolerance, that kind of philistinism. These days I have to carry around with me a kind of thermometer. I usually prefer to park it in the armpit, just checking my pulse and my temperature all the time to see if I am going to become an old curmudgeon. And I have occasion to use this thermometer several times a day for symptoms of encrustation and curmudgeonhood. But I have to tell you that it gets worse.

Recently in Tucson, Arizona, I was invited to speak at the opening of the local arts theater on my film about the crimes of Henry Kissinger—the war crimes, crimes against humanity and crimes against the U.S. Constitution. There was a showing of the film *The Trial of Henry Kissinger* and then I was asked to respond to what was a pretty large and enthusiastic audience. And then someone got up (this was about the beginning of February 2003) and said to me from the front row, "By what right does our U.S. government go around the world deposing elected governments?" And I thought, well, we're still talking about Henry Kissinger so I can't be sure of the tone of the question. So I asked him, "May I ask you which episode you mean?" He might have been referring to Chile in 1973 or Greece in 1967 or Indonesia in 1965. And he looked at me as if I were stupid and said, "I mean the government of Saddam Hussein, which was an elected government." So I said, "You don't do it enough honor actually. It not only recently had a referendum which had 100 percent vote in favor of Saddam Hussein but it also recorded what had been hitherto unprecedented, 100 percent turn out. So you're perhaps not praising the Baath party sufficiently." You can always try irony. If it doesn't hurt them it doesn't hurt you.

What did I get for saying that? He said, "That's more than you can say of George Bush." In a split second it taught me to think, well you're going to meet every now and then someone who thinks that Saddam Hussein was democratically elected and George W. Bush wasn't. Get used to it. I am used to that. I became aware that this remark had been drowned in applause. It wasn't the remark, in other words, it wasn't the stupidity of the remark, it was the warmth and generality of the applause in Tucson, Arizona, where a point against Saddam Hussein became a point at my expense and at the expense of the president. And it gave me to worry very much. I've had to worry about the same point since.

In early 2003 the *San Francisco Chronicle* featured the front-page headline "U.S. Occupation Forces Have Deprived the Iraqi People of Their 20th of April Annual Holiday." The 20th of April holiday celebrates the birthday of Saddam Hussein; it is a compulsory holiday, a holiday of fear, a holiday on which any teacher who doesn't bring her students to the square and make them clap is in real danger for her life. But the *San Francisco Chronicle* finds yet another violation of Iraqi rights. They have lost their national holiday on April 20th. A deadpan headline.

There are people who say that North Korea may be evil now but it wasn't evil until George W. Bush said it was. It only began to behave badly after it had been upset and offended by a speech that called it by its right name. This seems to me to be extraordinary. What Orwell teaches us, among other things, is that certain key words are in our lexicon for a reason. They are in our vernacular for a reason. *Evil* is one of them. Some people commit cruelty for its own sake. Some people do it gratuitously; they do it because they like it. And we have to have a word for it. I tried to advise the president in the *Washington Post* a few months ago that he would have done better in his first speech on this matter to describe his foes as an "axis of lesser evil," because at least then he would have had a chance of getting half of the Democratic party on his side right there. Evil can be used. It turns out we need it. The word *evil* is in our language for a reason, but it can only be used in relativist terms. That is what we are up against.

There is a reason to pay tribute to Orwell. I would like to disagree very respectfully with Daphne Patai's essay. When some of us invoke the name of George Orwell in contemporary politics for contemporary reasons we do so not in the hope of acquiring his reputation for honesty and courage. After all, a moment's thought will tell you that I can lay no such claim. And no one would believe me if I tried to emulate someone who took such risks and was willing to endure such hardship for his convictions. There's another reason, which I would describe as a literary reason, why Orwell remains alive to us. His favorite texts, ones that he could usually quote from memory and often did so with very small mistakes, were the canonical works of William Shakespeare, the prayer book of Archbishop Cranmer, and the King James Bible. Those texts too contain phrases, thoughts, simple offhand descriptions that come to us when we need them, that stay in our cortexes because of the exquisite care with which they were composed. No one saying "I do not believe that the powers that be are ordained of God" is expecting to have it believed by the audience that he has made up this term himself or is claiming the mantle of St. Paul. He is arguing about a proposition, the wording of which everybody knows. And in my view, the reason for the enduring legacy of Orwell is precisely that. And here's the contradiction: when we try to struggle against totalitarianism, not just as a system or a threat but in our own minds and the bad habits it inculcates, we also strive to avoid the obvious. We strive to avoid catch-phrases and stale phrases. Orwell pointed out two beauties I remember offhand about Nazism: the jackboot has been thrown into the melting pot, and on another occasion: the fascist octopus has sung its swan song. The people who use slogans of this kind have ceased to think about the meaning of words. These are examples of what the French used to call the *langue du bois*—the wooden tongue. Claud Cockburn, Orwell's great enemy and great antagonist in Spain and father of Or-well's leading critic in the United States, when he worked for the *Daily Worker* saw that one article in the magazine in a communiqué from Moscow said that the leading organs of the party should begin to penetrate the backward parts of the proletariat. In response, the editors said, "that's from Moscow, you can't change that." The fear that people have not just of recognizing totalitarianism as a threat or calling evil by its right name arises in part because if these threats are true and if these evils are existent, they themselves may be called upon to witness or to fight or to do something about it.

There is an element of denial in the refusal to admit that the threat has arisen in the first place. Orwell puts one on one's guard against that tendency to euphe-mism and he does it in phrases that are memorable and that are drawn from the great wellsprings of English writing. His atheism was Protestant, in other words. He believed that the struggle for a Bible that was in English and understood by the people was a great struggle for free speech and that the inner part, the priesthood, should never possess or have exclusive claim on what was sacred in order to make it more profane. And those of us who are journalists are always striving to avoid the cliché or the obvious retort.

John Burns of the *New York Times,* whom I regard to be the exemplar of the journalist in this day, recently had to write from Baghdad about that Saddam referendum. John avoids the obvious whenever he can, but he had to use the word *Orwellian.* He had no choice but to use the word *Orwellian* when describing this referendum and its turnout, its result and the hysteria, the self-loathing humilia-tion. The sadomasochism involved in conscripting people one last time to abase themselves at the foot of a statue of the image of a mediocre and wicked human being. I will quote what I wrote myself from North Korea a few years ago. I am quite well up on evil countries and axis countries. I've been to most of them, and I am probably one of a few people who have been to Iraq and North Korea in the recent past. I'll quote some of what I wrote from Pyongyang.

> In the closing months of the twentieth century, I contrived to get a visa from North Korea. Often referred to as 'the world's last Stalinist state', it might as easily be described as the world's prototype Stalinist state. Founded under the protection of Stalin and Mao, and made even more hermetic and insular by the fact of a parti-tioned peninsula that so to speak 'locked it in', the Democratic People's Republic of Korea still boasted the following features at the end of the year 2000. On every public building, a huge picture of 'The Great Leader' Kim Il Sung, the dead man who still holds the office of President in what one might therefore term a necrocracy or mausolocracy. (All other senior posts are occupied by his son, 'The Dear Lead-er', Kim Jong Il—'Big Brother' was a perversion of family values as well.) Children marched to school in formation, singing songs in praise of aforesaid Leader. Photo-graphs of the Leader displayed by order in every home. A lapel-button, with the

features of the Leader, compulsory wear for all citizens. Loudspeakers and radios blasting continuous propaganda for the Leader and the Party. A society endlessly mobilized for war, its propaganda both hysterical and—in reference to foreigners and foreign power—intensely chauvinistic and xenophobic. Complete prohibition of any news from outside or any contact with other societies. Absolute insistence, in all books and in all publications, on a unanimous view of a grim past, a struggling present, and a radiant future. Repeated bulletins of absolutely false news of successful missile tests and magnificent production targets. A pervasive atmosphere of scarcity and hunger, alleviated only by the most abysmal and limited food. Grandiose and oppressive architecture. A continuous stress on mass sports and mass exercise. Apparently total repression of all matters connected to the libido. Newspapers with no news, shops with no goods, an airport with almost no planes. A vast nexus of tunnels underneath the capital city, connecting different Party and police and military bunkers.

There was, of course, only one word for it, and it was employed by all journalists, all diplomats and all overseas visitors. It's the only time in my writing life that I have become tired of the word 'Orwellian.'[2]

I was once arrested in Czechoslovakia in the old days. And I thought, whatever I do, I am not going to use the name Kafka. I'm just not going to do it. I am going to be the first reporter from Prague who doesn't do it. And then the secret police smashed into this secret meeting I was attending and said, "OK, everyone freeze; you're under arrest." They took us one by one and I said, "Well, can I know what the charges are, why we've been arrested." They said, "No, we're not telling you." And I thought, damn, now I have to do it. They *make* you do Kafka. North Korea makes you do Orwell. Winston and Julia would never find a private flat for a moment of squalid delight in North Korea. There would be no chance. And there is no reason at all not to notice how often this comes up.

In Zimbabwe recently, where collectivized farming is being used to reward the members of the ruling party with stolen property, the local African opposition paper reproduced without comment for seven days, chapter by chapter, *Animal Farm.* On the seventh day their offices were blown up by a land mine that is only available to the Zimbabwean army. What strikes me is the fact that *Animal Farm* was reprinted without comment and that nobody failed to get the point or needed it rammed home.

On my last trip to the Middle East, I was reading a local Arabic newspaper, in translation I'll add, but I saw yet again the Ministry of Education had renewed the ban on the publication of *Animal Farm* because in *Animal Farm* not only are there pigs but there are pigs who drink alcohol. You might say that that was a keyhole criticism of *Animal Farm* or you might think that this regime had a particular reason for wanting to stop publication, but believe me a book that is to us a cliché in the sense of being a children's story is still a story with explosive possibilities. It is censored for excellent reasons across vast tracts of the known world. Author to author tributes are not that refulgent sometimes and not that common. I would nominate as the greatest compliment made from one author to another the remark made by Czeslaw Milosz in his book *The Captive Mind,* which was written in 1951 and published in the West in 1953. Milosz was then a cultural official of the Polish communist regime, but he had begun internally to dissent and to compose the essays that make up *The Captive Mind,* which is a book that bears extensive rereading. And Milosz wrote, about the moral and political atmosphere of Stalin's Warsaw, the following:

A few have become acquainted with Orwell's *1984;* because it is both difficult to obtain and dangerous to possess, it is known only to certain members of the Inner Party. Orwell fascinates them through his insight into details they know well and through his use of Swiftian satire. Such a form of writing is forbidden by the New Faith because allegory, by nature manifold in meaning, would trespass beyond the prescriptions of socialist realism and the demands of the censor. Even those who know Orwell only by hearsay are amazed that a writer that never lived in Russia should have so keen a perception into its life.[3]

Now think about that. Orwell died as he was finishing, and seeing into the press, *Nineteen Eighty-Four.* He never saw it become a success. It describes a party regime where the inner party possesses a secret book that may possibly tell them what the truth of the matter is. Within two years in Stalin's Warsaw, the man who is now accepted by all as the great national literary laureate of Poland but was then a struggling member of the bureaucracy writes that there is a book within the Polish inner party that has circulated and that is *Nineteen Eighty-Four.* This is an extraordinary tribute and I think an unparalleled one. And I want to comment quickly on why I think Milosz was slightly wrong. In fact, Orwell had understood and had had the experience of living in a totalitarian society. In a very small way, and I don't mean this to sound flippant, in a very small way he had had it by being at a very authoritarian, bullying, and sadistic little boy's school that he described as a tender lad in his wonderful essay "Such, Such Were the Joys." I've had the experience of being at such a school at the same age. I was luckier than he was, but not by that much. I remember thinking it was good preparation for living in extreme times. The experience was not wasted on him. The way in which people will betray one another. The way in which power and cruelty can exert a pull of attraction, not just fear, upon those upon whom it is exerted. He had been a policeman in colonial Burma and had worked out that there is a dirty secret at the heart of power. There's a dirty secret and it is this: The most qualified Indian or Burmese person would never get, if he was a man, into the English club no matter how well he spoke English and no matter how many degrees and qualifications he had. He would never be admitted by the front door even, as a guest. But the most unqualified Burmese girl could be admitted to the villa of the British official as long as it was by the back door and as long as money changed hands.

Indeed in *Burmese Days,* Orwell describes a police officer—clearly himself— as having bought his Burmese mistress from her family. I believe myself that he resigned from the service of the police because he was afraid that if he kept on with it he would become a sadist and robot and someone governed by racial prejudice. He understood that, and he had also seen a political witch hunt and a show trial and a reign of terror in Catalonia in Barcelona during the Spanish Civil War. In fact, he had seen two reigns of terror—one from the fascist side and one from the communist side.

Milosz did not know that this was so. All he knew was that some Englishman had captured the moral atmosphere of Stalin's Europe without living there. But there are ingredients that went into *Nineteen Eighty-Four* and these are the insights that I think are very unlikely to become tedious to us or unworthy of further consideration. These are not, in other words, historical considerations; they are alarmingly contemporary. And on top of these experiences—because many people had the experience of both brutality and brutalization, which are not, as you know, the same thing—Orwell had an instinct for language. He wrote that he knew from the start, as soon as he read the first pamphlet and the first proclamation from the USSR, that by the language you could tell that something hideous was being done there. Actually, you could be tipped off pretty easily. Anything that is called a great "experiment" is going to be pretty nasty because we don't use humans for experiments and we don't, on the whole, respect people who do. Always attend to the language. He didn't have to visit, in other words, even though he had ancillary and corollary experience. By the language he could tell what was filthy and dangerous and mean and doomed about this system. So he got the three greatest issues of the twentieth century right in part because he got other things wrong.

I want to talk a little bit about the essential nature of contradiction in this subject. I'll try and materialize the contradiction. You can as a pedantic matter say that Orwell got right the three great questions of empire, fascism, and Stalinism and he did it quite early. Quite early in the 1920s, he saw that the Englishman's day in India and Burma was done. And that was a struggle with himself. So was the struggle to expose the great lie of communism among his intellectual friends, not just as an illusion but as a delusion, a falsehood, a foul propaganda that should be exposed, not pitied. And then about the struggle against fascism. When I talk about struggle within himself, I mean this: Orwell was born into a family that helped run the drug trade. His father was involved in the British colonial business of forcing China to buy opium made in India. That's why Orwell later refers to British society as a family where there is a terrible conspiracy of silence about the source of family income. That's why he never mentions his father or a father figure in anything he writes, only a big brother. He was brought up to dislike and despise Jewish people. He was brought up to distrust the great unwashed and the proletarians and the masses. If he wasn't brought up to be misogynistic, his upbringing was enough to make him very suspicious and fearful of women. And for reasons we may never fully understand, he was evidently very distraught at the mention of male homosexuality.

So how right, really, was Orwell on the three main questions? On empire he was wrong. He believed it was merely a racket. He thought that the British people would be poorer if India and the colonies were given up. That the English people would have to live on potatoes and herrings if they didn't exploit the colonies. He knew nothing about investment, trade, and innovation in the imperial economy. But he was morally right in that he saw that the white man's day was done, that there was no God-given right for European countries to run as their property Africa, India and other underdeveloped regions. And he was very right in his contemporary challenge to the chauvinism of the British labor movement (there was at least someone more exploited than themselves).

On fascism, Orwell barely wrote anything. He seems to have assumed that nobody needed to be persuaded about fascism. At one point he did say that fascism was indistinguishable from democracy and plutocracy. And several times he said that imperialism was worse than fascism. He was wrong about it, in other words, while being right. He was morally right. In the energy, the horrible energy of national socialism, everything that he couldn't stand—bullying, exploitation, racism, hierarchy—was distilled, double distilled and distilled again into a system of cruelty and hatred, and Orwell felt the physical need to go and block its path with his own body in Spain. Being morally right about fascism is good enough, even if he was sometimes analytically wrong. And he was willing to fight and to kill and, much more important, the test of a revolutionary, to die in the struggle.

On communism, we know how clear-sighted he was in many ways. Though I believe I might have to stand a challenge on this—I don't think that anyone has pointed out that in neither *Animal Farm* nor *Nineteen Eighty-Four* is there any Lenin figure. There is only a Trotsky and a Stalin. There's only Snowball and Napoleon. There's only Goldstein and Big Brother. The Lenin phase of the argument on the left about what went wrong with Marxism and with the revolution is by Orwell amazingly and interestingly and reprehensibly skipped. But he did see the point that remains with us, which is that any attempt to trade freedom for security contains a death trap within it. The one who can be persuaded or tries to persuade others that if you give up a little liberty you'll have a few more rations or a bit more protection runs the risk of losing both the freedom and the liberty *and* the security.

And so when we are recalled to Orwellism and our memory of him by hearing ugly, euphemistic phrases, pretty names for nasty things such as "collateral damage," we should also bear in mind far more seductive phrases such as "homeland security," or the idea of security at all, or the idea of a homeland. All of these things need to be scrutinized and not just accepted. So Orwell's struggle with himself is extremely worth studying. His realization of his own contradictions and negations is part of the honor that I think is due to him.

And it is the same with the idea of the personal and the political. He wrestled massively with his prejudice against Jewish people and overcame it and wrote material on the roots and nature of anti-Semitism that could not have been written by someone who had never been a sufferer and that will stand as an extraordinarily clever and insightful and mordant critique of the most vulgar and most sinister mother of all prejudices. He may have had a distorted relationship with womanhood, but he married two very intelligent, tough-minded, independent, and highly educated women: Eileen O'Shaugnessy and Sonia Brownell. (The biography of Sonia Brownell by Hilary Spurling I very much commend to you.[4]) Orwell got over his fear of the masses. He ceased to despise the working class in his country or the peasantry of others, perhaps even overcompensating, if anything, and being too sure of the wisdom of the people. Do misogynists like women too much or too little? It is not a question that I can resolve here but it is a question that might be decently asked. Overcompensating in the other direction is what has to be suspect about my original subject—the liberal softness on totalitarianism. Orwell was clever about patriotism. He knew enough to know that he suspected it and that it was suspect. But he also knew that it is an indispensable part of the human makeup. His argument was the following: You may think you've given up your own patriotism and have nothing but contempt for your own country. That doesn't mean you've given up patriotism altogether. So basic is this identification that it will be transferred to something else. You will begin to admire other people, other states, other communities for their solidarity, for their unity, for their brave leadership, for their martial qualities. This will be transferred into a vicarious admiration for others. As indeed it was by the intellectuals of the day into either fascism or communism. They only despise the martial and patriotic qualities of their own societies, but they couldn't destroy the instinct toward patriotism in themselves.

I know I will be telling you nothing you don't know if I tell you that recently people who know better have been describing the country of Iraq as an Arab country, as a Muslim one, and describing any policy designed to change the government as an affront to the idea of Arabism or Arab nationalism or to Islam, knowingly falsifying the fact that even the Iraqi constitution defines Iraq as a state of Arabs and Kurds. It is by no means an Arab society. Until 1948, there were more Jews in Baghdad than there were in Jerusalem. There were innumerable other minorities as well. It is what Western liberals in any other context would describe as a multicultural, multiethnic, gloriously diverse county. And yet Western liberals repeat the robotic slogans of its own regime about uniformity and conformity and they have transferred their feeling of national and patriotic identification onto a psychopathic regime of aggression and repression. I don't owe all of that insight to George Orwell, but I don't think that I would have noticed as acutely and with such pain as I did without his work.

A thing that I am no longer interested in is the question of whether or not George Orwell would take my view or anyone else's if he was still with us. In 1984, it was actually possible that Orwell could have lived that long. We are now at the point that we are as far from him as he was from Dickens. We have to say goodbye to him as a contemporary and ask why it is, therefore, that he remains so vivid and actual in our own lives. My feeling is this and only this. Suppose it were possible to have this conversation. Suppose one could find out what he thought and more importantly, how he thought about any matter. All I can say for sure is that it would be a pleasure to disagree with him. And that is not a compliment I find one can very often bestow these days.

NOTES

1. Saul Bellow, *Mr. Sammler's Planet* (New York: Viking Press, 1970), 42–43.
2. Christopher Hitchens, *Why Orwell Matters* (New York: Basic Books, 2002), 73–74.
3. Czeslaw Milosz, *The Captive Mind,* trans. Jane Zielonko (New York: Knopf, 1953).
4. Hilary Spurling, *The Girl from the Fiction Department: A Portrait of Sonia Orwell* (New York: Counterpoint Press, 2003).

5

On the Ethics of Admiration—
and Detraction

JOHN RODDEN

I

You see the placards waved at every rally of the Christian Right, as well as in many gatherings of the Catholic Church and the mainline Protestant sects: "W.W.J.D.?" And yet secular intellectuals are not without their own oracle, and (with the exception of the Marxist Left) the coveted (and presumed) patronage of their patron saint knows no bounds. "The most heterogeneous following a writer can ever have accumulated," said his close friend, George Woodcock, about Orwell's "faithful."[1] "W.W.G.O.D.?" they ask recurrently. (Why not simply an Orwell website, a cyberspace hotline named www.GOD.net?) As a headline in the *New York Times Book Review* did indeed phrase it in September 2002, on the one-year anniversary of al Qaeda's attacks, "What Would Orwell Do?"[2]

Yes, that question seemingly arises whenever a public issue provokes a major intellectual debate and splits the ranks of the Left and/or Right. Then "St. George" is called to arms, with the battle-certified catchwords from *Animal Farm* and *Nineteen Eighty-Four* of the "Big O" packed in the polemical arsenals of his self-appointed mouthpieces, ready to be fired off at the drop of his name. (Indeed, just days after "9/11," the conservative British critic Geoffrey Wheatcroft suggested that British soldiers shipped out to Afghanistan should pack Orwell's essays in their knapsacks.)

One could multiply the examples, but the point is clear: More than a half century after his death, Orwell remains "a writer well worth stealing," as he once said of Dickens. Since his death in January 1950, Orwell's soul has been up for grabs. Today, polemically minded intellectuals are still playing what Ben Wattenberg recently referred to in his PBS talk show devoted to Orwell as "that wonderful parlor game" called "How Would Orwell Stand Today?"[3] (One is tempted to reply: Being one hundred, he wouldn't.) Nonetheless, the "game" often has its illicit darker sides: mantle stealing, body snatching, and political grave robbing.

It's an ideological shell game (usually with clever sleight of hand), whereby the participants move Orwell's coffin to the left or right.

II

One recalls the comment of the poet William Empson, Orwell's wartime colleague at the BBC and the author of *Seven Types of Ambiguity* (1930), on reading *Animal Farm*: "You must expect to be 'misunderstood' on a large scale. . . ." Yes—and he has been. Empson himself reported that his young son, a supporter of the Conservative Party, was "delighted" with *Animal Farm* and considered it "very strong Tory propaganda."[4]

Similar misreadings have occurred with *Nineteen Eighty-Four*—for instance, during the early cold war era, the last four digits of the John Birch Society's telephone number were "1-9-8-4." And, as happened with both *Animal Farm* and *Nineteen Eighty-Four,* sometimes the author himself inadvertently contributes to such misreadings. "Orwellian" misreadings have occurred partly because readers have identified so strongly with him that they have projected their own needs and aspirations on him. Their identifications have been variously induced by Orwell's appeal to readers as a "rebel" and an intellectual's "common man," by the perceived moral heroism of his radical humanism, and by the seeming "purity" and simplicity of his literary style, among other factors. And then there are also the darker reasons for confusion: because the catchwords of *Nineteen Eighty-Four* could be easily turned back on him, because his aggressive "conscience of the Left" stance could seem like a renegade's antisocialism, and because politically savvy intellectuals noticed the pilgrim crowds swarming toward his grave—and thus deemed it "well worth stealing."

Should we then partly "blame Orwell" for cooperating with his kidnappers? Or for a lack of foresight as to the uses and abuses to which his work has been put since his death? Not at all. Rather, the scrupulous reader's task is to get down to particulars and see how writers sometimes invite or participate in their own appropriation, to see why a writer was so susceptible to such Orwellian "facecrime," as Winston Smith would have (proudly) termed the "Orwellian" distortions.

So all this does not imply that a political writer such as Orwell should somehow become a farseeing prophet and anticipate both how the course of events may alter and how his work may become liable to abuse beyond the grave, any more than it means that he must tame his style and never exhibit partisanship. Rather, the mantle snatching of Orwell serves as a warning and a summons to his readers— above all, to the intellectuals who interpret his work and influence the culture's perceptions of it—to approach him and his legacy with particular care. For the politics of reception cannot be divorced from the *ethics* of reception. In fact, we might speak here of an "ethics of admiration" (and even detraction), whose precise formulation and vigilant observance form a special responsibility of intellectuals.

Indeed, perhaps the cultivation of such a moral awareness is not just the "responsibility," but rather part of the *vocation* of the historically minded intellectual in the postideological age—an era that has witnessed not the "end of ideology" but, rather, such an all-pervasiveness of ideology that any putatively "objective" claim is deemed intellectually naïve or outrageously polemical.

Such distinctions are important. To observe that all interpretations have degrees of validity, and that "some are more equal than others," is not obtuse or crude. Instead it is merely to insist that positions on an issue can be embraced with differing levels of confidence and accuracy, depending on the available evidence— and based on whatever criteria such evidence is deemed admissible.

III

If the foregoing reflections sensitize readers to aspire to a more judicial (and judicious) sensibility and, indeed, invite intellectuals above all to adopt a heightened moral consciousness toward controversial political figures such as Orwell, two questions necessarily arise: What specific concerns should occupy the serious admirer or respectful enemy of an artist's work? And what concrete guidelines should shape his hermeneutic "code of ethics"?

Let the following criteria serve as a prolegomena to an ethics of reception. Among the considerations governing such an ethics, which in Orwell's case might indeed be better termed an ethics of admiration (and detraction), could be the following four precepts.

First precept: avoid anachronistic interpretation. Take care to assess the historical context in which the writer has lived. Measure his work against the standards of his own day. Beware the fallacy of presentism. For instance, by the standards of today, numerous respectable contemporaries of Orwell—especially conservatives and Catholics—such as G. K. Chesterton, Christopher Dawson, and T. S. Eliot— subscribed to an unconscionable anti-Semitism. All of them have been posthumously castigated for this failing. The failing is real and it is important to cite; but it is equally important to note that we live today by cultural norms very different from those that prevailed in the genteel literary circles of prefascist Europe. Similarly, Orwell himself was, at least early in his career, mildly anti-Semitic. And yet, Orwell's own emphasis on the importance of historical context, when he defended Eliot (whom his good friend and *Tribune* colleague T. R. Fyvel had criticized as anti-Semitic) is worth noting.

> One has to draw a distinction between what was said before and what after 1934. Of course all these nationalistic prejudices are ridiculous, but disliking Jews isn't intrinsically worse than disliking Negroes or Americans or any other block of people. In the early twenties, Eliot's anti-Semitic remarks were about on a par with the automatic sneer one casts at Anglo-Indian colonels in boarding houses. On the other hand if they had been written after the persecutions began they would have meant something quite different. . . . Some people go round smelling after anti-Semitism all the time. I have no doubt Fyvel thinks I am anti-Semitic. More rubbish is written about this subject than any other I can think of.[5]

By current standards, Orwell was also both homophobic and antifeminist. But such judgment says nothing about his positions in view of his own historical and cultural horizons. Nor do they absolve present-day readers of the obligation to research their claims via painstaking investigation of the life and times of historical and biographical subjects.

Such empirical work reflects a healthy respect for historical and cultural difference—and a recognition of our own limitations (and inevitable presentist bias). For we need to learn better to honor and even to admire that which differs from us, whether the differences owe to an historical gulf or to cultural factors, rather than simply to esteem those ways in which the writer is similar to us or how he or she anticipated the values and standards of the present.

In other words, as I stressed in my critique of the feminist reception of Orwell in *The Politics of Literary Reputation*,[6] one must understand the figure in relation to his contemporaries. Often this will mean to examine closely the historical context in which his opinions were formed as well as how events broke in a different direction at the time of his death and subsequently. And that will, in turn, entail a nuanced understanding of both the attitudes that existed in Orwell's day and how those attitudes evolved and have contributed to a different climate of opinion and values in our own day. For instance, Orwell's attitudes toward gays, women and feminism, and Jews were formed in the 1920s and 1930s, before the current recognition of minority oppression and before minority rights were widely extended to these groups. Orwell was not ahead of his time in these areas. He was a man of his time on such issues—as well as of his class and gender.

Consider, for instance, gender. Discussing *The Road to Wigan Pier,* the Marxist feminist Beatrix Campbell has explained the near-absence of working-class women as evidence of Orwell's "toxic scorn" toward women, especially female socialists. I devoted a chapter in *The Politics of Literary Reputation* to the historical context in which Orwell was writing, and I concluded there that he was not misogynistic but, rather, merely conventional on gender issues for his time and place. So it is heartening to see Peter Davison write: "What must be borne in mind in considering the relative nonappearance of women in *The Road to Wigan Pier* is that this is absolutely typical of such studies, even those by women, in the first 50 years of the twentieth-century." Davison cites several works including Left Book Club publications written by women, all of which devote women miners and wives of miners scant attention. A 1948 book, for example, discusses seventy-five cases of working-class miners; not a single one is a woman. On gender issues, Orwell was unexceptional, a man and a writer of his time.[7]

My larger point is that we need empathy for our predecessors, who, as Milan Kundera observes in *Testaments Betrayed* (1985), always walk "in a fog," by which he means they participate in events whose outcome is obscure. They make decisions, "especially decisions involving large historical events remote from their sphere of control," as one proceeds in a fog. He adds: "I say fog, not darkness. In the darkness, we see nothing, we are blind, we are defenseless, we are not free. In the fog, we are free, but it is a limited freedom, the circumscribed freedom of a person in a fog: he sees fifty yards ahead of him, he can clearly make out the features of his interlocutor, can take pleasure in the beauty of the trees that line the path, and can even observe what is happening close by and react."

So our predecessors proceeded in a fog. But what about us latter-day critics and historians as we look back from the present on our forerunners? When we judge people of the past, says Kundera, we usually see no fog on their path. "From our present, which was their faraway future, their path looks perfectly clear to us, good visibility all the way. Looking back, we see the path, we see the people proceeding, we see their mistakes, but not the fog." And Kundera then pleads: "Yet all of them—Heidegger, Mayakovsky, Louis Aragon, Ezra Pound, Gorky, Gottfried Benn, St.-John Perse—all were walking in fog, and one might wonder: Who is more blind? Mayakovsky, who as he wrote his poem on Lenin did not know where Leninism would lead? Or we, who judge him decades later and do not see the fog that enveloped him?" Kundera concludes: "Mayakovsky's blindness is part of the eternal human condition. But for us not to see the fog on Mayakovsky's path is to forget what a human being is, forget what we ourselves are."[8]

But *should* Mayakovsky have known where Leninism might lead? That is how the prosecutorial critic proceeds further. And without a rich understanding of the historical context—that is, the fog—the verdict is, invariably: Guilty. So here again, we come full circle: the responsible critic must honor the limits of our foggy human condition.

And what about the prosecution of George Orwell?

I raise the issue of Orwell's testament, here and elsewhere, via Kundera because it reminds us how relatively clear-sighted on the big issues Orwell really was—and yet also that the author of the mildly anti-Semitic *Down and Out in Paris and London* (1933) did not envision the fate of European Jewry in the next dozen years. Nor did the author who enthusiastically cooperated with the British and American intelligence services to translate and distribute *Animal Farm* anticipate that it would soon be denuded of its allegorical correspondences with USSR history and presented instead as a general attack on all forms of socialism. Or that "1984" would become such a red-scare symbol that the John Birch Society would soon be using those numerals as the last four digits in its national hotline. So Orwell was, on some issues, blinded by the fog—but let us see the fog as well as his limitations and errors.

IV

My other three corollary precepts flow from the first. A second precept of an ethics of reception involves the acceptance of human imperfection. This means that we acknowledge character blemishes as the inevitable price of heroic achievement. We do not insist—as Kingsley Amis once put it about the need to tolerate Orwell's shortcomings—"on ten out of ten" for our culture heroes.

All this suggests that we must learn not just to look at—but also to *overlook*—some minor flaws in the intellectual and spiritual physiognomy of our literary models. As I have already noted, such a wide-angle view entails no whitewashing of any shortcomings. Instead, it mandates both their compassionate recognition and balanced assessment as part of the writer's struggle. In that light, they can then be understood as distinctive features in the context of his life and work rather than narrowly focused upon and thrust into the sensationalistic glare of the spotlight. Such a "field focus" approach enables us to better see the whole man and not focus too much on one part, whether good or bad.

Indeed any ethics of detraction would necessarily mean that the judicially minded critic avoid "*the forgetting of everything not a crime,*" as Kundera puts it. He adds that we must not "reduce the writer to a defendant" and the art of biography to "*criminography*" as does Victor Farias (whose *Heidegger and Nazism* is "a classic example" of criminography). According to Kundera, Farias locates the roots of the philosopher's Nazism in his early youth, "without the least concern for locating the roots of his genius"; Kundera adds that, on the left, to punish someone accused of ideological deviations, "Communist tribunals would put *all* his work on the index (thus, for instance, the ban on Lukács and Sartre in Communist countries covered even their pro-Communist writings)."[9]

So, radical adversaries of Orwell such as Scott Lucas should hesitate to condemn his cooperation with British intelligence services in 1949[10] even as his admirers need to be careful to avoid reducing him to the plaster "St. George." One needs to remind oneself that Orwell lived in an era at least as complicated as our own—he was no icon but a very human individual with very human foibles and failings.

A third precept: discriminate between the man and the work. Learn to distinguish the writer's personality from his writings and intellectual achievement. This is an imperative task in the case of a writer such as Orwell, who, critics claim, lived what he wrote and wrote what he lived. Such a writer is frequently perceived by his admirers to have so fused his literary work and public personality that the two form a seamless whole. But these perceptions are usually judgments formed at a distance from the life of the writer. The closer the biographical scrutiny, the greater the likelihood that one eventually observes discrepancies, some of them sharp—as has happened with each new biography of Orwell (and has also occurred with the aforementioned examples of Chesterton, Dawson, and Eliot).

Here too, however, this realization need not entail any condemnation of the writer for such inconsistencies. Rather, it invites us to understand the interrelations between the man and his work in all their complexity—and not to insist on an appealing, simplistic figure. Instead we can distinguish better between self-actualizing and demeaning literary models, between creative and slavish intellectual hero worship.

None of this means yielding to what Kundera calls "the *biographical furor,*" including questions such as: "What was his vice or his weakness?" Such questions leads us to forget the writer's work and instead interrogate his life, following what Kundera calls a "quasi-police method." Kundera cites Proust's condemnation of the critic who "surrounds himself with every possible piece of information about a writer, to check his letters, to interrogate people who knew him. . . . "

Yet, says Kundera, surrounded "with every possible piece of information," the critic who immerses himself in such a plethora of circumstantial data embraces a positivistic method that usually skews his approach. Readers often find that, by overfocusing on writers' lives, such critics inevitably miss their work. Why? Because "a book is the product of a *self other than* the self we manifest in our habits, in our social life, in our vices"; "the writer's true self is manifested in his books *alone.*"

I realize that, in our postmodern and post-structuralist era, talk of a "true" self seems hopefully naive. Even literary artists of the stature of Kundera and Proust have trouble getting away with it. Nonetheless, Kundera and Proust are clear: the biographical method is "blind to the author's *other self,* blind to his aesthetic wishes, to his creative genius, his daimon."[11]

Fourth precept: beware all bounty hunters. Weigh—and discount—the influence of both supporters and skeptics. Judge a political writer not by those who claim or disclaim him for their own side. Adopt instead the motto: "The enemy of my enemy is *not*—on that account alone—my friend."

Orwell attacked Stalinism in *Nineteen Eighty-Four,* and prominent conservatives did likewise, but surely that does not mean that Orwell would have sanctioned the John Birch Society's use of "1984" in its telephone numbers—or Norman Podhoretz's use of "Orwell Press" in the 1980s as the name for the publishing imprint of the neoconservative Committee for the Free World. Orwell specifically dissociated himself from an anticommunist Conservative group in a 1945 letter to the Duchess of Atholl: "I cannot associate myself with an essentially Conservative body that claims to defend democracy in Europe [against Stalinism] but has nothing to say about British imperialism. I belong to the Left and must work inside it, much as I hate Russian totalitarianism."[12] (The John Birch Society was certainly among Orwell's concerns when he noted that Ingsoc refers not just to "English socialism" but to "hundred percent Americanism.") And yet, "working within the Left" clearly also had its limits for Orwell—as his attacks on the progressives of his day evince. So the fact that both Orwell (in *Lion and the Unicorn*) and the Marxist Left—or Maoist Left—denounced corporate capitalism does not mean that Marxists and Maoists are Orwell's bedfellows—or that Orwell admirers such as Noam Chomsky are either.

For in an inescapably ideological age such as our own, any significant figure will inevitably be tagged with positions other than the ones that he formally embraced. Admirers and detractors will smear him with charges and convictions at wide variance from those he upheld and even attribute to him beliefs that he could not have fathomed during his lifetime. This is another form of intellectual grave robbing that has become standard practice with Orwell.

That means that one resists equally the hagiographic urge to canonize Orwell into St. George and the iconoclastic temptation to trash him, which might prove oneself a greater skeptic and rebel than he was, a daring intellectual outsider capable of challenging the historical consensus that Orwell was the "conscience of his generation." Succumbing to that iconoclastic temptation was Louis Menand in a January 2003 feature essay in *The New Yorker.* Titled "Honest, Decent, Wrong: The Invention of George Orwell," Menand's piece denounced the left- and right-wing pieties about Orwell, his "army of fans all eager to suggest that a writer who approved of little would have approved of them."[13]

So far, so good: Menand is on the lookout for bounty hunters. But he goes on to commit the historical misjudgment of implying that there was no fog, only clear blue and true North in the 1930s when he writes that the notion that "Orwell was right" about imperialism, fascism, and Stalinism was nothing exceptional: "Many people were against them in Orwell's time," says Menand. But that is historically misguided—Orwell was one of the few intellectuals in the mid-1930s to stand loudly and firmly against all three.

Meanwhile, an example of hagiography that I consider to be what Orwell would call just on the "right side" of hero worship was Leon Wieseltier's column in the *New Republic* in February 2003, a reply to Menand. Wieseltier argued that Orwell is worth caring about, is even worth fighting over, because he warned against the possibility that "objective truth is fading out of this world." Wieseltier drew important distinctions that Menand's postmodernist sensibility had effaced, distinctions especially relevant to the emerging historiographical battle about the Iraqi war: "not all wars are jihads, indeed there are just wars as well as holy wars; not all moral certainties are terroristic impulses, not all objectivity is proto-fascism." "Whom to be like?" asks Wieseltier. And he answers, diffidently yet with unmistakable admiration: "There are many greater mistakes than the aspiration to be like George

Orwell. For a long time, admiration of Orwell has been one of the most encouraging features of our political and cultural situation. There are worse masters, much worse."[14]

I agree—Orwell is worth fighting over—which doesn't mean that intellectual war crimes in the W.W.G.O.D. game are tolerable. Hence this proposal for an ethics of admiration and detraction, which might serve as a preliminary set of honorable guidelines for conducting such battles.

V

So the question remains: Who to be like? That is the question implied by all critical acts or intellectual judgments that pass via biography toward what Lionel Trilling called "the bloody crossroads where literature and politics meet."[15] Such a question takes Orwell's work, as well as his life and legacy, seriously. It does not assure, let alone assert, that he was a "saint" or a moral exemplar. Whatever our conclusions about Orwell's ethical conduct and intellectual integrity, it is clear today that George Orwell was no "saint." Like all of us, he was a human being with flaws, fables, and failings—especially in his personal life. He was an unfaithful husband with an ambiguous attitude toward Jews and homosexuals, yet he was also a loyal friend, a courageous militiaman, a generous supporter of struggling writers, a master of plain prose, a champion of freedom of speech, and an outspoken scourge of both capitalist profiteers and Stalinist ideologues. A conflicted man, not a plaster saint or pure hero. So let us decanonize and rehumanize George Orwell. Properly skeptical of the hagiography of Orwell's admirers, we can remain impressed by this noble, impressive, and flawed man; we can appreciate the contradictions between Eric Blair's ambiguous life and George Orwell's radiant reputation.

I believe that, after a careful reading of his work and of the historical record, Orwell's writings hold up in an unusually powerful and compelling way. Whatever the claims and counterclaims about Orwell, he is indeed uniquely attractive as an ideological patron and political mentor. Unlike two other contemporaries, Ignazio Silone and Arthur Koestler, both of whom have been tarred by recent scandals,[16] Orwell's reputation still stands high (despite scattered calls since 1996 to condemn him for cooperating with British intelligence services in the early days of the cold war). In fact, among contemporary British intellectuals who have been admired and claimed by the Right, Left, and Center, only Isaiah Berlin compares; among postwar American intellectuals, only Lionel Trilling. And both Berlin and Trilling (who coveted Berlin's status) are much narrower figures than Orwell—they are intellectuals rather than men of letters. And they are little known to the wider public or outside their native countries.

Amid all this, Orwell remains standing as an intellectual model, perhaps the leading twentieth-century exemplar of the public intellectual.[17]

VI

Who to be like? I suppose my own intellectual and scholarly pursuits—namely, four books devoted to Orwell's legacy—serve as an obvious personal answer to that question. Indeed, readers' responses to Orwell are almost invariably personal and even passionate. George Orwell's own directions and buttoned-down common-sense style somehow invite one to speak personally about him. So let me close here with an unguarded acknowledgment of what I have learned from Orwell—and what I acknowledge gratefully has been his invaluable legacy to me—whereby I am simply honoring the fact of my own intensely personal response to both the man and his work.

Indeed I am responding to the question so often put to me by my family and friends: "So then, what is it like to have lived with George Orwell?!" It's a question that several other writers at this conference—doubtless including his biographers—could perhaps answer even better.

My own response will satisfy no one. It satisfies me least of all, let alone the Orwell of my imagination. For my debt to him is incalculable, and it cannot be repaid or discharged but merely acknowledged. And it is best acknowledged by my own practice of the code of ethics of admiration that I have outlined in this short essay.

The indebtedness is literary and political—but also existential and even spiritual. It has to do with clear writing and plain speaking, with a comradely insistence on holding one's own side to the highest standards. But more importantly, it owes to Orwell's repeated emphasis on—and inspiring enactment of—intellectual integrity. And it has also to do with his clear-sighted recognition of its complexity and its difficulty, of the manifold temptations to succumb to la trahison des clercs.

How both the writer gave voice and the man gave life to such excruciating intellectual integrity has taught me lessons that can only be learned by living with such a presence as Orwell—lessons about truth telling, about groupthink, about vocation, and about the life of the mind. They are lessons that are hard won and easily forgotten, invaluable lessons that must be repeatedly discovered, honored, and learned anew. Fortunate is the person who learns them by word and deed from an intellectual big brother.

NOTES

1. George Woodcock, *The Crystal Spirit: A Study of George Orwell* (Boston: Little, Brown, 1966), 53.
2. Judith Shulevitz, "What Would Orwell Do?" *New York Times Book Review,* September 8, 2002, 12.
3. Ben Wattenberg, host of the PBS program "The Orwell Century," broadcast March 2002.
4. Quoted in Bernard Crick, *George Orwell: A Life* (London: Secker and Warburg, 1980), 430.
5. Letter from Orwell to Julian Symons, October 29, 1948, in *the Complete Works of George Orwell,* ed. Peter Davison (London: Secker and Warburg, 1998), 19:461.
6. John Rodden, *George Orwell: The Politics of Literary Reputation* (New Brunswick, N.J.: Transaction, 2002 [1989]), 211–26.
7. See my discussion of Campbell and Daphne Patai in *George Orwell: The Politics of Literary Reputation,* chap. 4. Peter Davison notes in his *George Orwell: A Literary Life* (Basingstoke: Macmillan, 1996): "Orwell (relatively rarely in his day, especially in a working-class family) was not the kind of man who would not wash up; he willingly changed young Richard's nappies at a time when few men did such things. But he was writing about

a society which was dependent on the man working and, in working-class society, orientated to that end far more than was the world of the middle-class. Examination of a number of books of the first half of the twentieth century that have obvious parallels with *The Road to Wigan Pier* reveals few working women" (219).

8. Milan Kundera, *Testaments Betrayed* (New York: HarperCollins, 1985).

9. Kundera, *Testaments Betrayed.*

10. Scott Lucas, *George Orwell and the Betrayal of Dissent* (London: Pluto Press, 2003).

11. Kundera, *Testaments Betrayed.*

12. Orwell, *The Collected Essays, Journalism, and Letters,* ed. Sonia Orwell and Ian Angus (London: Secker and Warburg, 1968), 4:30.

13. Louis Menand, "Honest, Decent, Wrong: The Invention of George Orwell," *The New Yorker* (January 2003).

14. Leon Wieseltier, "Aspidistra," *New Republic,* February 17, 2003.

15. Lionel Trilling, "Reality in America," in *The Liberal Imagination: Essays on Literature and Society* (New York: Viking, 1950), 11.

16. Revelations about Koestler's mistreatment of women—his alleged rape of Jill Craigie, among other assaults—have destroyed his reputation as a humanist and champion of the dispossessed. Silone's radical credentials have been soiled by evidence that he was an informant to the fascists in the 1930s as well as knowledgeable about CIA funding of the Congress for Cultural Freedom (and other anti-Soviet postwar activities of the Western intelligence services in the "cultural Cold War").

17. That is the verdict of Richard Posner in his *Public Intellectuals* (Cambridge: Harvard University Press, 2001).

6

The Public Intellectual as Connected Critic: George Orwell and Religion

Ronald F. Thiemann

> The Kingdom of Heaven has somehow got to be brought on to the surface of the earth. We have got to be children of God, even though the God of the prayer book no longer exists.
> —*George Orwell, "Notes on the Way"*

> The real problem here is how to restore the religious attitude while accepting death as final.
> —*George Orwell, "Arthur Koestler"*

To compose an essay on Orwell and religion is, one might imagine, to write a very short piece indeed. Orwell is generally understood to be an agnostic, a humanist whose most well-known utterances about religion are sardonic, sarcastic, and occasionally even contemptuous. He had a particular dislike for the Roman Catholic Church, an institution he compared to both Nazism and Communism in its totalitarian aims. He expressed equal disdain for Anglo-Catholicism, abhorring its vain and empty ritual and noting the proclivity for Anglo-Catholic writers to embrace aspects of fascist ideology.[1] Among his favorite epithets is "creeping Jesus," by which he seems to mean a person of evangelical persuasion whose piety he found to be intellectually and ethically offensive.

At the same time Orwell, like most Englishmen of his time, was steeped in the religious culture of Britain; he had a particular love of church architecture, a decent knowledge of the Bible, and an appreciation for some of the values Christianity had instilled in the English working class. Like most "upper lower middle class" persons of his time, Orwell was baptized, confirmed (by the socialist bishop Charles Gore), and married in the Church of England. (On his marriage day Orwell wrote to a friend, "I have been studying [the prayer book] for some days past in hopes of steeling myself against the obscenities of the wedding service."[2]) In his will, to the surprise of many of his friends, he specifically requested a burial "according to the rites of the Church of England" and insisted that he not be cremated.

In this essay I focus on the development of Orwell's thoughts on religion during the crucial period of 1932 to 1936. These five years encompass a number of significant changes in Orwell's life, not least of which was his decision to change his name from Eric Blair to George Orwell. At the outset of this period he emerged from his four-year tramping expedition in London and Paris facing serious and sustained poverty. He suffered the second publisher's rejection of the manuscript that would finally become *Down and Out in Paris and London*. He experienced a serious sexual affair, one that ended unhappily when the woman who was the object of his desire married another man. In order to support himself he took up a teaching post, one that provided much of the detail for *A Clergyman's Daughter,* a novel he wrote during this period. These years also marked his engagement with members of the Independent Labour Party, an encounter that helped to shape his peculiar form of left-wing, egalitarian, noncommunist Marxism. And this period concludes with his tour of the coal mining regions of northern England and the publication of his important but controversial *The Road to Wigan Pier.*

I argue that Orwell emerged from these years confirmed in his judgment that he could not adopt the beliefs of traditional Christianity but with an equally firm commitment to the "spiritual" (his word) aspects of socialist practice. The "religious attitude" that was crucial to the vitality of British culture could only be sustained, he believed, by a form of nonideological socialist practice that would be relevant to the working-class people of England. In his grasp of socialism as a set of moral practices designed to promote freedom and equality, Orwell manifests a humanist faith without illusions, a "religious attitude" that accepts "death as final" but never ends its quest for social justice.[3]

THE YEARS OF UNCERTAINTY, 1932–1934

At Christmastime 1931 Eric Blair, having returned from the journeys described in *Down and Out in Paris and London,* was living in tenement housing along the Thames River across from Westminster. Though he had no regular source of income, he still harbored strong hopes of becoming a published writer. Those hopes suffered a serious setback, however, when he received on February 19, 1932, a letter from T. S. Eliot in behalf of Faber and Faber Publishing Company. "Dear Mr. Blair," it read,

> I am sorry to have kept your manuscript. We did find it of very great interest, but I regret to say that it does not appear to me possible as a publishing venture. It is decidedly too short, and particularly for a book of such length it seems to me too loosely constructed, as the French and English episodes fall into two parts with very little to connect them.
>
> I should think, however, that you should have enough material from your experience to make a very interesting book on down-and-out life in England alone.
>
> With many thanks for letting me see the manuscript.
> I am,
> Yours faithfully,
> T.S. Eliot[4]

Whatever solace we might take from the fact that a rejection letter from one great writer to another bears all the marks of the standard letter every writer or scholar has received, it certainly was a great blow to Blair's desire to continue in his craft. So, after a brief stay with his sister and brother-in-law in Leeds, he took up an offer to become headmaster of a small boys school in Hayes, Middlesex, north of London.

The experiences at The Hawthorns provided much of the material included in his novel *A Clergyman's Daughter.* Dorothy's teaching adventures at Ringwood House Academy for Girls were a mildly exaggerated version of Blair's own experiences at The Hawthorns, and her famous encounter with the noxious glue pot while making costumes for a church play reflected Blair's own venture of making handmade costumes for a play he wrote and produced at the school. But the most important influence on George-Orwell-in-the-making during this time was his friendship with the vicar of the parish church in Hayes, the Rev. Thomas Brownbill James Parker. Despite his continuing skepticism about matters religious, Blair regularly attended mass at the Anglican church, and, according to Rev. Parker's widow, Madge, assisted with communion distribution and even helped the vicar to administer last rites to the dying.[5] She further reports that he helped to wash dishes after Church Guild meetings, chopped wood for the stoves, and filled coal buckets for the furnaces. She described him as "the kind of person who fits into a kitchen and helps you with everything in your own house, didn't stand on ceremony."[6] She also recalled that he had cleaned the crown of a statue of the Virgin Mary, an incident Blair himself confirms in a letter to his friend and soon-to-be-lover, Eleanor Jaques.

Sir Bernard Crick, one of Orwell's biographers, reports "Mrs. Parker is indignant at the idea that he was not a genuine believer. She argues that her husband looked him over very carefully indeed,"[7] since the previous head had been removed for financial fraud, and the new head had to assist in bringing other local clergy on to the school board. In addition, the Parkers were burgeoning Christian socialists and they shared with Blair a deep concern for the plight of the poor and unemployed. While Crick has no reason to doubt the accuracy of Mrs. Parker's memories, Blair himself gave a somewhat different account of his time in Hayes, one that affirms his genuine friendship with the Rev. Parker but raises doubts about the authenticity of his piety.

> Hayes . . . is one of the most godforsaken places I have ever struck. The population seems to be entirely made up of clerks who frequent tin-roofed chapels on Sundays and for the rest bolt themselves within doors. My sole friend is the curate—High Anglican but not a creeping Jesus & a very good fellow. Of course it means that I have to go to Church, which is an arduous job here, as the service is so popish that I don't know my way about it and feel an awful BF when I see everyone bowing and crossing themselves all around me & can't follow suit. The poor old vicar, who I suspect hates all this popery, is dressed up in cope and biretta and led round in process with candles etc. looking like a bullock garlanded for sacrifice.[8]

Blair's confirmation of the statue story is told in a rather different tone from that suggested by Mrs. Parker. "I have promised to paint one of the church idols (a quite skittish-looking B.V.M, half life-size, & I shall try & make her look as much like one of the illustrations in *La Vie Parisienne* as possible)."[9] His concluding remarks show little sign of authentic faith. "I would 'communicate' too, only I am afraid the bread might choke me."[10]

What are we to make of the sharp differences between Mrs. Parker's memories and Blair's own account in his letter to Ms. Jaques? If we grant integrity to both accounts, it is probable that Blair is exaggerating his skepticism in his remarks to Eleanor, since she was a notable freethinker and religious agnostic in her own right. Since he was also courting her favor in these days, one might well imagine that he thought that she might especially appreciate the humor in his compromising situation. For he wrote again, in October of 1932, "I take in the *Church Times* regularly now and like it more every week. I do so like to see that there is life in the old dog yet—I mean in the poor C. of E. I shall have to go to Holy Communion soon, hypocritical tho' it is, because my curate friend is bound to think it funny if I always go to Church but never communicate."[11] How these comments square with Mrs. Parker's claim that he actually assisted in the distribution of communion is hard to say. But Blair's clear and consistent sardonic tone in these letters leads the reader to doubt whether his piety was anything more than a concession to the religious practice of his sole friend in "godforsaken" Hayes.

Still, there is some evidence to suggest that Blair struggled with the question of religious faith during these years. He certainly reviewed a number of religious works for publication and remarked to Eleanor in a subsequent letter that he is "reading a book called *Belief in God* by Bishop Gore–late Bishop of Oxford, who confirmed me." He also engaged in a brief published exchange with one of Britain's most distinguished Christian socialists, the Jesuit ethicist C. C. Martindale. In his 1932 review of Martindale's book *Catholic Social Guild,* Blair opined, "Father Martindale, being committed to the statement that faith is reasonable, can neither stand up to his difficulties nor ignore them. Consequently he evades them, with considerable nimbleness. He sails over the theory of evolution in a sort of balloon flight with common sense flying overboard for ballast; he dodges past the problem of evil like a man dodging past his creditors' doorway."[12] Martindale did not reply directly to Blair's critique of his own work but, rather, wrote a letter to *The New English Weekly* in which he characterized Blair's criticisms of Karl Adam's *The Spirit of Catholicism* as "disingenuous." Blair responded briefly in the next issue of the journal simply reversing the charge and calling Martindale "disingenuous" in his own remarks.[13] Despite the snippiness of this brief exchange, there is evidence that Orwell and Martindale remained in contact throughout the years. Orwell, despite his disagreements with the Jesuit socialist, apparently respected both his intellect and his moral judgment. In a letter of July 8, 1932, he wrote, "I have had a small controversy with Fr. Martindale, S.J. & he wrote & told Mrs. Carr that he would like to meet me as I was deeply in error & he could put me right. I must meet him sometime if possible."[14]

Blair also wrote a poem in 1932 that was published in March 1933 in the *Adelphi.* Here he reflects on the reality of death and the possibility of faith before "the silent grave."

> Sometimes in the middle autumn days,
> The windless days when the swallows have flown,
> And the sere elms brood in the mist,
> Each tree a being, rapt, alone,
>
> I know, not as in barren thought,
> But wordlessly, as the bones know,
> What quenching of my brain, what numbness,
> Wait in the dark grave where I go.

And I see the people thronging in the street
The death-marked people, they and I
Goalless, rootless, like leaves drifting,
Blind to the earth and to the sky;

Nothing believing, nothing loving,
Not in joy nor in pain, not heeding the stream
Of precious life that flows within us,
But fighting, toiling as in a dream.

So shall we in the rout of life
Some thought, some faith, some meaning save,
And speak it once before we go
In silence to the silent grave. . . .[15]

While such existential sentiments are rare in Orwell's writings, they do remind one of the concluding section of *A Clergyman's Daughter,* the novel that Orwell wrote in its entirety during these years. Most observers consider this novel Orwell's least distinguished, and Orwell himself had grave doubts about its artistic quality. "It was a good idea," he wrote to Leonard Moore, "but I am afraid I have made a muck of it—however, it is as good as I can do for the present. There are bits of it that I don't dislike, but I am afraid it is very disconnected as a whole, and rather unreal."[16] While most critics would agree that this book is "the least successful of Orwell's novels,"[17] I find myself in concurrence with Christopher Hitchens's judgment that "*A Clergyman's Daughter* is a finer novel than Orwell believed it to be."[18] Granted that the novel relies upon a hackneyed plot device of an amnesiac blackout and centers upon a pallid heroine of "watery personality,"[19] still the book has many redeeming literary qualities.[20] Of more importance for my own purposes, it also gives us a brief window into Orwell's own reflections on the question of the faith's viability in the modern world.

In his depiction of Dorothy Hare, the subservient and repressed daughter of the Rev. Charles Hare, Orwell shows his talent for sympathetic identification with characters who find themselves trapped in circumstances not of their own making. While Orwell clearly struggles with Dorothy's own inner motivations, he still manages to evoke in the reader a genuine sense of connection to her plight. Her behavior demonstrates the thoroughness by which she has internalized the suffocating and repressive environment in which she lives. In the early stages of the novel she goes about rather mindlessly acting in ways in which her father has instructed her. But Orwell's control of his narrative art allows him to describe Dorothy's masochistic actions in a good-humored manner that makes her an engaging character even in her self-flagellating moments. "Her body had gone gooseflesh all over. She detested cold baths; it was for that very reason that she made it a rule to take all her baths cold from April to November. Putting a tentative hand into the water—and it was horribly cold—she drove herself forward with her usual exhortation. Come on, Dorothy! In you go! No funking, please!"

Orwell's description of an early morning mass is a minor classic that clearly draws on his own experiences in the parish church of Hayes. As Dorothy enters the church she notices that the only other communicant is "old Miss Mayfill, of the Grange."

Miss Mayfill was very old, so old that no one remembered her as anything but an old woman. A faint scent radiated from her—an ethereal scent, analysable as eau-de-Cologne, mothballs and a subflavour of gin. Dorothy drew a long glass-headed pin from the lapel of her coat, and furtively, under cover of Miss Mayfill's back, pressed the point against her forearm. Her flesh tingled apprehensively. She made it a rule, whenever she caught herself not attending to her prayers, to prick her arm hard enough to make blood come. It was her chosen form of self-discipline, her guard against irreverence and sacrilegious thoughts. With the pin poised in readiness she managed for several moments to pray more collectedly.[21]

Dorothy's plight becomes even more dire, however, as she realizes that she may have to commune from the common cup *after* Miss Mayfill has already done so. Orwell's power of description combines with his sense of humor to create an atmosphere of comic dread that actually makes Dorothy, even in her masochism, an appealing and sympathetic person.

Dorothy remained on her feet a moment longer. Miss Mayfill was creeping toward the altar with slow, tottering steps. She could barely walk, but she took bitter offence if you offered to help her. In her ancient, bloodless face her mouth was surprisingly large, loose and wet. The under lip, pendulous with age, slobbered forward, exposing a strip of gum and a row of false teeth as yellow as the keys of an old piano. On the upper lip was a fringe of dark, dewy moustache. It was not an appetising mouth; not the kind of mouth that you would like to see drinking out of your cup. Suddenly, spontaneously, as though the Devil himself had put it there, the prayer slipped from Dorothy's lips: "O God, let me not have to take the chalice after Miss Mayfill!" The next moment, in self-horror, she grasped the meaning of what she had said, and wished that she had bitten her tongue in two rather than utter that deadly blasphemy upon the very altar steps. She drew the pin again from her lapel and drove it into her arm so hard that it was all she could do to suppress a cry of pain. Then she stepped to the altar and knelt down meekly on Miss Mayfill's left, so as to make sure of taking the chalice after her.[22]

Orwell's vivid but wry style allows him to depict Dorothy in a critical yet sympathetic manner that presages his discussion of faith and faithlessness in the concluding section of the novel. There, once Dorothy had returned from her days in London, the hops fields, and teaching, she finds herself again in the presence of Mr. Warburton, the man whose sexual advances had triggered her initial fall into amnesia. As they travel back to Dorothy's home in a first-class train carriage bound for Knype Hill, she and Warburton engage in a fascinating debate about faith and doubt. Orwell's own views emerge only in the dialogue between the two and should not be identified with just one or the other character. Sometimes he speaks through the caustic irreverence of Mr. Warburton.

"Surely I don't take you to mean that you actually *regret* losing your faith, as you call it? One might as well regret losing a goiter. . . . Is it the hypocrisy that's worrying you? Afraid that the consecrated bread might stick in your throat, and so forth? I shouldn't trouble. Half the parsons' daughters in England are probably in the same difficulty. And quite nine-tenths of the parsons, I should say. . . . What you're trying to do, apparently, is to make the worst of both worlds. You stick to the Christian scheme of things, but you leave Paradise out of it. And I suppose, if the truth were known, there are quite a lot of your kind wandering about among the ruins of the C. of E. You're practically a sect in yourselves," he added reflectively, "the Anglican Atheists. Not a sect I should care to belong to, I must say."[23]

At other times Dorothy's struggles seem to echo Orwell's own, or at least Orwell's concern about the fate of Christian culture.

"I don't believe in it any longer, if that's what you mean. And I see now that a lot of it was rather silly. But that doesn't help. The point is that all the beliefs I had are gone, and I've nothing to put in their place. . . . But don't you see—you must see— how different everything is when all of a sudden the whole world is empty? . . . Yes . . . I suppose that's what I do mean. Perhaps it's better—less selfish—to pretend one believes even when one doesn't, than to say openly that one's an unbeliever and perhaps help turn other people in to unbelievers too."[24]

Finally, and perhaps most importantly, Orwell seems reflected as well in the voice of the narrator.

What she would have said was that though her faith had left her, she had not changed, could not change, did not want to change, the spiritual background of her mind; that her cosmos, though now it seemed to her empty and meaningless, was still in a sense the Christian cosmos; that the Christian way of life was still the way that must come naturally to her. . . . Beliefs change, thoughts change, but there is some inner part of the soul that does not change. Faith vanishes, but the need for faith remains the same as before. . . . Life, if the grave really ends it, is monstrous and dreadful. No use trying to argue it away. Think of life as it really is, think of the *details* of life; and then think that there is no meaning in it, no purpose, no goal except the grave. . . . Either life on earth is a preparation for something greater and more lasting, or it is meaningless, dark and dreadful.[25]

It is, of course, speculative to suggest that the struggle between Dorothy and War-burton reflected a struggle within Orwell's own soul. Still the themes enunciated in these three sections of text—irreverent skepticism, well-intentioned hypocrisy, faith and meaning at the edge of the grave—all echo aspects of his life and work during these two years of uncertainty. I do not intend to take these biographical speculations any further. Rather, I want to suggest that the issues that emerge at the end of *A Clergyman's Daughter* presage the urgent questions he will ask about the future of secularized British culture and the place of humanistic socialism within it. What will sustain the moral sensibility of British citizens once the explicit influence of Christianity has disappeared? What will sustain a commitment to freedom and justice within the socialist movement if there is no place for a "spiritual dimension" within socialist practice? How will socialist practice engage the working classes of Britain who have been shaped by Christian culture and exhibit the virtues attributable to that culture? Orwell's own zeal for equality and his equally zealous critique of the British Left must be understood in part against the background of the existential questions he posed to himself during these two years of uncertainty. Thus the quotations posed at the outset of this essay return to set the stage for my consideration of the next two years of Orwell's life. "The real problem here is how to restore the religious attitude while accepting death as final. . . . The Kingdom of Heaven has somehow got to be brought on to the surface of the earth. We have got to be children of God, even though the God of the prayer book no longer exists."[26]

SOCIALISM'S SPIRITUAL SIDE: A COMMITMENT TO JUSTICE AND COMMON
DECENCY, 1934–1936

Sometime late in 1932, shortly before the publication of *Down and Out in Paris
and London,* Eric Blair changed his name to George Orwell. Given the alternatives
he was considering at the time—Kenneth Miles and especially H. Lewis All-
ways—posterity should be grateful that Blair chose the name of a small English
river for his new identity. The summer of 1933 witnessed two other important
changes in his life. Eleanor Jaques, with whom he had carried on a long-distance
relationship, became engaged to another man, and The Hawthorns was sold to a
new owner who immediately changed headmasters. Orwell then took up another
teaching position at a larger school in Uxbridge. It was there, after being soaked
by a cold mid-December rainstorm, that Orwell was hospitalized for the first time
with pneumonia and thus began his battle against the lung ailments that would
finally take his life sixteen years later.

Teaching clearly was not Orwell's vocation, and so in the fall of 1934 he
accepted a job as a clerk in a bookshop owned by Francis and Byfanwy Westrope,
two prominent members of Britain's Independent Labour Party (ILP). It was through
the Westropes and their acquaintances that Orwell was introduced to the form of
socialism that would shape his political views for the rest of his life. The ILP
positioned itself firmly between traditional liberalism on the one hand and communism on the other.[27] It understood itself as providing a peculiar form of ethical
socialism as a leaven to the purely economic approach characteristic of the traditional labor movements. It was "[l]eft-wing, egalitarian, a strange English mixture
of secularized evangelism and non-Communist Marxism."[28] The party attracted
significant numbers of Christian socialists, especially those in the nonconformist
churches and others associated with the Labour Church Movement.[29] The ILP was
both anticapitalist and strongly democratic. It anticipated and welcomed a left-
wing revolution that would bring down Western capitalist economies, but it parted
company with the communist doctrine that "bourgeois liberty" should be destroyed
in the process. The ILP urged the expansion of liberty to all classes of society,
thereby achieving the equality central to the socialist platform. The ILP was am-
bivalent on the question of war, recognizing war as an implement of capitalist
domination that would ultimately bring about capitalism's demise yet recognizing
the horrors that inevitably accompany armed conflict. The party thus tended to be
antimilitarist though not quite pacifist, but often found itself in alliance with pacifist movements in opposing state-sponsored violence. Finally, the ILP saw in both
Soviet Communism and fascism similar forms of totalitarian state monopoly economies. Both regimes stood under the condemnation of the ethical socialism es-
poused by the ILP. We know that Orwell often attended ILP meetings and even
participated in retreats sponsored by the *Adelphi* that focused on the "mystic Marxist
or Christian Socialist"[30] aspects of ILP ideology. The resonances between the ILP
platform and Orwell's more mature socialist reflections are obvious, and thus it is
safe to say that Orwell's emerging political beliefs were nurtured in the context of
the peculiar form of ethical socialism represented by the ILP.

Orwell found his own political voice, however, when he decided to undertake
another road expedition, this one focusing on the workingmen and -women living
in poverty in England's industrial north. From January 31 through March 30,

1936, Orwell lived with and among working-class people in the cities of Wigan, Barnsley, and Sheffield. The result was one of the most graphic descriptions of working-class poverty ever written, *The Road to Wigan Pier*. Combining historical narrative, ethical analysis, and ideological critique, this book allowed Orwell to hone his skills as a social critic to razor-sharp precision. In this early work we see the emergence of the distinctive qualities that mark Orwell as a superior writer and an insightful critic: vivid descriptive prose, political and ethical purpose, social critique in narrative form, ideological impatience, and engaged self-critical analysis. *The Road to Wigan Pier* reveals Orwell as a prophetic social critic of the highest order.

"The first sound in the mornings was the clumping of the mill-girls' clogs down the cobbled street."[31] With this simple but evocative sentence Orwell began to open the world of the northern mining country to his readers. With its deceptive simplicity and alliterative repetition, the sentence simultaneously describes the sounds that awakened the author every morning and reproduces those sounds in the readers' ears in the hopes that their eyes might also be opened to the abject poverty of this place. Orwell had few peers who could rival the power of his descriptive narrative art. With acute attention to the minute details of the world in which he lived, Orwell provided a realistic but ethically charged account of his own experience. His prose simultaneously described that world and evoked a sense of identification with it in his readers. His gaze was relentless, taking in even the gruesome details and laying them before his audience. "The meals at the Brookers' house were uniformly disgusting. For breakfast you got two rashers of bacon and a pale fried egg, and bread-and-butter which had often been cut overnight and always had thumb-marks on it. However tactfully I tried, I could never induce Mr. Brooker to let me cut my own bread-and-butter; he *would* hand it to me slice by slice, each slice gripped firmly under that broad black thumb."[32] Orwell's descriptions were interlaced with narrator's comments designed to enhance and intensify the feelings evoked by the descriptions themselves. He was acutely attuned to matters of the senses and often remarked upon the power of smell. "[T]his is where it [i.e., industrialized civilization] all led—to labyrinthine slums and dark back kitchens with sickly, ageing people creeping round and round them like blackbeetles. It is a kind of duty to see and smell such places now and again, especially smell them, lest you should forget that they exist."[33]

No passage more clearly illustrates the power of Orwell's morally engaged narrative than one that appears toward the end of the first chapter of *Wigan Pier*.

> The train bore me away, through the monstrous scenery of the slag-heaps, chimneys, piled scrap-iron, foul canals, paths of cindery mud criss-crossed by the prints of clogs. This was March, but the weather had been horribly cold and everywhere there were mounds of blackened snow. As we moved slowly through the outskirts of town we passed row after row of little grey slum houses running at right angles to the embankment. At the back of one of the houses a young woman was kneeling on the stones, poking a stick up the leaden waste-pipe which ran from the sink inside and which I suppose was blocked. I had time to see everything about her—her sacking apron, her clumsy clogs, her arms reddened by the cold. She looked up as the train passed, and I was almost near enough to catch her eye. She had a round pale face, the usual exhausted face of the slum girl who is twenty-five and looks forty, thanks to miscarriages and drudgery; and it wore, for the second in which I

saw it, the most desolate, hopeless expression I have ever seen. . . . She knew well enough what was happening to her—understood as well as I did how dreadful a destiny it was to be kneeling there in the bitter cold, on the slimy stones of a slum backyard, poking a stick up a foul drain-pipe.[34]

This is realistic narrative at its best. The meaning of this passage depends upon the careful account Orwell gives of even the smallest details. By attending to the slag heaps, the cindery mud, and the blackened snow, Orwell evokes a vivid but desolate scene for the reader. By focusing initially on the houses, the clogged drained pipe, and woman kneeling on the stones, he slowly directs our attention from the grim natural surroundings to the equally forlorn human environment. Only once he has done that does he attend to the woman's round, pale, and exhausted face, one that reflects in her identity the desolation of the surrounding scene. It is as if we are watching Annie Leibowitz or Diane Arbus develop a black and white photograph. The details of the human visage emerge slowly from the blurred background, but as the silver bromide works its magic we find ourselves confronted by a human face from which we cannot avert our eyes. The words "how dreadful a destiny" have impact precisely because we see in the face of this no-longer-young girl something of ourselves. Thus the moral impact of the prose emerges only when the full narrative description is complete. This is no jeremiad; rather this is ethically informed social critique with a narrative shape.

It is also realistic narrative that serves a moral and political purpose[35] and should not be confused with *mere* historical description. One of Orwell's great accomplishments was to break down the artificial barriers between the essay, the story, and the novel. It would be no exaggeration, nor criticism, to characterize Orwell's novels as extended essays in narrative form. The historical, political, and ethical meaning of his writing cannot be extracted from the narrative descriptive itself. There is no extractable moral to these stories. The moral meaning is found only in, with, and under the narrative account.

This literary form was, of course, a perfect vehicle for the kind of ethical socialism that Orwell wanted to advance. The first half of *Wigan Pier* was designed to depict simultaneously the plight of the working-class poor and their courage, good humor, and dignity. "A working class man does not disintegrate under the strain of poverty as a middle-class person does. . . . [T]hey realise that losing your job does not mean that you cease to be a human being. . . . Families are impoverished but the family-system has not broken up. The people are in fact living a reduced version of their former lives. Instead of raging against their destiny they have made things tolerable by lowering their standards."[36] Even when we note the "dreadful destiny" of the poor young woman poking her stick up the drainpipe, we do not see her merely as a victim. Orwell skillfully granted agency to the persons he described in the north of England, even as he indicted those whose lives benefited from the labor of the poor. "[A]ll of us *really* owe our lives to poor drudges underground, blackened to their eyes, with their throats full of coal dust, driving their shovels forward with arms and belly muscles of steel."[37]

Orwell's literary and ethical procedure in the first half of *Wigan Pier* is essential to understanding the oft-criticized and controversial second half. By depicting the poor of northern England as genuine persons with families, clogged drainpipes, and dilapidated living quarters, Orwell hoped to give them a particularity that generalizations like the "proletariat" could not illumine. He approached socialism "from below," by a consideration of the actual conditions in which the poor lived, worked, made love, and reared children. For him socialism was primarily a set a moral practices designed to create a world in which children were no longer malnourished and society's resources were more equitably distributed among all classes. He rebelled against highly theorized versions of socialism because he was convinced that they blinded their advocates to the plight and personhood of the poor—the real poor and not simply the "poor" as constructed by socialist theory. In this sense, then, Orwell advocated a nonideological understanding of socialism. He shared the goal of all socialists: equality across all classes of society, but he understood socialism to be "a moral code in action"[38] that could not be fully articulated through traditional socialist theory. He believed that he had seen this moral code embedded in the culture of the working-class poor with whom he lived in northern England. Thus Orwell extolled "the irreducible belief in decency that exists in the hearts of ordinary people. . . . [E]verywhere, under the surface, the common man sticks obstinately to the belief that he derives from Christian culture."[39] For Orwell, "Socialism means justice and common decency,"[40] a point he repeats again and again in *The Road to Wigan Pier.* Socialism, understood as a set of moral practices designed to promote justice and common decency, could, he believed in 1936, "bring the Kingdom of Heaven down to the surface of the earth," i.e., provide ethical orientation and moral motivation in the struggle for justice in a post-Christian culture.

"[I]n order to defend Socialism it is necessary to start by attacking it."[41] Many critics, including Orwell's editor Victor Gollancz, have taken great exception to his sharp criticisms of socialism in the second of half of *The Road to Wigan Pier.* By contrast I want to argue that Orwell's critique of socialism grows naturally and directly out of his commitment to socialism as moral practice. In engaging in this form of critique Orwell exemplifies a practice I have called "connected criticism."[42] Connected criticism is a form of critique that oscillates between the poles of criticism and connection, solitude and solidarity, alienation and authority. Connected critics are those who are fully engaged in the very enterprise they criticize yet alienated by the deceits and shortcomings of their own community. Because they care so deeply about the values inherent in their common enterprise, they vividly experience the evils of their society even as they call their community back to its better nature. Connected critics recognize the fallibility that clings to the life of every political or social organization, and they seek to identify both the virtuous and the vicious dimensions of the common life in which they participate. Connected critics exemplify both the commitment characteristic of the loyal participant and the critique characteristic of the disillusioned dissenter. This dialectic between commitment and critique is the identifying feature that distinguishes acts of dissent that display genuine moral integrity from those that represent mere expediency or self-interest. Connected critics are socially situated within the community to which their criticisms are directed yet still find within the common life of the society principles of justice that serve as the basis for hope. Living in a state of "antagonistic connection," the connected critic discerns the principles of justice that provide the basis for both critique and hope.

I know of no thinker who exemplifies this category with greater integrity than does Orwell. He begins his criticism of socialism by implicating himself in the very community he is about to critique. "I was born into what you might describe as the lower-upper-middle class."[43] With that sentence Orwell identifies himself within the class system that he believes must be dismantled if Britain is to gain genuine equality. In contrast to many British socialists, however, Orwell understands the class system to be as much cultural as economic. "The fact that has got to be faced is that to abolish class-distinctions means abolishing a part of yourself. . . . What is involved is not merely the amelioration of working-class conditions, nor an avoidance of the more stupid forms of snobbery, but a complete abandonment of the upper-class and middle-class attitude to life."[44] As long as theoretical and solely economic understandings of socialism predominate, the deeper problems of class division cannot be adequately addressed. If the cultural aspects of the class system remain untouched, an economic revolution will fail to bring about genuine justice and equality.

Orwell's concern about the primacy of culture also reflects itself in his insistence on the importance of the "spiritual" side of politics. Socialists fail to understand the attraction of the British to fascism because they "tacitly assume that the spiritual side of it is of no importance. . . . With their eyes glued to economic facts, they have proceeded on the assumption that man has no soul, and explicitly or implicitly they have set up the goal of a materialist Utopia."[45] As long as socialists fail to grasp the importance of the cultural, spiritual, and soulful aspects of human life, they will be at a huge disadvantage in the fight against fascism. As long as socialism itself remains disconnected from the deeper cultural values of post-Christian England, it will fail to win the *hearts* of the very people they say they want to rescue. Thus true self-critical socialists must face a very uncomfortable truth. "The only possible course is to examine the Fascist case, grasp that there is something to be said for it, and then make it clear to the world that whatever good Fascism contains in also implicit in Socialism."[46] In order to do that, however, socialism must move beyond its narrow materialist theory and reassert "the underlying ideal of Socialism: justice and liberty. . . . Justice and liberty! *Those* are the words that have got to ring like a bugle across the world."[47]

By the end of 1936 George Orwell had emerged from a period of serious self-examination to become a formidable social critic with a clear moral vision. While he had rejected, once and for all, the belief system of Christianity, he continued firm in the conviction that the most important values represented by Christianity, particularly human decency and a commitment to justice and equality, must be incorporated into the form of ethical socialism he so fervently advocated. Operating as a connected critic, he sought to develop an internal critique of theoretical materialist socialism that would awaken British socialists to the cultural and spiritual aspects of human life. He feared that without a full engagement with the matters that engaged human souls, socialism would lose the battle with fascism. Moreover, he saw that socialism itself was threatened by its own totalitarian materialist obsessions. If it failed to make a place for the spiritual within its own practice, then its humanitarian aspirations could never be achieved, and thus it would provide no real alternative to the totalitarianism of the Right. Thus we can glimpse in these early years the critique that would finally take full flower in Orwell's later novels. It was in the name of and for the sake of decency and justice that Orwell sought, without full success, "to restore the religious attitude" and to bring "the Kingdom of Heaven to the surface of the earth." Whether it is possible in this time of fundamentalist fanaticism to achieve the kind of modest humanistic "faith" that Orwell exemplified seems very much in doubt. Some of us will, none-theless, continue to aspire to such lives of commitment, criticism, and conviction. And that George Orwell should serve as an inspiration, a goad, perhaps even a curmudgeon for us in our own struggles seems a very good thing indeed.

NOTES

1. He made similar critiques of the Roman Catholic Church. In an otherwise quite respectful review of F. J. Sheed's *Communism and Man* he makes this telling point. "For some time past the Church has been in an anomalous position, symbolized by the fact that the Pope almost simultaneously denounces the Capitalist system and confers decorations on General Franco." *The Complete Works of George Orwell,* ed. Peter Davison (London: Secker & Warburg, 1998), 11:323.

2. *The Complete Works of George Orwell,* 10:485.

3. In this regard Orwell's reflections bear a striking similarity to the musings of Dietrich Bonhoeffer on "religionless Christianity" in his *Letters and Papers from Prison* (New York: Macmillan Publishing Company, 1981). I will explore these similarities further in my forth-coming book, *Prisoners of Conscience: Public Intellectuals in a Time of Crisis.*

4. Bernard Crick, *George Orwell: A Life* (London: Penguin Books, 1980), 214.

5. This is reported by Bernard Crick, *George Orwell,* 226–27.

6. Crick, *George Orwell,* 226.

7. Crick, *George Orwell,* 227.

8. Orwell, *The Complete Works,* 10:249.

9. Orwell, *The Complete Works,* 10:249.

10. Note the similarity to a line uttered by Mr. Warburton in *A Clergyman's Daughter.* "Is it the hypocrisy that's worrying you? Afraid that the consecrated bread might stick in your throat, and so forth?" 298.

11. Orwell, *The Complete Works,* 10:271.

12. Orwell, *The Complete Works,* 10:247.

13. Orwell, *The Complete Works,* 10:251, 10:252.

14. Orwell, *The Complete Works,* 10:253. I can find no evidence that the two men ever met, although I have discovered in the Orwell archive an unpublished letter Martindale wrote in April 1939 in response to a letter from Orwell. It appears that Martindale wrote a favorable review of *The Road to Wigan Pier* and that Orwell responded with a rather lengthy reply of his own. Their discussion seems to revolve around the question of whether Orwell's assertions concerning justice in his vivid descriptions of the horrible conditions of poverty in the North of England can be thematized into a more philosophical discourse. "You will understand why I like all this part of your book which describes facts, because it is 'first hand' and because it makes my own desire for justice, understanding and kindness more active, and also your 'de-bunking' of jargon wherever it is heard. . . . I thought that one might get further than you did in this crystalizing 'liberty' and 'justice.' It would be from this end that the Catholic philosopher would like to be of service." This exchange suggests a serious and mutually respectful discus-sion on the topic of social ethics between Orwell and this prominent Christian socialist. Unfor-tunately, Orwell's own letter has disappeared and neither the Orwell archive nor the Martindale archive has any record of it. Thomas McCoog, S.J., the current archivist of the British Province of the Jesuits, surmises that the letter might have been lost during the war, since Martindale's residence was destroyed during the Battle of Britain. Thus the one substantial positive engage-ment Orwell had with Christian ethics has tragically vanished.

15. Orwell, *The Complete Works,* 10:306.

16. Orwell, *The Complete Works,* 10:351. Other self-deprecating comments include the following. "I am so miserable, struggling with the entrails of that dreadful book and never

getting any further, and loathing the sight of what I have done. *Never* start writing novels, if you wish to preserve your happiness" (10:344). "That book is bollox, but I made some experiments in it that were useful to me" (10:382).

17. Jenni Calder, *Chronicles of Conscience* (London: Secker & Warburg, 1968), 89.

18. Christopher Hitchens, *Why Orwell Matters* (New York: Basic Books, 2002), 182.

19. The phrase is Jenni Calder's. *Chronicles of Conscience,* 87.

20. Orwell and his critics agree that the most successful literary section of the book comes in chapter 3 with the vivid depiction of London's homeless trying to sleep on the cold benches in Trafalgar Square. In a letter to Brenda Salkeld Orwell wrote, "As you will see, it is tripe, except for Chapter 3, part 1, which I am pleased with." Orwell, *The Complete Works,* 10:382.

21. George Orwell, *A Clergyman's Daughter* (New York: Harcourt Brace, 1936), 12–13.

22. Orwell, *A Clergyman's Daughter,* 14–15.

23. Orwell, *A Clergyman's Daughter,* 296, 298, 299.

24. Orwell, *A Clergyman's Daughter,* 296–97, 298.

25. Orwell, *A Clergyman's Daughter,* 308, 315–16.

26. George Orwell, "Arthur Koestler," *The Complete Works,* 16:399; Orwell, "Notes on the Way," *The Complete Works,* 12:126.

27. See David James, Tony Jowitt, and Keith Laybourn, *The Centennial History of the ILP* (Krumlin: Ryburn Press, 1992).

28. Crick, *George Orwell: A Life,* 252–53.

29. Leonard Smith, "Religion and the ILP," *The Centennial History,* 32–48.

30. Crick, *George Orwell,* 273.

31. George Orwell, *The Road to Wigan Pier* (New York: Harcourt, 1958), 5.

32. Orwell, *The Road to Wigan Pier,* 15.

33. Orwell, *The Road to Wigan Pier,* 17. Orwell, of course, received strong criticism for his reference to the smell of the working classes in the second part of *Wigan Pier.* The entire passage reads, "Here you come to the real secret of class distinctions in the West. . . . It is summed up in four frightful words which people nowadays are chary of uttering, but which were bandied about quite freely in my childhood. The words were: *The lower classes smell.* That was what we were taught—*the lower classes smell* (127–28). Orwell is clearly describing a prejudice, and one with which he strongly disagrees even though he acknowledges that he was taught the prejudice as a boy. Thus it is quite unfair for Victor Gollancz to say in the foreword, "I have in mind in particular a lengthy passage in which Mr. Orwell embroiders the theme that, in the opinion of the middle class in general, the working class smells!" (xiii). Orwell's embroidery, if one can even call is that, is designed to show how deeply this class prejudice in engrained within British culture.

34. Orwell, *The Road to Wigan Pier,* 18.

35. "And looking back through my work, I see that it is invariably where I lacked a *political* purpose that I wrote lifeless books and was betrayed into purple passage, sentences without meaning, decorative adjectives, and humbug generally." George Orwell, "Why I Write," *A Collection of Essays* (New York: Harcourt, 1946), 316.

36. Orwell, *The Road to Wigan Pier,* 87–88.

37. Orwell, *The Road to Wigan Pier,* 35.

38. Raymond Williams, *Orwell* (London: Fontana, 1991), 3.

39. Orwell, "Notes on the Way," 12:125.

40. Orwell, *The Road to Wigan Pier,* 176.

41. Orwell, *The Road to Wigan Pier,* 172.

42. The term was coined by Michael Walzer in his *Interpretation and Social Criticism* (Cambridge, Mass.: Harvard University Press, 1987)) and employed again in *The Company of Critics* (New York: Basic Books, 2002), a work in which he treats Orwell under the category of "connected critic." I have developed the term further in my *Religion in Public Life: A Dilemma for Democracy* (Washington, D.C.: Georgetown University Press, 1996)

and it will also structure the argument in my forthcoming book, *Prisoners of Conscience: Public Intellectuals at a Time of Crisis.*

43. Orwell, *The Road to Wigan Pier,* 121

44. Orwell, *The Road to Wigan Pier,* 162. In no way does Orwell exempt his own kind of socialist from this dilemma. "The middle-class I.L.P.'er and the bearded fruit-juice drinker are all for a classless society so long as they see the proletariat through the wrong end of the telescope; force them into any *real* contract with a proletarian . . . and they are capable of swinging back to the most ordinary middle-class snobbishness" (163).

45. Orwell, *The Road to Wigan Pier,* 187, 214.

46. Orwell, *The Road to Wigan Pier,* 214.

47. Orwell, *The Road to Wigan Pier,* 216.

7

Orwell, Pacifism, Pacifists

LAWRENCE ROSENWALD

Orwell's honesty demands a comparable honesty, or at least an attempt at it, on the part of anyone venturing to write about him. So I'll begin this essay on Orwell and pacifism by making clear the standpoint from which I'm writing it. I'm a longtime pacifist, and a fairly extreme one—a war tax resister and a member of the War Resisters League, whose creed is that "war [is] a crime against humanity." I'm also a longtime admirer of Orwell, not just for his honesty but also for his unhampered perception, his "power of facing unpleasant facts,"[1] and his sympathy with the feelings and judgments of "ordinary decent people." And I'm aware that these two commitments of mine are at odds with each other and that Orwell was, for much of his life, a relentless critic of pacifists, both politically and ethically.

Now my pacifism is probably more deep-rooted than my admiration for Orwell, and if I had to give up one or the other, it's the pacifism I'd strive to hold on to. But the goal of this essay is not to defend pacifism against Orwell's critiques. It is, rather, to find the ideas in Orwell's remarks about pacifism that pacifists can *use*—the ideas expressed both in his abundant critiques and in his occasional praises. A Yiddish proverb says *"ver's shmeykhlt iz a faynd, ver's shtroft iz a fraynd"*—enemies smile, friends rebuke. In that sense, Orwell is a great friend to pacifism, and my essay is an exploration of the ideas his friendship yielded.

I

In the late 1930s, Orwell was a consistent opponent of war. His opposition was largely on socialist grounds: that wars were fought in the interests of "the moneyed classes," and that opposing those classes meant opposing their wars. In 1937, for example, reviewing a pacifist manifesto called *The Men I Killed*, by Brigadier-General F. P. Crozier, Orwell vigorously stated "the two facts . . . which should be made the centre of all anti-war agitation":

> 1. That war against a foreign country only happens when the moneyed classes think they are going to profit from it.

111

2. That every war when it comes, or before it comes, is represented not as a war
but as an act of self-defence against a homicidal maniac ("militarist" Germany in
1914, "Fascist" Germany next year or the year after).[2]

Orwell wrote an antiwar pamphlet in 1938; it's now lost (1:357), but presumably
it included among its arguments the claim Orwell made in a 1938 letter to the *New
English Weekly,* that "modern war is a racket" (1:332). Even as late as 1939, when
the nature of Hitler's fascism was clear to him, he was still adventurously conspiring with Herbert Read to procure material and supplies for an antiwar printing
press, against the time when such presses would be made illegal (1:378).

Even at this time, though, it's pretty clear that Orwell doesn't like pacifists—in
much the same way that, in *The Road to Wigan Pier,* he holds socialist principles
but doesn't like socialists. He praises General Crozier's pacifist book partly because it refutes "the widespread notion that every pacifist is a Creeping Jesus"
(1:283)—a notion Orwell clearly shares.[3] He regards the central task, for those
committed to "producing an effective anti-war movement in England," as being
that "of mobilising the dislike of war that undoubtedly exists in ordinary decent
people, as opposed to the hack-journalists and the pansy left" (1:332). Paraphras-
ing and extrapolating from these two phrases, we might say that what Orwell
doesn't like about pacifists before the war is that they're sanctimonious, hypocritical, abject, elitist, and not masculine enough.

II

Orwell ceased being a member of the antiwar party in 1939, when England entered
the war. He explains his shift of position in a candid, complex 1940 essay, "My
Country Right or Left"; he reveals there both a new political analysis and new
motives.

The analysis is stated simply: "there is no real alternative between resisting
Hitler and surrendering to him, and from a Socialist point of view I should say that
it is better to resist" (1:539). It rests, however, on Orwell's complicated belief in
"the possibility of building a Socialist on the bones of a Blimp, the power of one
kind of loyalty to transmute itself into another" (1:540). That is, for Orwell to
support the war "from a Socialist point of view," he must believe that fighting for
England against Hitler can be made to be part of the same process as fighting
against "Chamberlain's England" for "the England of tomorrow,"—a socialist
England. He must, that is, believe that the socialist principles that had previously
led him to oppose wars can now be realized by supporting one.[4]

Orwell's motives are more complicated and probably more important; they have
to do with character, with psychological style. Supporting the war lets Orwell
acknowledge and deploy traits of character and deeply held aspirations that being
against the war would suppress and that he already believes pacifists characteristically lack: toughness, fitness, masculinity, what Orwell calls "vastness of . . .
experience" (1:538). This last is especially interesting, because Orwell associates
it with the veterans of World War I—with men who fought in a war that he is not
justifying as a struggle against fascism. For this particular virtue, it seems, any war
will do. And in the essay's final sentence Orwell writes of "the spiritual need for

patriotism and the military virtues, for which, however little the boiled rabbits of the Left may like them, no substitute has been found" (1:540). Again, this argument is almost independent of the political one; the "spiritual need for patriotism and the military virtues" would presumably exist even without the threat posed by Hitler.

III

Once engaged in the war effort, Orwell turned against pacifism and pacifists with a vengeance. Like the reflections in "My Country Right or Left," some of his critiques are political, and some are psychological and ethical. The principal ones are as follows.

1. As noted, pacifism amounts to capitulation: "there's no real choice between resisting Hitler and surrendering to him" (1:539).

2. Pacifism is not just capitulation, it is in fact "objectively pro-Nazi" (2:167). Orwell says this first in a 1941 review of Alexander Comfort's novel *No Such Liberty.* But his clearest explanation of it comes in a celebrated 1942 debate in *Partisan Review,* in which "objectively" is explained as meaning something like "in effect if not in intention." In responding to a mean-spirited letter from the pacifist poet D. S. Savage, Orwell writes:

> Pacifism is objectively pro-Fascist. This is elementary common sense. If you hamper the war effort of one side you automatically help that of the other. Nor is there any real way of remaining outside such a war as the present one.[5] In practice, "he that is not with me is against me." . . . Mr. Savage remarks that "according to this type of reasoning, a German or Japanese pacifist would be 'objectively pro-British.'" But of course he would be! (2:226)

Moreover, Orwell argues, the net effect of pacifism in the struggle between a democratic state and a fascist one will be in favor of the latter: "in so far as it takes effect at all, pacifist propaganda can only be effective *against* those countries where a certain amount of freedom of speech is still permitted; in other words it is helpful to totalitarianism" (2:226).

3. Pacifism is intellectually "irresponsible" (2:89), because pacifists can't imagine running things. Orwell writes this in 1940, in "The Lion and the Unicorn," and expands the idea in a 1941 letter to the Reverend Iorwerth Jones, clarifying certain points in that work: "Government cannot be conducted on 'pure' pacifist lines, because any government which refused in all circumstances to use force could be overthrown by anyone, even any individual, who *was* willing to use force. Pacifism refuses to face the problem of government and pacifists think always as people who will never be in a position of control, which is why I call them irresponsible" (2:111).

Those are Orwell's chief political critiques of pacifism. They're important, clearly. But they don't feel as important as the psychological and ethical critiques, the critiques Orwell directs against pacifist *character.*

4. Of these, the first is the one already noted, that pacifists characteristically lack certain important virtues and emotions: patriotism, courage, comradely

solidarity, suffering, self-sacrifice. Orwell states this view most vividly in a couple of passages in which he's attempting, interestingly enough, to explain why "ordinary decent people" are attracted to Hitler. In a 1940 review of *Mein Kampf,* for example, he writes:

> [Hitler] has grasped the falsity of the hedonistic attitude to life. Nearly all western thought since the last war, certainly all 'progressive' thought, has assumed tacitly that human beings desire nothing beyond ease, security and avoidance of pain. In such a view of life there is no room, for instance, for patriotism and the military virtues. The Socialist who finds his children playing with soldiers is usually upset, but he is never able to think of a substitute for the tin soldiers; tin pacifists somehow won't do. (3:14; see also 3:141)[6]

5. Pacifists are unwilling to make a distinction of value between Nazi Germany and 1941 England. They're guilty of a false moral relativism.

6. Worse still: to the extent that pacifists *do* make sharp moral distinctions, they direct their critiques more against democracies than against totalitarianisms. In other words, pacifists are pro-Nazi not just objectively but also subjectively. Thus in 1942 Orwell writes, "with the out-and-out, turn-the-other-cheek pacifists you come upon the much stranger phenomenon of people who have started by renouncing violence ending by championing Hitler" (2:180). Again, in a 1944 letter to the noted pacifist John Middleton Murry: "many remarks you have made in recent years seem to me to imply that you don't object to violence if it is violent enough. And you certainly seem or seemed to me to prefer the Nazis to ourselves, at least so long as they appeared to be winning" (3:185; see also 3:8).

Orwell dislikes this not just because it amounts to being on the side of great evil but also because it reveals pacifists as hypocrites and cowards. The correspondence with Murry provides the most vivid examples: "you are wrong," he writes, "in thinking that I dislike wholehearted pacifism, though I do think it mistaken. What I object to is the circumspect kind of pacifism which denounces one kind of violence while endorsing or avoiding mention of another" (3:191). Later he develops the point:

> A courageous pacifist would not simply say "Britain ought not to bomb Germany." Anyone can say that. He would say, "The Russians should let the Germans have the Ukraine, the Chinese should not defend themselves against Japan, the European peoples should submit to the Nazis, the Indians should not try to drive out the British." Real pacifism would involve all of that: but one can't say that kind of thing and also keep on good terms with the rest of the intelligentsia.[7] It is because they consistently avoid mentioning such issues as these, while continuing to squeal against obliteration bombing etc, that I find the majority of English pacifists so difficult to respect. (3:204)[8]

7. Orwell claims repeatedly that pacifism is attractive only to people in sheltered positions (3:89, 3:111, 3:170). This by itself might simply be an empirical claim: that pacifists tend to be people living in safe places, for example, in nations with effective armies, nations not often subject to invasion, or nations separated from other nations by large bodies of water; that pacifists tend to be people in soft economic situations, members of the comfortable middle class. Clearly the claim

is more than that, though. The fact that pacifists are sheltered means to Orwell that their authenticity in political debate is compromised. The suggestion is that "pacifists are people who haven't faced the unpleasant facts of life, either economically or politically; if they did face those facts, they wouldn't be pacifists for long."

8. Pacifists are also sheltered intellectually; being a pacifist, says Orwell, requires not knowing what you're living on. "Rightly hating violence, [pacifists] do not wish to recognise that it is integral to modern society and that their own fine feelings and noble attitudes are all the fruit of injustice backed up by force. They do not want to learn where their incomes come from" (2:170; see also 2:187).

IV

Those are Orwell's principal charges against British pacifism and pacifists during the war. This seems the right place, then, to assess them historically—to ask, that is, how accurately British pacifism and pacifists are described by them.

One of the charges, though, doesn't need to be assessed, because Orwell withdrew it. The charge in question is the famous one, that pacifism is "objectively pro-Nazi." That charge is quoted frequently, and for the most part without any reference to Orwell's change of position, so it's important to describe that change clearly.[9] It is announced in December of 1944. Orwell is writing about propaganda, and he sees "the same mental atmosphere" everywhere: "nobody is searching for the truth, everybody is putting forward a 'case' with complete disregard for fairness or accuracy, and the most plainly obvious facts can be ignored by those who don't want to see them" (3:288). Then, with remarkable generosity, he takes as an example of this mental atmosphere his own use of the word "objectively":

> I draw attention to one very widespread controversial habit—disregard of an opponent's motives. The key-word here is "objectively." We are told that it is only people's objective actions that matter, and their subjective feelings are of no importance. Thus pacifists, by obstructing the war effort, are "objectively" aiding the Nazis: and therefore the fact that they may be personally hostile to Fascism is irrelevant. I have been guilty of saying this myself more than once. . . . This is not only dishonest; it also carries a severe penalty with it. If you disregard people's motives, it becomes much harder to foresee their actions. (3:289)

Orwell withdraws the charge for two reasons, then: it's "dishonest," which is a very bad thing to be in Orwell's lexicon, and it leads to a sharply limited view of the world, in which motives are disregarded and actions harder to understand.

In the charges that remain, Orwell seems to me significantly wrong about most British pacifists. But he is also significantly right about them; and the pacifists he's most right about are the ones I myself most care about and most resemble, namely, pacifist intellectuals—who are also the ones that pacifism most needs if it's to become a vital political position.

One aspect of British pacifism Orwell is wrong about is its demography. Many British pacifists, in particular many prominent British pacifists, were women. Reading Orwell, it's impossible to see that. He never refers to a woman pacifist, never engages one in debate.[10] Moreover, many British pacifists came to pacifism through religious belief. Orwell mentions a few of these, notably Canon Dick Shepard, the founder of the Peace Pledge Union (PPU), but religious pacifism isn't something he's really interested in.

There's a revealing exchange about this in the *Partisan Review* debate. D. S. Savage writes, "[Orwell] sees pacifism primarily as a political phenomenon. That is just what it isn't. Primarily it is a moral phenomenon. Political movements are based on programme and organisation. With pacifism, programme and organisation are quite subsidiary. Pacifism springs from conscience—i.e., from within the individual human being" (2:221). Savage is smugly self-contented here, but he's not wrong, especially if we substitute for "moral" the less guarded word "religious." Orwell, though, dismisses the question, writing frankly, "I am not interested in pacifism as a 'moral phenomenon'" (2:226). He needn't be, of course, to argue against a pacifist political program; but his lack of interest compromises his accounts of pacifist character.[11]

Orwell is also significantly wrong about much pacifist behavior. For one thing, British pacifists were less aggressive than he makes them seem; Martin Ceadel, one of the leading historians of British pacifism, points out that "the good reputation of the peace movement was finally assured by the generally self-effacing wartime behavior of both the [Peace Pledge Union] . . . and the conscientious objectors . . . of 1939–1945."[12] British pacifists were respectable, well-spoken, sometimes persons of distinction. Some, during the so-called Phony War, took actions to hinder the war effort: they propagandized against the war, breached the Defence Regulations by publicly urging men to refuse to fight, picketed outside local employment exchanges where men were registering for the draft. They also counseled potential and actual conscientious objectors. That's about as far as their antiwar work went, though. They certainly were not doing Berrigan-style civil disobedience. They weren't, for the most part, doing civil disobedience at all.[13]

As the war continued and intensified, moreover, pacifists and conscientious objectors did less to oppose the war and more to support their neighbors and, in noncombatant ways, their neighbors' war.[14] They established "a rest centre where evacuees from Liverpool could sleep";[15] supported German refugees, some of them interned as enemy aliens; were guinea pigs in medical research; created small agricultural communities; got involved "in a number of pressure-group efforts concerned with mitigating the effects of war,"[16] bearing in particular on the famines created by blockades and on saturation bombing; and launched the Food Relief Campaign in 1941 that later gave rise to Oxfam. Some were working on farms and doing forestry work. Some were doing noncombatant military services, notably in the Friends Ambulance Unit. Peter Brock and Nigel Young sum up the situation as follows:

> One should not turn to absolutists to find the representative type of [conscientious] objector. One must look rather to those who worked on the land as farm laborers or in forestry units or as market gardeners, to those who served in the understaffed hospitals as porters, orderlies or ambulance drivers, to those who chose civil defense or the Auxiliary Fire Service as the field of their alternative service, or those engaged in social work of the kind carried on, for instance, by privately organized Pacifist Service Units among the depressed sections of the population in large industrial cities like London, Liverpool, Manchester or Cardiff.[17]

The people doing these activities could not be justly described as objectively or subjectively pro-Nazi. They were not moral relativists, they neither worshipped power nor preferred totalitarianism to democracy, they did useful work for England.

On the other hand, though, there's little in the history of these pacifists to suggest that they had an answer for Orwell's charges against pacifism as a political program. They were not figuring out what it might mean to resist Hitler but not to fight him. They were not imagining how pacifists might govern. They were often sheltered and comfortable people.[18] The forms of pacifism they devised during the war did not for the most part expose them to the challenges faced by soldiers and did not therefore cultivate the virtues that Orwell found lacking in pacifism as a way of life. Andrew Rigby writes persuasively that "there can have been few pacifists who had not experienced periods of doubt about their stance, some degree of shame that they were avoiding the pain and discomfort that others in the services were facing, some concern that maybe they had no non-violent answer to the Nazi aggression other than 'peace at any price.'"[19]

Moreover, and depressingly, the British pacifist intellectuals whom Orwell is really thinking of when he refers to "pacifists" deserve most of the censures he directs against them. (They're also flagrantly rude when engaging Orwell in debate; it's amazing that so many of them remained friends with him.) Alexander Comfort, for example, is in fact a moral relativist, or at any rate the unironized narrator of his novel is:

> Looking out across London, I knew that all the talk of strength I heard and all the assurances of the popular songs, as I came to understand them, how happy and strong and right and cultured you are, were the same as the assurances that I'd left plastered on the complaining walls of Cologne by the Rhine, and that they'd blossom the same things—injustice and enormity. It's not that you of London are evil; it's not that the infection has gone so far that you beat and jail men, individual men, who tell you that the bacteria of your disease are there. But they are there. And I know that they must, and they will grow, till you are as we, and fear has redoubled itself.[20]

D. S. Savage is in fact an admirer of Hitler: "Whereas the rest of the nation is content with calling down obloquy on Hitler's head, we regard this as superficial. Hitler requires, not condemnation, but understanding. This does not mean that we like, or defend him. Personally I do not care for Hitler . . . there would be a profound justice, I feel, however terrible, in a German victory" (2:222). That's just plain nauseating. Orwell records meeting a young pacifist in the Café Royal in 1940, an aspiring painter who is simultaneously foolish, cowardly, and self-serving (3:131–32).[21] Stuart Morris, for a while the general secretary of the PPU, joined an undercover Nazi organization called The Link. "It is hard," writes David Lukowitz, "to escape the conclusion that there was too much sympathy [among PPU pacifists] for the German position, often the product of ignorance and superficial thinking. There was also a complete failure to grasp the nature of . . . Germany's policies with regard to colonies, Austria, Czechoslovakia and Poland . . . [and] the . . . ruthless spirit . . . of the Nazi state."[22]

All of which is to say that though British pacifists are a rather different group than Orwell presents them as being, they do not offer a satisfactory model for someone who's trying, at this present moment, to imagine a stronger pacifism, a pacifism that can stand up to Orwell's charges.

V

For that we need to look at Gandhi's work, and at the striking change in Orwell's view of it, from harsh to almost sentimental. In 1941, Orwell regards Gandhi's nonviolence as cooperation with the British empire. He writes in a letter that "it was always admitted in the most cynical way that Gandhi made it easier for the British to rule India, because his influence was always against taking any action that would make any difference" (2:111). In 1942, he claims, "it always makes me shout with laughter to hear . . . Gandhi named as an example of the success of nonviolence" (2:227). He thinks Gandhi is insufficiently antifascist, that is, insufficiently in support of the Allied cause: "Gandhi would certainly advise us to let the Germans rule here rather than fight against them—in fact he did advocate just that. And if Hitler conquered England he would, I imagine, try to bring into being a nation-wide pacifist movement, which would prevent serious resistance and therefore make it easier for [Hitler] to rule" (2:112).[23] Orwell also thinks that Gandhi is a hypocrite: "rejection of the machine is, of course, always founded on tacit acceptance of the machine, a fact symbolised by Gandhi as he plays with his spinning-wheel in the mansion of some cotton millionaire" (2:312). And Orwell goes so far as to acknowledge "a sort of apocalyptic truth in the statement of the German radio that the teachings of Hitler and Gandhi are the same" (2:315).

By 1949, though, when Orwell wrote his "Reflections on Gandhi," everything seems to have changed. Maybe the change was in Orwell's mood, with the ending of the war letting him generously reexamine old judgments. Maybe it was the developments in Gandhi's career and the astonishing liberation of India. Maybe it was just Orwell's open-minded reading, and in part rereading, of Gandhi's remarkable autobiography. Whatever the cause, though, "Reflections on Gandhi" is one of the sanest, most challenging, and most generous essays ever written about a great pacifist.

Orwell admires Gandhi because he finds him so unlike the pacifists of England. He likes Gandhi's honesty, for one thing. He likes his physical fearlessness. He likes his worldly intelligence: "inside the saint . . . there was a very shrewd, able person who could, if he had chosen, have been a brilliant success as a lawyer, an administrator or perhaps even a businessman" (4:463).[24] Orwell also likes the fact that Gandhi, unlike the pacifists Orwell accuses of moral relativism, "was honest enough to see that in war it is usually necessary to take sides. He did not—indeed, since his whole political life centred round a struggle for national independence, he could not—take the sterile and dishonest line of pretending that in every war both sides are exactly the same and it makes no difference who wins" (4:468). And, in a sentence that comes as close to being sentimental as anything I can recall in Orwell's work, he praises Gandhi's ability to regard human beings as individuals: "even when he was fighting what was in effect a colour war he did not think of people in terms of race or status. The governor of a province, a cotton millionaire,[25] a half-starved Dravidian coolie, a British private soldier, were all equally human beings, to be approached in much the same way" (4:464).

Maybe it's because of this personal admiration that Orwell is willing to make several extraordinary concessions in judging Gandhi's pacifism. First, he admits the possibility that Gandhi's pacifism can be separated out from the rest of his views. That admission is crucial. If one can be a Gandhian pacifist only by adhering to the whole of Gandhi's ethical program, then Gandhian pacifism hasn't much of a future, because the demands on the potential pacifist are too great: no meat, no milk, no alcohol, no tobacco, no spices or condiments, no sex except for procreation, no sexual desire, no particular friendships. Nor is it just that these demands are too great; they're also repellent. As Erik Erikson writes in his great letter to the then long-dead Gandhi,

> it is important to affirm unequivocally that what you call Satyagraha must not remain restricted to ascetic men and women who believe that they can overcome violence only by sexual self-disarmament. For the danger of a riotous return to violence always remains at least latent if we do not succeed in imbuing essential daily experiences with a Satyagraha-of-everyday-life.[26]

It would have been easy for Orwell to argue that Gandhi's views come all together or not at all, and then to argue that as a collected set they need to be rejected. In fact, though, he argues precisely the contrary: "Gandhi's pacifism can be separated to some extent from his other teachings. Its motive was religious, but he claimed also for it that it was a definite technique, a method, capable of producing desired political results" (4:467).

A second concession: it's a common claim that, as Orwell put it, Gandhi "did not understand the nature of totalitarianism" (4:468). Orwell agrees with that claim, but he makes it in an unusual way. For him, the point isn't that the British treated Gandhi "forbearingly" (or, conversely, that a totalitarian government would have shot Gandhi out of hand); it is, rather, that in British India, "[Gandhi] was always able to command publicity" (4:468). That means that for Orwell, the question of whether Gandhian nonviolence could have an effect in a totalitarian society can be answered empirically, and on a case-by-case basis, rather than categorically and once and for all.

Finally: an important critique of pacifism is that it doesn't have a strategy of intervention—or, in Orwell's language, "applied to foreign politics, pacifism either stops being pacifist or becomes appeasement" (4:469). Orwell might have used that critique to dismiss Gandhi's work. In fact, though, he doesn't. Rather, he backs off, and seems willing to wonder what strategies of pacifist intervention Gandhi might have devised and willing to admit that they might have been useful.

> These and other kindred questions need discussion, and need it urgently, in the few years left to us before somebody presses the button and the rockets begin to fly. It seems doubtful whether civilisation can stand another major war, and it is at least thinkable that the way out lies through non-violence. It is Gandhi's virtue that he would have been ready to give honest consideration to the kind of question that I have raised above. . . . One feels of him that there was much that he did not understand, but not that there was anything that he was frightened of saying or thinking. (4:469)[27]

The essay on Gandhi reveals the extent to which Orwell's critiques of pacifism are *personal.* When he's dealing with pacifists whom he doesn't respect, he doesn't respect pacifism either. When he's dealing with Gandhi, with a pacifist whom he does respect, he thinks pacifism is worth consideration. It's as if he were saying, to paraphrase his great brief summary of Dickens's political philosophy, "If [pacifists] would behave decently [pacifism] would be worth taking seriously" (1:428).

VI

Which leaves only the final and crucial questions: does the history of pacifism, the pacifism preceding Orwell and the pacifism following him as well as the pacifism he himself observed, offer satisfactory responses to the full range of his critiques of it?[28] If it does, how does that help us to identify what traditions of pacifism are most alive? If it doesn't, how does that help us to identify what tasks pacifists need to set themselves?

1. Orwell's right: there's no choice between resisting Hitler and surrendering to him. That doesn't mean, though, that resisting Hitler, that resisting evil generally, needs to be violent. What Orwell is contemplating in Gandhi is the idea that certain nonviolent practices can be formidably resistant, as uncompromising as battle. (This is an idea that Western pacifists learned from Gandhi and often didn't like learning; Gandhian resistance seemed to them excessively coercive, too close to violence for comfort.[29]) The sit-ins and jail-ins and boycotts of the American civil rights movement, which was strongly influenced by Gandhi, are forms of coercion. When Denise Levertov writes of peace as being "an energy field more intense than war," it's perhaps this Gandhian mode of nonviolent resistance that she has in mind. And developing this mode of resistance is the chief aim of Gene Sharp's ambitious three-volume work, *The Politics of Nonviolent Action,* in the preface to which Sharp writes,

> it appeared evident that both moral injunctions against violence and exhortations in favor of love and nonviolence have made little or no contribution to ending war and major political violence. It seemed to me that only the adoption of a substitute type of sanction and struggle as a functional alternative to violence in acute conflicts . . . could possibly lead to a major reduction of political violence in a manner compatible with freedom, justice and human dignity.[30]

But then: can that resistance work against totalitarian regimes? As noted, Orwell puts this question undogmatically; but he does put it. So it's important here to evoke the admittedly few but quite thought-provoking stories of nonviolent resistance practiced against, precisely, Hitler's Nazis and those under their control. The most celebrated of these took place in the French village of Chambon-sur-Lignon, the inhabitants of which saved five thousand Jews from deportation and the death camps. The inhabitants' motives remain enigmatic; their pastors, though, were avowed pacifists, who encouraged their congregations to employ *les armes de l'esprit,* the weapons of the spirit, and the actual resistance and rescuing in Chambon were in fact conducted nonviolently.[31] A still more telling example, because geographically closer to the center of Nazi power, was the 1943 protest conducted in Berlin. Non-Jewish women whose Jewish husbands had been taken into custody assembled on the Rosenstrasse, by the collection center where their husbands were being held before being deported. The women numbered anywhere between six hundred and six thousand. They chanted, simply, "give us our husbands back." They were threatened with machine guns, they stood their ground, they yelled "murderer, murderer, murderer." And in the end, two thousand of the imprisoned Jews were freed and were allowed to survive till the end of the war—partly because, as Nathan Stoltzfus points out, the protest was so public, so successful at, in Orwell's phrase, "commanding publicity."[32]

2. It's not true, in the long history of pacifism, that pacifists as a group "do not want to learn where their incomes come from." Certainly some pacifists haven't; a recent letter from a pacifist friend very forthrightly complains of this: "the peace movement, for the most part, wants to have its cake and eat it too. They by and large refuse to recognize their own complicity."[33] But Orwell's point, that pacifists' fine feelings, noble attitudes, and gracious lifestyles "are all the fruit of injustice backed up by force," is in fact a point that pacifists themselves have often made, especially those pacifists for whom nonviolence is not a tactic but a way of life.

The history of pacifism includes a tradition of voluntary poverty, poverty chosen at least in part because pacifists have in fact found out where their incomes come from and then striven to be bound as little as possible to those sources. This was certainly true of Gandhi, and of many people influenced by him. (Orwell does not comment on this aspect of Gandhi's program.) It was true of the eighteenth-century American pacifist John Woolman, was and is true of the Catholic Worker pacifists from Dorothy Day and Peter Maurin down to the present day and is true of many American pacifists practicing war tax resistance, both religious and secular. Attend any gathering of war tax resisters, and you'll find people fretting about every detail of their getting and spending, imagining or practicing alternative economies, devising ways out of the cash nexus, finding sources for clothing other than sweatshops; you'll also find people who, with something of Henry David Thoreau's handyman virtuosity, make things rather than buying them or hold things in common rather than individually—clothing, gardens, houses, land—precisely out of an acute discomfort with "where their incomes come from."

That may not be what Orwell wanted, of course. His critique seems intended to push pacifists away from pacifism rather than toward voluntary poverty.[34] But a great strength of the pacifist movement, in my view, is precisely this perception, which it shares with Orwell, that it's important to know where the money that you spend is coming from, and equally important, if it turns out that it's all "the fruit of injustice backed up by force," to make as sparing and judicious a use of it as possible.

3. This same tradition of voluntary poverty, combined with a far more militant tradition of nonviolent civil disobedience than anything Orwell's British pacifists were conducting, offers something of an answer to Orwell's more general charge that pacifists are "sheltered" and perhaps the beginning of an answer to his charge that being a pacifist does not allow the exercise of the military virtues. Such an answer is famously articulated in Williams James's 1910 pacifist essay, "The Moral Equivalent of War," in which James, anticipating Orwell's language, argues that "a conscription of the whole youthful population to form for a certain number of years a part of the army enlisted against *Nature* . . . would preserve in the midst of a pacific civilization the manly virtues which the military party is so afraid of seeing disappear in peace."[35]

Other pacifists have imagined other ways of bringing those virtues into play. The extreme voluntary poverty called for by Dorothy Day, the risks undergone by

Gandhian activists in India and by civil rights workers in the American South, the beatings and sometimes fatal attacks they suffered, the time they spent in prison, the time spent in prison by ultraresisters during the Vietnam War and the campaigns against nuclear weapons, the risks undergone, and sometimes succumbed to, by those who've done accompaniment in Latin America and the Middle East, worked against timber companies in the Northwest, been "human shields" in Iraq—whatever judgment one might make of the wisdom or folly of taking these risks, whatever one thinks of voluntary poverty and privation as a way of conducting a life, it's clear that pacifists who purposely expose themselves to risk, pain, poverty, assault, and death can't be justly described as "sheltered" and are able to, are in fact forced to, deploy some of the military virtues Orwell is talking about. They have need of courage and solidarity and camaraderie and self-sacrifice. And in developing those virtues, they seem to me pacifism's best answer to Orwell's critique of it in this regard.

4. A difficult charge of Orwell's to answer is one that he expressed somewhat tentatively, toward the end of the reflections on Gandhi: "how does one put [nonviolent resistance] into practice internationally? . . . Applied to foreign politics, pacifism either stops being pacifist or becomes appeasement" (4:469). What Orwell is talking about is the difficulty of nonviolent intervention. It is possible, that is, to imagine, and has been possible in some cases to carry out, nonviolent resistance against one's own government, against an occupying army, even when the government or the army is part of a totalitarian regime. But suppose what you want to do is to defend not yourself but someone else, someone far away. Suppose—to take an obvious and pressing example—that what you had wanted to do, as a pacifist in January 2003, was both oppose U.S. military action against Iraq and intervene nonviolently on behalf of the oppressed Iraqi people.

That's hard; violence has a long history of having large effects at a distance, whereas the great triumphs of nonviolence have been local and intimate. But there have been hints of what pacifist intervention would look like. Orwell's British pacifists had begun to discuss the practice that is now called accompaniment. They proposed, for example, the idea of a "Peace Army," to be "recruited from volunteers ready to stand without weapons between the opposing forces . . . . [This] emerged in 1932 at the time of the Sino-Japanese conflict over Manchuria."[36] But nothing came of it. Again, "at the time of the Munich crisis, the PPU sponsors offered to send five thousand pacifists to the Sudetenland as a nonviolent presence."[37] Nothing came of that either. Today we have the pacifist interventions of Peace Brigades International and now, with greater risk, those of the International Solidarity Movement in Palestine. It's too early to say whether anything will come of these attempts, I think. They may turn out, in retrospect, to have been the fumbling beginnings of a great human invention; they may turn out to have been steps down a dead-end street. In either case, whatever tradition of pacifism ends up offering the best answer to Orwell's charge here will also end up, I think, being the tradition of pacifism that has the longest future and greatest influence.

5. Two of Orwell's charges remain, both bearing on the relations pacifists might have with the nations they live in: the charge that pacifists can't govern, can't even imagine governing, and the charge that they can't feel patriotism.

A modest answer to the first question would rest on the fact that many pacifists, even War Resisters League pacifists, are willing to make a distinction between police force and state military force, accepting the former and rejecting the latter. Those who make such a distinction can imagine governing, within the domestic sphere, in a quite familiar way. They would, of course, need to conduct foreign policy rather differently. But the business of arresting murderers and drug dealers would proceed as usual.

Other pacifists are less easy about police force; they refuse, for example, to call the police even when personally threatened. How such pacifists would face the problem of governing is less clear. It's possible that they would admit the truth of Orwell's charge but would suggest that it bears on governing large states rather than small communities, in which it's easier to see how militant nonviolence could be an adequate substitute for militant violence. Pacifism then would lead to a critique of large states, precisely as requiring violence to maintain. In doing so, it would ally itself with the decentralist tradition associated with E. F. Schumacher.

A modest answer to the second question is that pacifists could be patriots in pacifist states; that is, if the first question could be answered, the answer to the second question would follow. A more challenging answer would agree with Orwell that pacifism and patriotism are in fact at odds. Pacifists have for the most part refused to make a distinction not between good and wicked states but between the value of one human life and another—in particular, between the value of a fellow citizen's life and the life of a citizen belonging to one's country's antagonist. How do you know, asks the Talmud, whether your enemy's blood is less red than yours? Maybe it's just as red, or even redder! But patriotism often rests on this distinction. And as Susan Sontag writes in a recent *Nation* article, "it is hard to defy the wisdom of the tribe, the wisdom that values the lives of members of the tribe above all others. It will always be unpopular—it will always be deemed unpatriotic—to say that the lives of the members of the other tribe are as valuable as one's own."[38]

I'm not claiming that the modes of pacifism I present as offering responses to Orwell's charges are, at the moment, pacifism's dominant modes. I'm not claiming that the responses they offer are entirely satisfactory. I am claiming that if we who cherish pacifism take Orwell's charges seriously, and in considering them take a long, eclectic look at pacifist history, we can find in certain traditions of that history some compelling answers to his charges. And we may want to conclude that those traditions are, precisely because they can provide such answers, the traditions that might nurture a stronger pacifism than the one Orwell knew, and the one we have now.

NOTES

1. Quoted and well commented on in Christopher Hitchens, *Why Orwell Matters* (New York: Basic Books, 2002), 13.

2. Orwell, *The Collected Essays, Journalism, and Letters,* ed. Sonia Orwell and Ian Angus (Jaffrey, N.H.: David R. Godine, 2000; orig. pub. New York: Harcourt Brace, 1968), 1:283. Sources for subsequent quotations from this edition will be given by parenthetical citation in the body of the text.

3. The shorter OED defines "creeping Jesus" as "an abject or hypocritical person."

4. Later Orwell candidly acknowledged he'd been wrong in this belief and in the predictions accompanying it; but looking around him in 1944, he was not distressed by what he saw: "The fact that we were fighting for our lives has not forced us to 'go Socialist,' as I foretold that it would, but neither has it driven us into Fascism. So far as I can judge, we are somewhat further from Fascism than we were at the beginning of the war" (3:295).

5. It's not clear how much of Orwell's sense of pacifism is dependent on his being situated "in a war like this one," i.e., in a war in which an enemy comparable in power to one's own country has in fact physically attacked that country. It's good to remind oneself, though, that that is the sort of war England was in fact involved in; such a reminder should at least slow down the process of claiming Orwell in support of any war that is distinctly *not* "like this one."

6. Such passages almost justify Alexander Comfort's sarcastic remark that Orwell was "the preacher of a doctrine of Physical Courage as an Asset to the left-wing intellectual" (2:225).

7. Note the implication, in the phrase "the *rest* of the intelligentsia," that pacifists are themselves members of that group. On Orwell's tendency to talk of "pacifists" when what he really has in mind is pacifist intellectuals, see 2:225.

8. Orwell's respect for "wholehearted pacifists" seems to embrace not just pacifists who denounce all state violence but even pacifists who support the Nazis, if only their pacifism is purged of what he regards as its "forensic" character, its evasiveness. If pacifists admit that they are helping the Nazis, he writes in 1941, "then the long-term case for pacifism can be made out. You can say: 'Yes, I know I am helping Hitler, and I want to help him. Let him conquer Britain, the USSR and America. Let the Nazis rule the world; in the end they will grow into something different.' That is at any rate a tenable position. It looks forward into human history, beyond the term of our own lives" (2:169).

9. E.g., Roger Kimball, "Failures of Nerve," *The New Criterion* 21:3 (November 2002), *http://www.newcriterion.com/archive/21/nov02/aa-kimball.htm;* Jonah Goldberg, "Safire's Courage," *National Review Online,* January 7, 2002, *http://www.nationalreview.com/goldberg/goldberg010702.shtml;* Michael Kelly, "Pacifists Are Not Serious People," *Washington Post* September 26, 2001, *http://www.townhall.com/columnists/michaelkelly/mk20010926.shtml.*

10. On women pacifists see Josephine Eglin, "Women Pacifists in Interwar Britain," in *Challenge to Mars: Essays on Pacifism from 1918 to 1945,* ed. Peter Brock and Thomas Socknat (Toronto: University of Toronto Press, 1999).

11. In 1945 Orwell does write that "the majority of pacifists either belong to obscure religious sects or are simply humanitarians who object to taking life and prefer not to follow their thoughts beyond that point" (3:374). That, though, is the only passage I'm aware of in which he acknowledges this. It's a grudging acknowledgment, too; presumably by "obscure religious sects" Orwell means Quakers, among others, but why, given the strong history of British Quakerism, does he call them "obscure?" (Nor were Quakers the majority among British pacifists; the highest percentage of that group were, in fact, Methodists.) In any case, in the following sentence Orwell returns to the pacifists he's actually thinking about: "but there is a minority of intellectual pacifists whose real though unadmitted motive appears to be hatred of western democracy and admiration for totalitarianism."

12. Martin Ceadel, "A Legitimate Peace Movement: The Case of Britain, 1918–1945," in *Challenge to Mars,* 142.

13. Thus Andrew Rigby refers to "the [PPU] leadership's refusal to contemplate any form of civil disobedience" ("The Peace Pledge Union: From Peace to War, 1936–1945," in *Challenge to Mars,* 172). An interesting exception: Norma Page, who'd been doing *voluntary* fire-watching, refused to do *compulsory* fire-watching and was sentenced to fourteen days in prison (178).

14. Orwell came to recognize this also, writing in 1945 that "it has been made easy for COs to choose non-military jobs, and the number refusing all kinds of national service has been tiny" (3:385). But he didn't consider the implications of these facts.

15. Rigby, "Peace Pledge Union," 177.

16. Rigby, "Peace Pledge Union," 181.

17. Peter Brock and Nigel Young, *Pacifism in the Twentieth Century* (Syracuse, N.Y.: Syracuse University Press, 1999), 168.

18. On the demography of conscientious objectors, see Brock and Young, *Pacifism,* 164–66.

19. Rigby, "Peace Pledge Union," 182.

20. Comfort, *No Such Liberty* (London: Chapman & Hall, 1941), 108–9.

21. This is the only case, in what I've read at any rate, of Orwell's meeting a pacifist in person, and moreover of his meeting a pacifist he didn't already know.

22. Quoted in Brock and Young, *Pacifism,* 133.

23. See also Orwell's 1943 review of Lionel Fielden's *Beggar My Neighbor:* "the idea put forward by Gandhi himself, that if the Japanese came they could be dealt with by sabotage and 'non-cooperation,' is a delusion, nor does Gandhi show any very strong signs of believing in it. Those methods have never seriously embarrassed the British and would make no impression on the Japanese. After all, where is the Korean Gandhi?" (2:310).

24. Similarly: "underneath his less ordinary qualities one feels all the time the solid middle-class businessmen who were his ancestors" (4:465).

25. This is a significant revision of Orwell's earlier attitude, when Gandhi's friendship with the wealthy Sarabhai family seemed to count for him as hypocrisy. On that friendship see Erik Erikson, *Gandhi's Truth* (New York: Norton, 1969).

26. Erikson, *Gandhi's Truth,* 234.

27. A further manifestation of Orwell's generosity, though less directly related to the question of pacifism, is his overall judgment of Gandhi's life work. It's a common thing to say about that work that "[Gandhi] had lived just long enough to see his life work in ruins" (4:469). But Orwell rejects that critique too: "it was not in trying to smooth down Hindu-Moslem rivalry that Gandhi had spent his life. His main political objective, the peaceful ending of the British rule, had after all been attained" (4:470).

28. I'm presuming in what follows that certain of Orwell's critiques can be regarded as already answered, either because he withdrew them, or because Gandhi's example is an implicit refutation of them, or because all that needs to be done to refute them is to say, e.g., "pacifists who refuse to make a distinction of value between Churchill's England and Hitler's Germany are being bad pacifists."

29. See Leila Danielson's regrettably unpublished essay, "'In My Extremity I Turned to Gandhi': American Pacifists, Christianity, and Gandhian Nonviolence, 1915–1941." On the relation between nonresistance and resistance in nineteenth-century American pacifism, see my "Thoreau's Essay on Civil Disobedience: Sources, Argument, Influence," in *A Historical Guide to Henry David Thoreau,* ed. William E. Cain (New York: Oxford University Press, 2000).

30. Gene Sharp, *The Politics of Nonviolent Action* (Boston: Porter Sargent, 1973), v–vi.

31. Philip Paul Hallie, *Lest Innocent Blood Be Shed: The Story of the Village of Le Chambon, and How Goodness Happened There* (New York: Harper & Row, 1979), and Pierre Sauvage, *The Weapons of the Spirit* (Los Angeles: Friends of Le Chambon, 1989).

32. See on this Nathan Stoltzfus, *Resistance of the Heart: Intermarriage and the Rosenstrasse Protest in Nazi Germany* (New Brunswick, N.J.: Rutgers University Press, 2001).

33. Aaron Falbel, personal communication, February 19, 2003.

34. It would be interesting, in this context, to think about how Orwell's experiences of poverty do and don't resemble the sort of voluntary poverty practiced by pacifists. For acute reflections on Orwell's thinking about the matter, see Margery Sabin's chapter in this volume.

35. James, "The Moral Equivalent of War," in *Nonviolence in America: A Documentary History,* ed. Alice Lynd and Staughton Lynd (Maryknoll, N.Y.: Orbis, 1995), 73.

36. Brock and Young, *Pacifism,* 116.

37. Rigby, "Peace Pledge Union," 172.

38. Susan Sontag, "On Courage and Resistance," *The Nation,* May 5, 2003, 11.

8

Varieties of Patriotic Experience

TODD GITLIN

I. PATRIOTISM OUT OF THE BLUE

To tell the truth, the jolts of September 11, 2001, jammed my mental circuits, and I spent much of the ensuing year trying to get them unjammed. This was as much an intellectual as an emotional undertaking, if, indeed, it makes any sense to separate the two. To devote yourself to such a task, you must resist what is called "closure." You must open yourself to the shock, again and again, and refuse to let any ideology take possession of it. You must not shy from bewilderment, from unprecedented feelings and thoughts, neglected topics, whole shelves full of cans of worms. When you ask *What?* and *Why?* and *What follows?* and the subject under discussion is mass murder, you must not be satisfied to rummage through your mental file cabinet of prepackaged answers—not if you want to be alive to the shock, that is, to reality. You know that all the preprinted labels are wrong. You refuse to honor the shallow thought that the images of atrocity "looked like an action movie." You do not classify deliberate massacre as an "understandable" response to an objectionable foreign policy or, for that matter, as a singular outburst of evil directed against a people innocent of evil. You do not try to dispel your immediate feelings, horror and astonishment, because your feelings are your links to reality, even if sometimes they throw you for a loop. It was through my emotions that I found myself in contact with—thinking about—questioning—and taken by—patriotism.

Proximity wasn't the cause. It wasn't that I or my family was in danger directly—we lived a mile north of the ruins of the Twin Towers, a sizable distance, as these things go, though close enough to see and hear the second explosion. A day and a night later, and for weeks to come, we were breathing the World Trade

Some passages in this essay are drawn from articles published in 2001 and 2002 in the *New York Times* and on www.openDemocracy.net and www.motherjones.com, and some appear in a different form in Todd Gitlin, *Letters to a Young Activist* (New York: Basic Books, 2003); reprinted by permission of the author.

Center, the acrid smoke, the vaporized remnants of thousands of computers, copy machines, phones, glass, steel, carpets, desks, asbestos, and God knows what—corpses too, but it took time to realize that. But the fumes of catastrophe, however deeply they sink into your lungs, don't make you rethink your principles. Fear—fear that this one-time event might not turn out to be a one-time event—comes closer to accomplishing that. But fear was only one feeling and there were others, surprising ones. Love, for example.

Thinking about that crystalline, desperate morning forever enshrined by a number, I have tried to hold on to the astonishment and deepen it with reflection, not to flee from the downright shock. Experience that astonishes is not the sole truth, but it is an indispensable truth—the truth of "wild history," in the historian Richard Slotkin's phrase,[1] history that did not have to happen but that, once having happened, changes not only the future but also the history that happened before. The risk of such an endeavor is that you become trapped in the trauma, fixated on the suppurating past. You can sink into a state of mental arrest, where trauma rivets you to memory, but memory is selective, and there is a danger that when you remember, you screen out the inconvenient stuff.

My memories are of strangers and their losses, but no less of solidarities. I think of a distraught young woman, red-haired, staggering up the sidewalk from the direction of the vanished Twin Towers, a continuous cascade of tears flowing down her face. I think of the handbills posted everywhere in lower Manhattan, the photos of the missing, *Have you seen* —?, the desperate listings of phone numbers to call, the candles burning on the sidewalks next to the fire stations, the hand-printed signs: THANK YOU TO OUR HEROIC FIREFIGHTERS. I recall a homeless woman on the subway declaring her sympathy for my wife, whose home, after all, was a mile from the rubble. Strangers wished each other good luck. It's not too much to say that I, and they, felt love for each other—love of a people who would endure. I think of mourners and mutual aid, in other words, not of the dead themselves. I also think of an open mike in Union Square where people already debated the American response, people who disagreed vehemently but were willing to hear each other out.

I did not, as they say, "lose anyone." But I hope it does not sound either callous or self-congratulatory to say that in those awful days I *found* people—a people to whom I belonged. Not the lost, but those who were working feverishly not only to repair losses but also (in a phrase of James Baldwin's used by Richard Rorty to entitle his book about the patriotism of the Left[2]) to "achieve our country." Around five o'clock the afternoon of September 13, my wife and I walked down to the perimeter of the ruins along the West Side of lower Manhattan and fell in with a crowd that was greeting and applauding rescue workers—police officers, firefighters, phone and gas company people, ironworkers and welders, most driving slowly northward out of the smoking Ground Zero area as other trucks drove south, heading in. Some came trudging out of the zone, their boots caked in gray ash. Some people came around handing out pictures of lost loved ones.

Out of the zone of ruins walked a man and woman in their early thirties, handsome, clear-eyed, wearing yellow slickers and boots. They were trying to figure out how to get to the subway. We advised on directions and fell in with them. Mary and Dean had driven down from Syracuse, 250 miles away, to volunteer, and had just spent thirty-six hours in the belt of destruction, digging in

rubble, dispersing whenever horns sounded to signal that buildings were in danger
of collapse. They'd been directing themselves, more or less. Now the federal
managers were coming in to take over.

They said it hadn't been easy to get into the damage zone: in fact, they'd had to
trick their way in. They had reported to the main volunteer depot at the Javits Convention Center a mile and a half north. They found three hundred people lined up in front
of them. So they attached themselves to an upstate fire company, got their yellow
slickers, boots, and smoke-protection masks, and made their way to Ground Zero.
They didn't know George W. Bush had made his appearance that afternoon (or that
he'd been given a far less vigorous reception than Mayor Giuliani), nor were they
impressed. At the time, they'd been catching a couple of hours' sleep. Soaked by the
first rain in days, they'd gone first to the shell of a nearby hotel, but there had been a
stench and somebody walked up and told them not to sleep near the bodies.

I asked Dean what he thought the United States ought to do now. "We have to
do something," he said, "but it's not easy. We have to be careful about retaliating.
We need diplomatic pressure. We can't go bomb a lot of innocent people. *Then
we've done what they've done.*" That same week, I was also struck by a third-
generation New Jersey flag factory owner, Gary Potenzone, who was interviewed
on ABC. He said that he sold 27,000 flags in a single day, adding: "It's not like the
Gulf War. That was, 'Get 'em, get 'em.' This is more solidarity. I'm very happy to
see true patriotism. This is so much warmth."[3]

I loved these strangers, and others I met in those days, and didn't feel mawkish
about it—these new, less-aggressive New Yorkers, speaking in hushed voices, or so
it seemed, lining up to give blood at the local hospitals from day one, disappointed
that no one was collecting it; the cabbies driving in unaccustomed silence, all the
gratuitous horns stilled; New Yorkers without their carapaces, stripped down to
their cores, no longer islands unto themselves. I took inspiration from the patriotic
activists who seem to have brought down Flight 93 over Pennsylvania and probably saved the White House. *They* hadn't waited for authorities to define their
patriotism for them. They hadn't trifled with symbolic displays. It dawned on me
that patriotism was the sum of such acts.

Patriotism is not only a gift to others but also a self-declaration: It affirms that
who you are extends beyond—far beyond—yourself or the limited being that you
thought was yourself. You are not an isolate. Just as you have a given name and a
family name, you also have a national name. It gives you a past and a future. You
are in solidarity with strangers: their losses are your own. One deep truth about
September 11 is that a community was attacked, not an assortment of individuals.
A second truth was that the community of survivors was a *political* community, a
community where diversity is not a feel-good slogan and debate is lifeblood. At
war, it is important to know what you are at war for, even when you are not the one
declaring the war. The night of September 11, in search of clarity and shoring up,
I reread George Orwell's 1945 essay "Notes on Nationalism," wherein Orwell
distinguishes between the English patriotism that he affirms in the name of the
values of the Left and the bombastic nationalism that is the cowbird version. "By
patriotism," he wrote, "I mean devotion to a particular place and a particular way
of life, which one believes to be the best in the world but has no wish to force on
other people. Patriotism is of its nature defensive, both militarily and culturally. . . .
Nationalism, on the other hand," he wrote, "is inseparable from the desire for

power."[4] Orwell leaves some difficult questions in abeyance: Can you be patriotic if you don't think the place and the way of life you are devoted to are the best in the world? Can you think some aspects (democracy and human rights) are most definitely worth spreading, even at times by force, come to that, and others most definitely are not? I'll come back to these difficulties later, but the important thing is that they complicated the devotional feeling I had but didn't erase it.

No surprise, my wife and I decided a few days later to hang an American flag from our terrace. It was a straightforward household decision—hardly a decision at all, because no one in the house felt like debating it. We didn't send out a press release. There was no controversy and we didn't consult anyone. The flag was a plain affirmation of membership. We did not put it up to claim that the United States of America deserved to rule, or war on, anyone else. (As it happened, we supported the use of force against al-Qaeda and the Taliban in Afghanistan, though with plenty of worries about terrible consequences that might ensue, but the worries were neither here nor there.) A few days later, Clyde Haberman, a metropolitan columnist of the *New York Times,* called to round up a quote about flag bearers. When I told him that we had put up a flag, that we had never thought we would undertake such a display, that it was not meant as support for the policies of George W. Bush but as an affirmation of fellowship with an injured and resolute people, then our private fact was transformed into a news fact and featured prominently in Haberman's column of September 19,[5] whereupon a lot of friendly mail came my way, and some not so friendly: some tut-tuts, some insults. An appreciative friend—a human rights activist, as it happens—who teaches at a prominent liberal arts college told me that he had mounted a flag on his office door, whereupon a student had complained to college authorities that this constituted an abuse of professorial authority. I heard later that on a couple of campuses, the fact that I had put up the American flag was cited as a reason why it was, at the very least, not forbidden for someone on the Left to fly an American flag.

But the interesting question is, why this fervent debate in the first place? Why did left-wingers of my generation get into arguments with their children, who wanted to fly flags from their windows? Why should the flying of the flag have been seen as a betrayal? What was it betraying?

2. WHAT PATRIOTISM RUBS RAW

A history, but also a belief.

If you belong to a certain class—call it the cosmopolitan class, middle- to upper-middle in income, college educated and beyond, university and culture-industry based—patriotism has been robbed of its allure. This history is connected to—in a single phrase—the "Vietnam generation," though Vietnam only launched the problem. But there are other factors that get in the way of patriotism, make it at the least weightless and irrelevant or, even more, laughable, demeaning, *embarrassing,* even infuriating. Why should this be?

To understand why patriotism is (or has been) tainted, it will help to consider the opposite concepts against which patriotism is counterposed, for they suggest what people think they are turning toward when they turn away from patriotism. One is individualism, and the other is cosmopolitanism.

First of all, patriotism gets in the way of individualism, a declaration of identity that is as fundamental for critics of rugged individualism as it is for the most fervent advocates. For patriotism affirms that we are bounded, attached, unfree. It places value on a certain conformity. Nietzsche called the shots on this when he associated patriotism with the herd instinct.[6] We pride ourselves on being individuals, after all. This is an article of faith, our modern gift and glory. We are self-created (or trying to be). However and wherever we were born, with whatever roots and equipment, into whatever class, race, religion, region, or nationality, we insist that we remain free to choose the essentials of our lives, that our freedom is inalienable, that whoever tampers with it is our enemy. Choice is our mantra. As women and men with reproductive rights, we declare ourselves pro-choice. As voters, believers, advocates, and consumers, we are nothing if not free—or so we firmly believe. Even as religious souls, Americans like to imagine that they are born-again, affirming a choice to *accept* Jesus Christ, something they can do or not, something that wasn't preordained by their parents.

But patriotism decrees that we are not free. We are obliged. Patriotism is sticky. It is imperious about its imperatives. It values a certain unfreedom, for it declares that in a crucial way we are not free to choose the condition we were born into. Unless we are naturalized citizens, we did not choose our obligation. We are free to imagine our country any way we like, but we are not free to deny that it *is* our country. In fact, American patriotism is an especially compelling and demanding sort of patriotism, because the American nation is founded on an idea, not on blood. The idea is an apparent paradox—that we are most ourselves when we affirm our roots, that we are free now because we are bound by the American past. What we are loyal to is the condition of our freedom, and yet when we are loyal, we have renounced our freedom.

All of this is to say that if you believe that you are free and that it is important to be free, patriotism, to the degree that it claims your loyalty, is unnerving. The more insistent the claim, the more unnerving it is. One way to ward off the claim is with cosmopolitan disdain. Patriotism is parochial. The cosmopolitan impulse is to declare that patriotism is for other people—lesser people, really. Superpatriots, we call them. They are the herd of the weak. They live by cant. Why? How can they live that way, how can they talk the way they talk? They've been brainwashed. They've succumbed to propaganda. This is partly because they're surrounded by propaganda but, let's face it, it's only possible because their character is degraded. They're gullible, or stupid. Some of these attributes we infer but there are others that are highly visible. Patriots, to get down to it, are people of bad taste. Part of what marks our class is good taste, and we distinguish ourselves as people of good taste—we collect, confirm, and multiply our "cultural capital," to use the sociologist Pierre Bourdieu's phrase[7]—by scorning people of bad taste. So patriotism is objectionable because it's tacky. It means vinyl and trailer parks. It means slogans and lapel pins. It means klutzy rituals at ball games and truculence in policy debates. It means bluster and sentimentality. It means myopia, willful ignorance. If we forgive the patriots flying their flags during the Gulf War or after September 11, 2001, in depressed areas like upstate New York, it is because patriots are pitiable. Let them have their flags if flags make them feel better. The nation is what they have—or fancy they have—when they don't have much else.

Worst of all, from this point of view, patriotism means obscuring the whole grisly truth of America under a polyurethane mask. It means covering over the

Indians in their mass graves. It means covering over slavery. It means overlooking America's many imperial adventures—the Philippine, Cuban, and Nicaraguan occupations, among others—as well as abuses of power by corporations, international banks, and so on. It means disguising American privilege—even when America's good fortune was not directly purchased at the cost of the bad fortune of others, a debatable point. So from this point of view, patriotism betrays the truth. It's a story, all right, but a story in the sense of a lie. It can't help spilling over into what Orwell thought was the harsh, dangerous, and distinct phenomenon of nationalism, with its aggressive edge, its implication of superiority. Scrub up patriotism as you will, the cynic asserts, and nationalism, as the political theorist John H. Schaar put it in a prophetic (and for a man of the Left, courageous) 1973 essay, remains "patriotism's bloody brother."[8] Was Orwell's heroic distinction not, in the end, a distinction without a difference? Didn't his patriotism, disdaining aggressiveness, still insist that the nation he affirmed was "the best in the world?" What if there is more than one feature of the American way of life that you do *not* believe to be "the best in the world"—the national bravado, the pride some Americans take in their ignorance, the overreach of the marketplace. The very emphasis on difference—I belong to *this* nation—might well be the door through which you march with the rest of the conformists to the beat of a national anthem.

So it follows that patriotism deserves to be unmasked. It is the recourse of scoundrels. It deceives. It masks interests. It defends privilege. It masks pettiness. So patriotism is for small people, not for the likes of you and me, reader, unless we submit to diminish ourselves. Patriotism's morality is bad faith, because it assigns to someone else the moral initiative that is properly mine; it beggars my freedom, alienates rights that are fundamentally inalienable. Nietzsche made this point more than a century ago and it has lost none of its force.

But, so goes the complaint, patriotism betrays not only the small and the personal but also the large and impersonal. Affirming the larger unit, it picks the wrong one—it doesn't think big enough. The term *patriotism* is often paired off against *cosmopolitanism,* whose root by one definition in *The American Heritage Dictionary of the English Language* means "so sophisticated as to be at home in all parts of the world." Cosmopolitanism embraces the cosmos, patriotism the parish—it is parochial. When the global environmentalist declares "Think globally, act locally," the locality she has in mind is not the nation. It might be the county, perhaps, or the bio-region, or as far as the eye can see, but it is not the nation, let alone the state. The impulse to disdain the nation is a recognition of the arbitrariness and pettiness of the nation. If war is the health of the state, as Randolph Bourne wrote against the carnage that started the twentieth century off with a bang,[9] then the rejection of the state (and therefore the nation that tags along with it) is the beginning of the end of war.

No surprise, then, that in the wake of the Vietnam War, a generation of post-Vietnam skeptics about the nation-state fell upon the work of the political anthropologist Benedict Anderson, who neatly argued in a book called *Imagined Communities* that that is what nations are, that they are not natural, organic, primordial, objective, or anything of that sort, but the creatures—"constructions"—of intellectuals and the stories they tell about history and culture.[10] In the more vernacular rendition, a nation was an entity possessed of an army, a navy, and a dictionary. The implication that some readers drew was that nations, being con-

structed, were superficial, not deep; artificial, not natural; malleable, not traditional and thus lacked moral standing. So patriotism seemed a presumption, an un-
earned imposition.

I have been making a case abstractly, on first principles, about a logic conducive to a culture clash that afflicted—was bound to afflict—those of us who value
individualism and cosmopolitanism. But for a large bloc of Americans my age and
younger—too young to remember World War II, the generation for whom "the
war" meant Vietnam and possibly always would, to the end of our days—the case
against patriotism was not an abstraction. There was a powerful experience underlying it: as powerful an eruption of our feelings as the experience of patriotism is
supposed to be for patriots. Indeed, it could be said that in the course of our
political history we experienced a very odd turnabout: The most powerful public
emotion in our lives was the *rejection* of patriotism.

3. Loving and Leaving

America is a nation that invites anxiety about what it means to belong, because the
national boundary is ideological, hence disputable and porous. Part of what it has
meant to be American has been to participate in a debate about what it means to
be American. As the first constitutional republic, America has been not just a
homeland but a land of ideas, of American*ism*. At its best, affirming American*ism*
has entailed affirming a lineage to 1776. Thus did Lincoln declare, on his way to
take office in the White House, "I have never had a feeling politically that did not
spring from the sentiments embodied in the Declaration of Independence."[11] Later
he refined this idea into the stark propositions of the Gettysburg Address. Lincoln
was affirming what John H. Schaar called "covenanted patriotism"[12]—as opposed
to the blood-and-soil variety. But under stress, the covenant is prone to wear thin.
Civic patriotism, which demands self-rule, collapses into the follow-the-leader
principle. Under strain, authoritarians conclude that questioning authority is an
unaffordable luxury. Like the citizens of race-based regimes, even citizens of the
democratic American republic have been, from time to time, acutely vulnerable to
the accusation that their membership is not authentic after all and that by expound-
ing the wrong ideas they have forfeited their membership. They are prone, in other
words, to be accused of un-Americanism.

Astoundingly, the 1960s upended this accusation and turned it into a mass
movement of pride. From membership and anger combined came a tradition of
antitraditionalism. During most of the 1960s, and frequently since, I have groped
for words to express, in the right proportions, the membership and the anger at
once—the anger deriving from the membership, of course, the membership an
intimate fact, making it easy to feel that the nation, by acting contrary to justice,
violates its very right to exist, and that this is a fact on which I am bound to act,
for ultimately it is not anyone else's doing. I, as a citizen, cannot shake responsibility. If the covenant turns out shallow, if humanity is betrayed by those who
would purport to be its saviors, there is no one to rectify the wrong but those of
us who understand how deep the betrayal goes.

For me, the anger and the horror predated the Vietnam War. I launched into
activism as a campaigner against the American nuclear weapons stance in 1960,

and my estrangement from national policies only deepened under the pressure of the Bay of Pigs invasion of Cuba, American collusion in South African apartheid, and, most of all, the egregious war in Indochina. But for some reason one particular moment in March 1965 stands out. I was twenty-two, living among the Students for a Democratic Society (SDS) circle in Ann Arbor, Michigan, helping organize the first national demonstration against the Vietnam War. The war was already a daily assault on brains and conscience, so I could scarcely bear to watch the TV news. But one evening, for some reason, I turned on NBC News and saw pictures of American Marines occupying Santo Domingo while young Dominicans protested. It was, on the scale of enormities, only a tiny exercise in old-fashioned imperialism, this expedition into the Caribbean to shore up a military régime blocking the restoration of an elected social-democratic government that it had deposed. There was no napalm, no white phosphorus, no strategic hamlets. I don't know why these particular pictures of young Dominicans resisting the Americans stirred me so deeply, but I know I identified with them. I don't know what I felt more keenly: horrified disbelief, that my country could be waving the wrong flag, betraying its better self, or horrified belief that my country could only be doing something so appalling because it—not its policies, not this or that wretched decision, but, in the core of its dark heart, my country itself—was committed to suppressing the rights of inconvenient peoples. Gunboat diplomacy, we learned to call this, in my high school history class. How do you reform a leviathan?

I remember writing a poem that night—not a good one, but a sincere one. I was a nonviolent twenty-two-year-old and I wanted to stand with the young anti-Americans in the Dominican Republic. The poem ended with a romantic line about "a rifle and a sad song." Another phrase I like better sticks out in my memory: "I would only curse America, like a drunkard his bottle." America, love it and leave it at once. A nice trick, though it may put a kink in your lower back.

I have felt such moments of horrified recognition countless times since that night in 1965, and I have devoted many waking hours to fighting against imperious American foreign policies. I am not speaking of my ideas here, but of feelings, deep feelings. In the second half of the 1960s and early 1970s, I was choking on the Vietnam War. It felt to me that the fight against the war had become my life. The war went on so long and so destructively, it felt like more than the consequence of a wrongheaded policy. My country must have been revealing some fundamental core of wrongness by going on and on with an indefensible war. I was implicated because the terrible war was wrapped in my flag—or what had been my flag. Then why persist? Why not surrender title, and good riddance? Right! The American flag did not feel like my flag, even though I could recognize—in the abstract—that it made sense for others to wave it in the antiwar cause.

I was a tactician. I could argue—I did argue—against waving the North Vietnamese flag or burning the Stars and Stripes. But the hatred of a bad war, in what was evidently a pattern of bad wars (though none so bad as Vietnam) turned us inside out. It inflamed our hearts. You can hate your country in such a way that the hatred becomes fundamental. A hatred so clear and intense came to feel like a cleansing flame. By the late 1960s, this is what became of much of the New Left. Those of us who met with Vietnamese and Cuban communists in those years were always being told that we had to learn to love our people. In my case, it was a communist medical student in Cuba who delivered the message in 1967. Love our people! How were we supposed to do that, another SDSer and I argued back, when our people had committed genocide against the Indians, when the national history was enmeshed in slavery, when this experience of historic original sin ran deeper than any class solidarity, when it was what it meant to *be* American? Lessons in patriotism taught by communists—a definitive New Left experience drawn from the comedy of the late 1960s. Well, we would try.

We would go looking for historical lessons, for one thing. Revisionist historians went looking for "history from the bottom up"—heroic seamen during the American Revolution, slaves in revolt, Native Americans, union organizers, jailed World War I socialists, Wobblies. But the America of Richard Nixon was not conducive to our invention of *this* tradition. The American flag did not feel any more congenial as Nixon widened the Vietnam War into Laos and Cambodia and connived in the Pinochet coup; or in the 1980s, as Reagan endorsed the Nicaraguan contras and the Salvadoran and Guatemalan death squads. To put it mildly, my generation of the New Left—a generation that grew as the war went on—relinquished any title to patriotism without much sense of loss because it felt to us that the perpetrators of unjust war had run off with the patrium. The nation had congealed into an empire whose logic was unwarranted power. All that was left to the Left was to unearth righteous traditions and cultivate them in universities. The much-mocked "political correctness" of the next academic generations was a consolation prize. We lost—we squandered—politics but won the textbooks.

Read history with open eyes and it is hard to overlook the American empire. Honest conservatives acknowledge imperial power too—though enthusiastically. What is the idea of Manifest Destiny, if not a robust defense of righteous empire? What was the onetime California Senator S. I. Hayakawa's brag about the Panama Canal, "we stole it fair and square,"[13] if not a sly recognition of the truth? You need not subscribe to the Left's grandest claims that America from its birth is essentially genocidal and indebted to slavery for much of its prosperity to acknowledge that white colonists took the land, traded in slaves, and profited immensely thereby; or that the United States later lorded it over Latin America (and other occasional properties, like the Philippines) to guarantee cheap resources and otherwise line American pockets; or that American-led corporations (among others) and financial agencies today systematically overlook or, worse, damage the freedoms of others. If all this lording over does not rise to the level of colonialism in the strict sense, and if it can be acknowledged that empires may have benign consequences, even for far-flung peoples far from the metropolitan core, then still, American wealth, access to resources, military power, and unilateralism qualify as imperial reach. Add to that the fact that America, counting less than 5 percent of world population, uses about one-quarter of the world's nonrenewable, environment-wrecking, fossil-fuel energy—and the Bush administration proposes to keep doing so as long as it pleases.

The tragedy of the anti-American Left is that, having achieved an unprecedented victory in helping stop an appalling war, it proceeded to commit suicide. It helped force the United States out of Vietnam, where the country had no constructive work to do—either for Vietnam or for itself—but did so at the cost of disconnecting itself from the nation. To a considerable degree it substituted the pleasures of condemnation for tactics designed to pursue further improvement. The orthodoxy was that "the system" precluded reform—never mind that the antiwar movement had already demonstrated that reform *was* possible. Human rights, feminism, environmentalism—these worldwide initiatives, American in their inception, flowing not from the American establishment but from our own American movements, were not in the picture. The only America in the picture was the America of wealth and weaponry—the corporations, the Pentagon, the CIA. According to the anti-imperialist dogma, the wholesale, indiscriminate anticommunism that led to imperial overthrows in Iran, Guatemala, Chile, Nicaragua, El Salvador, and elsewhere was the essential America, the inevitable consequence of a history poisoned at the root. When, in the 1990s, the Clinton administration mobilized armed force on behalf of Bosnia and then Kosovo against Slobodan Milosevic's genocidal Serbia, the hard Left could only smell imperial motives. In their eyes, the democratic, antigenocidal motive for intervention was a paper-thin mask. Milosevic's Serbs were cast as deserving victims.

In short, just as America seemed trapped in an essence, so did its opposition. By the 1970s, the outsider stance had become second nature. Even those who had entered the 1960s in diapers came to maturity thinking patriotism a threat or a bad joke. It did nothing for them. To be on the left meant to negate it. But anti-Americanism was, and remains, a metaphysics more than a politics. Indeed, the demonology substituted for politics, because politics was delusional, entangled with a fatally flawed system. Viewing ongoing politics as contemptibly shallow and compromised, the demonological attitude naturally ruled out patriotism. There was no reason for deep engagement in the political life of the country and every reason to avoid it. This Left prided itself on *dis*connection from a history ruined from the start by original sin. Marooned (often self-marooned) on university campuses, in left-wing media and other cultural outposts—all told, an archipelago of bitterness—what sealed itself off in the post-1960s decades was what Richard Rorty calls "a spectatorial, disgusted, mocking Left rather than a Left which dreams of achieving our country."[14]

From this outlying point of view, the attacks of September 11, 2001, revealed a symmetry that the hard-bitten Left had long expected. America was condemned by its history. The furies were avenging, chickens were flying home, American detonations were blowing back. No one could see the truth but the saved. They had little time, little interest, little hard-headed curiosity to comprehend a fanatical Islamist sect that set no limits to what and whom it would destroy. Whoever was killed in America, Americans must still end up the greatest of Satans. Thus did Noam Chomsky belittle the September 11 attacks so incredibly far as to claim, in a Belgrade radio interview as the ash still rained on lower Manhattan, that the United States had, after the attacks, "demanded that Pakistan kill possibly millions of [Afghani] people who are themselves victims of the Taliban,"[15] and, in subsequent interviews and writings, that the United States was responsible for vastly more deaths—"several tens of thousands"—in Sudan after the possibly mistaken bombing of a pharmaceutical plant in 1998[16]—and all on the strength of the thinnest of evidence and the thickest of rageful passions. Intent on blaming America first, these anti-Americans bent and selected the reports and rumors that suited them to find respectable reasons for anti-American sentiment, which they regarded as strictly derivative—not blameless, exactly, not necessarily quite justifiable, but always, "ultimately," traceable to American malfeasance. From the legitimate fear that misguided American policy had the effect of recruiting more terrorists, the hard anti-Americans leaped to the unwarranted assumption that terrorists were not terrorists. Soft anti-Americans did not go so far but were quick to change the subject.

Their moral balance was badly askew, but the anti-Americans shared with the rest of America the revelation that there is more than enough destructive power to go around. There are connoisseurs of apocalypse in the world, forces like al-Qaeda that are more than willing to slaughter Americans (not to mention inconvenient others) in the name of their own version of empire. Indisputably, there are forces in the world that, if victorious, would leave the world far worse off than under American power. You don't have to look any further for examples than the Nazi and Japanese empires or the Islamist totalitarianism that al-Qaeda evidently longs for (insofar as it troubles to offer what the American Declaration of Independence called a "decent respect to the opinions of mankind" and "declare the causes which impelled them" to their massacres).

A patriotic Left disputes American policies. But it criticizes, however vociferously, in an insider's voice, without discarding the hope, if not of redemption, at least of improvement. It deplores the deplorable in a tone that displays the critic's shared membership with the criticized. It acknowledges—and wrestles with—the strange dualities of America: the liberty and arrogance twinned, the bullying and tolerance, myopia and energy, standardization and variety, ignorance and inventiveness, the awful dark heart of darkness and the self-reforming zeal. It wants to address the whole of America, but not from the outside looking in. It does not labor under the illusion that the world would be benign but for American power or that capitalism is uniformly the most damaging economic system ever. It lives inside, with an indignation born of family feeling. Its anger is intimate.

4. Lived Patriotism

To repeat: patriotism is conventionally understood as a combination of feelings and ideas. Words are its proofs. We recognize patriotism when it is professed, we bemoan its absence when it is not professed. But patriotism in this sense is claimed too easily. The ease devalues the real thing and disguises its deep weakness. The folklore of patriotism lends itself to symbolic displays wherein we show one another how patriotic we are without exerting ourselves too strenuously. We sing songs, pledge allegiance, wave flags, display lapel pins, mount bumper stickers, attend (or tune in to) memorial rites. We think we become patriotic by declaring that we are patriotic. This is activity, but of a limited, I would say desiccated, sort. It is striking how many of these touchstones we have now—how rituals of devotion are folded into ball games and concerts, how flags adorn the most commonplace of private activities. Their prevalence permits foreign observers to comment on how patriotic the simple-minded Americans are. But such displays are not such straightforward proofs of patriotism at all. They are at least equally substitutes. John H. Schaar's stricture is apt here: Patriotism "is more than a frame of mind. It is also activity guided by and directed toward the mission established in the founding covenant."[17] Patriotic activity starts with a sense of responsibility but does not discharge it with tributary rites of celebration and memory. Patriotism in this sense, genuine patriotism, is not enacted strictly by being expressed in symbolic fashion. It is with effort and sacrifice, not pride or praise, that citizens honor the democratic covenant.

To put it this way is to erect an exalted standard. Yet to speak of the burdens of patriotism points to something not so flattering about the patriotism Americans so strenuously claim. Perhaps we celebrate our patriotism so energetically because when we get past the breast-beating our actual patriotic experience is thin on the ground. Perhaps Americans feel the need to tout Americanism and rout un-Americans precisely for this reason—not because we are such good patriots but because our substantial patriotic activity is weak. Ferreting out violations is the lazy person's substitute for a democratic life. If civic patriotism requires activity, not just symbolic display, Americans are not so patriotic after all.

What do I mean by substantial patriotic activity? I mean the work of civic engagement—the living out of the democratic commitment to govern ourselves. Actual patriotic experience in a democracy is more demanding—far more so—than the profession of sentiments; it is more easily advertised than lived up to. Whatever Woody Allen thinks of life, 90 percent of patriotism is not just showing up. Democratic patriotism is also far more demanding than signifying loyalty to the régime. In a kingdom, the patriot swears loyalty to the monarch. In a totalitarian society, the patriot is obedient in a thousand ways—participating in mass rituals, informing on enemies, joining designated organizations, doing whatever the anointed leader requires. But democratic loyalty is something else, stringent in its own way. If the nation to which we adhere is a community of mutual aid, a mesh of social connections, then it takes work, engagement, and time on the part of its citizens. It is likely to take money. It may take life. It is a matter, to borrow a magnificent phrase of 1776, of pledging "our lives, our fortunes, and our sacred honor." Most disturbing of all to the prime commitments of our private lives, it may well require that we curb our individual freedoms—the indulgences that normally we count as the highest of values.

In other words, lived patriotism entails sacrifice. The citizen puts aside private affairs in order to build up relationships with other citizens, with whom we come to share unanticipated events, risks, and outcomes. These citizenly relationships are not ones we choose. To the contrary. When we serve on a jury or in Teach for America or ride the subway, we do not choose our company. The community we partake of—like the whole of society—is a community of people whom we did not choose. (Thus the embarrassment to the liberal ideal of self-creation, already discussed.) The crucial difference here is between a community, consisting of people crucially *un*like ourselves, and a network or "lifestyle enclave," made up of people *like* ourselves.[18] Many "communities" in the sense commonly overused today— "the business community," "the academic community"—are actually networks, a fact that the overused term disguises. Cosmopolitanism is also usually lived out as a network extension: it invites connections with people like ourselves (writers, academics, liberals, members of the same profession, what have you) who happen to live in other countries.

Undemocratic societies require sacrifice, too, but unequally. There what passes as patriotism is obeisance to the ruling elite. Democracy, on the other hand, demands (for one thing) a particular sort of sacrifice: citizenly participation in self-government. This is not the place to explore the difficult questions of where participation must stop and professional management must start; but the important principle is that the domain of popular involvement should be as large as possible, the question of possibility itself deserving to be a vexatious one. At the very least, at the local level, the citizens should approve the agenda for governmental action. The result is twofold: not only policy that takes distinct points of view into account but also a citizenry that takes pride in its identity as such. When the citizen enters the town meeting, the local assembly, or, for that matter, the jury, disparate qualifications hardly disappear, but they are tempered, counterbalanced by a common commitment to leave no voice unattended.

Decision making aside, democratic life also requires spheres of experience where citizens encounter each other with equal dignity. Put it another way: A democratic culture is one in which no one is exempted from common duties. Commonality and sacrifice are combined. This is the strong side of what has become known as communitarianism, which has also been called civic liberalism. As Mickey Kaus argued in *The End of Equality,* social equality requires bolstering three spheres: the armed forces and national service; public schools; and adult public domains (transportation, health, day care, public financing of elections). The operative word, of course, is "public." It is in these sectors that the republic's commonality lives, on the ground, in time and space. In the armed forces, life is risked in common. In national service, time is jointly invested in benefits that do not accrue to self-interest. When loopholes are closed, class mixing becomes integral to life. Privilege, however extravagant in the rest of life, can't buy you everything. In public schools, privilege doesn't buy superior opportunities. In amenities like public transportation, governments provide what private interests would not, and individuals experience themselves as sharing a common condition. As these public spheres dwindle, sheer wealth and income grow in importance and vice versa. (For purposes of this argument it doesn't matter which comes first.)[19]

We also need some common sacrifice of our self-indulgences—not to test our Puritan mettle but to prevent ecological breakdown. Having proven averse to eco-efficiency in production, consumption, and transportation, despite our robust achievements in global warming and air and water pollution, Americans have a particular responsibility to lean less heavily on the earth. Since oil dependency is a considerable factor behind some of America's most egregious foreign policies, true patriotism is fully compatible with, indeed intertwined with, ecological sanity that lowers fossil fuel guzzling and promotes sustainable sources like solar and wind power. Yet Detroit automakers steadfastly resist hybrid gas-electric cars and increased fuel efficiency, and Washington permits them to get away with their profligacy. Patriots ought to endorse environmentalist Bill McKibben's suggestion that "gas-sucking SUVs . . . should by all rights come with their own little Saudi flags to fly from the hood."[20]

Overall, egalitarian culture is patriotism's armature. No matter how many commemorations Americans organize, no matter how many pledges we recite and anthems we rise for, the gestures are inessential. At times they build morale—most usefully when the suffering is fresh—but they do not repair or defend the country. For that, the quality of social relations is decisive. And the contrary follows, too: The more hierarchical and less equal the nation becomes, the less patriotic is its life. Not that the culture as a whole should be in the business of enforcing egalitarian norms, the ideal that populism defended and Stalinism made murderous. But there must be zones of social life, important ones, where the same social goods are at stake for everyone and individual distinction does not buy exemption. The most demanding, of course, is the military—and it is here, where the stakes are highest and the precedents most grievous, that universality is most important. It must not be possible to buy substitutes, as the Union's wealthy did in the Civil War. Many are the inequalities that are either morally legitimate or politically unbudgeable, but there must be equalities of sacrifice and encounter—not in order to strip the high and mighty of their individuality but purely and simply to treat everyone equally. Financial sacrifice on the part of the privileged is a proof that money cannot buy anything—it may not even be able to buy the most important thing, namely, personal safety. As long as equality prevails in one central phase of life— the most dangerous phase—the inequality of rewards in other phases does not become the be-all and the end-all of existence.

Many liberals will be inclined to demur. For whatever its merits, conscription surely grates upon the ideal of self-control—that is precisely one of its purposes. Let's face it: Most of us don't like to be told what to do. Moral preachments not only grate but also offend our sense that the only authority worth taking seriously is the authority of our own souls (or senses). Moral preachments about our duty sound to many Americans, left, right, and center, like claxons of a police state. To live our patriotism we would have to pick and choose, to overcome—selectively— some of the automatic revulsion we feel to laying aside some of our freedoms in the name of a higher duty. It isn't clear how many of us are willing to overcome our inner frolickers. I think of myself as rather civic-minded, but much of the time it isn't clear to me how much of my own initiative *I* will gladly surrender for the common good.

Which raises this related question: Where does a onetime antiwar activist and would-be conscientious objector get off defending conscription now that he is several decades away from vulnerability? (At the very least, I am not the only man of my generation to have rethought the principle of the draft. I wonder, though, whether any of the so-called chicken hawks, who defended the Vietnam War but not for themselves—Dan Quayle, George W. Bush, Dick Cheney, Trent Lott, Tom DeLay, Paul Wolfowitz, and Richard Perle, to name only a few recent Republican office holders—has rethought his own stance. "I had other priorities in the '60s than military service," Vice President Cheney has said.[21]) This is no mere debater's point. The principle of universal conscription not only is an abstract tribute to equality—worthy as that would be—but also undermines arbitrary warfare. If the citizens asked to support a war (or their relatives) are the ones who will have to fight it, the chicken hawk factor weakens—such as the fervent endorsement of war in Iraq, for example, by Republican leaders who thought the Vietnam War a "noble crusade" (Ronald Reagan's term) that they in their own persons somehow never found time for. The principle that wars must be popular with their soldiers is a good democratic requirement. Let it not be forgotten that Richard Nixon terminat- ed the draft not to end the war—in fact, he continued the war from the air, killing at a pace that exceeded Lyndon Johnson's, often in secret (as in Cambodia)—but to insulate it from public exposure and dissent.

Equal sacrifice of liberty in favor of conscription ought to dovetail with equal civic opportunity of other sorts. We talk a lot about equality of opportunity, but as a nation we are ill-prepared to amplify the principle—to enlarge it to the right to be healthy, to be cared for, to participate in government. As the election of 2000 demonstrated, we are not even terribly serious about guaranteeing the right to vote and have one's vote counted. In a formula: Lived patriotism requires social equality. It is in the actual relations of citizens, not symbolic displays, that civic patriotism lives. In these palpable relations no one is elevated. Status does not count, nor wealth, nor poverty. One person, one vote. Absent these ideals in action, patriotism lapses into gestures—pledges of allegiance, not the allegiance itself.

Considering the shallowness of patriotic experience, there is a particular pathos in expecting the current president, so little of whose life has been concerned with public service, to ignite civic virtue. A unifying logic links many of George W. Bush's public statements on and after September 11, 2001. There is the inadvertently comic spectacle of this man, who spent much of *his* September 11 flying aimlessly around the country as his staff fabricated security threats, soon thereafter appearing on a television commercial urging people to get back on planes and visit Disney World.[22] In July 2002, pooh-poohing the significance of corporate corruption and therefore the need for political remedies, he resorted to these words: "I believe people have taken a step back and asked, 'What's important in life?' You know, the bottom line and this corporate America stuff, is that important? Or is serving your neighbor, loving your neighbor like you'd like to be loved yourself?"[23] No contradiction here: the mediocre oilman with the triumphal career expresses the logic of a business civilization—consumption *as* citizenship; political withdrawal as a noble act. His not so comic equivalent was urging Congress to stick with tax-cut legislation of which almost all of the benefits would flow to the rich. How striking the contrast to World War II's dollar-a-year men, who attested by financial sacrifice—and noblesse oblige—to the cause's transcendent virtue (though romantics should not forget that war profiteering remained common)! Even trivially, children during that war collected scrap metal to link their fate to the country they loved. Air raid wardens did their part. So, of course, did soldiers, sailors, and war workers. So did those who accepted their rations without resorting to the black market. Yet in a drastic break from precedent, Bush proposed to cut taxes (especially for the better off) in wartime, promoting "bombs and caviar," in the words of the *Los Angeles Times*'s Ronald Brownstein, and guaranteeing "bigger federal deficits and a larger national debt, which amounts to shifting to defending the nation onto our children. . . . With this push to slash taxes during wartime, Bush broke from 140 years of history under presidents of both parties."[24]

Forget Afghanistan: After September 11, 2001, millions of Americans wanted to enlist in nation-building *at home.* They wanted to fight the horror, to take their fate in their hands, to make community palpable. They wanted to rescue, save, rebuild, restore, recover, rise up, go on. From their governments, nothing much materialized by way of work for them, for the principal version of patriotism on offer today demands little by way of duty or deliberation but much by way of bravado. What duty might ignite if it were mobilized now, we do not know. How Americans might have responded if their political leadership had invited them to join in a Marshall Plan that would, among other things, contain anti-Americanism and weaken the prospects of terror, we do not know. How they would have responded if told that it was now a matter of urgent self-defense as well as environmental sanity to free America from oil dependency, we do not know. These invitations were not issued. After the week of mutual aid, patriotism dwindled into symbolism. It was inert, unmobilized—at most, potential. In the current state of desiccated patriotism, Election Day is all the politics most citizens can manage and for most of them, that single day is not the culmination of their political activity but the sum of their political activity.

Take it as symbolic, then, that September 11, 2001, was, among other things, New York City's primary day for Democratic mayoral candidates. The primary was the least missed loss of that day. Terrorists smashed up our political life as well as our economic and personal lives. Our professionals, our public institutions, and our volunteers roared into action. Our police officers, our firefighters, our ironworkers, our emergency workers threw themselves into action in a style that deserves to be called noble. A mayor previously unmarked by eloquence responded eloquently. Take it as symbolic that our official politics, and our loss of them, didn't seem to matter much. Politics didn't live. America's survivors did.

5. PATRIOTISM UNEMBARRASSED?

A few weeks after September 11, my wife and I took down our flag. The lived patriotism of mutual aid had fallen off and the symbolic substitute felt stale. Leaving the flag up was too easy, too easily misunderstood as a triumphalist cliché. It didn't express my patriotic sentiment, which was turning toward political opposition of various sorts (though not in the key of the antiwar Left). The unexceptionable part of the war on al-Qaeda and the Taliban was in place, and while the United States proceeded to commit several terrible wrongs in Afghanistan and many vexatious questions remained about how to proceed there, these were not questions that could have been asked, let alone answered, without the intervention.

But with the passage of weeks, the hardening of American foreign policy and the Democratic cave-in produced a good deal more triumphalism than I could stomach. The patriotism of the activist passengers of Flight 93 slipped into the background; the spectacle that replaced them in my imagination was of unnamed, unrepresented detainees turned deportees. Deep patriotism, patriotic activity, was not bouncing back. Americans were watching more news, even more foreign news, but the political debates about means and ends that needed to happen were not happening. Democrats were fearful of looking unpatriotic—in other words, patriotism was functioning in the most poisonous way, chauvinistically, as a silencer. We needed defense, absolutely—lurking in the background was the most interesting question as to why we had not had it on September 11, 2001—but what *was* a "war on terror" that was, in effect and in principle, interminable, unlike the righteous war against imperial Japan and Nazi Germany, for it would be declared won (as Secretary of Defense Rumsfeld declared soon after the attacks) when and only when Americans *felt* safe? What kind of war was that, and what did missile defense and the reckless demolition of such treaties as Kyoto and anti-ballistic-missile defense have to do with it, and was there not the disconcerting fact that five or six individuals without a legitimate claim to democratic rule were calling all the important shots? By the time George W. Bush declared war without end against an "axis of evil" that no other nation on earth was willing to recognize as such (indeed, against whomever the president might determine we were at war against, just when he said so), declared further the unproblematic virtue of preemptive attacks, and made it clear that the United States regarded itself as a one-nation tribunal of "regime change," I felt again the old estrangement, the old shame and anger at being attached to a nation—*my* nation—ruled by runaway bullies, indifferent to principle, their lives manifesting supreme loyalty to private (though government-slathered) interests, quick to lecture dissenters about the merits of patriotism.

So once again patriotic sentiment bangs up against a wall of small-mindedness. Not since the last big bank loan to Argentina has credit been squandered as rapidly as when the administration of George W. Bush drained away the moral capital that came America's way after the massacres of that bright, scorched day of September.

For good and bad reasons people love to hate, love, and otherwise be transfixed by America, so it was not altogether predictable that instantly in September 2001, as the acrid stench still hung over lower Manhattan, millions of people on every continent would stand up to declare that they identified with America and Americans. Mirabile dictu! In candlelight vigils and front-page headlines, they declared a common humanity. *(Libération:* "We Are All New Yorkers." *Le Monde:* "America Struck, the World Seized with Dread," with a photo of the Statue of Liberty over the smoke and void.) To feel this solidarity, people had to move their grievances—and everyone has grievances against the imperial center—to the back burner, and many millions of people did that, did it spontaneously and, I think, sincerely. It was as if the awfulness of mass murder drove them not only to share in the losses but also to remember who they were and to draw a sharp existential line. On *this* side, the best of the American idea. On *that* side, the abyss of apocalyptic violence. Even as anti-Americans came forward to insinuate that time spent grieving for the American lost was time stolen from the more deserving victims of American power, anti-Americanism had never looked so ugly, petty, and frozen.

The outpouring of plain human solidarity was all the more impressive because to that date the Bush administration had already piled up a considerable bill due from the moment of its anointing by the Republic majority of the Supreme Court, delighting in go-it-alone crusades, its blustering imperiousness so unremitting in its unilateralism, so contemptuous of "a decent respect to the opinions of mankind," that it seemed to have lasted twenty-one years, not a mere twenty-one months, at the moment when the fuel-laden jet missiles exploded us into a new epoch. Osama bin Laden had, at a stroke, given anti-Americanism a bad name. When I spoke to Greek students at an American studies conference in Athens in April 2002, arguing that theirs too was the cause of the West against absolutism, that it was possible to dissent, as I do, from much of American foreign policy without changing sides, I was happily struck by their openness to my case. Greeks have a propensity to look for "dark forces" at work, frequently American, frequently Zionist, but by comparison with the suspicions circulating in recent years, I was pleasantly surprised at the straightforward sympathy, the absence of rancor.

Most of this goodwill is gone. Monumental arrogance is the hallmark of Bush's foreign policy—it *is* his foreign policy. Not surprisingly, anti-Americans are back in gloat mode. Hi-Yo Silver, the Lone Bully rides again. So I find myself thrown back on the familiar old brew of emotions—pain at the losses, love of Americans, suspicion of power, fury at the enemies of humanity who hijacked the jets and would cheerfully commit more mass murders, fury at their apologists who had not a moment to spare to mourn—and a vigorous dissent from Bush's recklessness. Patriotism must make room for a robust no, too.

If mobilized—it hasn't yet been—liberal patriotism would find many friends among troubled Americans. Perhaps surprisingly, the American public cares about acting abroad through alliances and with the sanction of the United Nations. It rejects—though not actively, by and large—Bush's go-it-alone adventures. On the domestic front, little love is now lost for the corporate chiefs, those of gargantuan appetite for whom this administration so loyally fronted until they were shocked, shocked to discover there was gambling going on in the casino. With the bursting of the stock market bubble, deregulation no longer looks like an economic cure-all. Whom do Americans admire now, whom do we trust? Americans did not take much reminding that when skyscrapers were on fire, they needed fire fighters and police officers, not Enron hustlers or Arthur Andersen accountants. Yet we confront an administration that passes out capital gains and inheritance tax cuts to the plutocracy, whose idea of sacrifice is that somebody in a blue collar should perform it for low wages.

Surely many Americans are primed for a patriotism of action, not pledges or SUVs festooned with American flags. The era beginning September 11, 2001, would be a superb time to crack the jingoists' claim to a monopoly of patriotic virtue. Instead of letting minions of corporate power run away with the flag (while dashing offshore, gobbling oil, and banking their tax credits), we need to remake the tools of our public life—our schools, social services, transport, and, not least, security. We need to remember that the exemplary patriots are the members of the emergency community of mutual aid who brought down Flight 93, not the born-again war devotees who cherish martial virtues but somehow succeeded in getting themselves deferred from the armed forces.

Post-Vietnam liberals have an opening now, freed of our 1960s flag anxiety and our automatic rejection of the use of force. How to feel—and live—pride in the nation when the nation's power is hijacked? Only by working to ripen our institutions. To live out a democratic pride, not a slavish surrogate, we badly need liberal patriotism, robust, unapologetic, and uncowed. For patriotic sentiment, that mysterious (and therefore both necessary and dangerous) attachment to the nation moves only in one of two directions: backward, toward chauvinistic bluster and popular silence, or forward, toward popular energy and democratic renewal. Said the French essayist Charles Péguy: "Everything begins in mysticism and ends in politics." Patriotism, as always, remains to be lived.

It's time for the patriotism of mutual aid, not just symbolic displays, not catechisms or self-congratulation. It's time to diminish the gap between the nation we love and the justice we also love. It's time for the real America to stand up.

NOTES

1. Richard Slotkin, personal communication.
2. James Baldwin, *The Fire Next Time* (New York: Dial, 1963).
3. ABC News, *Good Morning America,* September 14, 2001.
4. George Orwell, "Notes on Nationalism," www.resort.com/~prime8/Orwell/nationalism.html.
5. Clyde Haberman, "60s Lessons on How Not to Wave Flag," *New York Times,* September 19, 2001, A20.
6. Friedrich Nietzsche, *Beyond Good and Evil,* trans. Walter Kaufmann (New York: Vintage, 1966), part 8, ¶241.

7. Pierre Bourdieu, *Distinction: A Social Critique of the Judgement of Taste,* trans. Richard Nice (Cambridge, Mass.: Harvard University Press, 1984).

8. John H. Schaar, "The Case for Patriotism," *American Review* 17 (1973): 59.

9. Randolph Bourne, "The State" (1918), available at http://www.antiwar.com/bourne.php.

10. Benedict Anderson, *Imagined Communities: Reflections on the Origin and Spread of Nationalism* (London: Verso, 1983).

11. Lincoln in *Collected Works of Abraham Lincoln,* ed. Roy P. Basler (New Brunswick, N.J.: Rutgers University Press, 1953), 4:240, quoted in Schaar, "The Case for Patriotism," 70.

12. Schaar, "The Case for Patriotism," 68.

13. Cited by Anthony Lewis, "A Failure of Reason," *New York Times,* December 16, 2000 (available at http://www. legitgov.org/Lewis_failure_reason.htm).

14. Richard Rorty, *Achieving Our Country: Leftist Thought in Twentieth-Century America* (Cambridge, Mass.: Harvard University Press, 1998), 35.

15. Noam Chomsky, interview with B-92 Radio, September 19, 2001, http://www.b92.net/intervju/eng/2001/0919-chomsky.phtml.

16. Chomsky, interview with Suzy Hansen, January 16, 2002, http://www.salon.com/people/feature/2002/01/16/chomskky/index.html, and "Terror and Just Response," July 2, 2002, http://www.zmag.org/content/showarticle.cfm?SectionID=11&ItemID2063. At that, the evidence Chomsky alluded to was skimpy and at least partially misattributed. See the letter to *Salon* by Carroll Bogert of Human Rights Watch, http://www.salon.com/people/letters/2002/01/22/chomsky/index.html.

17. Schaar, "The Case for Patriotism," 72.

18. Robert N. Bellah et al., *Habits of the Heart: Individualism and Commitment in American Life* (Berkeley, Calif.: University of California Press, 1985), 72, uses the term "lifestyle enclave." The commonplace use of "network" came later.

19. Mickey Kaus, *The End of Equality* (New York: Basic, 1992). Kaus argued that liberals are mistaken to overemphasize economic inequality, and I do not follow him all the way to his bitter end. Surely the appalling inequalities in the ratio between CEO and worker salaries, for example, of the order of five hundred to one, do not serve the entrepreneurial purposes that laissez-faire advocates rejoice in. The fact that it would take confiscatory tax rates to eliminate this discrepancy does not mean that lesser reductions are pointless. Reducing the high-low income gap would work toward the principle of social equality.

20. Bill McKibben, "It's Easy Being Green," *Mother Jones* (July/August 2002): 36.

21. See http://abcnews.go.com/sections/politics/DailyNews/BUSHPICK_PROFILE.html, citing a 1989 piece in the *Washington Post.*

22. Speaking to airline workers in Chicago on September 27, 2001, Bush said: "When they struck, they wanted to create an atmosphere of fear. And one of the great goals of this nation's war is to restore public confidence in the airline industry. It's to tell the traveling public, 'Get on board. Do your business around the country. Fly and enjoy America's great destination spots. Get down to Disney World in Florida. Take your families and enjoy life, the way we want it to be enjoyed.'" Available online at http://www.whitehouse.gov/news/releases/2001/09/20010927-1.html.

23. Judy Keen, "Bush Trying to Ride out Corporate Flap," *USA Today,* July 12, 2002, 4A.

24. Ronald Brownstein, "Bush Breaks with 140 Years of History in Plan for Wartime Tax Cut," *Los Angeles Times,* January 13, 2003, A10.

9

Vulgar Nationalism and Insulting Nicknames: George Orwell's Progressive Reflections on Race

Anthony Stewart

Questions of race rarely come up in discussions of George Orwell, or if they do, he is normally gathered unflatteringly into that familiar fraternity (Kipling, Forster, and Conrad, principally) who are so insufficiently critical of the empire as to appear in favor of it. Orwell's five-year stint in the Indian Imperial Police, from 1922 through 1927, further aids in this somewhat reductive association. Ranajit Guha, for instance, states that *Burmese Days,* Orwell's first novel, "has no room in it even for the standard liberal value of racial tolerance. It is peppered with phrases that speak explicitly of his disapproval of the Burmese not only for the color of their skin but for what he obviously perceived as their cultural and moral inferiority."[1] Speaking of Orwell's Burmese writings—"A Hanging," "Shooting an Elephant," and *Burmese Days*—Douglas Kerr sees a cognitive pattern emerging:

> First, what is Burmese is seen as grotesque and alienating. Then, a romantic epiphany reveals a kinship between the (male) observer and the object of observation, seeming to offer a romantic integration into a kindly and unalienated natural life. But to glimpse this possibility is also to see that it is impossible to sustain, for the constraints of ideology—the roles provided for him by his place in the imperial project, by his race, his gender, his class and profession—drive him back into postures of antagonism, and acts of violence.[2]

Elsewhere, Kerr makes a broader observation about Orwell's ostensible superiority complex, noting "a passionate belief in equality" which is "at war with an ineradicable disbelief in it, so that his most eloquent statements of the right of all people to be treated equally, as human beings, are haunted by the suspicion that some people are more human than others."[3] Certainly, one need not look far in *Burmese Days* for evidence of a problematic racial attitude. The question that arises for me, though, is whose attitude is it? Is the racial attitude "obviously," to use Guha's word, that of Orwell or, for that matter, is the pattern of romantic epiphany, kinship, and then antagonism that of Orwell? It seems more likely that the novel expresses the representative attitudes of a contemporaneous narrator of an anti-imperialist novel set in an outpost of the empire. Since the narrator need not be Orwell, to equate him with the views stated or, for that matter, implied by the narrator oversimplifies the complicated relationship between the author and the narrator, a particularly fascinating relationship in Orwell's fiction.

Phyllis Lassner, in describing the challenges of authorial positioning when representing a cultural experience the author does not share, invokes Orwell's essay "Marrakech" when she asks the following question about Phyllis Bottome's 1950 novel, *Under the Skin:* "can the white colonial writer represent an authentic or indigenous colonial experience if her representation can only be figured in the European political history and cultural traditions that constitute her language?"[4] I will return to Lassner's question at the end of this essay. For now, the question serves as a critical first step in a more nuanced understanding of Orwell's views regarding race. Lassner's attention to the onus that is necessarily borne by the white colonial writer suggests that there is at least room to consider just how much one can infer about a novelist's attitudes toward a particular group by reading one of his or her novels. In Orwell's case, basing such inferences on *Burmese Days* alone is all the more suspect, since his voluminous nonfiction (which was widely available even before the publication of the twenty-volume *Complete Works of George Orwell* in 1998), in which he speaks in something more closely approximating his own voice, includes topical statements on race that make his progressive attitudes and intentions quite clear.

But the questions surrounding *Burmese Days* and Orwell's putative attitude toward the Burmese are interesting ones and worth some attention before moving on to the issues surrounding the author's position, as expressed in his nonfiction, regarding race. Even if we accept for the moment an equation between Orwell and the narrator, the characterizations within the novel still bear a more subtle reading when the text is given close attention. While a much longer discussion regarding this subject is possible in the context of *Burmese Days,* a couple of examples from the beginning of the novel will, I hope, be suggestive.

U Po Kyin, the scheming Burmese magistrate who engineers the downfall of the British protagonist, John Flory, is described at the beginning of the novel as physically enormous, "and yet shapely and even beautiful in his grossness; for the Burmese do not sag and bulge like white men, but grow fat symmetrically, like fruits swelling" (2:1).[5] This willingness to generalize self-assuredly the attributes of an entire group of people ("the Burmese") as well as exoticizing these attributes as "beautiful" is certainly unsettling to early twenty-first-century eyes. But U Po Kyin is identified, in fact, as quite unusual within the Burmese population of the novel. He is the only obese character and is said to be "quite proud of his fatness," seeing his "accumulated flesh as the symbol of his greatness. Obesity is a sign of accomplishment. He who had once been obscure and hungry was now fat, rich, and feared. He was swollen with the bodies of his enemies; a thought from which he extracted something very near poetry" (2:11). This added qualification of U Po Kyin's physical description goes beyond merely generalizing about "the Burmese" and instead locates the magistrate quite particularly within a specific cultural context. This description makes a telling political point. Within a population distinguished by poverty and starvation, obesity signifies differently than it would for "white men."

This early description of a central Burmese character suggests U Po Kyin is rare among the Burmese, and yet he is also apparently representative of a "trait" of Burmese people, their characteristic swelling like fruit instead of bulging and sagging "like white men" (2:1). The relation between U Po Kyin as one individual and as a representative of what "the Burmese" are like in general typifies the problem of rendering members of groups to which one does not belong, the problem Lassner points out. The comment about how "white men" grow fat attracts our attention much less than that about "the Burmese" because Orwell was a white man and, whether consciously or not, it's as easy to assume his authority on white men's growth patterns as it is to impugn his knowledge of, and criticize his willingness to generalize about, the physical characteristics of "the Burmese."

This tension, and more importantly, what it proves or does not prove about Orwell's racial attitudes, becomes more obvious still as we sample other descriptions of U Po Kyin. When the narrator, for instance, describes the magistrate this way, "His brain, though cunning, was quite barbaric, and it never worked except for some definite end; mere meditation was beyond him" (2:4), we must ask ourselves if U Po Kyin is being described for the purpose of establishing this character within the novel or if this assertion, like the swelling attribute, is another generalization about some essential quality, this time something that might be called the "Burmese mind." Since no other character, Burmese or English, schemes in the novel quite as U Po Kyin does (although a case might be made for Mrs. Lackersteen's attempts to find her niece, Elizabeth, a husband), we are safe in assuming that this cunning barbarity of mind is attributable only to him. In fact, bearing in mind how the novel concludes, establishing U Po Kyin's cunning barbarity is essential to constructing the plot. Does such a conclusion imply that other Burmese are not of a similar "mind"? That such cunning barbarity is, in fact, rare among Burmese people? What of the English characters in the novel? Is cunning and a lack of meditativeness characteristic of them or of oppressors in general? It does not appear that any conclusion may confidently be drawn on this subject, except that U Po Kyin—one Burmese character—is possessed of such a mind.

This brief consideration of the introductory descriptions of U Po Kyin leaves us with a sense of how the relationship between the author and a character from a background the author does not share inevitably exposes the author to charges of bigotry. It is true that Orwell bears something of a historical onus, by dint of being English, middle-class, and male at the height of the British Empire, a constellation of personal attributes that—in countless others who shared the same cultural inheritance—resulted in the feelings of moral and cultural superiority typical of the bigot. But even if we accept the dubious equation between Orwell and the narrator as a pretext for a reading of *Burmese Days,* the novel still reveals subtleties regarding race that are frequently overlooked, subtleties that do not reveal anything "obvious" about Orwell's racial attitudes.

However, the equation of the narrator and Orwell is not the point here, although an engagement with the assortment of brief statements he makes about race in his nonfiction suggests that he was actually possessed of a quite sophisticated appreciation of questions pertaining to race, which adds force to an argument about the subtleties in *Burmese Days.* In addition, as with his critiques of totalitarianism, imperialism, and middle-class socialism, Orwell was unsparing in his attempts to convey to his readers, principally other members of the English middle class, that improving one's attitudes toward members of groups to which one does not belong and becoming more aware of one's own prejudices are essential to life in the twentieth century. His nonfiction shows him to have a quite progressive view of race, and reading these excerpts contributes to a fuller understanding of this complex and still-relevant figure.

That Orwell had quite strong opinions pertaining to questions of race within the British Empire is hardly surprising. His five years as an Indian Imperial Police officer put him in close and extended contact with at least one of the empire's subject groups and gave him ample opportunity to consider the morality—as well as the long-term efficacy—of imperialism. In "Marrakech," written in 1939, he offers the following quite well-known reflection: "When you walk through a town like this—two hundred thousand inhabitants, of whom at least twenty thousand own literally nothing except the rags they stand up in—when you see how the people live, and still more how easily they die, it is always difficult to believe that you are walking among human beings. All colonial empires are in reality founded upon that fact" (11:417). The essay ends with a cautionary pronouncement on the nature of imperialism: "But there is one thought which every white man (and in this connection it doesn't matter twopence if he calls himself a Socialist) thinks when he sees a black army marching past. 'How much longer can we go on kidding these people? How long before they turn their guns in the other direction?'" (11:420). This last observation points up the intense feelings of injustice that are part and parcel of any enterprise of systematic racial oppression. The imperialist's profound knowledge that he is unwelcome reinforces his awareness that he is also unsafe. This combination of injustice and fear requires of the imperial officer actions that he himself knows to be wrong as well as the self-delusion to hide the injustice from himself.

Orwell's invention of doublethink in *Nineteen Eighty-Four* might usefully be applied to this mechanism of imperialist self-delusion, since the most important element of doublethink is "to forget whatever it was necessary to forget, then to draw it back into memory again at the moment when it was needed, and then promptly to forget it again; and above all, to apply the same process to the process itself" (9:37). This last part, "consciously to induce unconsciousness, and then, once again, to become unconscious of the act of hypnosis you had just performed" (9:37–38), is characterized by the narrator of *Nineteen Eighty-Four* (who is not necessarily Orwell!) as "the ultimate subtlety" (9:37). This kind of subtlety, as Orwell makes clear in "Marrakech," is absolutely imperative to the maintenance of empire.

Orwell also wrote an essay called "Charles Dickens" in 1939. "Charles Dickens" typifies the character of most of Orwell's observations about race—brief, almost offhand remarks on the way to making some other point. But again here, the remark is telling. While characterizing Dickens as a "free intelligence, a type hated with equal hatred by all the smelly little orthodoxies which are now contending for our souls" (12:56), Orwell digresses in order to make the following point about what he praises as Dickens's lack of "vulgar nationalism":

> All peoples who have reached the point of becoming nations tend to despise foreigners, but there is not much doubt that the English-speaking races are the worst offenders. One can see this from the fact that as soon as they become fully aware of

any foreign race, they invent an insulting nickname for it. Wop, Dago, Froggy, Squarehead, Kike, Sheeny, Nigger, Wog, Chink, Greaser, Yellowbelly—these are merely a selection. Any time before 1870 the list would have been shorter, because the map of the world was different from what it is now, and there were only three or four foreign races that had fully entered into the English consciousness. (12:34)

Apart from the shock value of the extended catalog of racial epithets—the sort of strategy only available to an author quite certain of his own feelings (for better or worse, it should be said) about race—Orwell's criticism of vulgar nationalism highlights the pernicious ways in which such naming works. He asserts that the entry of foreign races into the "English consciousness" leads inevitably to the naming of these others by the English. By listing this catalog of insulting nicknames, he makes clear his awareness that epithets diminish the subjectivity of the group being named by designating that group in the eyes of the empowered English instead of acceding to the group's wishes to be designated according to its members' own preferences. The catalog also maximizes the possibility that just about any contemporary British reader might eventually stumble upon some name that he or she has intemperately used, adding to the rhetorical effect of the passage by exposing the reader's own lapses into vulgar nationalism.

A related observation occurs in an "As I Please" column from December 10, 1943,[6] in which Orwell addresses what he calls the "horrors of the colour war." Conceding first that the many complex issues that militate against the arrival of the socialist revolution are larger than the power of any one person, he recommends a couple of small gestures that each individual might make to improve relations between the privileged and the disenfranchised in the meantime. He counsels that his readers "at least remember that the colour problem exists," and "avoid using insulting nicknames" (16:24). The column concludes by criticizing the habitual but hurtful language usage that many engage in without realizing its effects. The column indicts writers who, Orwell feels, should know better than to traffic unthinkingly in names that are hurtful to members of other groups:

It is an astonishing thing that few journalists, even in the Left wing press, bother to find out which names are and which are not resented by members of other races. The word "native," which makes any Asiatic boil with rage, and which has been dropped even by British officials in India these ten years past, is flung about all over the place. "Negro" is habitually printed with a small n, a thing most Negroes resent. One's information about these matters needs to be kept up to date. I have just been carefully going through the proofs of a reprinted book of mine [*Burmese Days*], cutting out the word "Chinaman" wherever it occurred and substituting "Chinese." The book was written less than a dozen years ago, but in the intervening time "Chinaman" has become a deadly insult. Even "Mahomedan" is now beginning to be resented: one should say "Moslem." These things are childish, but then nationalism is childish. And after all we ourselves do not actually like being called "Limeys" or "Britishers." (16:24)

This "As I Please" column shows a writer who has done his homework and is now urging others to realize that there is still more work to be done and that can be done on an individual basis.

Randall Kennedy, in his remarkable book *Nigger: The Strange Career of a Troublesome Word,* notes how African Americans "furiously objected to Negro being spelled with a lower- as opposed to an uppercase *N,* and on March 7, 1930, the editors of the *New York Times* announced that the paper would henceforth capitalize the *N* in Negro."[7] This editorial decision, in other words, is taken some thirteen years before Orwell's "As I Please" column and yet he still feels called upon to point out the practice of journalists who continue to call groups of people by anachronistic names they have grown to resent. That naming is, in his words, something that "needs to be kept up to date" (16:24) imputes a benevolence to some contemporary writers that they may not have deserved but also makes clear that for those inclined to update their information periodically, the objective is hardly insurmountable.

Orwell's own employment of racial epithets has made him the subject of revision by the scholar who has probably done the most recently to consolidate his literary stature. The revision highlights not only the unavoidable sensitivity but also the prospect for good intentions to go awry when the subject is race and the legacy of an iconic figure is at stake. Orwell's essay entitled "Not Counting Niggers," a review of Clarence K. Streit's book *Union Now,* was published in *Adelphi* in July 1939, only two months before the Second World War broke out. In *The Collected Essays, Journalism and Letters of George Orwell,* edited by Sonia Orwell and Ian Angus, published in 1968, Orwell's essay was included under its original title. The shocking title cannot help but draw one's eye in the table of contents of volume one of the four-volume collection. However, in *The Complete Works of George Orwell,* edited by Peter Davison, and completed in 1998, the same essay is included under the remarkably benign title "Review: Clarence K. Streit, *Union Now,* July 1939," delivering—it is fair to say—hardly the same rhetorical punch as the original title.

Davison's footnote regarding the essay's title—that it was "originally published with the ironic title 'Not Counting Niggers'"—is an inadequate gloss to say the least. While it is true that volumes ten through twenty of the *Complete Works* adhere to a format that lists the entries according to genre ("Letter," "Article," "Review," and so on), and so the essay is listed as a review, the alteration of the title robs the essay of its initial power to shock its reader into attention, a strategy Orwell used intentionally and, it should be said, courageously in giving the essay the title he chose. In July 1939, as the world readied itself for a conflict intended, at least in part, to stand against the Nazi doctrine of racial superiority, the decision by a white, English writer to include the word "niggers" in the title of a book review was a significant and deliberate one. To relegate the original title to a two-line footnote suggests the ongoing ability of the word "nigger" to cast suspicion on anyone who uses it, even when he or she invokes it in order to make a crucial point *against* racial injustice.

It is worth speculating that perhaps the reason this remarkable essay is so rarely discussed by critics might be that the use of the word may appear to reflect badly on Orwell, giving aid and comfort to those inclined to make assertions about his racial insensitivity. I would argue instead, though, that the title uses a shocking word in order to expose another, equally shocking, injustice that was able to continue as long as the white subjects of the British Empire were not forced to confront it.

To alter the title of this particular essay, even in the interest of formal consistency, reiterates the conspiracy of silence around a hateful word for perhaps no greater reason than to spare the author, specifically the author's reputation, some perceived embarrassment. Moreover, Sonia Orwell and Ian Angus had as much justification to elide the offending word in 1968 as did Davison thirty years later. Memories of the Nottingham and Notting Hill race riots of 1958, as well as the Tory election slogan from the 1960s, "If you want a nigger neighbour, vote Labour," would have still been fresh at the time of the completion of *The Collected Essays, Journalism, and Letters of George Orwell,* suggesting an atmosphere in Britain rife with racial tension. And yet, they chose to leave the original title intact.

Of course, it's fair to speculate that perhaps the editors of the 1968 collection determined that the sense of the essay would justify the title. (There is no editorial comment about the title in the 1968 collection.) In 1998, with the ethnocultural makeup of potential readers—both academic and popular—having changed quite substantially since 1968, it is most probable that, for Davison, the altered title is a gesture of sensitivity, albeit one that carries with it the unexpected effects I have tried to set out here. While I gladly extend to Davison's editorial decision the benefit of the doubts I have raised here, I nevertheless support the original title and will use it here.

"Not Counting Niggers" announces in no uncertain terms the importance of race to Orwell's thinking and how critically he viewed relationships between the powerful and the disenfranchised. Bernard Crick is one of the very few critics who mentions the essay at all, although he diminishes it as merely "another violently anti-war article" by Orwell and as a part of the writer's "anti-militarism or crypto-pacifism" in the months leading up to the war.[8] But the essay's remarkable intensity is felt most strongly within the context of a discussion of Orwell and race. "Not Counting Niggers" takes issue with Clarence K. Streit's proposal that the democratic nations—"the USA, France, Great Britain, the self-governing dominions of the British Empire, and the smaller European democracies, not including Czechoslovakia" (11:359)—form a union of free trade and mutual economic and military support. Orwell cannot overstate his opposition to such a proposal: "Like everyone of his school of thought, Mr Streit has coolly lumped the huge British and French empires—in essence nothing but mechanisms for exploiting cheap coloured labour—under the heading of democracies!" (11:360). Calling Britain and France democracies offends Orwell deeply because of the ways in which these imperial powers have treated their dark-skinned subjects.

From this point he widens his attack, targeting what he sees as the double standard employed by those who argue for a socialist revolution on the one hand, but who are unwilling or unable to conceive of the empire's colored subjects as worthy of equal treatment as human beings, on the other.

> In a prosperous country, above all in an imperialist country, left-wing politics are always partly humbug. There can be no real reconstruction that would not lead to at least a temporary drop in the English standard of life, which is another way of saying that the majority of left-wing politicians and publicists are people who earn their living by demanding something that they don't genuinely want. They are red-hot revolutionaries as long as all goes well, but every real emergency reveals instantly that they are shamming. (11:358)

As with the "As I Please" column from December 10, 1943, in which he laments the "colour war," Orwell points out what he feels should already be apparent to those who supposedly observe their culture most closely, namely, other intellectuals. He finds instead the same self-interest that enables imperialist oppression based on the imposition of a racial hierarchy to continue.

The attack on Streit's proposal of a military and economic union of democracies reaches its boiling point when the essay compares Britain and France—unfavorably—with Nazi Germany:

> Mr Streit is letting cats out of bags, but *all* phrases like "Peace Bloc," "Peace Front," etc contain some such implication; all imply a tightening-up of the existing structure. The unspoken clause is always "not counting niggers." . . . What we always forget is that the overwhelming bulk of the British proletariat does not live in Britain, but in Asia and Africa. It is not in Hitler's power, for instance, to make a penny an hour a normal industrial wage; it is perfectly normal in India, and we are at great pains to keep it so. One gets some idea of the real relationship of England and India when one reflects that the *per capita* annual income in England is something over £80, and in India about £7. It is quite common for an Indian coolie's leg to be thinner than the average Englishman's arm. And there is nothing racial in this, for well-fed members of the same races are of normal physique; it is due to simple starvation. This is the system which we all live on and which we denounce when there seems to be no danger of its being altered. (11:360–61)

This passage is remarkable for a number of reasons, not the least of which is how rarely it is cited when we consider its content, the time in twentieth-century history when it was written, and how much has been written about its author in general. Giving voice to the usually unspoken clause breaks the taboo that conventionally disrupts reflection upon the stakes underlying expressions like "peace bloc" and "peace front." Pointing out that the unjust working conditions endured by Indians and Africans has nothing to do with Hitler implicitly compares the injustice that undergirds the empire to the injustice that the empire is set to confront on the battlefield. Finally, the observation about the Indian "coolie's" leg and the average Englishman's arm lends further context to the ethnographic extrapolations about the Burmese swelling like fruit instead of bulging and sagging like "white men" that begin *Burmese Days*. In this essay, published five years after the novel, the Indian and the Englishman are held in a common physiology when both are "well-fed." Perhaps this commonality is only breached when members of each group are overfed, as is U Po Kyin. (Just as likely, though, Orwell's own observations may again be seen as distinguishable and much more politically sensitive than are those of the novel's narrator.) In "Not Counting Niggers," the physiological comparison is made in order to highlight the starving of one group as a result of the self-interest of the other.

Both the exploitation of nonwhite labor and the unwillingness or inability of intellectuals to note this exploitation appear again in "Culture and Democracy," a lecture Orwell delivered on November 22, 1941, as part of a lecture series organized by the Fabian Society. Because there were problems with the publication of the lecture in book form along with some of the other lectures from the series, Davison warns that "Culture and Democracy" should be read with the caveat that Orwell was unhappy with its final printed version. That said, the section that concerns me here is completely consistent with his comments in the "As I Please" column discussed earlier in this essay and with "Not Counting Niggers."

In "Culture and Democracy," Orwell argues that one of the "worst things about democratic society in the last twenty years has been the difficulty of any straight talking or thinking" (13:69). His example is "the basic fact about our social structure. That is, that it is founded on cheap coloured labour. As the world is now constituted, we are all standing on the backs of half-starved Asiatic coolies. The standard of living of the British working class has been and is artificially high because it is based on a parasitic economy" (13:69). While it would be easy to hold the upper classes solely responsible for the structural inequities he describes and, by extension, equate the plight of the working class to that of Britain's nonwhite imperial subjects, Orwell's argument is most notable for its willingness to cast the working class as complicit in the empire's racial oppression. This criticism is more remarkable still as it breaches Orwell's well-documented sympathy for the British working class in order to make a point that he feels supersedes this allegiance. "The working class is," he says, "as much involved in the exploitation of coloured labour as anybody else, but so far as I know, nowhere in the British Press in the last twenty years—at any rate in no part of the Press likely to get wide attention—do you find any clear admission of that fact or any straight talking about it" (13:69–70). Whereas in "Not Counting Niggers," the interests of the working class and the oppressed subjects of India and Africa are equated— Africans and Indians are described there as "the overwhelming bulk of the British proletariat," who just happen to live outside Britain—here, Orwell's critique of imperial oppression goes a step farther, as he contrasts the interests of the British working class to those of Indians and Africans in order to emphasize the injustice perpetrated upon the latter, in part by the selfishness of the former.

"Culture and Democracy" sketches two "policies" open to a nation "living on coloured labour" (13:70). One is the "master-race" policy, keeping in mind that "that is how Hitler talks to his people, because he is a totalitarian leader and can speak frankly on certain subjects" (13:70). The master-race policy announces that the English should "get together and squeeze as much out of [the "inferior" races] as we can" (13:70). Obviously, equating this policy to Hitler's makes its own criticism of the policy itself. As in "Not Counting Niggers," the point is that it is the self-interested immorality of rank-and-file Britons, not the treachery and evil of Hitler, that is the prime mechanism keeping so abominably low the living standards in the colonies inhabited by subjects whose cultural inheritance may not be traced back to Europe. Germany's dictator serves as a useful rhetorical prop in emphasizing the enormity of the racial injustice that Orwell sees.

The other policy, call it the "justice" policy, argues that the English "cannot go on exploiting the world for ever, we must do justice to the Indians, the Chinese and all the rest of them, and since our standard of living is artificially high and the process of adjustment is bound to be painful and difficult, we must be ready to lower that standard of living for the time being" (13:70). This second policy—the one, obviously, favored by Orwell—attempts to reactivate the senses of morality and justice that the machinery of imperialism must impede in order to allow it to continue functioning.

As I've already said, the social, political, and historical contexts in which Orwell found himself made it likely that he would have some strong opinions regarding race, at least within the British Empire. But it is quite remarkable how his interest in such questions extended to the treatment of the African American soldiers who arrived in Europe during the war and, from there, to the experience of African Americans living in the United States, a nation he never visited.

In an "As I Please" from May 26, 1944, Orwell discusses the phenomenon of personal advertisements—British women and men advertising in publications like *The Matrimonial Post and Fashionable Marriage Advertiser* in the attempt to find spouses. The pretext for his discussion, though, is his opening remark about anti-British feeling in the American army. Part of this sentiment seems to be the result of what the Americans perceive as an overly permissive attitude towards interracial romance. A young American soldier tells Orwell that upon asking an American military policeman, "How's England?" after landing in the country, the MP replied, "The girls here walk out with niggers" (16:230). Orwell comments on this exchange, "That was the salient fact about England, from the M.P.'s point of view" (16:230). He continues by talking about anti-British feeling in general, but his decision to commence the piece with an observation about what appears to be a substantive difference between Great Britain and the United States, a difference that expresses itself along racial lines, enables him to register an important political point before continuing his discussion of marital ambitions among the English.

While he does not reflect any further on this incident in that particular column, Orwell returns to the question of racial treatment, specifically by Americans, a few months later, in another "As I Please," this one from August 11, 1944. Here, he addresses the problem of "colour bars," in which people of color are disallowed from entering or turned out from dance halls, restaurants, and other places of amusement, "presumably to please the American soldiers" (16:328) who form an important part of the establishments' clientele. This column is particularly interesting because in it Orwell takes an explicit stand against color prejudice and, more importantly, exhorts his readers to do likewise. "It is immensely important," he writes, "to be vigilant against this kind of thing, and to make as much public fuss as possible whenever it happens. For this is one of those matters in which making a fuss can achieve something" (16:328). A very hopeful and progressive sentiment, Orwell's advice regarding the protest of segregation accords with his well-known opposition to behaviors born of convention.

What he says next, however, shows that while he is determined to draw his readers' attention to the injustice of bigotry he does not come at these issues from a particularly sophisticated or experienced point of view. He contends that there is no "legal disability against coloured people" in England, adding "what is more, there is very little popular colour feeling" in his country at all (16:328–29). When we remember that the "As I Please" columns were topical pieces written for *Tribune* over the four-year period from 1943 through 1947, it must also be remembered that some of the observations he makes in the column are just opinions, sometimes registered while moving toward some other, more central, point. This particular column exhibits this topical weakness, as he seems to hurry to correct his sweeping, and improbable, announcement about the lack of "popular colour feeling" in England by adding, parenthetically, "This is not due to any inherent virtue in the British people, as our behaviour in India shows. It is due to the fact that in Britain itself there is no colour problem" (16:329). Interestingly, even as he qualifies the initial statement, he reiterates its substance, thus solving nothing. This kind of logical sloppiness was uncharacteristic of Orwell's writing and invites some speculation on its possible causes.

One might ask why he would make such a muddle of a seemingly straightforward, if misguided, assertion. The answer may lie in Orwell's strong sense of patriotism. It is noticeable that whenever he recounts an incident in which someone is being insulted because of his or her race it is always the fault of "a very small minority" (16:329) or the actions of "the tiny percentage of colour-snobs who exist among us" (16:329). Of course, as often as not, by Orwell's reckoning, at least, the offending bigot is an American, further reinforcing, it would appear, the assertion that the British are not afflicted by such problems.

Asserting that these are the bigoted actions of a very small minority or a tiny percentage of British people achieves two effects. First, it reassures the reader that he or she is more than likely not guilty of such actions (thus creating the opposite effect from that accomplished in "Charles Dickens," in which the extravagant listing of racial epithets cannot help but eventually include one the reader might have used in an intemperate moment). This appeal to a sense of British solidarity resists the "bad name" (16:329) they might otherwise get from the actions of an ostensible few. Second, and equally importantly, it makes the objective of exposing such prejudice and (so the logic goes) eliminating it seem all the more possible, instead of a mere wish, since only a very few people are guilty of it in the first place. As he ends his reflections on the matter of the "colour-bar," he reiterates this point about what is possible, stating that "the ordinary Indian, Negro or Chinese can only be protected against petty insult if other ordinary people are willing to exert themselves on his behalf" (16:329).

In trying to understand the nature of Orwell's proclamation about the lack of color feeling in Britain, we must also acknowledge the particular historical moment during which the remark was made. He was writing his "As I Please" columns in the last days before the beginning of large-scale migration into England from the Caribbean, which began in 1948. Many of the motivations for racial animosity that are expressed toward immigrant populations when they appear in a new land in any noticeable numbers ("they're taking our jobs," "they don't live the way we live," "we've always done things our way and their ways are different," "I don't want my daughter to marry one") do not obtain as much when the minority population is only a temporary novelty, as the African American soldiers were to Britons during the war. Put bluntly, the Brits knew the American blacks weren't staying. They were citizens somewhere else and so there was less incentive to behave negatively toward them as became the case post-1948, when race relations within England quickly became a source of conscious tension and, occasionally, violence.

By contrast, the complex history of race relations in the United States was simply transferred across the Atlantic Ocean, to be renewed on the other side, war or no war. As Eric Sundquist points out in his companion to Ralph Ellison's *Invisible Man,* "The campaign for what was called the 'Double V'—victory abroad in the military, and victory at home against racism and discrimination—became a focal point for political organizing and a theme in many books and essays aimed at the overthrow of segregation."[9] So the double vision Orwell seems to have in talking about the experiences of African American soldiers in Britain aptly expresses the schizophrenia of being black and American, which is further compounded by living, temporarily, in a society that tolerates your presence without the explicit hostility to which you have become accustomed at "home."

The mixed messages conveyed by this "As I Please" suggest further the nature of Orwell's untutored and hard-won progressiveness on matters of race. Christopher Hitchens describes Orwell's self-examining work to overcome his own inherited prejudices. Orwell

> had to suppress his distrust and dislike of the poor, his revulsion from the "coloured" masses who teemed throughout the empire, his suspicion of Jews, his awkwardness with women and his anti-intellectualism. By teaching himself in theory and practice, some of the teaching being rather pedantic, he became a great humanist. Only one of his inherited prejudices—the shudder generated by homosexuality—appears to have resisted the process of self-mastery. And even that "perversion" he often represented as a misfortune or deformity created by artificial or cruel conditions; his repugnance—when he remembered to make this false distinction—was for the "sin" and not the "sinner."[10]

The rather pedantic autodidacticism Hitchens describes cannot accommodate comfortably the prospect that it might have been more than a mere few among the British who were making nonwhites feel unwelcome in the dance halls and restaurants of wartime Britain. And yet, for all of this, Orwell could still exhibit a quite subtle understanding when it came to prejudice as experienced by a population with whom he had little in common, from a nation he'd never seen. This ability is probably at its clearest in his 1940 review of Richard Wright's novel *Native Son*.

In his reading of Wright's groundbreaking novel, Orwell shows a rare ability to extrapolate beyond his own experiences to those of America's black population. His observations about Bigger Thomas's mental state are especially astute. Orwell's reading seizes upon the most subtle elements of Thomas's fate: "The instant that suspicion falls on him he is hunted down and condemned to death in a fury of race-hatred that does away with any pretence at justice" (12:152–53). That Orwell has no experience of the lynch mob or the mentality that spawns it does not impede his ability to see the relationship between perception and reality for someone who, because so disenfranchised, is guilty when the mob says he's guilty, irrespective of his own motivations or the mitigating factor that Thomas's killing of Mary Dalton was an accident.

Bigger Thomas's motivations, though, are part of what makes *Native Son* so compelling, and again Orwell is able to tease out what is most significant about the book and the experience it represents. "Society has so hemmed him in that he can only express himself, only feel that he is really alive, by committing some horrible crime. The author shows this by making him commit another murder, a real one this time, almost immediately afterwards. He had not killed the white girl, *but he had had the will to kill her,* because she was white and even more because she had tried to befriend him" (12:153, emphasis added). The notion of will in the face of prejudice is crucial to Orwell's reading of the novel. His subtle distinction between Thomas's accidental act at the expense of Mary Dalton and the preexisting will that, under other circumstances, might have led Thomas to murder her deliberately, exhibits a deep appreciation of the effects of the protagonist's disenfranchisement. Orwell clearly understands how easily oppression can manifest itself in destructive behavior on the part of the oppressed.

When Orwell describes Thomas's mental state at the end of his discussion of the novel, he highlights what is best and most perceptive about his own reading of *Native Son* as a whole:

[Bigger Thomas] has always "known" that sooner or later he would commit a murder; in other words he has always wanted to commit one. Only in the 24 hours of crime and flight does he feel himself a full human being, controlling his own destiny, acting instead of being acted upon. The dreadful thing that he has done actually gives him a feeling of release. No white person grasps this, except the Jewish lawyer who defends him, and he shrinks from the knowledge. (12:153)

The statement that "no white person" could grasp Bigger Thomas's inner desire to kill is striking because of how similar it is in its tone of certainty to the statement Orwell makes four years later in "As I Please," the assertion that Britain has no racial feeling. The certainty with which he makes that impeachable pronouncement helps put into context the force with which he makes this one about *Native Son.* Here, though, the tone of certainty is warranted, as Orwell implicitly includes himself (as a white person) when he refers to the difficulty of grasping the effects of the exclusive and excluding experience of racial oppression.

While acknowledging the horror expressed in *Native Son,* Orwell does not shrink from the knowledge of the homicidal rage inside a Bigger Thomas because he can see clearly where it comes from. Even though, or perhaps because, he has never visited the United States, he can extrapolate from Wright's novel and derive a clear picture of the effects of oppression on a group of people. When he says, "So long as colour-feeling exists the white race can't, in fact, look on the negro quite as a human being; they can only look on him as a slave or as a pet animal" (12:153), he takes it upon himself to do what he says in "As I Please" must be done. When there is an injustice, individuals must make a fuss. When he makes this statement about how "colour-feeling" affects how whites see blacks, he is no longer simply reviewing a novel. He is using the review to make a political point. He turns his review of Wright's novel into an opportunity to make a fuss, in effect to translate for his British *Tribune* readers what Wright is presenting to them from inside the American context.

Orwell appears to have learned at least one thing from Wright's novel, and this lesson manifests itself most famously in the pigs' social status toward the end of *Animal Farm.* As a final expression of the pigs' superiority over the other animals in the years after the rebellion that ousts Jones and brings Napoleon to power, the pigs are segregated from the other animals in a manner that brings to mind the Jim Crow laws under which Bigger Thomas lives and against which he finally, murderously, rebels:

It was announced later, when bricks and timber had been purchased, a schoolroom would be built in the farmhouse garden. For the time being the young pigs were given their instruction by Napoleon himself in the farmhouse kitchen. They took their exercise in the garden, and were discouraged from playing with the other young animals. About this time, too, it was laid down as a rule that when a pig and any other animal met on the path, the other animal must stand aside: and also that all pigs, of whatever degree, were to have the privilege of wearing green ribbons on their tails on Sundays. (8:75–76)

Separate schools, separate playgrounds, the discouragement to play with disfavoured "others," the social dictum to stand aside whenever a member of the empowered group is encountered—all of this would no doubt have a familiar ring for any African American who endured the daily indignities of Jim Crow America.

Iris Marion Young describes the dynamics of privilege in terms that throw into relief Orwell's determination to overcome his own inherited class and racial positions.

> Social and economic privilege means, among other things, that the groups that have it behave as though they have a right to speak and be heard, that others treat them as though they have that right, and that they have the material, personal, and organizational resources that enable them to speak and be heard in public. The privileged are usually not inclined to protect and further the interests of the oppressed, partly because their social position prevents them from understanding those interests and partly because to some degree their privilege depends on the continued oppression of others.[11]

From Young we can see what is remarkable about Orwell's views of race. From his own position of inherited privilege—his ability to behave as though he has a right to speak and be heard—he attempts to make a fuss in the interest of the disempowered.

Young's description also returns us to the questions Phyllis Lassner asks regarding Phyllis Bottome's *Under the Skin* and that I have been asking in turn about Orwell: can the white colonial writer represent an authentic or indigenous colonial experience if the representation can only be figured in the European political history and cultural traditions that constitute his or her language? The answer, in Orwell's case, is that he cannot offer an "authentic or indigenous colonial experience," nor should he try. Such a posture would probably come across as disingenuous, at least, and fraudulent, at worst. This particular white, male, British writer, born at the height of the British Empire, can offer instead a much more optimistic example than "authenticity" might produce. His nonfiction demonstrates an intellect working to overcome its own inherited prejudices, arguing actively against prejudice by pointing out the breadth of its injustice, and drawing to our conscious minds our own prejudices as well as our failings in struggling against them. Although these examples from Orwell have not been examined to any extent before now, they are noteworthy and crucial to add to discussions about him. If we are going to draw inferences regarding Orwell's views on race, we should at least consider those inferences in the context of the explicit statements he makes in his nonfiction. Once we do this, we derive an increasingly subtle and nuanced understanding of this important figure.

Notes

1. Ranajit Guha, "Not at Home in Empire," *Critical Inquiry* 23:3 (Spring 1997): 489.

2. Douglas Kerr, "Colonial Habits: Orwell and Woolf in the Jungle," *English Studies* 78:12 (March 1997): 152.

3. Douglas Kerr, "Orwell, Animals, and the East," *Essays in Criticism* 49:3 (July 1999): 239.

4. Phyllis Lassner, "A Bridge Too Close: Narrative Wars to End in Fascism and Imperialism," *JNT: Journal of Narrative Theory* 31:2 (Summer 2001): 140.

5. All references to Orwell's works are taken from *The Complete Works of George Orwell,* ed. Peter Davison (London: Secker and Warburg, 1998). Volume number and page number, separated by a colon, will be cited parenthetically in the text.

6. Orwell wrote a wide-ranging weekly column entitled "As I Please" for *Tribune* from December 3, 1943, until April 4, 1947.

7. Randall Kennedy, *Nigger: The Strange Career of a Troublesome Word* (New York: Pantheon, 2002), 114.

8. Bernard Crick, *George Orwell: A Life* (London: Penguin, 1992), 376–77.

9. Eric J. Sundquist, *Cultural Contexts for Ralph Ellison's Invisible Man* (Boston: Bedford, 1995), 10.

10. Christopher Hitchens, *Why Orwell Matters* (New York: Basic, 2002), 9–10.

11. Iris Marion Young, "Polity and Group Difference: A Critique of the Ideal of Universal Citizenship," in *Throwing Like a Girl and Other Essays in Feminist Philosophy and Social Theory* (Bloomington: Indiana University Press, 1990), 124.

10

Orwell's "Smelly Little Orthodoxies"— and Ours

JIM SLEEPER

In the dark London spring of 1944, George Orwell was having an eerily difficult time finding an established publisher for *Animal Farm*. He had expected—and gotten—a rejection from his regular publisher, Victor Gollancz, a parlor leftist who was also enough the public liberal to deny hotly Orwell's suggestion, in a letter to him, that fealty to the Soviet Union had had anything to do with the decision. Biographer Bernard Crick recounts that Orwell and some friends felt sure Gollancz was warning other publishers that the book's Swiftian send-up of Stalinism endangered Britain's vital interests, what with Hitler still just across the channel and the Eastern Front so critical to national survival. Subsequent rejections of *Animal Farm* were by turns mealymouthed and candid about its political risks, deepening Orwell's suspicions. The publisher Jonathan Cape had been enthusiastic at first but informed him that on a second reading—undertaken after an unexplained consultation with the Ministry of Information—he realized that the book was a satirical reprise of Soviet history and so was unworkable even as a fable. Especially irksome to the Russian ally, Cape suggested, would be Orwell's representation of the politbureau and commissars as pigs.

It wasn't only book publishers who were letting Orwell down. He suspended his own weekly *Tribune* column because, he told a friend, the newspaper's Labourite editorial codirector Aneurin Bevan "was terrified there might be a row over *Animal Farm* which might have been embarrassing [to the Labour Party]."[1] *The Manchester Evening News* rejected a review of Orwell's that faulted Harold Laski's *Faith, Reason, and Civilization* for its blindness to Stalin's "purges, liquidations, the dictatorship of a minority [and] suppression of criticism."[2] Crick stops just short of saying that Orwell felt himself the victim of some vast, left-wing conspiracy.

If these guardians of "highbrow" book publishing and popular journalism weren't in thrall to Stalinism, they were at least paralyzed by a cowardice before it that puzzled and exasperated Orwell. He probed it in "The Freedom of the Press," a preface he wrote for *Animal Farm* as he contemplated publishing the book privately with subventions from friends. In the preface he described the weakness he sensed in editors and public discourse all around him and traced the balance he was trying to maintain. But he withheld "The Freedom of the Press" when *Animal Farm* was accepted by Secker and Warburg, a moderately leftist, anti-Stalinist publisher, well-enough established to allay fears that the book would sink into oblivion. The preface didn't see print until 1972, when Crick resurrected it from the papers of one of the firm's principals and brought it out in *TLS*.

The best-known sentence of "The Freedom of the Press" is a declaration any dissenter might utter: "If liberty means anything at all it means the right to tell people what they do not want to hear." But what if some of the things people "do not want to hear," such as fascist or Stalinist lies and smears, are destructive of public trust and, with it, of liberty itself? Orwell might have answered that liberty can't be defended by prejudging which utterances will prove out in debate and which will be shown up as serpentine lies. Why, then, do publishers and editors who claim to prize liberty keep denying hearings even to reasonable, well-presented views like Orwell's? He gets this far toward an answer: "If publishers and editors exert themselves to keep certain topics out of print it is not because they are frightened of prosecution but because they are frightened of public opinion. In this country intellectual cowardice is the worst enemy a writer or journalist has to face, and that fact does not seem to me to have had the discussion it deserves."[3]

Orwell is probing for causes of intellectual cowardice that run deeper than Stalinism and for "cowards" besides those in the highbrow "intelligentsia" who preoccupy him at the moment. He is struggling, as he would in *Nineteen Eighty-Four*, against a broader despair of the public and of democracy itself, as if both harbored a malignancy of which editors may be carriers and accelerants but not causes. This long struggle against despair of democracy had absorbed Orwell from his first encounters with British colonialism (and colonials themselves) in Burma, and from his time "down and out" in Paris and London, tramping with Britain's "underclass," sojourning with workers at Wigan, and fighting alongside proletarian and peasant soldiers in Spain. And that preoccupation would consume him in Winston Smith's emblematic rendering of it in *Nineteen Eighty-Four*: "[I]f there was hope, it lay in the proles. You had to cling on to that. When you put it in words it sounded reasonable; it was when you looked at the human beings passing you on the pavement that it became an act of faith."[4] Not an illusion, mind you, and not even a revolutionary act of sacrifice, but an almost stoical, tragical, perhaps even faintly Christic act of faith, a burden so heavy and at times frightening that many would do almost anything but bear it—even if they were just publishers turning down manuscripts whose force and integrity made readers face up to the responsibilities and risks of being free.

Reading Orwell this way revivifies three truths that are sometimes finessed by political writers. First, there is something so inherently dangerous to freedom in democracy itself that the two cannot be conflated. Second, what a political writer needs most isn't the courage to stand for "equality" with the Left against the Right or for "freedom" with the Right against the Left, but the more elusive courage to illuminate truths about freedom that may anger both sides or, worse, be taken up by both opportunistically. Third, that kind of courage depends in turn on a willingness to strip oneself of protections that come with the insulations of class (or the nursed injuries of class) and with ideological partisanship. Even writers brave enough to seek out dangerous encounters with "freedom" and "equality" they could well have avoided (and who have bodily scars to show for it) may spoil their efforts by sparring with other writers about whose stigmata are bigger. They may even get into arguments about whether Orwell himself always kept a train ticket home to a comfortable flat. What matters more, I think, is whether a writer exposes oneself somewhat or not at all. One writer's moral imagination may be deeply shaken and instructed by moderate leaps and risks that would seem a Sunday outing to another.

Orwell didn't end up despairing of all public discourse and politics, but he certainly stared into that abyss. I want to suggest here that had he been able to engage Americans' fraught experiences with freedom and equality by sojourning here in person or at least by reading Alexis de Tocqueville's *Democracy in America,* his own chiaroscuro of despair and hope, of dire prediction and mere warning, might have been even richer than it already is for us in liberal capitalist democracies. John Rodden has shown that wherever *Animal Farm* and *Nineteen Eighty-Four* were circulated, samizdatlike, in the totalitarian countries of Central and Eastern Europe, the books struck readers with the force of dark revelation or epiphany; even now in those countries they remain as ubiquitous as Bibles (or anti-Bibles), evoking and exorcising the nightmares of the recent past. The books swept Western Europe and America, too, of course, especially during the cold war, but we needed then a rendering of Orwell's dystopic vision that would show, as Tocqueville had, that even an apparently benign democracy can curdle or decay not only in party coups or statist terror, as in Eastern Europe, but in something more like what Gibbon saw in ancient Rome: the slow, subtle weakening of the vitals of an apparently triumphal republican felicity. I think that it was Tocqueville, not Gibbon or Orwell, who showed best that a democracy could become so "democratic" it would be almost wholly unfree and that it could become so owing to a division in the human heart that cannot be explained only by analyses of oppression, grinding inequality, and other exogenous constraints. One must be careful in saying this, and Orwell says it unforgettably in *Nineteen Eighty-Four.* But I still wish that he had read Tocqueville, who, incidentally, anticipated that American editors would be even less free than the British ones who vexed Orwell.

Orwell reconnoiters the problem in his 1944 preface about the British publishers' mishandling of his manuscript and reviews:

> The sinister fact about literary censorship in England is that it is largely voluntarily. Unpopular ideas can be silenced, and inconvenient facts kept dark, without the need for any official ban . . . because of a general tacit agreement that "it wouldn't do" to mention that particular fact. . . . It is not exactly forbidden to say this that or the other but it is "not done" to say it. . . . Anyone who challenges the prevailing orthodoxy finds himself silenced with surprising effectiveness. A genuinely unfashionable opinion is almost never given a fair hearing either in the popular press or in the highbrow periodicals.[5]

At the moment, he notes, the main orthodoxy of Britain's "intelligentsia" proscribes all criticism of the Soviet Union. As if anticipating Ronald Reagan, he writes, "For quite a decade past, I have believed the existing Russian regime is a mainly evil thing," but he adds, "I claim the right to say so in spite of the fact that we are allies with the USSR in a war which I want to see won."[6] Here is the ideologically elusive courage I've mentioned: He sounds, by turns, like a conservative moralist ("a mainly evil thing"), a moral liberal ("I claim the right to say so"), a patriot ("a war which I want to see won"), and even, perhaps, a progressive ("we are allies with the USSR"). Such complexity is discomfiting to partisans. Something in the fellow-traveling publishers' discomfort with Orwell suggests a desperation to sustain the conceit that they are independent thinkers, not the foot soldiers he thinks some of them actually are in the wars of more powerful people.

He finds especially galling their indulgence of crude "literary" enforcers like the *Daily Worker's* Harry Pollitt, who, Orwell recalls, had explained his *Homage to Catalonia* by describing Orwell as a "disillusioned little middle class boy."[7] Orwell notes in his preface that apparatchiks more practiced than Pollitt in "the art of denigration will not attack [a book] on political grounds but on literary ones. They will say that it is a dull, silly book and a disgraceful waste of paper. This might well be true" of his own work, he adds with impish modesty, but such reviewers never criticize trash that follows their own political line.[8] Anyone who has sojourned in political journalism knows this is far from the worst of it, as Orwell learned in Spain and made excruciatingly clear in *Homage*.

But that still doesn't explain why anyone enjoying the liberties of Western book publishers and newspaper editors would do what they did to Orwell and do now to challengers of certain orthodoxies here. "It is important to realize that the current Russomania is only a symptom of the general weakening of the western liberal tradition," he writes, but still he doesn't go far beyond noting that editors "are afraid of public opinion."[9] Seven times in this four-thousand-word preface he accuses them of "intellectual cowardice," "sheer cowardice," harboring "a cowardly desire to keep in with the bulk of the intelligentsia," "timidity," "fear," and "servility" to conventional wisdom. He calls them "circus dogs" who jump even when no whip is cracked by government or private interests. And that is restrained compared to his rebuke to Stalin-friendly "English leftwing journalists and intellectuals" in a *Tribune* column at the time: "Do remember that dishonesty and cowardice always have to be paid for. . . . Once a whore, always a whore."[10]

Crick calls the preface itself "intemperate," acknowledging that "it had to be, considering how badly temperate, civilized and responsible [publishers and editors] had behaved." Still, Orwell was "wise to decide against publishing 'The Freedom of the Press' in front of *Animal Farm,* which might have lost its resonance as a fable and appeared to be an attack only on Stalin. The universality of its reflections on power and corruption might have seemed just the projection of a literary quarrel."[11] Yet the preface doesn't seem so "intemperate" when read alone now with an eye to what had provoked it. Orwell sounds exasperated, yes, but even more puzzled, like a diagnostician facing a strange malignancy he can't quite identify or explain.

At one point he alters the diagnosis enough to make one wonder if there is even a disease: "You could, indeed, publish anti-Russian books," he acknowledges, even if "to do so was to make sure of being ignored or misrepresented by nearly the whole of the highbrow press"[12] So his was not quite as "totalitarian" a suppression as *Nineteen Eighty-Four* readers might think. It is only "highbrow" gatekeepers who affront and preoccupy Orwell; there *are* other publishers, some successful even if disdained by those among whom he has generally taken his bearings. Orwell shares that disdain: "There was a huge output of anti-Russian literature, but nearly all of it was from the Conservative angle, and manifestly dishonest, out of date and actuated by sordid motives";[13] even with Animal *Farm* being silenced by a tacit understanding among liberals, he rejected an offer to serialize it in the right-wing journal *Time and Tide*. Still, on the left and in the centrist prestige press, "there was an equally huge and almost equally dishonest stream of pro-Russian propaganda and what amounted to a boycott on anyone who tried to discuss all-important questions in a grown-up manner."[14] He leaves us with little more than that last, prosaic, almost wistful phrase; reading it, I can't help but recall Turgenev's more portentous lament: "The honest man will end by having to live alone."[15]

For Orwell in 1944, politics "in a grown-up manner" could be imagined only somewhere beyond the ideological partisanship of both Left and Right. Certainly he was more bitterly disappointed in leftists' and liberals' betrayals of liberty than in conservatives' throne-and-altar mystifications of oppression: "In our country . . . it is the liberals who fear liberty and the intellectuals who want to do dirt on the intellect."[16] Yet the more we know of Orwell's complex courage to be scathing of both sides, the more we grasp why so many other writers and editors avoid such independence or only feign it. What Orwell saw early was that while both the Left and the Right have credible claims on certain truths, each tends to cling to its own claims so tightly that they become half-truths which soon curdle into lies, leaving each side right only about how the other is wrong. At any historical moment, one side's claims may be the more liberating in struggle against the other's institutionalized carapaces and cant; Orwell sought liberation through democratic socialist movements in the dark, protofascist Europe of the interwar years, and indeed his sympathies abided with workers throughout his life, albeit sometimes against their self-proclaimed leaders as well as against Tories. But he never forgot that both sides tend to get stuck in their imagined upswings and disappoint in the end: The Left's almost willful misreadings of human nature make it founder in swift currents of nationalism and religion, pitching from sweeping denials of their importance to abject and hypocritical surrenders: "Socialism in One Country"; Marxism the secular eschatology. Not for nothing did Orwell, the social democrat, label the progenitor of Big Brother "Ingsoc" (*English* Socialism), not Stalinism. Yet neither did he doubt that the corporate capitalist state and its ministries of information could pose *Nineteen Eighty-Four*–ish dangers. He remained conservative enough to look sympathetically into nationalism, patriotism, and religion and to savor the life in their interstices. He was always on the left enough to seek solidarity in struggles against capitalist overreach, but he also held to an irreducible personal dignity and responsibility that balk at solidarity itself. Another way of characterizing his political balance might be to say that just as a healthy person walks on both a left foot and a right one, a society needs both a left foot of social equality and social provision—without which neither the individuality nor the communal bonds which conservatives honor could exist—and a right foot of personal liberty through responsibility, without which any leftist social reorganization would reduce persons to clients, cogs, or worse.

Why then, after all, were "highbrow" editors and publishers afraid to join Orwell in sustaining this balance? Perhaps, knowing that they were tethered to a capitalism dark and foreboding, they were trying to offset their discomfort through flights of socialist imagination. Because those flights were never as well grounded as Orwell's, they had to be kept insulated from reports of reality in order to be sustained. Like other links in a long chain of leftist-intellectual exoticisms, including attractions to demagoguery in third world countries from Cuba to Tibet, philo-Stalinism was really a displacement of social hope onto something so distant it could be sustained by a highly moralized ignorance; the more distance, the more certitude.

Surely some editors were merely opportunistic in promoting such flights. Others may have been driven less by opportunism than by upper-class self-loathing. Orwell understood them. He had entered adulthood wearing their clothing and lenses, and his unrelenting search for better drove him to tramps, workers, and Spanish peasant and proletarian freedom fighters. What parlor intellectuals only fantasized he engaged, at greater risk. But what seems to have put off Orwell's editors wasn't just the bothersome truth that he'd made himself more vulnerable and therefore unpredictable than they let themselves be but also a reality that was bothering him, too: uncertainty about "the people" as a beacon of social hope.

Here is where I wish that Orwell had been able to try on the lenses Tocqueville had worn a hundred years earlier while surveying the United States' unprecedented effort to reconcile untrammeled individual liberty with the self-government of a vast demos. It was Tocqueville who most memorably observed and imagined that the more "democratic" a society in the colloquial, "we're all equal" sense, the more susceptible to despotism its members are actually likely to be. It is a dark, and for Americans somewhat counterintuitive, warning, tracing back though it does to Benjamin Franklin's misgivings about the viability of a republic. Had Orwell encountered such American warnings earlier than he did, he might have cautioned even more compellingly about tendencies in the "free world."

Tocqueville observed that freedom and equality aren't as mutually reinforcing as Americans often innocently believe, and he insisted on this even in the America of the 1830s, where a fortuitous alignment of the stars seemed to have unleashed democratic passions for both freedom and equality whose nearness to realization resembled nothing before. The passion for equality was so torrentially strong that it swept aside every care about the costs and prerequisites of freedom. Americans had little to fear from the highly centralized nation-state that had replaced feudalism in much of Europe. Shielded by two oceans from proximate enemies of the kind that shaped nationalism there, Americans were free, as well, of the standing armies that nourish authoritarianism. Americans traded and governed themselves locally, with little intervention from a tiny, distant federal government. They debated one another in local newspapers and forums, enjoying what struck Tocqueville as unprecedented freedom of the press. Religiously, they communed, if at all, not through the sacraments of an established ecclesium but in a dissenting Protestant "priesthood of all believers," in which equality came straight from God. Equality was championed as well in the unprecedented universal white, male citizenship of the liberal, constitutional polity, displacing socialism's allure for a caste-hobbled Europe. And when equality or freedom faltered, there was always the American frontier, with its promise of an earthly yet oddly sacralized deliverance from despotism and the injuries of class.

Or so it seemed, and Tocqueville was too acute an observer to leave the picture that rosy. Yet his evocations of equality's potency and intimacy in the America of 1835 anticipate nothing better than Orwell's own account, a hundred years later, in

Homage to Catalonia, of his bracing first encounters with revolutionary equality in Barcelona. There, he was uncharacteristically exultant about equality's first flush among men long constrained by caste but now unafraid to look one another in the eye, if only for a breakthrough moment. Read Tocqueville on young America and, with some stylistic allowances, you can hardly tell which man is talking:

> The first and most intense passion which is produced by the equality of condition is, I need hardly say, the love of that equality. . . . This passion for equality is every day gaining ground in the human heart. . . . Equality every day confers a number of small enjoyments on every man. The charms of equality are every instant felt, and are within the reach of all; the noblest hearts are not insensible to them, and the most vulgar souls exult in them. Men cannot enjoy political liberty unpurchased by some sacrifices, and they never obtain it without great exertions. But the pleasures of equality are self-proffered: each of the petty incidents of life seems to occasion them; and in order to taste them nothing is required but to live.[17]

But it is Tocqueville's forebodings about this that make *Democracy in America* so riveting. He feared that Americans' untempered passion for equality would suppress liberty and degrade their public life into a tyranny of fickle majorities driven only by soul-narrowing cupidity. That wasn't the danger worrying Orwell even in the equality-mad international Left of the 1930s and 1940s and certainly not in the familiar British delusions of hierarchy, militarism, and inbred cultural elitism amid economic depression and war. Reading Tocqueville's reflections would have accelerated and perhaps deepened the most heartbreaking lesson of Orwell's long, personal revolt against "knowing your place" in a class society: that having *no* place in a classless society could be even worse.

Because the America Tocqueville studied had no medieval estates or other countervailing powers to resist the tyranny of the majority, it had too few of the precious interstices and eccentricities that countervailing powers do accommodate and that made even throne-and-altar England seem more humane in the little ways Orwell portrayed so endearingly. He dreaded the dissolution of those redoubts, whether under socialism or corporatist fascism, which would atomize civil society. So prescient had Tocqueville been about precisely such perils in America that while he had opened with paeans to the passion for equality, his anticipations of the despotism of public opinion seem almost a prolegomenon to *Nineteen Eighty-Four.* He understood, more starkly than Orwell would, that the dystopia lurking in the febrile heart of equality is more than the trahison des clercs which Orwell encountered in "the intelligentsia." It is more, too, than an unfortunate consequence of the fact that "capitalist oppression" may damage "the people" more than it ennobles or equips them for freedom. For Tocqueville, the most nightmarish vision of social organization lurks in the nature of democratic man, a nature divided and corrupt in ways that antedate capitalist alienation all the way back to the Garden of Eden—or to the Edenic American heartland that Tocqueville surveyed.

He lamented that by diffusing political and other powers so widely and minutely that they eclipse higher authorities and standards, "[d]emocratic republics extend the practice of currying favor with the many, and introduce it into all classes at once."[18] They make people ever unsure of their standing in ways that diminish character and opinion. Not everyone is heroically self-making enough to become Emerson's "Man Thinking" or even just Orwell the home gardener and furniture-maker. Melville, Hawthorne, and Thoreau shared Tocqueville's fear that while untrammeled democracy and commerce might liberate the strong they would also engender gnawing vulnerabilities and a chronic hunger for security among many who would lead "lives of quiet desperation." They would be the more susceptible to clever marketing or soft demagoguery in a "majority" culture more constraining of the individual than was the old monarchy and an established church. As if anticipating Orwell's intimations of the "fear of public opinion," Tocqueville wrote that

> no monarch is so absolute as to combine all the powers of society in his own hands, and to conquer all opposition, as a majority is able to do, which has the right both of making and of executing the laws.
>
> In America, the majority raises formidable barriers around the liberty of opinion: within these barriers, an author may write what he pleases; but woe to him if he goes beyond them. . . . [H]e is exposed to continued obloquy and persecution. His political career is closed forever, since he has offended the only authority which is able to open it. Every sort of compensation, even that of celebrity, is refused to him. Before publishing his opinions, he imagined that he held them in common with others; but no sooner has he declared them, than he is loudly censured by his opponents, while those who think like him, without having the courage to speak out, abandon him in silence. . . .[19]

While a monarch might attack the body in order to subdue the soul, Tocqueville observed,

> such is not the course adopted by tyranny in democratic republics; there the body is left free and the soul is enslaved. The master no longer says, "You shall think as I do, or you shall die"; but he says, "You are free to think differently from me and to retain your life, your property, and all that you possess; but you are henceforth a stranger among your people. . . . Your fellow-creatures will shun you like an impure being; and even those who believe in your innocence will abandon you, lest they should be shunned in their turn."

We are at least partly back to Orwell's warning of 1944 that writers faced not government censorship but publishers' fear of public opinion in "accepting the principle that a book should be published or suppressed, praised or damned, not on its merits but according to political expediency."[20] Expediency was determined not only by the crown, church, or lords but also by a Fourth Estate that claimed to serve the people, sometimes in collaboration with their self-anointed "revolutionary" vanguard. Watching that collaboration, Orwell complained that "others who do not actually hold this view [of what is expedient] assent to it from sheer cowardice," so that a writer who declares the Soviet regime "evil" finds himself shunned as an impure being.[21]

Yet, he concluded, "One can only explain this contradiction [of proclaiming freedom while betraying it] by a cowardly desire to keep in with the bulk of the intelligentsia."[22] And it is here that I think Orwell could have learned from Tocqueville and America, earlier than he eventually did learn it, that often it's the other way around: It's the intelligentsia that is trying to "keep in" with an unguided, elusive, and fickle but pervasive majority. In America it need not be only a liberal intelligentsia that does this; the country's conservative elites, most of them really classical liberals, not throne-and-altar Tories, hunger for "silent majorities," "moral majorities," and worse. As Tocqueville foresaw, consumer sovereignty has consumed so much else that only a bigger market share or a winning (i.e., bought and paid-for) electoral majority seems to carry cultural or intellectual force.

Has it really come to this? At first glance, the silencing and shunning Tocqueville and Orwell bemoan seem not to characterize today's American public discourse, with its cacophony of shouts in a "crossfire" between "Left" and "Right" and of cries from myriad religious, ethnic, racial, and other groupings that seem to defy the floor plan of the nineteenth-century French Chamber of Deputies. But lost, if not suppressed, in this buzzing, blighting confusion are voices that don't roar in a Manichaean way—voices reminding us that everyone has both a left foot and a right one and urging us to walk politically in what Orwell called "a grown-up manner." It's not that the conglomeration of public discourse has imposed an ideological or party line in the nineteenth- and mid-twentieth-century manner of Orwell's "intelligentsia." Rather, when the only party line is the bottom line, every other public priority, including freedom of speech, is innundated by distractions fomented by corporate entities that are not the thinking beings whose political speech the First Amendment was meant to protect. Their "ideas" are merely tactically deployed reiterations of one unexamined imperative—the pursuit of profit and market share. Their ability to overwhelm and deform public discourse, buying up political debate while assembling huge audiences for profit, swamps democratic deliberation in titillation and gross degradation that moves socially and emotionally atomized consumption. As the promotion of such "consumer sovereignty" displaces political sovereignty, a quiet riot of self-regarding consumption displaces the subtle, canny self-discipline of a civic discourse that might lift everyone's sights to the good of the whole. Such lifting is an art. People need to be trained to do it to stimulate one another in achieving a good in common that they cannot know alone.

Against such Tocquevillian forebodings, Orwell sounds almost archaic when he grounds his 1944 appeals for freedom of speech and publishing in Milton's "known rule of ancient liberty." It is deeply embedded in Western thought and tradition, he argues. But even then he must have known that invocations of Milton were little more than incantations against the tyranny which he foresaw and which Tocqueville had long since forecast. Perhaps it was Orwell's immersion in a lingering British civility, still graven in the heart (and in "wholesome" boys' weeklies) and not merely in law, that inclined him to rely on Milton's "known rule." But in the United States today, surely, the written Constitution, no longer very decently draped by Burkean custom, may have the paradoxical effect of stimulating endless, anomic litigation within ever more slippery webs of contracts and rights. That would appall Orwell, as the prospect of it did Tocqueville. Within the uncontested sovereignty of a faceless majority, law can't protect and may even undermine the social amenities and decencies Orwell loved. If the legislation that is ground out like sausages in Washington becomes the *only* embodiment of social order, what defense of comity and indeed order itself can it offer against media that "morph" commercial initiative into casino gambling, cultural entertainments into mob circuses resembling the prolecult of *Nineteen Eighty-Four*, and public discourse into hate-mongering—all while catering to "majority" impulses for higher quarterly returns?

Like Tocqueville in early nineteenth-century America, Orwell had the courage to face such bleak prospects and to expose the corruption of all that had kindled his social and political imagination in Barcelona. But he also contended that even if we lose a romantic faith in "the people" as we uncover evil in the irreducible divisions of the human heart, still we must choose between a stoic "act of faith" in the people or surrender to the security of Authority. If Orwell's example is any guide, at least the inevitable disillusionment need not subvert an almost stoical ability to carry on. But that may depend in part on the integrity of publishers and editors who present new social visions when old paradigms are crumbling and brighter social prospects seem dim. Those choices seem especially fateful just now in America, not only because the United States is so powerful but also because, if Tocqueville's and Orwell's warnings are right, "tyranny of the majority" is so advanced that soon it may need only a Big Brother to persuade everyone that his whims embody their will.

Each of us comes in his or her own way to prospects like those Tocqueville and Orwell confronted. In 1977, after twelve years spent mostly in and around universities, I moved to inner-city Brooklyn, New York. There I lived for five years with mostly black and Hispanic neighbors in tenement walk-ups, losing myself in local neighborhood politics and activist journalism enough so that on my rare forays into Manhattan, the density of white faces was disorienting. In time I ran a now-long-defunct small weekly newspaper in the Williamsburg and Greenpoint sections of Brooklyn (my column in it was called "At Large") and later wrote for the then-still-bohemian, muckraking *Village Voice* and Irving Howe's democratic-socialist quarterly *Dissent.* Later, for more than two years, I wrote a thrice-weekly op-ed-page column for the New York *Daily News,* whose reading "intelligentsia" consisted of local politicians; parochial and public-school teachers; community leaders in neighborhoods like Archie Bunker's white-ethnic redoubts, and the Roman Catholic prelates of the Bronx, Brooklyn and Queens. The latter's pews were filling with Spanish-speaking immigrants; and, finally and most poignantly for me, older black New Yorkers who'd had decent high school educations and would mail me back my columns with their underlinings and notes in the margins.

I describe this odyssey briefly in *The Closest of Strangers.*[23] But only years after writing that book did I read, for the first time, and well into middle age, *Down and Out in Paris and London* and *Homage to Catalonia* and discover that I had written my own homage to Brooklyn. It wasn't just political innocence that I had lost there, as Orwell had in Catalonia. Living and working with nonwhites who had some power over my immediate prospects boiled out a campus radical's racial romanticism and brewed deeper interracial affinities and bonds. Far more than I had expected, my interest in a common American identity and in an American democratic exceptionalism was shared by nonwhite neighbors and coworkers. A surprising number of them felt diminished by liberal oversolicitude almost as much as by the conservative racism that dominates the liberal imagination. That distanced me from what seemed earlier incarnations in Cambridge and New Haven: One night, when my unpaid-for telephone could only receive calls, not make them, a Yale classmate trading currencies for Citibank rang me up to ask for an alumni contribution. Sitting on the floor of my apartment in the smoky Brooklyn dusk, I explained I had only a subsistence living. Taken aback, he gently wished me well. I hadn't words to add that I was deeply, darkly contented and that Yale was a million miles away.

The Orwell who sojourned at Wigan and in the slums of his own London might have understood how quickly a place very close to home can become one's bleeding Spain, how inner-city Brooklyn became my Catalonia. Many of the same harsh social and political truths emerge, and while there are crucial differences—otherwise, I would not be wishing that Orwell had spent time in the United States—I can't help but wonder if some talented, morally acute, upper-middle-class young American writers aren't running from problems that feel oddly too close for comfort when they skip over domestic probings like Orwell's at Wigan to report—as he also did—on more dangerous conflicts far away. Might there be a vague need to correct an older generation's displacements of American political frustrations and fantasies onto "third world" peoples and problems?

Certainly if one wanted to bear witness to a politics of death, one could have moved in the 1980s to parts of Brooklyn where the sense of living in a war zone and of negotiating its duplicities got coded into my body language and would remain for years. In the bleeding, beautiful Brooklyn of those years I witnessed a precipitous decay of opportunity, authority, and civility and an ascendancy of force and fraud in calculations of everyday life. By the time of the 1989 mayoral election that produced David Dinkins, a glittering Manhattan real estate boom had receded, exposing not just the perennial ethnic clashes and jockeyings of elites but also a frightening disintegration of families and neighborhood institutions amid reports of soaring child abuse and housing abandonment. Everywhere, it seemed, were encroachments of the drug economy, of roaming packs of violent youths, and of the homeless and mentally helpless, human wreckage which no one knew how to repair. In a growing civic vacuum, politics moved increasingly in cycles of tribal recrimination, along racial lines.

Even as newcomers whose understandings of race were more fluid and ecumenical than those of American blacks and whites promised a new cosmopolitanism, the city's public racial disputes turned less on the hopeful claims of the civil rights movement, or for employment, housing, schools, and welfare, and more instead on death, on emblematic, murderous interracial assaults in the streets. Howard Beach, Tawana Brawley, Bensonhurst, the Central Park Jogger, Crown Heights; long before the Rodney King and O. J. Simpson psychodramas convulsed Los Angeles and riveted the nation in a politics of racial paroxysm, the New York I knew learned, as Orwell had in Catalonia, that a politics turning on a discourse of death heralds only the death of politics.

New York had 2,500 homicides annually through most of my time of inner-city immersion. Some were terroristic, as in the Son of Sam serial murders and the gunning down of more than a dozen children caught in the crossfire of warring drug gangs. Some were riotous, as during the mass lootings of neighborhoods I worked in during the 1977 electrical power blackout. A large number were almost random, in that they were committed on strangers in encounters untempered by anything like the twinge of compassion Orwell felt for the humanity of an "enemy combatant" he saw running across a ridge in Spain, trying to hold up his pants. I stepped over two still-warm bodies on Brooklyn streets in those years and saw an elderly man pull a gun on a young mugger on a subway platform. I watched whole underground transit passageways slip rhythmically in and out of civil authority, like provinces in a country gripped by a guerrilla war. My apartment was cleaned out by burglars twice. By the time an unassuming white computer technician named Bernhard Goetz shot four black youths who had been harrassing him on a crowded subway car in 1987, I understood viscerally what most of the city's intelligentsia would not acknowledge: that something more and less than racism was in play, something more and less, too, than what goes into battlefield and political shootings. Polls suggested that, had one of Goetz's victims died, a surprisingly large proportion of New Yorkers, black as well as white, would have considered it a "necessary murder"—the term Orwell rebuked W. H. Auden for using with reference to some of the political killings in Spain.

Tout comprendre ce n'est pas tout pardonner; when I say that I understood, it is not that I approved. I learned, rather, that understanding is worth more than ideological moralizing ginned up for political action. Whatever the historical and structural explanations for the violence and the racial street theater collecting around it, an apolitical coldness in the killings dimmed the coordinates of political action in Brooklyn. No matter how nuanced and compelling the New York left's causal analyses, it repeatedly and almost defiantly displayed its helplessness before these accessions of thanatos or nihilism. Slowly I concluded that even in the midst of oppression—indeed, in order to organize against oppression—lines of personal responsibility must first be drawn and policed, morally and legally, even as they are being tested spiritually or politically. Nelson Mandela, Malcolm X, Martin Luther King Jr. and even Louis Farrakhan understood very well that the least one can do to affirm the dignity of the oppressed is hold them to the basic human standards one would set for one's own children.

Rudolph Giuliani understood this, too, and was willing to be called a conservative and a racist to say so. And hunger for such candor, not racism, was the main reason why, in 1993, with some guarded support from my perch at the *Daily News,* he defeated the city's first African American mayor. Racism there was, of course, but the politics of antiracism had imploded by so obviously hedging the truths I have just mentioned: Giuliani became mayor because liberals had lost the art of public deliberation that affirms those basic truths and lift people's sights.

Nowhere was this clearer than in the hideous failure of the *New York Times* to be the "paper of record" of anything but an over-solicitude about race that had so clearly become one of liberal Democrats' liabilities among decent New Yorkers of all colors. The central problem, visible so clearly through my "down and out," Orwellian lenses—as I explained relentlessly and to no avail for a decade in many venues and with varying shades of humor, satire, and sober analysis—was that the paper's young publisher, Arthur Sulzberger Jr., had joined his own impish, vaguely countercultural moralism to the intensely penitential, often retributive southern racial liberalism of his editorial-page editor and, briefly, executive editor, Howell Raines. Both men shared a larger misapprehension to whose correction I had devoted *The Closest of Strangers*: Few New Yorkers, black or white, conservative or liberal, who followed the city "on the ground" could rely on the *Times*'s iconographically "correct" coverage or commentary on any of the signal crises involving race.

For example, even as the *Times* published an average of three stories a day for eight months and many hectoring editorials about the police killing of the African immigrant Amadou Diallo, sparing no effort to amplify a cacophony of long-pent-up Giuliani-hatred orchestrated by Al Sharpton, it could not or would not report that in Giuliani's then-seven years as mayor the number of black New Yorkers killed by police officers had been half that of Mayor David Dinkins's four-year term. Under the tutelage of the publisher and editorial-page editor, reporters simply were not inclined to ask about these numbers or, hearing of them, to consider them relevant. And although the general murder rate, too, had been halved, it mattered to no gatekeeper of New York City's public discourse—at least it was never mentioned by any—that thanks to the controversial new policing policies, thousands of blacks and Hispanics who would otherwise have been killed were up and walking around. Like the fellow-traveling "intelligentsia" in London during Orwell's time, New York's chattering classes simply would not process this information, let alone argue about what it might mean.

In 1997, I devoted a chapter of a new book, *Liberal Racism,* to warning, explicitly and specifically, that the strange symbiosis between Sulzberger's political correctness and Raines's florid, penitential racialism was responsible for a long train of such myopic reporting and for setting up the sort of journalistic debacle that occurred six years later in the disgrace of Jayson Blair, the young black reporter whose fabrications were overlooked by dozens of editors desperate to promote him in the name of "diversity."[24] For writing this chapter and defending and expanding its arguments in other venues, I had to undergo some of the shunning Tocqueville anticipated and Orwell experienced.

American editors who silence writers this way are committed not so much to a "liberal" or leftist ideology as they are to sniffing the company wind, which tracks the publisher's understanding of how to reconcile certain moral conceits with the bottom line. They seek writers whose work will bring the desired "market" of readers to the publication's advertisers. Of course, even vapid publications have an ideology of sorts. But, in a double irony, the only remaining American publishing counterpart to the Stalinist cohort Orwell faced is today's conservative-corporate media combine—dubbed the "Con-intern" by *Slate* editor Jacob Weisberg—over which owners such as Rupert Murdoch hold so much sway.

The conservative news media's political contradictions and moral hypocrisies are quite as yawning as those of the leftist publishers Orwell faced: They pretend to uphold cultural values that in the long run cannot be reconciled with the corporate priorities, morality, and behaviors to which their editors and publishers are joined at the hip. The media's "party line" is a kind of hyper-bottom line—not just of profit but of the relentless *celebration* of profit—even if this or that magazine survives only on subventions drawn from the other profits of ideologically driven owners. Joined at the hip: The Calvin Klein fashion-cum-kiddie-porn ads that showed up on New York City public buses in 1995 weren't put there by liberal elites or sexual liberationists, as the Con-intern's kept conservative cultural warriors charged, but by private investors in free markets. Only nonmarket civic forces rallied to yank them off, as most conservatives stood speechless. Similarly, it is not leftists but huge corporations that pump pornography into hundreds of thousands of American hotel rooms and Internet screens, along with spectacles of the live degradation and humiliation of Americans before television-studio audiences on live daytime shows.

Left and Right are sometimes complicit in these assaults on civic culture, the Left as an addled junior partner that has abdicated its noble ideals of insurgency by mistaking seductive gyrations for political action: American Indian "tribes," some virtually concocted by activist-entrepreneurs and investor-friendly officials, use their "sovereignty" to set up casinos that, in a bitter poetic injustice, hook busloads of flaccid whites on gambling as surely as whites once hooked Indians on firewater.

The Left, flummoxed by racialist fantasies of liberation, and the Right, flummoxed by free-market idolatry, are speechless about the spread of this addictive, regressive tax of casino betting. Living at the edge of a white-ethnic, working-class neighborhood in Brooklyn, I often saw blue-haired Ediths and paunchy Archies boarding "luxury" buses to the casinos.

Within parameters like those I have just sketched, conservative media team players virtually mimick Stalinists such as the *Daily Worker*'s Harry Pollitt or Victor Gollancz, whether in braying "the people's" resentments against selected targets to deflect attention from their own more dubious goals, as Pollitt did, or in crying piously about (their own) freedom of speech and other liberal protections. Barely a level or two below the Cheshire-cat grins of Murdoch's *Weekly Standard* editor Bill Kristol swarm "movement" operatives whose behavior and prose Orwell would have recognized at the *Daily Worker*. But even outside such ideologically defined limits, the players are bound so tightly and unthinkingly to the consumer *sovereigniste* mind-set that they are satisfied to feign public discourse if participants can be induced to shout loud enough to draw an audience. Such an audience, in Walter Lippmann's view, is no longer a deliberating public because it is a "buying" public and therefore a fickle one.[25] The simulacrum of combat is what sells, not the serious thinking about our common destiny that may come out of one school of thought or another.

Faith in "highbrow" editors and publishers has been a major casualty among beliefs about politics and race I carried from Cambridge to Brooklyn. I have learned that romantic or ideological projections of political liberation onto the "oppressed" reflect little but moral self-indulgence. White liberals of a certain temperament, such as Sulzberger and Raines, become passionately committed to busing or racial preferences because they need to re-stage morality plays that pass through the white conviction of the sin of racism; penitence; and then conditional, edgy absolution. Some join in these morality plays to sustain their own shaky self-regard or their moral self-importance, often with the cynical assistance of impresarios of the racial street theater like Sharpton, who enact them in real time, at the expense of real people and justice. Journalists write these morality plays into their stories, political choices, and even friendships. Pity the objects of such solicitude. As if enduring racism hasn't been enough, now they must endure being turned into props.

A closely related casualty of my Brooklyn experiences has been faith in leftist schemes for organizing the oppressed by prescriptions based on class analysis or on using race as a stand-in for class. Such strategies lead to the telling of many lies, which the dissemblers themselves come to believe and which too many decent but distracted citizens suborn out of a diffuse racial guilt or cowardice like that which Orwell described in his preface. Although racism and capitalist exploitation are real, some of what passes for antiracism and anticapitalism among otherwise-intelligent "progressive" political chroniclers and activists is unreal because it is self-referential enough to do subtle but corrosive harm to the dignity of its intended beneficiaries through the articulation of a common destiny.

Learning to know when and how this is so, and saying so, can put one at odds with the "antiracist" orthodoxy that is this country's most powerful analogue of the anticapitalist orthodoxy Orwell defied. I have taken this brief personal excursion in order to revivify, with an American twist, at least something of what I cannot help but believe he endured. Let me close by proposing some Stations of the Cross that I see in Orwell's journey as I read him after taking my own.

The first such station on a leftist political writer's road toward strength amid disillusionment is the unforgettable first flush of one's encounter with "true" equality—in Barcelona for Orwell, but for others in Russian collective farms of the early 1930s, Israeli kibbutzim of the early 1950s, Cuban sugar cane harvests and American black-power struggles of the 1960s, *and* on. A second station marks the encroachment of disillusionment itself, not so much with "the people" as with any overly ideologized faith in "the oppressed," or in "race and class" analysis as a road map to justice. The readers of that map are so wishful that soon enough they are telling lies. The damage reinforces Tocqueville's caution, and Orwell's chastened discovery, that the most furious pursuit of equality blinds its celebrants to abdications of freedom and falsifications of fraternity.

A third station: Part of becoming disillusioned is being shunned by keepers of orthodoxy, including academics, editors, and other members of the self-avowedly liberal, independent intelligentsia whom Orwell derided in his preface for *Animal Farm.* They avoid writers like him and anyone who reminds them—as Orwell surely did in writing about Spain and the workers of Wigan—that as parlor champions of "the people" they have stopped thinking precisely where they should have begun. These increasingly self-insulating apologists—for Stalinist anticapitalism in Orwell's time, or for race-industry "antiracism" in our own—include several types. There are smooth interpreters of orthodoxy, like Orwell's sometime publisher Gollancz, some of them avuncular arbiters of what is safe now for progressive people to say. They are deft enough in deploying the larger society's reigning liberal pieties and forms of address to suggest that they're open to grounded decency like Orwell's. They are not.

There are also ingratiators, like the jittery Jonathan Cape, who turned down *Animal Farm* on second reading, struggling earnestly to sustain their liberal respect but unable to deviate from orthodoxy in the end. And there are ideological enforcers like the *Daily Worker*'s Pollitt. And there are legions of academic, literary, journalistic, and political hacks like those with whom Orwell had to deal in order to get work. They do not so much take political positions as look over their shoulders before positioning themselves. These are the diminished, conformist "democrats" whom Tocqueville found bereft of any independent thought or expression and of whom Orwell wrote, simply: "they are afraid of public opinion."[26]

The more such placeholders comport themselves (and think of themselves) as independent professionals, the more assiduously they shield themselves against the moral discomfort of their servility to the orthodoxy of the day. The isolation that so puzzled and frustrated Orwell as he wrote "The Freedom of the Press" had come to him simply because he irritated and even frightened these people by sharing his observations, which had the effect of showing how myopic the editors and publishers had become. The irony in his literary isolation that spring of 1944 is that while he stood for ordinary people, he had no illusion he actually spoke for them (or even to them, at least before *Animal Farm*). He did not consider himself their tribune; *Tribune* was the name of the newspaper he wrote for, but his column there was called "As I Please." It is because he refused to shield himself with higher pretensions that he wound up speaking so reliably for others.

Another Station of the Cross marks the temptation to fall into the arms of the Right upon becoming disillusioned with the Left, or, less often, the converse. The morphology of minds that flip this way doesn't change with the switch; it is reinforced, because they yearn always to be rising against evil cant and convention. When the first ideological sodality isn't liberating anyone and isn't even right about how the other side was wrong, the quivering hurt of that discovery can make the other side seem better than it is. The real enemy, Orwell wrote in the preface, is "the gramophone mind, whether or not one agrees with the record that is being played at the moment."[27]

The gramophone mind, which has jumped from one orthodoxy to another without ever really thinking for itself, accounts for the uncanny resemblance between so much of today's American conservative opinion journalism and the media Stalinism of Gollancz and Pollitt: Many of the tactics and tropes one finds in the work of today's Con-intern mirror those recounted in *The Age of Suspicion,* an acute, humorous account of habits of mind in the Stalinist, Comintern-run American left of the 1930s and 1940s by my cousin James Wechsler, the anticommunist liberal who edited *The New York Post* before Murdoch turned it into a daily reminder that Australia was founded as a penal colony.[28]

When one has reached the Stations of the Cross through which writers Orwell and Wechsler passed, one can tell pretty quickly which station any opinion journalist is writing from. One appreciates why the most important courage is the kind that is willing to anger true believers on all sides. One learns, too, that although it is lonelier to be shunned by both sides than by one, one is freer to stand for the liberal civic center that still respects "the known rule of ancient liberty" and sustains some hope, however chastened, in "the people." That is the only morally trustworthy basis of politics, but because it is so fragile it has too few friends who can address political questions "in an adult manner."

To become a chastened liberal after an ordeal like Orwell's is also to become a connoisseur of bad faith and simple weakness. It is to discover that what left-leaning cultural gatekeepers like those whom Orwell disdained call "politics" is a compensatory moralism—gestural, deceitful, counterproductive, and sometimes even oppressive. On the left, it is the default position of the cohort who, like the British intelligentsia of Orwell's time, blame capitalism for all evil and their own alienation; they find more obvious villains, such as Hitler or George W. Bush, and sacralize its opponents like Stalin or . . . Well, since there is no new "Uncle Joe," this Left has little to say.

In the London of the 1940s this leftist default position escaped Orwell's condemnation because it could not spare its holders the harsh burdens of war against fascism; he confronted it mainly in his last two novels. But in the far more secure and insulated America of the last thirty years of the twentieth century, gatekeepers of what Murray Kempton called "progressive goodthink"[29] discovered racism, and then sexism and homophobia, as the most compelling, if complicated, moral representations of evil, and these have served not only as perfectly legitimate targets but also as mere foils to moral posturing. Keepers of this orthodoxy place undue reliance on gestures and symbols of moral redress because they will never do the heavy lifting to describe, let alone redress, the inequities and injustices of a political economy which they dare not actually oppose yet cannot quite bring themselves to defend.

I have spent too many years offering too many definitive accounts of the American racial orthodoxy not to know that no "genre" of appeal—investigative, ingratiating, humorous, satirical, or jeremiadic—will loosen its grip before events conspire to drive the point home. For now, Orwell's insistence that liberty is the right to tell people what they do not want to hear figures mainly as a maxim for distant places and or a drapery for titillations closer to home. His insistence is honored only in the breach, contained and dismissed in the few slots that are licensed to dissent for the sake of appearances. And this strategy, which suffuses even the craft of reporting, is what makes so much in the American news media so disappointingly vapid. The news media and publishing worlds are weakened further by the understaffing and overwork that keep editors and reporters from thinking.

"Thought is not, like physical strength, dependent upon the number of its agents; nor can authors be counted like the troops which compose an army," wrote Tocqueville in a section of *Democracy in America* called "Liberty of the Press in the United States." "On the contrary, the authority of a principle is often increased by the small number of men by whom it is expressed. The words of one strong-minded man, addressed to the passions of a listening assembly, have more power than the vociferations of a thousand orators; and if it be allowed to speak freely in any one public place, the consequence is the same as if free speaking was allowed in every village. . . . Thought is an invisible and subtle power, that mocks all the efforts of tyranny."[30]

One might argue that the common inclination to join in "the vociferations of a thousand orators" is a consequence of alienation and despair that are unacknowledged or finessed, or of exploitation and bamboozlement, of the perversities of class and the playing fields of Eton. And one might argue—as I did for years—that if somehow this web of oppressions could be untangled, publishers and political actors would stand taller and the misleaders before whom so many cower would be shown up at last.

I don't know anymore. Like Tocqueville in America, Orwell traced the problem of slavery back to Eden, where no exploitation incited it. It would be good to have faith, as Orwell did fleetingly in Barcelona and as even the more aristocratic Tocqueville did at times in America, in democratic man's ability to lift himself and others from sinkholes of illusion and despair and to begin the world anew, as Tom Paine put it; there is some religion in that hope, these writers understood, even though I doubt that they prayed. One keeps trying—Orwell did—and at the last station of this secular cross, one moves from being disillusioned to being unillusioned. Perhaps one keeps faith with a Madisonian, constitutionalist, checks-and-balances realism that accepts the weakness in human nature but is willing to act a bit as if it didn't accept it, and that hedges its bets for the good, with a few protections against majority tyranny.

The figure ground of the journey for me is the hard-bitten journalist's wisdom, a stoical, for others sometimes Christic belief: No matter how hard you fight and how grand or noble your vision, the world will break your heart in the end, but how you bear yourself in the face of that certainty is the test of both friendship and politics. That faith is what confers the liberty to tell people what they don't want to hear, tell them forcefully but without a chip on your shoulder, satirically but not tauntingly, and, at bottom, simply and decently. Only if Tocqueville is still right about the power of "the words of one strong-minded man," and only if editors stand up for truth tellers like Orwell, will democracy in America or anywhere else live to fight another day.

NOTES

1. George Orwell, letter to Herbert Read, August 19, 1945, in *The Collected Essays, Journalism, and Letters of George Orwell,* ed. Sonia Orwell and Ian Angus (New York: Harcourt, Brace & World, 1968), 3:401.

2. Orwell, "The Freedom of the Press," with commentary by Bernard Crick, *Times Literary Supplement,* September 15, 1972, 1039.

3. Orwell, "The Freedom of the Press," 1037.

4. George Orwell, *1984* (New York: Penguin Putnam, 1950), 73.

5. Orwell, "The Freedom of the Press," 1037.

6. Orwell, "The Freedom of the Press," 1037.

7. *Daily Worker* (London), March 17, 1937, cited in Bernard Crick, *George Orwell: A Life* (New York: Penguin Books, 1980), 343.

8. Orwell, "The Freedom of the Press," 1038.

9. Orwell, "The Freedom of the Press," 1038.

10. Orwell, *The Collected Essays,* 3:180–81.

11. Bernard Crick, "How This Essay Came to Be Written," *Times Literary Supplement,* September 15, 1972, 1040.

12. Orwell, "The Freedom of the Press," 1038.

13. Orwell, "The Freedom of the Press," 1038.

14. Orwell, "The Freedom of the Press," 1038.

15. Ivan Turgenev, *Fathers and Sons* (New York: Oxford University Press, 1998), 258.

16. Orwell, "The Freedom of the Press," 1039.

17. Alexis de Tocqueville, *Democracy in America* (New York: Vintage Books, 1990), 2:96.

18. Tocqueville, *Democracy in America,* 1:264.

19. Tocqueville, *Democracy in America,* 1:264.

20. Orwell, "The Freedom of the Press," 1039.

21. Orwell, "The Freedom of the Press," 1038.

22. Orwell, "The Freedom of the Press," 1039.

23. Jim Sleeper, *The Closest of Strangers: Liberalism and the Politics of Race in New York* (New York: W.W. Norton & Co., 1990).

24. Jim Sleeper, *Liberal Racism* (New York: Viking, 1997).

25. Walter Lippmann, *Public Opinion* (New York: Free Press, 1997), 204.

26. Orwell, "The Freedom of the Press," 1038.

27. Orwell, "The Freedom of the Press," 1039.

28. James Wechsler, *The Age of Suspicion* (Westport, Conn.: Greenwood Press, 1953).

29. Murray Kempton, *Newsday,* March 20, 1991, 11.

30. Tocqueville, *Democracy in America,* 1:264.

11

Orwell in an Age of Celebrity

Jonathan B. Imber

George Orwell did not care outwardly what others thought of his opinion. He caused them considerable troubles in this regard, dedicated as they were both to the demands of ideology and to the people who imperfectly embodied them.[1] Orwell recognized the perilous demands of ideology—both Nazism and communism demanded perfection, and as pursuits undertaken by individual men they achieved their goals in the measure of human lives that they destroyed. As momentous as these evil pursuits were, Orwell could not overlook the domestic front out of which the garden varieties of evil grow into terror and genocide. His opposition to totalitarianism, *from the left,* still powerfully attracts those caught in the presumably uncomfortable position of appearing as dissenters against prevailing left positions (on war, for example), even as some notion of *the* Left remains a salient, even vital, perspective for those same dissenters.

Orwell was also a moralizer in the old-fashioned sense. If his opinions about women, homosexuality, and any number of matters presently make him more embarrassing than politically incorrect, it is because such opinions tend to be avoided or rationalized by admirers rather than "interrogated" and denounced by detractors. The relevance of Orwell today, I will argue, comes in his refusal to accept the world as it is, but not on the basis of one or another yet to be attained utopia. Rather, because human beings possess at best an imperfect moral sense about right and wrong, they must be reminded about the limits of their artfulness to be different, even perfect or perfectly awful. He was right on the big matters, but he was also uncannily right on many small ones. This is what confuses those admirers whose ideological predilections remain too strong and who pick and choose among his musings about how to understand an imperfect world.

THE PROBLEM OF ART AND ARTFULNESS

Orwell aspired to criticize art in ways that are now several standard deviations removed from the sophisticated disinterest of the postmodern critic. Criticism itself has grown exponentially in the past half century. The critics are numerous and mostly unknown, but what they criticize, when notice of it is made widely available, is the stuff of modern celebrity. The patron system of artistic creation of any kind has become the corporate system of artistic sponsorship and ownership. Orwell contended that "the golden age of the artist was the age of capitalism," indeed, laissez-faire capitalism, which he further contended was passing away, destroying the independent status of the artist who "must become either a spare-time amateur or an official."[2] Many "spare-time amateurs" are today kept by universities, who insofar as they accept awards from the National Endowment for the Arts, are quasi officials as well. The latest defiant independents who inhabit such cloistered arenas regard themselves over and against corporate-sponsored "art."

Orwell lived before the full expression of this configuration of opposition between state-funded and corporate-sponsored artistic creation. Yet he recognized how the artist's independence was not fundamentally tied to the distance established between art and bourgeois culture. In his admiration and concern for art, he downplayed the class sensibilities he brought so earnestly to the depiction of the lives of real, especially poor, people. Art and criticism of art were first and foremost didactic. Art teaches something, even when it fails. As the psalmist concluded, "From all my teachers I grew wise" (119:99). Orwell proved himself wise in his intense address to the life and work, and failure, of Salvador Dali.

Orwell's "Benefit of Clergy: Some Notes on Salvador Dali" was written in June 1944 and "made a sort of phantom appearance in the *Saturday Book* for 1944. The book was in print when its publishers, Messrs Hutchinson, decided that this essay must be suppressed on grounds of obscenity. It was accordingly cut out of each copy, though for technical reasons it was impossible to remove its title from the table of contents."[3] That the critic was censored because he carefully described what he was criticizing says something for English morals. The review did appear finally in 1946 in England in *Critical Essays,* and in America in *Dickens, Dali and Others.*

Orwell took particular exception to Dali's self-account of his life. He would not accept the neat separation between the character of the art created and the character of its creator. The shock to bourgeois sensibilities that Dali relished was intended to gain attention among a growing middle class no longer guided by institutional elites that could distinguish easily between the inherited criteria of greatness and the elusive but lucrative dynamics of fame. In the absence of a class capable of authoritative praise and condemnation, Orwell assumed such authority himself. He identified a dilemma of modernity in which the achievement of notice—or what today is called celebrity—is more important than who or what is noticed. He saw Warhol coming and so refused to become George Warhol.[4]

Orwell begins with a commentary on the meaning of autobiography "which is only to be trusted when it reveals something disgraceful. A man who gives a good account of himself is probably lying, since any life when viewed from the inside is simply a series of defeats." But, Orwell continues, "even the most flagrantly dishonest book . . . can without intending it give a true picture of its author. Dali's recently published *Life* comes under this heading."[5] He relates the reported events of cruelty and abuse by Dali toward others, especially women, to his surrealist art, which stands out for its "sexual perversity and necrophilia." Among other examples, Orwell describes Dali's literalness about excrement and urination, about decomposing animals and rotting corpses, and about a dying bat covered with ants, this last of which Dali claims to have put in his mouth and bitten in half, ants and all.

Dali's accomplishments as a draughtsman steer Orwell away from simply con-
demning his "personal life" (or by Dali's own account, "secret life"): "He is an
exhibitionist and a careerist, but he is not a fraud. He has fifty times more talent
than most of the people who would denounce his morals and jeer at his paintings.
And these two sets of facts, taken together, raise a question which for lack of any
basis of agreement seldom gets a real discussion." Orwell's moral conclusion is
decisive:

> The point is that you have here a direct, unmistakable assault on sanity and decen-
> cy; and even—since some of Dali's pictures would tend to poison the imagination
> like a pornographic postcard—on life itself. What Dali has done and what he has
> imagined is debatable, but in his outlook, his character, the bedrock decency of a
> human being does not exist. He is as antisocial as a flea. Clearly, such people are
> undesirable, and a society in which they can flourish has something wrong with it.[6]

What is wrong with such a society is defined in two ways. Orwell disparages those
critics of Dali and of art generally who cannot "admit that what is morally degraded can be aesthetically right," and says that such people are "especially dangerous
at a time like the present, when the Ministry of Information and the British Council put power into their hands."[7] In this way, the likes of Joyce, Proust, Lawrence,
and T. S. Eliot become vulnerable to such denigrators of art who see it as having
no real importance one way or the other. Orwell's criticism, including the word
"dangerous," is a presentiment of *Nineteen Eighty-Four,* in which art in the hands
of the state is neither critical nor truthful. He is compelled to defend Dali against
the much broader sweep of "high-brow baiting."

The second sense in which there is something wrong with a society that would
produce a Salvador Dali comes with those who would praise him precisely for
what Orwell considers worst about him: "If you say that Dali, though a brilliant
draughtsman, is a dirty little scoundrel, you are looked upon as a savage. If you
say that you don't like rotting corpses, and that people who do like rotting corpses
are mentally diseased, it is assumed that you lack the aesthetic sense."[8] Orwell
describes two fallacies: a good composition cannot be disgusting, and something
disgusting cannot be a good composition. In either case, there can be no relationship between art and morals, because art is either beyond morality or morality
determines what art is and so is indistinguishable from it.

Orwell wishes to propose a way to bring the question of the relationship between art and morals to bear on the judgment of both our art and our morals. In
so doing, he must ask what the nature of obscenity is. The "benefit of clergy" he
claims is used to exempt artists "from the moral laws that are binding on ordinary
people." As "art," what it depicts is excused from such judgment. Obscenity can
never be entirely a matter of "taste," despite the extraordinary degree to which all
forms of "deviance" have been, in Daniel Patrick Moynihan's memorable phrase,
"defined down," with the exception of the word "deviance" itself, which is now
considered politically incorrect.[9] Even, as in the case of pornography, "knowing it
when you see it," does not adequately guide in an understanding of *cultural* reaction to artistic expression.

This reaction is never based on aesthetic criteria alone. How could it be? The
halving of the National Endowment for the Arts budget in the early 1990s, after

several decades of governmental funding of independent artists and cultural institutions, is interpreted as an act of *politicization,* as if something genuinely cultural
is beyond any sort of political or moral judgment.[10] Orwell saw sooner and more
clearly how the highbrow defenders of aesthetic judgment would try to hide from
accountability to the larger society in which they operated, in the name of a purity
of art for art's sake. At the same time, the reaction to a Robert Mapplethorpe, or
Andreas Serrano, or Damien Hirst, in our own time, reminds us of Orwell's anxiety about the specter of any sort of ministry of information defining what is
offensive. The problem is that on either side of the culture war, too much credence
may be given to the dangers posed by the other side.

The question Orwell posed to his readers about the relationship between art and
morality was not one that can be easily taken up by partisans, perhaps because one
side is too thick-headed and the other too cynical. In either case, Orwell put it best
when he wondered, "If Shakespeare returned to the earth tomorrow, and if it were
found that his favorite recreation was raping little girls in railway carriages, we
should not tell him to go ahead with it on the ground that he might write another
King Lear."[11] Cultural genius does not excuse anything, least of all what is condemned in all others. Yet, benefit of clergy does extend in many ways to our
contemporary artists for whom the novelty of transgressing borders is nothing
more than being noticed for the act of transgressing.

Orwell took the example of Shakespeare having his way with little girls in
railway carriages one step further, arguing that even though Dali could be judged
an excellent draughtsman, he was also "a disgusting human being." The distinction
between technique and the person gifted with it is compared to the utility of a wall
and what it surrounds: "The first thing that we demand of a wall is that it shall
stand up. If it stands up, it is a good wall, and the question of what purpose it
serves is separable from that. And yet even the best wall in the world deserves to
be pulled down if it surrounds a concentration camp." The analogy seems to
threaten the very existence of Dali's work, but Orwell is insistent that as a critic,
he approves of neither the suppression of the work nor the genius of its creator.
Suppression strikes Orwell as evidence of too powerful a state, while deference to
genius can only be extended to an artist who "is also a citizen and a human
being."[12]

SURREALISM AND ITS DISCONTENTS

The question of Dali's connection to Surrealism is briefly remarked by Orwell at
the end of his essay: "Marxist criticism has a short way with such phenomena as
Surrealism. They are 'bourgeois decadence' (much play is made with the phrases
'corpse poisons' and 'decaying *rentier* class'), and that is that." Orwell still wishes
to know why Dali is attracted to necrophilia "and not, say, homosexuality," and
why "the *rentiers* and aristocrats should buy his pictures instead of hunting and
making love like their grandfathers."[13]

The historical question of how sexuality became a subject of broad cultural
exposure and comment has been answered well by Rochelle Gurstein in *The Repeal of Reticence,* which explores those aspects of life that, she concludes, should
remain private and out of public view "or the common world becomes literally

shameless and our shared existence without consequence."[14] Although Gurstein makes no mention of Orwell's similar concerns, his reflections on Dali inform her entire and thoroughgoing analysis of how a succession of elites capitalized on and eventually destroyed such a common world, leaving in its wake ever more publicly visible forms of the shamelessness and tastelessness that irritated Orwell so greatly. This is why the private lives of celebrities, once less open to unofficial public scrutiny, must now share along with all other "private lives" a full disclosure that is an egalitarian feature of democratic and commercial life. No one is permitted to be without a kind of shame that can be broadcast regularly and widely in a culture of shamelessness.

The origins of this peculiar dynamic may be attributed to many social forces and factors, but the public and commercially viable role of the artist is one of its most powerful sources.

Why has art developed as a challenge to bourgeois values even as it depends on the commercial machinery of communication indebted to those values to communicate its hostility and contempt? Jeffrey Meyers is probably not alone in observing that Orwell "naively rose to Dali's obvious bait, and unleashed his puritanical indignation at the artist who confessed that at the age of five he'd flung another little boy off a bridge . . . . He ignored the possibility that Dali's behavior and art were not a symptom of the world's sickness, but a powerful expression of it."[15] But all symptoms *are* expressions or they remain latent or hidden. Meyers's distinction neither clarifies nor debunks Orwell's important balancing of the interests of art and the public it serves but, rather, reinforces the argument that the critics of the critics of reticence are always depicted as the fomenters of "puritanical indignation." The evidence against Dali does not depend, as Meyers would have it, on whether Orwell could distinguish between fantasy and reality in Dali's self-reported episodes. In fact, Orwell states at the outset of "Benefit of Clergy" that "Which of them are true and which are imaginary hardly matters: the point is that this is the kind of thing that Dali would have *liked* to do."[16]

Orwell's critique of the bourgeoisie, quite apart from the surrealists', was indebted to a not often remarked insight that owes its strongest expression to Marx and Engels. The bourgeoisie, rather than challenging conventions, accepts those challenges as part of the necessary fabric of consumption. One does not have to engage in pornography to consume it. When Marx and Engels argued in *The Communist Manifesto* that "The bourgeoisie cannot exist without constantly revolutionizing the instruments of production, and thereby the relations of production, and with them the whole relations of society," they were describing a relationship between production and consumption as well.[17] Orwell's so-called puritanical indignation was directed toward the motivation to confront bourgeois sentiments that were, to his mind, deeper and more substantial than Marxist critics recognized. Those critics were not, as it turns out, on the same side as Orwell who asked instead *why* the rentiers and aristocrats were attracted to Dali in the first place. The answer seems to be a combination of thrill and boredom that marks a distinctive characteristic of a certain form of modern consumption. Orwell's concern was that the alternative between art dictated by the state and degeneracy advocated by socalled free artists was no alternative at all.

If Orwell takes up the "problem of culture" in a way that resides between these two unacceptable alternatives, then it remains only to ask how such culture is established and preserved over time without ossifying and oppressing on the one side or breaking up altogether on the other. Orwell realized that fame in itself was no sin, but the flammable mixture of provocative posturing and a public need to consume all that is noticeable even if it is not worth noticing led him to embody the very elements of judgment that culture requires. In so doing, those who come after him are faced with similar responsibilities taken up first as demands upon the judgment of character itself. Whether one is rewarded for responding to these demands is a matter not in any individual's complete control.

What is at stake finally is the ever-longer distance in our day between a vocation fulfilled and a life noticed by others. Surely in Orwell's own case, his enduring reputation depends on the intensity with which he lived his vocation despite the relative lack of notice and his early death. Today, the critics, talking heads, public intellectuals, and comfortable professors who compete for attention have devalued such notice sufficiently to ask whether its pursuit should be an end in itself or, like the lottery, something more akin to an unexpected dividend. The office of celebrity is ephemeral, and even if its offspring may be buoyed by nepotism, the tests of significance will likely remain the work accomplished rather than the person who accomplished it, the latter being a self-satisfying coincidence with the former and nothing more.

NOTES

1. Victor Gollancz's tortured account of the decision to publish *The Road to Wigan Pier,* which prefaces the book, is a case in point. Lionel Trilling's observations still stand: "He made no effort to show that his heart was in the right place, or the left place. He was not interested in where his heart might be thought to be, since he knew where it was." Lionel Trilling, *The Opposing Self: Nine Essays in Criticism* (London: Secker and Warburg, 1955), 172.

2. George Orwell, *The Collected Essays, Journalism and Letters of George Orwell,* ed. Sonia Orwell and Ian Angus (New York: Harcourt Brace Jovanovich, 1968), 3:229.

3. Orwell, *Collected Essays, Journalism and Letters,* 3:165.

4. A half century earlier, Oscar Wilde faced the institutional judgment of England. In contrast, Orwell's criticisms, like the life he criticized, were free-floating, tied only to notice by an anonymous public, without sanctions from institutional authorities other than the self-censorship of publishers. See Philip Rieff, "The Impossible Culture: Wilde as a Modern Prophet," in *The Feeling Intellect: Selected Writings,* ed. Jonathan B. Imber (Chicago: University of Chicago Press, 1990), 273–90.

5. Orwell, *Collected Essays, Journalism and Letters,* 3:156. Orwell was reviewing Salvador Dali's *The Secret Life of Salvador Dali* (New York: Dial Press, 1942).

6. Orwell, *Collected Essays, Journalism and Letters,* 3:159.

7. Orwell, *Collected Essays, Journalism and Letters,* 3:160.

8. Orwell, *Collected Essays, Journalism and Letters,* 3:160.

9. The idea of political correctness has outlived its usefulness. As an accusation, it was used against those who more often than not embraced an entirely relativistic moral sensibility beyond the spheres of their own immediate and absolutest experience. Those who are said to be most subject to political correctness are the ones who are the most intimidated by it, not those who claim to have been victimized by it. The victims, over time, have been largely vindicated, but this does not mean that bad manners are not judged as such. The sexual revolution provoked a cultural reaction, the legacy of which is a society that remains

highly judgmental about sex even under the stadium lights of the First Amendment. The other spiritual hot potato in the era of political correctness, race, is no longer too hot to handle. Racial grievances are now fatefully balanced between intimations of the bell curve and calls for reparations. That the latter is the flip side of the former will become more evident in years to come, both being profoundly antiliberal.

10. One of Dali's worthy successors, Andreas Serrano, the creator of a crucifix immersed in urine, brought the NEA to its knees in the culture war over arts funding that ensued.

11. Orwell, *Collected Essays, Journalism and Letters,* 3:161.

12. Orwell, *Collected Essays, Journalism and Letters,* 3:161.

13. Orwell, *Collected Essays, Journalism and Letters,* 3:164.

14. Rochelle Gurstein, *The Repeal of Reticence: A History of America's Cultural and Legal Struggles over Free Speech, Obscenity, Sexual Liberation, and Modern Art* (New York: Hill and Wang, 1996), p. 308.

15. Jeffrey Meyers, *Orwell: Wintry Conscience of a Generation* (New York: Norton, 2000), 269.

16. Orwell, *Collected Essays, Journalism and Letters,* 3:156.

17. Karl Marx and Friedrich Engels, *The Communist Manifesto* (New York: Penguin Putnam, 1998 [1848]), 54.

III

Of Biography and Autobiography

12

Writing about Orwell: A Personal Account

PETER STANSKY

At the George Orwell Centenary Conference, I was placed on a panel of Orwell's biographers. There is some irony in this, since I had originally intended to talk about Orwell as text, how in the fecundity and brilliance of his writings he seems to be able, like the Bible, to provide justification for such varying points of view. (In 1984 the most striking example was Hitchens versus Podhoretz. In 2003 it is Hitchens versus Menand.). But having discovered that I'd been placed on a panel with biographers, I took that decision as my mandate. I guess, for better or worse, William Abrahams and I became biographers of Orwell although that was not what we had started out being, and various myths—none of them very important—have arisen out of our transformation. If we were Orwell's biographers, we were in many ways the first; two of three major full biographies are represented on this panel, Michael Shelden having published his *Orwell,* proudly subtitled, at least in the English edition, *The Authorised Biography* in 1991 and Jeffrey Meyers's *Orwell: Wintry Conscience of a Generation* having appeared in 2000. Bernard Crick's *George Orwell,* subtitled on the dust jacket if not on the title page *The First Complete Biography,* was published in 1980. William Abrahams's and my *The Unknown Orwell* appeared in 1972. Our second volume, *Orwell: The Transformation,* came out in 1979. Such a study seems to emerge approximately once a decade. But in 2003 two new ones appeared: D. J. Taylor's *Orwell: The Life* and Gordon Bowker's *George Orwell.*

So as far as I know, there have only been four biographical studies (as distinct from studies that had some biographical content) of Orwell—with a fifth and sixth being published in 2003. And, as I shall discuss, Billy Abrahams and I rather backed into ours; indeed, it was never meant to be "complete": we always intended to end with Spain. Not that there hadn't been biographical information available about Orwell in published form before the publication of *The Unknown Orwell* in 1972. But previous studies had not had a primarily biographical purpose. The most considerable source, obviously, available along those lines was the extremely useful four volumes of *The Collected Essays, Journalism and Letters of George Orwell,* edited by Sonia Orwell and Ian Angus. These volumes appeared in 1968 and also contained a helpful chronology. It was known even at the time that there was much material in print that wasn't included in the four volumes, so the "collected" part of the title was somewhat misleading. Now we are deeply in the debt of Peter Davison, who in the twenty volumes recently published has made everything written by Orwell in publications, letters, interoffice memoranda at the BBC, and so on readily available. No doubt some missed items and some unpublished letters may yet be—perhaps already have been—discovered. But the man we celebrate at this conference has been well recorded, presumably, if he were in a position to comment, somewhat to his distress.

The earlier critical studies had paid some attention to Orwell's life, and that could hardly be otherwise as his writings were so autobiographical. For instance, in 1956 his Eton contemporary, Christopher Hollis, had published *A Study of George Orwell* with its revealing subtitle *The Man and His Works*. In 1960 Rayner Heppenstall had made Orwell one of his subjects, rather meanly, in his *Four Absentees*. That same year in *Twentieth Century* Elisaveta Fen had written her quite wonderful essay on Eileen, Orwell's first wife. Sir Richard Rees, the model for the editor in *Keep the Aspidistra Flying,* had published in 1961 his *George Orwell: Fugitive from the Camp of Victory.* George Woodcock's *The Crystal Spirit: A Study of George Orwell* appeared in 1967 and had as its first chapter "The Man Remembered," particularly dwelling on their interesting disagreements at the time of the outbreak of the Second World War. Raymond Williams had written his important section on Orwell in his *Culture and Society,* and the first version of his short study of Orwell appeared in 1971. Williams's ever-growing dislike of Orwell has been intriguingly chronicled in John Rodden's study of Orwell criticism. That same year, 1971, *The World of George Orwell* appeared in George Weidenfeld's series, *The World of . . . .* Edited by Miriam Gross, it contained eighteen mainly biographical essays by a very bright group of British writers, and one Burmese, Maung Htin Aung, who claimed that, as a school boy, he had been hit by Orwell. Aung went on to become an extremely distinguished historian of his country.

One might even say that one of the most important biographical takes—brief as it was—on Orwell had appeared as early as 1952 in Lionel Trilling's introduction to the first American edition of *Homage to Catalonia.* When originally published, *Homage* had been ignored to an extent and the reviews that appeared were mostly negative as it appealed, with rare exception, to neither the Right nor the Left range of opinions on the Spanish Civil War. Much of the stock was destroyed in the Blitz. One was deeply grateful that it reappeared in the early 1950s, and it undoubtedly did not decrease interest in it that it was, as were *Animal Farm* and *Nineteen Eighty-Four,* a central document in the cold war. Trilling's introduction was a wonderful piece of writing, and perhaps its most famous passage was as follows:

> It happened by a curious chance that on the day I agreed to write this introduction, and indeed at the very moment that I was reaching for the telephone to tell the publisher that I would write it, a young man, a graduate student of mine, came in to see me, the purpose of his visit being to ask what I thought about his doing an essay on George Orwell. My answer, naturally, was ready, and when I had given it and we had been amused and pleased by the coincidence, he settled down for some chat about our common subject. But I asked him not to talk about Orwell. I didn't

want to dissipate in talk what ideas I had, and also I didn't want my ideas crossed with his, which were sure to be very good. . . . Then, as if he could not resist making at least one remark about Orwell himself, he said suddenly in a very simple and matter-of-fact way, "He was a virtuous man." And we sat there, agreeing at length about this statement, finding a curious pleasure in talking about it.[1]

The graduate student was, it is said, Steven Marcus.

Although I have unlimited respect for both figures in that conversation so many years ago, in my own view it did George Orwell a disservice. It represents a major strand in both the biographical and critical approaches to Orwell. That this dispute is alive and well is made abundantly clear, I believe, in the present debate that has been going on about Orwell and in which Christopher Hitchens is the central figure and Louis Menand, Stefan Collini, and Leon Wieseltier have participated. In some senses it is, although those four jolly controversialists have not put it that way, a biographical dispute. It seems to me that in the last analysis Hitchens and Wieseltier are in the Trilling camp—and in many ways it is a highly honorable camp—of Orwell as the man of virtue. He is the man of virtue who got it right about imperialism, fascism, and communism. That is true, but is virtue Orwell's most important quality? Collini is more concerned about attacking Hitchens as the practitioner of what he calls the "Higher Bullshit Bullshit," playing on Hitchens's dedication in his Orwell book, and Menand has his own take on the Orwell who is, he says, "honest, decent, wrong."[2] I may be stretching things a bit to see Collini and Menand as supporters of the Orwell that I prefer to the Trilling one. That is the Orwell that is, in my view, something greater than a man of virtue, the "St. George" that figures in the subtitle of the first edition of John Rodden's study but has since been excised. What William Abrahams and I were concerned with in our two books was the making of Orwell, the artist and the writer. We believed that Orwell's caliber as an artist and as a writer was ultimately greater than even his virtue.

I hope it might be of interest to say something of how we came to write our books, which seems appropriate to this panel of biographers: the biography of a biography, if it is a biography. The origins of the books are very much on my mind at the moment as in a month's time I am to attend my fiftieth reunion at Yale, and it was at Yale that the study took its first shape, although it has its origins even earlier. When I was growing up one of my favorite records was the songs of the International Brigade of the Spanish Civil War sung by Ernst Busch. I particularly remember the heavily accented English in the verses by Brecht: "Zo left, two three! zo left, two three! . . . for you are a vorker too" and how moved I was by his rendition of "Freiheit!" When I was an undergraduate at Yale, the school's anglophilia helped lead me to combine my interest in the Spanish Civil War with an interest in Britain, reinforced by a two-week visit to England the summer after my sophomore year. I was also deeply influenced by a classmate, Russell Thomas, whose father had encouraged the young T. S. Eliot, a family friend. Russell introduced me—at quite a distance—to the wonderful ins and outs of the English literary world.

I became increasingly fascinated by the effort of trying to understand another world, both past and foreign, with which I had no connection of any sort. Wandering the stacks of the Yale library I took growing pleasure in the serendipity of finding appropriate texts. My original intention was to study in some sort of general way the English who had fought in the International Brigade. But I found myself quite quickly gravitating to the literary figures who were involved in the struggle—I continue to find my greatest interest where social, cultural, literary, and political life meet. I decided that I would write about four young Englishmen of the 1930s who went to Spain: John Cornford, Julian Bell, George Orwell, and Stephen Spender.

As I've noted, *Homage to Catalonia* had just recently become available. In the United States *Dickens, Dali and Others,* with some of his canonical essays had been published in 1946 and then *Shooting an Elephant and Other Essays* appeared in 1950. (The later 1930s works weren't published in the United States until the 1950s.) His great autobiographical essay, "Such, Such Were the Joys . . ." had just been published in 1952 posthumously in the *Partisan Review.* He had written it originally in 1947 for publication in Cyril Connolly's *Horizon* but it became too long to appear there, or so it was said. It was a devastating memoir of the boarding school, St. Cyprian's, that he had attended, as had Connolly, from the age of eight to fourteen. There has been some speculation that Orwell never meant for it to be published, but that seems unlikely as a writer writes to be published. And because of the stricter laws of libel in England. it could not appear there until 1968 in the four volumes after the death, at an advanced age, of the headmistress of the school, Mrs. Vaughan Wilkes.

When Billy Abrahams and I were working on our book and visited Cyril Connolly near Eastbourne, we hadn't realized that Mrs. Vaughan Wilkes was still alive and was still living in a school building left after a fire had closed the school. (Set by an old boy?) Connolly had insisted that we must go to see her, which provided us with one of our most memorable research experiences. We asked him if he had seen her, considering that he lived so close. He said it would be impossible for him to do so as he found the idea so terrifying, that he would be reduced to being a schoolboy again. That was pretty amazing coming from someone such as Connolly. I have a memory that at a later point he told us that he was one of the few people who attended her funeral—perhaps to make sure that she was dead.

So a lot of Orwell's writings were available when I became interested in him, yet there were many essays that were still only to be found through the joy of the hunt for periodicals in the Yale stacks. Orwell's reputation was considerable but had yet to reach the extraordinary heights in which it would seem that every school child, at least in America, read *Animal Farm* (or saw the cartoon version paid for by the CIA) and *Nineteen Eighty-Four.* I've always held a theory about why biographies of Orwell don't sell as well as one might hope—at least that has been my experience, perhaps my fellow panelists have had better luck. My theory is that high school students don't believe that actual people have written the books that they are required to read, and hence in later years, they have little interest in their biographies. Perhaps from the point of view of literature, that is all for the best.

In any case, I put my work as a senior at Yale aside, never thinking I might return to it. At a Christmas party in 1960 given by Richard Poirier I met Billy Abrahams. I was just finishing my Ph.D. dissertation on the British Liberal Party at the end of the nineteenth century. One topic I had material on but which hadn't formed part of my dissertation was the amusing question of who would succeed Tennyson as Poet Laureate—ultimately it was the dread Alfred Austin. Billy and

I wrote this up and it was virtually my first publication, in *History Today.* Billy then asked what we should do next and I showed him my jejune senior essay. Some time later, armed with a book contract, we then embarked upon a study that would discuss the same four men—Cornford, Bell, Orwell, and Spender—in Spain. Using the summers for research in England we worked on all four at the same time. We saw Spender quite a few times—Billy had met him earlier in the United States. For the other three, our main contacts were the two brothers, Christopher for John Cornford and Quentin for Julian Bell, and for Orwell, his widow, Sonia.

This was the early 1960s and, if I remember correctly, Sonia, though divorced, was still going under the name of Sonia Pitt-Rivers. Orwell was in some sense a nonexistent name; she had been married to a pseudonym. It was certainly our impression that Orwell didn't mean very much to her at that point. At first we got along extremely well, and Billy in particular was very taken with her. We had a glorious rather drunken lunch at the White Tower in which her refrain as we had another drink was "in for a shilling, in for a pound." I was attending a historical conference and eventually I staggered off, improbably, to a conference tea with the Archbishop of Canterbury at Lambeth Palace.

We were just interested at that point in Orwell in Spain. I had acquired a copy of his will from Somerset House where he indicated that "no biography shall be written." Richard Rees didn't think that he meant it very seriously and put it in because he felt, quite rightly, that no biography can fully recreate its subject. Also, as his writings are so frequently autobiographical, perhaps he felt that he had said what he wanted known. In any case, such a statement had a moral but not a legal standing. We did not intend to write a biography, so that was not a problem.

Sonia did not at that point seem to care one way or another, and she urged us to see people who would give us biographical information, most particularly her sister-in-law, Avril. In any case, some time before Sonia had commissioned Malcolm Muggeridge to write a biography, but he had given up the idea. Contrary to Jeffrey Meyers's inaccurate statement in a recent piece in the *Partisan Review,* we made no misleading statement in order to gain entry to the recently established archive at University College, London. No undertaking was required at that point, and no undertaking was given. The archive then was mostly a convenient gathering together of fugitive published pieces, although it was building up its manuscript holdings. Billy and I were instrumental in bringing into the archive a few items, but they were dramatic ones. We unearthed Orwell's first two publications, his patriotic poems about the war in 1914 and 1916 in the *Henley and South Oxfordshire Standard.* We may have first seen them in Mrs. Vaughan Wilkes's scrapbook. At our urging, Sir Steven Runciman sent to the archive the 1920 letter that begins the four-volume "Collected Works" of 1968, which describes unenthusiastically a tramping experience. On visiting Frank Jellinek in Switzerland we persuaded him to send to the archive his letter from Orwell, which Orwell signed first Eric Blair and then after it George Orwell, a rare instance when the two names appear at the same time. Those two signatures are embossed on the bindings of the four volumes of the collected works.

Through the generosity of their brothers and others, we discovered so much material about Julian Bell and John Cornford—both of whom had been killed in Spain—that we decided to make that a separate book—our favorite of the four we wrote together, *Journey to the Frontier,* published in 1966. It seemed to us that neither Orwell nor Spender fitted into such a study. In any case, there wasn't room. Although we did some research on the Spender part, that seemed to be fading as a possibility because Spender insisted that it would have to be a sanitized version, and it was his activities at the time of the Civil War that caused the controversy that he had some years ago with David Leavitt. One awaits with great interest the authorized biography of him by John Sutherland. Can it be that Spender's widow is causing delays, as apparently it was finished some time ago?

Billy and I did wish to write about Orwell. How to do so? Our interest had always been the significance of the Spanish experience for him. I've always been most interested in beginnings, in this case the making of Orwell, more so than in his years of triumph, the decade of the 1940s, so cruelly ending with his premature death. Some seemed to think that because of our fight with Sonia we had been prevented from writing a third volume. We never intended to do so. But we hadn't decided how to approach our subject. Naturally we sent Sonia a copy of *Journey to the Frontier.* We had intimations of problems; rumbles that *Journey* was biographical.

Now Sonia seemed much more concerned with the biographical wishes stated in Orwell's will. She was much more the widow Orwell than she had been when we first met. We would hear later from our friend Bob Treuhaft, Jessica Mitford's husband, who was also a good friend of Sonia's and, I believe, her American lawyer, that the Orwell contracts had been renegotiated. I think that under the American copyright laws of the time—the twenty-eight-year renewal stipulation—the rights for *Nineteen Eighty-Four* were now worth a lot more. Sonia was no longer happy with us, but we were to have dinner in Paris to see if we could work things out.

It was a disastrous evening. When we met for a drink at her flat before dinner we made two serious mistakes. We had seen quite a bit of Orwell's sister Avril very much at Sonia's suggestion at the time of our first meeting. Avril had been wonderfully helpful, but we never should have pointed that out to Sonia as there was no love lost between them. Also earlier in the day we had seen the beautiful Judy Innes, and dwelling on her beauty also did not warm Sonia's heart. We went on to dinner. Billy and Sonia argued about what the book would be like while I, in my insensitive way, ate my delicious and expensive chicken. Neither Billy nor Sonia touched their food. Sonia said we could go ahead and continue to be allowed to use the archive *only* if we would show her the manuscript and give her total approval. This was unacceptable, of course. The conversation grew quite emotional, and so we parted.

Access to the archive didn't matter much, as we had been in it already, particularly during my Guggenheim year in 1966–67 and there was valuable manuscript material elsewhere. It didn't hurt us with others that we were on bad terms with Sonia. We now felt that we could write whatever book we felt was right, and we would deal with the matter of quotation as best we could. We quoted less that we might have liked, but I think that biographers frequently rely too much on quotations and so I don't think the book suffered too much by that limitation. The lawyers advised us to take out one brief statement or a quotation—I don't remember which—that was exclusively based on material in the archive. Orwell's agent, Mark Hamilton, wrote us a stuffy letter when the book came out saying that, despite our acting badly, he would take no action. (Of course the risk of causing a fuss is that it would be likely to help sales as long as there weren't considerable legal costs.) Ironically, Hamilton particularly castigated us for quoting the complete poem about the death of Kitchener that we had discovered.

The Unknown Orwell appeared in 1972 to generally favorable reviews; particularly gratifying was Cyril Connolly in the *New York Times.* Stephen Spender wrote a prevaricating review in *The New York Review of Books,* typically trying to remain on good terms with both us and Sonia. Our book also helped precipitate further Orwell biographies. Sonia Orwell denounced us in a letter in the *Times Literary Supplement,* claiming that our book was full of errors that would be pointed out in due course. These were never listed. Bernard Crick informed his readers that some of his sources disagree with our account, as if writing a biography were not a matter of coming to a judgment about various competing accounts. Interviewees not surprisingly interpret polite silence as total agreement. Sonia was livid that the book had appeared and was determined to do something about it. In the fall of 1972, in both the *Times Literary Supplement* and the *New York Times,* Bernard Crick had written about a newly discovered introduction to *Animal Farm.* Crick was on the horizon as an Orwell scholar and Sonia appointed him the official biographer. Once his book was finished, she tried unsuccessfully to stop it. Later Michael Sheldon could deal with Mark Hamilton, Orwell's agent, because Sonia died in 1980, apparently cheated of most of the Orwell income by her accountant. And Jeffrey Meyers had the great advantage, as he acknowledges, of the work of Peter Davison.

The life of a writer is interesting. But in the last analysis, biographers of writers should be servants of the text. As a historian I am also particularly interested in what a life can tell one about the society in which the life was lived. Orwell, the patriotic radical, was in a particular English tradition and provides much material for those who are interested in the current preoccupation with questions of Englishness. I presume that my colleagues here would agree that the main reason for studying the life of a writer is to illuminate the work. To the extent that William Abrahams's and my contributions, written so long ago now but still in print, may have done so, we achieved our purpose.

NOTES

1. Lionel Trilling, introduction, in George Orwell, *Homage to Catalonia* (New York: Harcourt, Brace, Jovanovich, 1952), vii–viii.
2. Louis Menand, "Honest, Decent, Wrong," *The New Yorker,* January 27, 2003, 84–91.

13

Orwell: Unmasker of Underlying Realities

Dennis Wrong

There are, I gather, a few of us left who are venerable enough to have read close to the time they were first published many of Orwell's major nonfictional essays as well as the two later works of fiction that made him famous. In early 1939, at the age of fifteen, dining with my parents at an expensive restaurant in either Paris or Geneva (where we were living), I expressed awe at the décor and ambience; my father remarked that an English writer who had worked as a waiter in such posh places had reported that the waiters regularly stuck their thumbs in the soup and picked up to serve after brushing off only lightly steaks they had dropped in the dirty sawdust on the bespattered kitchen floor; this induced me to read *Down and Out in Paris and London* from my parents' library. The next autumn at boarding school in Canada I discovered the Penguin Books periodical *New Writing* edited by John Lehmann to which Orwell contributed essays on life and politics in wartime England, and I also read my first critical discussion of Orwell's work in a Pelican Book by Lehmann of the same title. These British publications were not then available in the United States, although Orwell's "London Letter" column in *Partisan Review* reprinted some of them in addition to a few of his regular "As I Please" columns from Aneurin Bevan's journal *Tribune.* I think I read *Homage to Catalonia,* the best of Orwell's book-length memoirs, at roughly the same time out of a special interest in the Spanish Civil War, a result of having gone to school in Geneva with the sons of the Spanish Republic's President Negrin, Foreign Minister Del Vayo, and Ambassador to London Azcarate. Azcarate became a leader of the Spanish Communist Party both when in exile in Paris and after the fall of Franco in Spain.

I decided to become an "intellectual," which at the time included adopting left-wing political views, right after the outbreak of the Second World War. This was in rebellion against the Canadian elite prep school where my parents had sent me as a boarder after two previous years in Geneva at an "international school" (that was its name) for the children of delegates to the League of Nations (my father being the Canadian delegate). American socialists, including Norman Thomas's party and not just the communists in the years of the Stalin-Hitler pact, opposed the war; however, as a believer in the "collective security" affirmed by the League of Nations and a passionate critic, like my parents, of the British-French "appeasement" policy capped by the 1938 Munich agreement, I strongly supported the eventual decision to go to war after Hitler had invaded Poland. Orwell instantly appealed to me both as a socialist who was also a supporter of the war, most notably in his essay "My Country Left or Right," which was later chosen for the title of the first volume of the posthumously published collection of his essays, journalism, and letters edited by Sonia Orwell and Ian Angus. The title perhaps suggests a self-sufficient patriotism, and Orwell was certainly an eloquent lover of England, especially its countryside, but he affirmed the justice and necessity of finally trying to curb militarily Hilter's aggressions and this was the basis of my attraction to Orwell.

In 1942, during my freshman year at the University of Toronto, I read "Inside the Whale," Orwell's justly famous essay on Henry Miller, belatedly published in the United States in a *New Directions* anthology. Of Orwell's other 1930s publications, unsurprisingly, I read neither the long-out-of-print *The Road to Wigan Pier* nor the four early novels until they were reprinted after *Animal Farm* and *Nineteen Eighty-Four* had made their author famous in the following decade. Those last two books were touted by ardent anticommunist conservatives during the early years of the cold war as well as by enemies of the postwar Labour government in Britain, although Orwell until the end of his life protested this use of his work and affirmed his commitment to "socialism," inevitably redefining it from time to time in response to changes in the world. Dwight Macdonald, who had printed Orwell in his short-lived left-wing journal *Politics* and carried on regular correspondence with him, gave me in 1948 a letter of introduction to Orwell when I was planning a summer visit to England. Macdonald told me that Orwell welcomed visits from young American (or Canadian) intellectuals. Alas, the letter arrived too late and I received it only after returning to graduate school in New York, though I doubt I could or would have traveled to the Scottish island where Orwell was living for most of that summer. He died just over a year later and I have ever since much regretted my failure to meet him. Like so many other young intellectuals of the anti-Stalinist Left as we called ourselves, he was a hero and "role-model," both politically and as a writer of prose.

Enough of these less than significant personal memories. In the two decades following his death in early 1950, memoirs and printed interviews by people who had known Orwell were published. Biographies, several of them massive, have appeared in each of the last three decades by authors who could not have known him personally, Jeffrey Meyers's Orwell biography, *Orwell: Wintry Conscience of a Generation* (2000), was followed by two published in 2003, *Orwell: The Life* by D. J. Taylor and *George Orwell* by Gordon Bowker. The clarity and directness of Orwell's prose, "clear as a pane of glass" as he said he wanted it to be,[1] have been amply noted, praised, and assigned as exemplary to writing classes in English. His "integrity" and "objectivity," his commitment to the truth however disturbing or banal, have often been extolled. These combined qualities of performance and of morality account for the unique appeal that has instantly struck so many readers: the sense that here was a writer who, in the later idiom of the 1960s, was truly "telling it like it is" without any hype, pretension, self-serving apologetics, or even literary adornment. There can hardly be much to add to the nearly universal rec-

ognition and affirmation of these qualities in his cultural criticism and political
essays.

I initially thought of entitling this piece "Orwell and the Decline of Political
Faith," but I chose the more general and abstract title because Orwell's gifts of
undercutting rhetoric and exposing false facades were not confined to politics, as
most notably shown in the nonpolitical *Down and Out in Paris and London,* his
very first book. Looking back at the historical context of Orwell's political writings, however, I am struck by how long ago it seems today that the most urgent
political issue was whether "totalitarianism," initially exemplified only by the Soviet
Union and Nazi Germany, represented "the wave of the future." It is generally
forgotten that that phrase was first used by none other than Anne Morrow Lindbergh, wife of the famous aviator and daughter of a Republican senator from New
Jersey, who used it in 1940 to characterize with approval Nazi Germany.[2] The
totalitarian label is often misused nowadays to refer to *any* undemocratic, authoritarian state, which trivializes the term and misses the distinctive historical resonance that accounted for its coinage and widespread adoption. Orwell, Arthur
Koestler, and Franz Borkenau were the first writers to project a fearsome negative
image of "totalitarianism" after observing as soldiers in the Spanish Civil War the
behavior of their Stalinist allies; Borkenau in 1940 wrote the first book with
"totalitarian" in the title.[3] The now-forgotten German refugee Emil Lederer, who
taught at the New School for Social Research's "University in Exile," was in 1940
the first theorist of totalitarianism. The word had previously been used approvingly
by several figures on both the right and the left, including Mussolini to describe
fascism and Gramsci to describe communism.[4] Hannah Arendt was the major
theorist of totalitarianism as a new historical phenomenon, but Orwell in *Nineteen
Eighty-Four* anticipated her by a few years in imagining a full-fledged version of
it.[5] They both even gave the same hypothetical example of the totalitarian power
over cognition itself: the power to dictate that 2 plus 2 equals 5 (though not the
best example in citing a purely analytic rather than an empirical synthetic statement). An admirer of Arendt, I have nevertheless always, like Orwell's first major
biographer Bernard Crick, been aggrieved by her Olympian stance as a German
philosopher in failing to give credit to Orwell, "plain Billy Brown from London
town" in Crick's words, for anticipating her vision by a few years. Both Orwell
and Arendt were certainly right to see totalitarianism as a permanent possibility in
advanced industrial society, a possibility since enhanced by new technologies of
communication and surveillance.

Yet "possibility" is a far cry from "probability" and the extinction in the West
of both fascism and communism has rendered Orwellian and Arendtian forebodings obsolescent. The age of apocalyptic utopian hopes transformed in attempts to
realize them into regimes arousing apocalyptic dystopian fears has surely ended.
Orwell was a major prophet of that age, coincident as it was with most of the past
century. Perhaps the discrediting of totalitarianism applies only to the West: regimes that might be described as totalitarian have recently flourished in Asia and
Africa, with Iraq under Saddam Hussein, allegedly an admirer of Stalin, being the
most notable recent example. But Arab nationalism and fundamentalist Islam,
however threatening to a vital resource and to regional nonaligned states, are
hardly equivalent to the threats posed by Germany and Russia in the previous
century. I do not mean to criticize Orwell in seeing him as a figure from a past he

understood so well that his name has become an adjective for aspects of it: few writers on politics ever achieve such a status. Indeed, his warnings were at least partially self-defeating in the signal contribution they made to the "end of utopia" (Russell Jacoby)[6] and its dystopian negations, to the discrediting of activist efforts to convert "the dream of the golden mountains" (Malcolm Cowley)[7] into reality. Orwell's conception in *Nineteen Eighty-Four* of new techniques of surveillance was actually quite modest: the most frightening imaginative feature of the book was his vision that rulers might dispense with *any* legitimating ideology at all, that is, with any invocation of noble ends to justify oppressive, even brutal, means, but that they might fully acknowledge and consciously accept what the critics of earlier tyrannical regimes had seen as the hidden underlying truths about their leaders' motivations. For example, in *Nineteen Eighty-Four*, O'Brien says, "The Party seeks power entirely for its own sake. We are not interested in the good of others; we are interested solely in power. . . . One does not establish a dictatorship in order to safeguard a revolution; one makes the revolution in order to establish the dictatorship. The object of persecution is persecution. The object of torture is torture. The object of power is power."[8] The full speech is relevant. Philip Rahv, in a brilliant review, may have been right that a ruling elite consciously capable of such cynical realism is psychologically implausible, but Orwell's grasp of the underlying motivations of totalitarian rulers made the book much more than a work of dystopian science fiction.[9]

The decline of comprehensive visions of utterly "new societies" inspiring and motivating believers as "secular religions" (Raymond Aron's phrase)[10] marks the period since the collapse of the Soviet Union and its satellites. As the late François Furet concluded a few years ago in what is likely to remain the best single history of "The Idea of Communism in the Twentieth Century" (the subtitle of his book): "The idea of *another* society has become almost impossible to conceive of, and no one in the world today is offering any advice on the subject or even trying to formulate a new concept. Here we are condemned to live in the world as it is."[11] I don't agree, however, with Furet's ensuing statement that this is a state "too austere and contrary to the modern condition to last." On the other hand, we have certainly not arrived at "the end of history" (Fukuyama)[12]: fierce political conflicts, even verging on violence, over particular government policies and territorial jurisdictions, as well as conflicts between classes and ethnic groups, will indubitably continue; moreover, I have already suggested that the abandonment of totalistic political claims may be confined to, or at least centered in, the West. Paul Berman is right to stress in his new book the similarities between radical Islamism and the various ferociously nationalist antiliberal movements in Europe after the First World War, though I do not find his inclusion of communism among these movements entirely convincing, granting the continuities between Russian nationalism and Stalinism.[13] Religion did not come to an end with the passing of the Age of Faith and the end of persecutions of rival religions and nonbelievers, even of adherents to variants of the same overall faith. It is, incidentally, misleading to conceive of the political "secular religions" as having come into being as substitutes for waning deistic religions: they had their own autonomous origin in the massive unplanned and unforeseen social changes since the end of the Middle Ages, Polanyi's "Great Transformation."[14] Nor is it true that human beings require faith in a totalistic worldview, sacred or secular, to which they become passionate-

ly attached, though minorities with such an outlook certainly have had a dispropor-
tionate influence on the course of history. But most people get along with pluralistic, compartmentalized orientations to reality. With the loss of belief in
all-embracing visions of radically different "social systems," actual or potential,
there is no reason why, Furet to the contrary notwithstanding, such a situation may
not endure indefinitely while political divisions over more limited issues persist.

But this may seem to be saying nothing new: after all, nearly half a century ago
Raymond Aron and Daniel Bell declared "the end of the ideological age."[15] They
had in mind the defeat of fascism and Nazism in war and their own early and far-
sighted discernment and rejection of Soviet totalitarianism. Though right in the
long run, they were a bit premature: the 1960s resurgence of the Left in both
Europe and America almost seemed to be a deliberate effort dramatically to refute
the "end of ideology" thesis. To continue the analogy with the Age of Faith, one
recalls that there were periodic religious revivals well after religion had begun "its
melancholy, long, withdrawing roar" (Matthew Arnold's great poem "Dover Beach").
The New Left struck me at the time as the end of something rather than a new
beginning, a willed attempt to breathe new life into a set of political and ideological tenets that had originated over a century earlier but that had no future. Their
demise became complete only with the quick and generally peaceful collapse of
communism in Russia and its satellites two decades later. Considering that most
socialists in the West had for decades been anticommunist, or at least noncommunist, repudiating any identification with the Soviet model as their goal, it is a bit
surprising and needs further explanation than it has received that it was not until
the Soviet collapse that the "death of socialism" fully transpired. There were
groups on the left who had argued that the political end of communism need not
mean the "restoration of capitalism," that is, the end of public or cooperative
"ownership" of the economy. But that is what happened in the Soviet Union and
its Eastern European satellites, quickly and with minimal violence. A few Western
socialists even argued that the end of communism would actually strengthen socialism by ridding it of delusive identification with the Soviet Union and its replicas. Nothing of the kind has occurred.

Orwell undoubtedly should still serve as a model for penetrating analysis of the
implications of commercial popular culture. One would like to have heard him on
the subject of television. But as a political analyst, he is primarily relevant to the
previous century. To have so discerned its most menacing aspects and the fearsome
additional potential they projected is an enormous achievement for which one
hopes he will receive eternal credit.

NOTES

1. George Orwell, *The Collected Essays, Journalism and Letters,* ed. Sonia Orwell and
Ian Angus (New York: Harcourt Brace Jovanovich, 1968).

2. Anne Morrow Lindbergh, *The Wave of the Future: A Confession of Faith* (New York:
Harcourt, Brace and Company, 1940).

3. Arthur Koestler, *Darkness at Noon* (New York: Macmillan, 1941); Franz Borkenau,
The Totalitarian Enemy (London: Faber and Faber, 1940).

4. See Benito Mussolini, "The Doctrine of Fascism," in Carl Cohen, *Communism, Fascism, and Democracy: The Theoretical Foundations* (New York: Random House, 1962).

5. Hannah Arendt, *The Origins of Totalitarianism* (San Diego: Harcourt Brace Jovanovich, 1979).

6. Russell Jacoby, *The End of Utopia: Politics and Culture in an Age of Apathy* (New York: Basic Books, 1999).

7. Malcolm Cowley, *The Dream of the Golden Mountains: Remembering the 1930s* (New York: Viking Press, 1980).

8. George Orwell, *Nineteen Eighty-Four* (New York: Plume, 2003).

9. Philip Rahv, "The Unfuture of Utopia," *Partisan Review,* July 16, 1949.

10. Raymond Aron, *The Dawn of Universal History: Selected Essays from a Witness of the Twentieth Century* (New York: Basic Books, 2002).

11. François Furet, *The Passing of an Illusion: The Idea of Communism in the Twentieth Century* (Chicago: University of Chicago Press, 1999).

12. Francis Fukuyama, *The End of History and the Last Man* (New York: Free Press, 1992).

13. Paul Berman, *Terror and Liberalism* (New York: W.W. Norton, 2003).

14. Karl Polanyi, *The Great Transformation: The Political and Economic Origins of Our Time* (Boston: Beacon Press, 2001).

15. Daniel Bell, *The End of Ideology: On the Exhaustion of Political Ideas in the Fifties* (Cambridge, Mass.: Harvard University Press, 2000).

14

Third Thoughts about Orwell?

DAPHNE PATAI

Years ago, I was an Orwell fan—a purely conventional one, admiring him for what I took to be his honesty, fair-mindedness, and passion for justice. Then, careful reading and rereading of his work, over many semesters during which I was teaching courses on utopian fiction, gave me second thoughts. These were set out in my book *The Orwell Mystique: A Study in Male Ideology,* published in 1984. The feminist reading of Orwell's work I undertook in that book produced an appraisal that found Orwell a most peculiar kind of moral exemplar and political hero.

My argument at the time was twofold: First, Orwell's famed decency, honesty, and political rectitude stopped well short of including questions of gender justice, though this was an important theme of his time, evident in the writings of well-known contemporaries such as Virginia Woolf and Vera Brittain; and, second, Orwell's overt political commitments were constantly undermined by his anxiety about eroding masculinity, which made him fear that socialism would lead to the sort of soft, feminized world that he distinctly despised. I supported these contentions with a very close reading of everything I could get my hands on written by Orwell, published and unpublished.[1]

Since then, two things have happened to make me reconsider Orwell's importance and to alter my opinion of his contributions and their worth. One is general and the other personal. The first is the spread of postmodernist rhetoric, with its pretended skepticism about everything, its attempt to reduce all reality to a "text," and its wild claims about the instability and self-referentiality of language. These uncannily recall Orwell's description of Ingsoc, with its denial of objective reality and embrace of an eternally mutable past. By contrast, Orwell's plainspoken assertions about language, and his conviction that it could adequately describe reality, seem more important to me now than they appeared to be a few decades ago when I had not yet been exposed to the vacuity of many academic intellectuals' pronouncements on this subject. I lack the space here to dwell on these ludicrous assertions (noting only that even postmodernists take antibiotics rather than disinfecting their discourse), but will merely refer to the hoax perpetrated in 1996 by Alan Sokal, which beautifully exposed the grandiosity and sheer stupidity of humanities' professors who somehow manage to reconcile their "correct" politics with a sweeping disavowal of reality. The dishonesty, pretentiousness, and viscosity of their positions naturally brought Orwell—the writer who celebrated lucidity and common sense—to mind.[2]

The second event that caused me to reconsider Orwell's work, although it was essentially personal, also relates to a general phenomenon in academe, and that is my own disillusionment with the role of feminism in teaching and research. The dismay I experienced in the course of spending ten years in a women's studies program is, of course, similar to the disillusionment that many other former loyalists have gone through as they have seen movements for which they once held great hopes succumb to orthodoxy, intolerance, and petty policing. In particular, it seems to me now that I had neglected to grasp the depth of the disappointment and irascibility that accompany such awakenings. Not surprisingly perhaps, this experience also made me think differently, and more sympathetically, about Orwell's trajectory.

Of course, Orwell was not the only dystopian writer or political essayist who has frequently come to my mind in recent years as I contemplated, and participated in, the academic scene. As often it was Zamyatin, especially his 1923 essay "On Literature, Revolution, Entropy, and Other Matters" and his novel *We* (first published, in English translation, in 1924), without which neither Aldous Huxley's *Brave New World* nor Orwell's *Nineteen Eighty-Four* would in all likelihood have been written. Zamyatin tirelessly warns against the entropy that invariably leads to rigidity and ossification of once vibrant social movements and ideas. He argues for the necessity of perpetual heresy if the tendency for new thought to become calcified is to be avoided, and he writes compellingly of the horrors of a panoptical world in which private space has been eliminated. The case he makes is for passion and imagination, as against the domination of mathematical reasoning. And to these appeals, writing in a different (ideologically stultifying and Stalinist) context, Orwell, in *Nineteen Eighty-Four,* added the case for reason, logic, and the ability to think for oneself as the foundations of a free society.

Actually, the two trends I found so disturbing—feminism and postmodernism—have joined forces in recent feminist attacks on logic, reason, and the primacy of facts. Let me give some examples of this collusion.

Not long ago I found myself defending the claim that sexual dimorphism in humans is a biological fact. The majority of contributors to a discussion of this subject, on the Women's Studies E-Mail List (which has 4,500 contributors, mostly academics in women's studies), challenged this view on the basis of the catch-all notion of "social constructionism." Sexual dimorphism, they argued, is a "social construct." Evidently, what these discussants were doing was simply defending a current orthodoxy of feminist teaching, which sees not only gender roles but also sexual difference itself (and, not least, heterosexuality) as a "social construct."[3]

Redefining terms has played, to be sure, a major role within feminism in recent decades. I have been present at departmental meetings at which a feminist colleague asked in all earnestness: "Who's to say what 'scholarship' really means?" This was, of course, an effort to promote the hiring of a poorly qualified candidate who was, however, a political activist of the right stripe. And I have heard feminists (and other political activists) defend Rigoberta Menchú's distortions—detailed by David Stoll in his now notorious exposé[4]—as insignificant, since (so they claim) "larger truths" (as long as they are the preferred ones) justify specific falsehoods.[5] I have observed too many feminists parrot Catharine MacKinnon's arguments that words *are* deeds—thus making sexual slurs tantamount to rape—

and that women in our society are not really empowered to give meaningful consent to heterosexual relations. And I have seen terms like *truth* and *logic* set in sneer quotes, the better to discredit them as a masculinist ruse, and incoherence celebrated as a daring challenge to the narrow linear (male) thinking that women are supposedly superior to—at least if they are the right kind of feminists. At some point, moreover, it became clear to me that these feminists were attacking science and reason opportunistically, their chief objective being to leave themselves free to make whatever claims they wished, without being held to any standard—all standards having been conveniently exposed as masculine contrivances.

And then there have been the blatant grabs for power. At my university, a philosophy professor and former head of women's studies, appealing to "equity for women," attempted to defend a large-scale plan to turn feminists into the supreme arbiters of curricular and personnel matters. When other faculty members objected to the proposed intrusion on their academic freedom, she stated—this was at a meeting of the Faculty Senate—"We can't lose track of the wider goal in order to defend some narrow definition of academic freedom, which might amount to a right not to have to respond to new knowledges that are relevant to someone's own field of expertise."[6] Similarly, campus activists have attacked free speech as nothing more than a form of white male privilege. On many campuses feminists are among those faculty members who have supported restrictive speech codes that would institutionalize clear double standards—this in accordance with the claims of critical race theorists that members of "historically oppressed" groups must be protected from verbal slights while they themselves must be free to say whatever they want to representatives of "historically powerful" groups. Thus, group identity and the ostensible needs of a given "community" are elevated above individual rights and freedoms, as if the twentieth century had never provided clear examples of the horrors that result from such commitments to political expediency.

I have also witnessed the spread throughout the country of sexual harassment policies, which (since they target "verbal or physical conduct") are in effect speech codes. Such policies do not distinguish between a look and rape. Instead, they allow offense to be judged by the complainant (recast in feminist literature as a "survivor"), and routinely include bans even on "third-party harassment," which may occur when someone has overheard a perhaps offensive joke, or feels personally aggrieved by someone else's "asymmetrical relationship." In this climate of vigilantism, I have seen due process given short shrift, so that some of the accused have a hard time even learning what the charges against them are or who has accused them.[7] Sometimes it has seemed to me that these feminist triumphs of the late twentieth century closely resemble Junior Anti-Sex League activities.

Many of these abuses have been perpetrated in the interest of advancing the feminist claim that "the personal is political." In utter disregard of the totalitarian potential of the principle behind such a slogan (exposed amply in both dystopian literature and in real-life fascist and communist regimes around the world), feminists have proudly embraced it as a means by which to efface the boundaries between the public and the private and have attempted to micromanage everyday life—all in the name of ushering in what they seem to see as a utopian future in which women would be safe from the depredations of the Patriarchy.

In the face of such assaults—and I'm speaking only of the privileged setting of the academy, not even of similar attacks occurring outside it—I have learned that clinging to reason, evidence, and clearly defined laws is a crucial counterstrategy. And, indeed, it was Orwell who, whatever his shortcomings, defended these claims over and over again.

Here, then, is my brief reassessment, in the light of my experiences since 1984, of the key points of my earlier critique of Orwell.

1. A man deemed to be the "conscience of his generation" and considered a moral exemplar should *not* have been hostile to basic feminist aspirations and to women in general, as his work clearly shows him to have been. In particular, his run-of-the-mill misogyny strikes me as unworthy of him. Of the many examples one could cite, I mention only one, a smug aside in a review Orwell wrote of a novel by Joseph Conrad: "One of the surest signs of his genius is that women dislike his books."[8] This is still, I believe, a significant and accurate charge against him, and it calls into question the hyperbole surrounding Orwell's reputation, which by now is far removed from the man himself.

2. Where my argument rested on a close reading of Orwell's work, it still has merit. For example, it is worth thinking about Orwell's incontrovertible ambivalence toward socialism because of his fear that it would make men "soft."

3. Where I went wrong in my book was whenever I extrapolated too much from Orwell's texts and made inferences and general statements conforming to the feminist framework to which I held at the time. Thus, for example, I argued that had Orwell been less mired in androcentrism, he would have seen that women, with their different, noncompetitive, more cooperative, less violent, way of doing things, represent hope. This image of women I can, alas, no longer believe. To have written such a thing in the 1980s seems to me today to have indulged in a naively hopeful or quasi-religious statement rather than one based on evidence.

Thus, my conclusion that Orwell's despair was the result of his androcentrism seems to me all wrong now. Or, at least, the prevailing mood in his works is matched these days by my own dismay over what feminism has brought us. My best guess today is that Orwell's pessimism was largely a matter of temperament and personal and historical circumstances, and that it had little to do with his distaste for feminist causes. Here was a clear case where I let my feminist politics dictate the results of my analysis. Experience has taught me better.

4. On the other hand, my application of game theory to *Nineteen Eighty-Four,* which helped me focus on the details of the interaction between O'Brien and Winston Smith, and my argument that this is the most important relationship in the book are still, I think, accurate.

5. My detailed analyses of Orwell's language, which revealed his attraction to war and its noises, his idealization of working-class men, and his denigration of women, are still, I think, of interest—in the way that all careful analysis that illuminates a literary work can be. Again, however, I see a discrepancy between the close readings and my larger claims—and it's the latter I would no longer want to defend since I myself have come to question so many of them.

Having attempted this reappraisal of my own arguments, I also think it important to note how Orwell continues to be used for the sake of political slam dunks (or efforts at these), regardless of the inappropriateness of the particular cause in which his name is being invoked. Toward the end of the preface to my 1984 book,

I wrote: "In the future, I think, interest in Orwell will focus not on his work but on the phenomenon of his fame and what it reveals about our own civilization."[9] Certainly, Orwell's reputation has been the subject of interesting work since then (most notably by John Rodden); however, there has been little letup in the tendency to idealize him and to borrow his moral authority in support of one's own positions, whatever these happen to be. The extent to which this is still true can be seen in the extraordinary use made of him in relation to the recent war in Iraq. A Google search on the Internet (on April 23, 2003) using the terms "Orwell + Saddam" turned up nearly fifteen thousand hits; a search under "Newspeak + Bush" turned up about five thousand, including some references to "Bushspeak." It appears that Orwell has been particularly useful for those wishing to attack the Bush administration[10]—though most everyone can and does borrow from Orwell as the occasion arises.

I am as convinced as I was twenty years ago that the habit of citing Orwell in defense or promotion of one's own causes is a way of asserting one's moral superiority—and clearly this is a game all sides can play. What is of greater interest to me in the present context is the disregarded Orwell, the one who can and did make the most outlandish statements without, somehow, having them threaten his moral authority or undermine his reputation for straight talk and honesty. Perhaps this is because he liked to adopt a "voice in the wilderness" persona and was in the habit of presenting his often idiosyncratic views as self-evident or prophetic truths that only he himself was courageous enough to proclaim or detect.

Here are a few examples, drawn from my book: In a letter dated December 28, 1938, Orwell wrote, remarkably: "I think it's really time someone began looking into Fascism seriously."[11] That so late in the 1930s Orwell should come to this realization is one of many indications, I think, of a peculiar habit of his: a tendency to believe that until something captured his own attention, it could not really be considered important. Contrast this with a 1933 essay by Joseph Roth, a well-known journalist and novelist who published, in the September/November 1933 issue of the Parisian journal *Cahiers Juifs,* an essay titled "The Auto-da-Fé of the Mind." Responding to the book burning and persecution that were occurring in Germany within a few months of Hitler's rise to power, Roth wrote this astonishing passage: "Let me say it loud and clear: The European mind is capitulating. It is capitulating out of weakness, out of sloth, out of apathy, out of lack of imagination (it will be the task of some future generation to establish the reasons for this disgraceful capitulation)."[12] But it wasn't only journalists such as Roth, or the *Manchester Guardian* reporter Frederic Voigt, who persistently took "seriously" the advent of fascism. Many novelists, too, including Storm Jameson, Naomi Mitchison, and Katharine Burdekin (from whom, I have argued, Orwell borrowed major elements for *Nineteen Eighty-Four*), were definitely looking seriously into fascism, long before Orwell declared that it was about time for "someone" to do so.[13]

In a similar tone, Orwell announced in a 1947 column that anti-Semitism "has never been looked into, or only in a very sketchy way."[14] Perhaps, in making such a strange claim, Orwell had in mind statements such as his own, in an entry in his wartime diary dated October 25, 1940: "What is bad about Jews is that they are not only conspicuous, but go out of their way to make themselves so. . . . What I do feel is that any Jew, i.e. European Jew, would prefer Hitler's kind of social system to ours, if it were not that he happens to persecute them. Ditto with almost any Central European, e.g. the refugees. They make use of England as a sanctuary, but they cannot help feeling the profoundest contempt for it. You can see this in their eyes, even when they don't say it outright."[15] Even in 1943, in a discussion of anti-Semitism filled with caricatures of pushy "Jewesses," Orwell still attributes such viewpoints about Jews to "many thoughtful people,"[16] That in 1945—1945!—Orwell wrote an essay critical of anti-Semitism does not undo the damage, for his admirers do not generally qualify their approbation by restricting it to particular moments or positions.

My point here is not to vilify Orwell but to suggest that we should think again about using him as a touchstone for decent opinions and good judgment. True, he was not alone in holding to such ideas (Virginia Woolf's anti-Semitic comments about her mother-in-law, for example, are a distinct blemish on her reputation, though they appear in her diaries, not in her published writings). But Orwell is unmatched in the moral authority he has been granted throughout the past half century, despite his often ordinary perceptions and prejudices. His writings are replete with dismissive pronouncements, and it is fascinating to see the convolutions undertaken by writers today as they attempt to deal with this reality. Christopher Hitchens, for example, in his recent book *Why Orwell Matters,* after quite rightly objecting to the cloying veneration of Orwell evident in many quarters,[17] nonetheless in the end attempts to redeem him. Hitchens distinguishes Orwell from "most intellectuals" of his time, who, says Hitchens, "were fatally compromised by accommodation to one or another" of the three great causes of the twentieth century—imperialism, fascism, and Stalinism.

But as Hitchens well knows, Orwell's thought was marred by his many prejudices—against feminists (and against birth control), against women in general, against homosexuals ("pansies" in particular), against militarists and against pacifists (at different times, of course), against vegetarians, against teetotalers. Except for homosexuality (toward which Hitchens admits that Orwell maintained an "unexamined and philistine prejudice"),[18] Hitchens seems satisfied that Orwell overcame his prejudices through conscious self-mastery.[19] Yet, typically, it is the whole man who is apotheosized, as when Hitchens, remarkably, asserts: "[I]t has lately proved possible to reprint [in the 20 volumes of the *Complete Works* edited by Peter Davison and published in 1998] every single letter, book review and essay composed by Orwell without exposing him to any embarrassment."[20]

Contra Hitchens, what seems to me to matter most is not to figure out how Orwell came around to this or that correct position but to be aware of the unvarying rhetoric Orwell maintained as he changed positions. This is something I analyzed in great detail in *The Orwell Mystique,* for it allowed me to see the constancy in the turn of mind (and of phrase) that persisted through shifts in political and other views. An important example, perhaps pertinent to the war in Iraq in relation to which Orwell has been so often cited, is apparent in Orwell's change of attitude regarding conflict with Germany.

In 1937 Orwell argued that British rule in India was just as bad as German fascism and went on to write: "I do not see how one can oppose Fascism except by working for the overthrow of capitalism, starting, of course, in one's own country. If one collaborates with a capitalist-imperialist government in a struggle 'against Fascism,' i.e. against a rival imperialism, one is simply letting Fascism in by the back door."[21] Compare this with Orwell's statement a few years later, in 1940: "Already it is common among the more soft-boiled intellectuals of the Left to declare that if we fight against the Nazis we shall 'go Nazi' ourselves. They might almost equally well say that if we fight against Negroes we shall turn black."[22]

The image of "soft-boiled intellectuals of the Left" is further clarified in another of Orwell's shifts of position that, again, failed to result in any change in his rhetoric. He opposed militarism as sarcastically in 1938–39 as he did pacifism thereafter (which explains why people today can use his words to defend both sides in the arguments over the war in Iraq). Thus, in 1938 we find Orwell blaming "the pansy left" and "hack-journalists" for stirring up war fever, and contrasting them with "ordinary decent people"—who, according to Orwell, opposed war.[23] By 1940, however, when Orwell himself had abandoned his antiwar stance, it wasn't ordinary decent people who opposed the war but, rather, once again, the "pansy left," and now also the "Fascifists" (Orwell's term for "pro-Fascist" pacifists), who were, Orwell claimed, trying to hush up "the fact" that the working class is almost always antifascist.[24] As I argued when I first discussed these examples two decades ago, the problematic values inherent in Orwell's assaults remain the same; only the targets change.

To follow the implications of this example further, consider that in 1938 and 1939, still in his brief antimilitarist phase, Orwell accused men who argued for war against Germany of not being real men. They promoted war, he said, because of the softness and security of their life in England. They thirsted for blood out of a lack of experience of it. But a few years later he was claiming the very opposite: "To abjure violence it is necessary to have no experience of it," he wrote, and this explains why the "real working class" is "never really pacifist"—because they do have experience of violence.[25] Orwell's sense of the proper manly virtues has evidently remained unchanged, allowing him at each point to portray his opponents as unmanly. So, in the 1940s, we find Orwell writing of "the spiritual need for patriotism and the military virtues, for which, however little the boiled rabbits of the Left may like them, no substitute has yet been found."[26] At this stage of his thinking, Orwell managed to make patriotism the crux upon which revolutionary socialism would be built, while also arguing that the war against Hitler could not be won "without introducing Socialism [into England]."[27]

Far from being a subtle thinker, then, Orwell often held simplistic and extreme views of complex questions. It is also significant, I think, that his most famous single line was lifted from another writer (he was an inveterate borrower, in fact). As Richard Mayne pointed out in 1982,[28] in Philip Guedalla's brief anticommunist satire "A Russian Fairy Tale," published in 1930, there appears a Good Fairy "who believed that all fairies were equal before the law, but held strongly that some fairies were more equal than others."[29]

Another aspect of Orwell's writing that I still find of great significance is his tone: self-righteous and judgmental. He had a marked preference for coercive discourse—that is to say, sweeping assertions and generalizations that tended to ward off criticisms by the sheer certainty with which they were declared, as when he attributes his current view (whatever it is at a given moment) to "all decent people," and to "everyone." An example of this technique can be seen in the following comment, from a notebook Orwell kept near the end of his life: "Who has not felt when talking to a Czech, a Pole—to any Central European, but above all to a German or a German Jew—'How superior their minds are to ours, after all?' And who has not followed this up a few minutes later with the complementary thought: 'But unfortunately they are all mad?'"[30]

Still, familiar though I was with Orwell's judgmentalism and coercive rhetoric, I remember clearly my dismay when, in May 1983, I sat in the Orwell Archives at University College, London, and held in my hands the list—or, as I called it in my notes at the time, the Notebook of Names—that Orwell kept toward the end of his life, in which he recorded the names and his appraisal of individuals he considered politically unreliable. When the archivist accidentally delivered to me this notebook, on the cover of which was clearly marked "Closed except with Mrs. Orwell's permission," in a box with other materials, I naturally read it quickly and quietly. Uncertain how to deal with this find at the time, I mentioned it briefly in my book on Orwell, but otherwise did not draw attention to it.

I do not want to dredge up the recent debate this notebook elicited when it came to light in the late 1990s,[31] except to comment that I think Alexander Cockburn—with whom I rarely agree—was right when, in his December 7, 1998, column for *The Nation,* he objected to the "forgiving" attitude of most Orwell admirers toward Orwell's "mini-diatribes," as Cockburn labeled them, against blacks, homosexuals, and Jews, and toward the very fact that Orwell compiled such a list.[32]

That day in the archive, twenty years ago, I was shocked by what I was reading. Despite having become a critic of Orwell in the several years during which I'd been working on him in the early 1980s, I still did not expect such a thing from someone who claimed to so abhor the vigilante mentality. After all, I knew Orwell's 1939 essay "Inside the Whale," in which he had written that what most frightened him about the war in Spain was the "immediate reappearance in left-wing circles of the mental atmosphere of the Great War," as people "rushed straight back into the mental slum of 1915. All the familiar war-time idiocies, spy-hunting, orthodoxy-sniffing (Sniff, sniff. Are you a good anti-Fascist?)."[33]

Yet ten years later here was Orwell, indulging in precisely such vigilantism. As I read his notebook of names, what most distressed me, beyond the mere existence of it—which would have been easy to explain innocently since I knew Orwell loved to make lists—was the smug tone, the sanctimonious manner of one enjoying total confidence in his own judgments and opinions, one ready to label scores of people according to the pettiest criteria, not just presumed political reliability in what might become critical circumstances, but labels such as Jew, Zionist, "probably venal," "tendency toward homosexuality," and "crippled hand."

This last comment was made of Alex Comfort, with whom Orwell had carried on a verse polemic in 1943. Comfort's name, like those of Naomi Mitchison, Max Lerner, and several dozen others, was omitted in Davison's 1998 version of Orwell's *Complete Works* (only recently the Orwell estate has finally granted permission to divulge the complete list). Of Comfort, Orwell wrote in his notebook of names: "Potential only. Is pacifist-anarchist. Main emphasis anti-British. Subjectively pro-German during war, appears temperamentally pro-totalitarianism. Not morally courageous. Has crippled hand." And then one additional (mitigating?) comment: "Very talented."

Especially interesting in this entry is the wording of Orwell's claim that Comfort was "subjectively pro-German" during the war, for in a review some years earlier, Orwell had called Comfort "objectively" pro-German. Perhaps late in his life Orwell backed away from the Leninist practice of labeling people "objectively" this or that, a habit which in the early 1940s had led him to classify pacifists as "objectively pro-Fascist."

As for Naomi Mitchison—who published an antifascist novel *We Have Been Warned* in 1935, several years before Orwell thought someone should "seriously" look into fascism,—Orwell wrote in his notebook of names, "Sentimental sympathiser only. Sister of J. B. S. Haldane (C.P.). Unreliable." Also interesting in Orwell's list is the frequency with which he labeled people "silly" or "stupid"—as if these, like Comfort's "crippled hand," had some political significance.

Peter Davison's nearly exhaustive editing of Orwell's complete works has made virtually every facet of Orwell's writing available to us. Now all can see the warts, the contradictions, as well as the strengths of this restless character. Yet Davison's volumes also have something of the fetishistic about them, as if the minutiae of everyday life could provide us finally with that sense, so elusive, of another person's reality. But do we really think we can better grasp a life once we have been allowed to read every last trivial notation made by its subject? In Doris Lessing's novel *The Golden Notebook,* the author's alter ego, Anna, attempts to capture the sense of everyday life by recording everything that takes place on a particular day, including changing her sanitary napkins; but she soon realizes the futility of all this as a means of registering a human life. There's more than a touch of absurdity, I think, in treating Orwell as if every passing remark reveals something significant. It seems to me that the texture of everyday life *is* its ordinariness, and we all are experts in that regard. Does knowing that on a certain day Orwell's cylinder of gas ran out really matter?[34]

But, like audiences' fascination with reality TV, the voyeurism implicit in wanting to read every last scrap that Orwell wrote suggests that somehow the reality of life always escapes us; hence we struggle to grasp it and think we can do so by observing other people's lives, as if they had a denser existence than our own. No; clearly Orwell's importance lies not in the minutiae of his life but in the constant appeal to his words and slogans made by people today, and this is much more an appeal to a symbol than to a person, as can be seen in the overuse of the term "Orwellian." Morris Dickstein, in a recent article, for example, praises the *Partisan Review* in the postwar years for its "Orwellian hatred of totalitarianism."[35] Evidently the adjective conveys a more compelling emotion than just a plain hatred of totalitarianism.

What is disturbingly new in our time is not the terror envisioned by Orwell at the end of *Nineteen Eighty-Four*—which always struck me as a bit ludicrous and incompatible with the rest of his understanding of power politics. It is not any such terror that endangers us today but the apparently voluntary abdication of reason and freedom by many intellectuals on the left. Rather, the danger now stems, as I see it, from the ordinary activism of supposedly well-intentioned people who, while enjoying the freedoms of our society, appear ready to renounce these very freedoms in the name of the "better" society they believe they are constructing. And although Orwell coined some excellent slogans and tags, and gave us a compelling—even if ultimately improbable—explanation of Newspeak as a language designed eventually to make "thoughtcrime" impossible, he can't really do much for us in the battle against this renunciation.

Many literary scholars these days pretend that, as the *Norton Anthology of Theory and Criticism* (which covers 2,500 years) tells us on the very first page of its preface, to do theory is "to engage in resistance."[36] Other professors claim that teaching is their form of "activism." In thrall to the notion that all education is political, contemporary academic vigilantes cultivate an ersatz politics from the safety of their tenured positions while being unwilling, it appears, to defend art and imagination except when they serve particular political commitments. And, in support of student censors, too many faculty members pretend that an unkind word or offending idea inflicts terrible damage on members of certain identity groups. As Harvey Silverglate and Greg Lukianoff recently wrote in the *Chronicle of Higher Education,* "The Foundation for Individual Rights in Education defines a speech code as any campus regulation that punishes, forbids, heavily regulates, or restricts a substantial amount of protected speech. Thus defined, speech codes are the rule rather than the exception in higher education."[37]

All this has forced me to see with a sharper eye the crucial distinction between politics and teaching, politics and art, and politics and scholarship. The point is to be able to distinguish one from the other, not to conflate them all into some simplistic and self-righteous bottom line of the sort students often indulge in as they engage in blame or praise of the authors they read and the historical figures they study.

We shouldn't fight these battles (those of us who want to) by appealing to figures who have acquired mythical status. We have to argue for free speech, truth telling, reason, logic, and the force of evidence on their own merits, defending them by reference not to authority but, rather, to historical alternatives, of which, lamentably, we have many examples. Orwell needs to be seen in the context of other British writers of the 1930s and 1940s, not as a uniquely heroic figure. Invoking him doesn't help us in our struggles. There is enough in his work to be useful to almost any side of most of the issues he addresses. To build one's case by citing Orwell at this late date is simply, and ironically, to abdicate the very habit of independent thinking for which he is being celebrated.

NOTES

1. See Daphne Patai, *The Orwell Mystique: A Study in Male Ideology* (Amherst: University of Massachusetts Press, 1984).

2. See Alan Sokal and Jean Bricmont, *Fashionable Nonsense: Postmodern Intellectuals' Abuse of Science* (New York: Picador, 1998).

3. See the discussion of this episode in Daphne Patai and Noretta Koertge, *Professing Feminism: Education and Indoctrination in Women's Studies,* rev. ed. (Lanham, Md.: Lexington Books, 2003), 307–16, 356–63, 399–400.

4. David Stoll, *Rigoberta Menchú and the Story of All Poor Guatemalans* (Boulder, Colo.: Westview Press, 1999).

5. See, for example, many of the essays in Arturo Arias, ed., *The Rigoberta Menchú Controversy* (Minneapolis: University of Minnesota Press, 2001).

6. See Daphne Patai, "Why Not a Feminist Overhaul of Higher Education?" *Chronicle of Higher Education,* January 23, 1998, A56.

7. For examples of the above, see Daphne Patai, *Heterophobia: Sexual Harassment and the Future of Feminism* (Lanham, Md.: Rowman & Littlefield, 1998).

8. *Collected Essays, Journalism and Letters of George Orwell,* ed. Sonia Orwell and Ian Angus (New York: Harcourt Brace Jovanovich, 1968), 1:227, henceforth referred to as *CEJL.* This edition is now superseded by Peter Davison's edition of *The Complete Works of George Orwell* (London: Secker and Warburg, 1998).

9. Patai, *The Orwell Mystique,* x.

10. See, for example, the comment by Paul Foot headed "Triumph of Doublethink in 2003: Orwell Warned against the Kind of Lies We Are Being Fed about Iraq," *The Guardian,* January 1, 2003 (available online at http://www.guardian.co.uk/Iraq/Story/0,2763,867153,00.html).

11. Orwell, *CEJL,* 1:370.

12. Joseph Roth, *What I Saw: Reports from Berlin 1920–1933,* trans. Michael Hofmann (New York: Norton, 2003; published in German in 1996), 207.

13. On this subject, see also Andy Croft's indispensable *Red Letter Days: British Fiction in the 1930s* (London: Lawrence and Wishart, 1990).

14. Orwell, *CEJL,* 4:311.

15. Orwell, *CEJL,* 3:377–78.

16. Orwell, *CEJL,* 2:290.

17. Christopher Hitchens, *Why Orwell Matters* (New York: Basic Books, 2002), p. 3. Philip French's review of Hitchens's book (published in England under the title *Orwell's Victory*) is titled, significantly, "A Saint Carved in Stone, Very Weathered." See *Times Literary Supplement,* June 7, 2002, 23.

18. Hitchens, *Why Orwell Matters,* 206.

19. Hitchens, *Why Orwell Matters,* 9.

20. Hitchens, *Why Orwell Matters,* 4; the other exception—Orwell's notebook of names—Hitchens discusses in a separate chapter called "The List," in which he goes to considerable lengths to defend Orwell.

21. Orwell, *CEJL,* 1:284.

22. Orwell, *CEJL,* 2:102.

23. Orwell, *CEJL,* 1:332.

24. Orwell, *CEJL,* 2:226–28.

25. Orwell, *CEJL,* 2:167.

26. Orwell, *CEJL,* 1:540.

27. Orwell, *CEJL,* 2:94.

28. Richard Mayne, *Times Literary Supplement,* November 26, 1982. I discuss this in *The Orwell Mystique,* 309, n. 18.

29. Philip Guedalla, "A Russian Fairy Tale," *The Missing Muse* (New York: Harper and Brothers, 1930), 206. Let me clarify that I would not consider this borrowing significant were it not for the fact that many critics refer to this line as a particularly felicitous example of Orwell's concision and clarity as a prose writer. See, for example, Raymond Williams, *Orwell* (Glasgow: Fontana/Collins, 1971), 4, who cites Orwell's version of this line as an example of the "exceptionally strong and pure prose" Orwell was "able to release" in *Animal Farm.* My own view is that Orwell had an excellent ear for slogans and catchphrases (his own and others'), and hence also understood the significance of propaganda.

30. Quoted in *The Orwell Mystique,* 10.

31. See, for example, the exchange of letters between Christopher Hitchens and Perry Anderson in the *London Review of Books,* January and February 2000 (in response to Anderson's article on November 25, 1999).

32. Alexander Cockburn, "St. George's List," *The Nation,* December 7, 1998, 9.

33. Orwell, *CEJL,* 1:517–18.

34. See Orwell's domestic diary for July 19, 1947, in Orwell, *Complete Works,* vol. 19, "It is what I think."

35. Morris Dickstein, "Waving Not Drowning," *Times Literary Supplement,* October 25, 2002, 14.

36. Vincent B. Leitch et al., ed., *The Norton Anthology of Theory and Criticism* (New York: W. W. Norton, 2001), xxxiii.

37. Harvey A. Silverglate and Greg Lukianoff, "Speech Codes: Alive and Well at Colleges . . . ," *Chronicle of Higher Education,* August 1, 2003, B7. See also Alan Charles Kors and Harvey A. Silverglate, *The Shadow University: The Betrayal of Liberty on America's Campuses* (New York: The Free Press, 1998). Silverglate and Kors went on to found FIRE—the Foundation for Individual Rights in Education—to defend civil rights on campus (disclosure statement: I am on the Board of Directors of this organization).

IV

Literary and Stylistic Issues

15

Orwell's Perversity: An Approach to the Collected Essays

WILLIAM E. CAIN

The question I want to raise and explore is, What gives Orwell's literary and political criticism its abiding interest and vitality? And in brief I think the answer is that it is perverse. In part the perversity exists in the bracing unexpectedness of Orwell's analyses and judgments but, even more, it is the result of his form of expression—the slant of his phrases, the shape of his sentences.

I am drawn to and curious about the operations of Orwell's language, and the dimension of it in particular that strikes me as perverse—the persistently oppositional and contradictory turns of his thinking, patterned in the style. Orwell's perversity makes his work as a literary and cultural critic extraordinarily good, yet it sometimes makes him predictable (a strange thing to say about such an independent mind) and hard to lay hold of.

Getting underway on this essay, I began reading volume 4 of *The Collected Essays, Journalism, and Letters.* The first essay in that volume, from November 1945, is "Revenge Is Sour," where Orwell describes acts of revenge taken by Jews against SS officers after Nazi control of the death camps had ended. Former prisoners could hardly be blamed for their behavior, he concedes, but he adds that his observations "brought home to me that the whole idea of revenge and punishment is a childish daydream": "Properly speaking, there is no such thing as revenge. Revenge is an act which you want to commit when you are powerless and because you are powerless: as soon as the sense of impotence is removed, the desire evaporates also."[1]

My first response was, Orwell is wrong: Countless people and nations have craved the power that would enable them to exact revenge, often through legal channels, but often too, as in Eastern Europe and Africa in the 1990s, through monstrously violent actions. Orwell's remote tone seemed wrong as well, oddly detached from the reality of Nazi victimization of Jews, which was itself a genocidal form of revenge—he gives this just a single sentence. But it then occurred to me that the more accurate term for Orwell's claim is *perverse,* and that, furthermore, perversity is his signature.

Perverse, like *perverted,* has through its Latin root a range of meanings—*turn,* but also *crooked, slanted, askew,* even *turned upside down or over. Perverse* implies

obstinate persistence and stubbornness, a deep disposition toward being oppositional and contradictory, and unpleasantly so. Orwell employs the word in this
sense, for example, in *Burmese Days* (1934): "It was the first time they [Flory and
Elizabeth] had definitely quarrelled. He was too miserable even to ask himself how
it was that he offended her. He did not realize that this constant striving to interest
her in Oriental things struck her only as *perverse,* ungentlemanly, a deliberate
seeking after the squalid and the 'beastly.'"[2] Later, Elizabeth lingers over Flory's
upsetting behavior: "For there had always been something dubious about Flory;
his age, his birthmark, his queer, *perverse* way of talking—that 'highbrow' talk
that was at once unintelligible and disquieting."[3]

In *Nineteen Eighty-Four,* Orwell gives *perverse* a political charge: "Goldstein
was delivering his usual venomous attack upon the doctrines of the Party—an
attack so exaggerated and *perverse* that a child should have been able to see
through it, and yet just plausible enough to fill one with an alarmed feeling that
other people, less level-headed than oneself, might be taken in by it."[4]

Perverse and affiliated words also appear in a number of Orwell's essays, in, for
instance, these two passages: "English is peculiarly subject to jargons. Doctors,
scientists, businessmen, officials, sportsmen, economists, and political theorists all
have their characteristic *perversion* of the language";[5] and "I am now reading a
new life of Dickens by Hesketh Pearson, which I have to review. It isn't awfully
good. There doesn't seem to be a perfect life of Dickens—*perverse* & unfair
though it is, I really think Kingsmill's book is the best."[6]

In Orwell's era and our own, *perverse* and *perverted* have been deployed as
demeaning words for homosexuals, and these words continue to be invoked as
designation and code for disturbed sexual imaginings and practices, as in Orwell's
essay on Salvador Dali: "But from his Surrealist paintings and photographs the
two things that stand out are sexual *perversity* and necrophilia . . . . He professes
an especial affection for the year 1900, and claims that every ornamental object of
1900 is full of mystery, poetry, eroticism, madness, *perversity,* etc."[7] This suggests
a path into sexual themes in Orwell's work—his uneasy comments about homosexuals, his account of Winston Smith's sadistic sexual fantasies, and related topics
pertaining to gender roles that Daphne Patai examines with a prosecutor's zeal in
The Orwell Mystique (1984). But I'm after something more general, closer to a
defining perversity of temperament and to the nature of Orwell's "peculiar and
impressive personality" (Stuart Hampshire's phrase)—his sense of himself and the
impact he made on other people and the effects he renders in his prose.

Commonly it is said that in Orwell's case the style is the man. But, in truth,
critics do not agree on the relationship of the life to the writing, the man to the
work. Lionel Trilling describes Orwell as one of those men "who live their visions
as well as write them, who *are* what they write, whom we think of as standing for
something as men because of what they have written in their books."[8] The political
scientist Ian Slater says, decisively, the opposite: "he was *not* what he wrote."[9] The
self presented in the books, Slater contends, calculatedly differs from the biographical self: the Orwell created on the page lives at a remove from the composite
Eric Blair/George Orwell whose actual experiences, opinions, friendships, and
sexual activities his biographers have traced.

I lean toward Trilling rather than Slater on this issue. But that is because I see
elements of perversity in both the writing and the life, complicatedly bonding

them together, and I doubt that Trilling would go along with that. Yet there is, among the recollections and anecdotes, a good deal of evidence for the term I propose. Many who knew Orwell have highlighted contradictions and tensions in his attitudes and behaviors that reached such a high degree they seemed perverse, or were saved from perversity only because his rare virtue and wholeness engagingly atoned for them.

"Orwell was original in himself," recalled Malcolm Muggeridge: "If not witty, he was intrinsically funny. For instance, in the extraordinary prejudices he entertained and the naïve confidence with which he propounded them. Thus, he would come out with the proposition: 'All tobacconists are Fascists!', as though this was something so obvious that no one could possibly question his statement."[10] Richard Rees describes Orwell as "strenuous and self-martyrizing" yet "diffusing" all the while an "atmosphere of cosiness."[11] Bernard Crick says: "Orwell saw himself as a violent unmasker of published pretentiousness, hypocrisy, and self-deceit, telling people what they did not want to hear; but in private he was a gentle and tolerant man."[12] Reviewing *Nineteen Eighty-Four,* Diana Trilling found herself "thrown off" by "something in the book's temper, a fierceness of intention, which seems to violate the very principles Mr. Orwell would wish to preserve in the world."[13] "A penchant for the painful, the demeaning and the repulsive," notes Dwight Macdonald more ominously, "runs throughout Orwell's work."[14] Orwell "turned his life into an experiment in classlessness," the critic Louis Menand states, "and the intensity of his commitment to that experiment was the main reason that his friends and colleagues found him a perverse and sometimes exasperating man."[15] In a similar vein, Timothy Garton Ash offers this brief biography: "The bare biographical facts are curious enough: a talented scholar at Eton perversely goes off to become an imperial policeman in Burma, a dishwasher in Paris, and a tramp in London; runs a village shop, fights in the Spanish Civil War, abandons left-wing literary London for a farm on a remote Scottish island and dies of tuberculosis at the moment of literary triumph, aged forty-six."[16]

The accent on Orwell's perversity is there, too, in Steven Marcus's reference to "Orwell's irresistible inclination throughout his life toward situations in which he would live in hardship, deprivation, and suffering."[17] One notices it in a comment by V. S. Pritchett, who, during the bombing of Britain, visited Orwell's flat on the top of a building in St. John's Wood: "He seemed to want to live as near to a bomb as possible."[18] "I think it's clear beyond all doubt that he didn't like himself much," remarks Christopher Hitchens.[19] This sounds accurate yet incongruous about a figure whom many, past and present, have admired, celebrated, wished they could become.[20]

Orwell, notoriously, angers and exasperates readers on the left, who find him extremely perverse, false, and dangerous, and their denunciations hit repeatedly at the perversity of his behaviors and views. The extreme personal distaste extends back and forth from Orwell to the positions he took. The foreign correspondent Alaric Jacob, for instance, says, "After coasting gently through Eton, earning no laurels but making no enemies, Orwell went tamely to Burma at the age of nineteen for lack of anything better to do. I could not understand how anyone of even moderate intelligence could have taken so retrograde a step."[21] Christopher Norris, commenting on Orwell's relation to "the broad tradition of British socialist politics," concludes, "He turned against that tradition while persistently claiming to speak for it; took over its most rooted assumptions in the service of antagonistic aims; and produced, in short, a point-for-point travesty of socialist argument."[22] Finally, Raymond Williams writes, "The recruitment of very private feelings against socialism becomes intolerable by *1984*. It is profoundly offensive to state as a general truth, as Orwell does, that people will always betray each other. If human beings are like that, what could be the meaning of a democratic socialism?"[23]

Critics like Williams find Orwell exasperating not only for the essays and books he wrote but also for the claims he made about his intentions in them. Referring to *Nineteen Eighty-Four,* Orwell observes: "My recent novel is NOT intended as an attack on Socialism or on the British Labour Party (of which I am a supporter) but as a show-up of the *perversions* to which a centralised economy is liable and which have already been partly realised in Communism and Fascism."[24] This, to those on the left, is perverse: they see Orwell in *Nineteen Eighty-Four* engaged in exactly the discrediting of socialism and the British Labour Party that he here denies.

Other readers—Left, Right, and Center—Orwell simply annoys. They do not warm to his quickness to take the other side, an inherent recalcitrance of mood that, they claim, verges on or edges into perversity. John Morris, a BBC colleague, found a "strange expression" in Orwell's eyes, "a combination of benevolence and fanaticism."[25] "Whatever was 'in' affected him with a kind of violent claustrophobia," says Mary McCarthy: "he wanted out."[26] Stephen Spender says: "Just as D. H. Lawrence disapproved of everyone else's sex, so Orwell disapproved of everyone else's socialism."[27] This, from John Bayley: "Like T. E. Lawrence in *Seven Pillars of Wisdom,* Orwell unconsciously strove both to be a man of action and destiny and to reveal what a fraud he was in that role." Pritchett, both impressed and suspicious, contends that Orwell's relentless regard for the truth was "perverse."[28]

As a writer Orwell is highly perverse, and I am interested in when that's a good thing and when it's not. It's nearly always a good thing when the perversity is in the detailed quality of observation—the direct seeing-and-saying capped with a flourish or given a keen edge that distinguishes Orwell's settings and scenes, as in this passage early in *The Road to Wigan Pier* where he depicts his lodgings at Mrs. Brooker's:

Downstairs there was the usual kitchen living-room with its huge open range burning night and day. It was lighted only by a skylight, for on one side of it was the shop and on the other the larder, which opened into some dark subterranean place where the tripe was stored. Partly blocking the door of the larder there was a shapeless sofa upon which Mrs. Brooker, our landlady, lay permanently ill, festooned in grimy blankets. She had a big, pale yellow, anxious face. No one knew for certain what was the matter with her; I suspect that her only real trouble was over-eating. In front of the fire there was almost always a line of damp washing, and in the middle of the room was the big kitchen table at which the family and all the lodgers ate. I never saw this table completely uncovered, but I saw its various wrappings at different times. At the bottom there was a layer of old newspapers stained by Worcester Sauce; above that a sheet of sticky white oilcloth; above that a green serge cloth; above that a coarse linen cloth, never changed and seldom taken off. Generally the crumbs from breakfast were still on the table at supper. I used to get to know individual crumbs by sight and watch their progress up and down the table from day to day.[29]

The brilliant perversity is in the Dickensian fantasia of the personified crumbs, as Orwell enlivens a dreary setting so that its pathos and degradation seem a bit sprightly. Frequently Orwell gives the bleakest place some lightly redemptive touch or comical exaggeration. He has the eye of a skillful cartoonist, as the sketch of Mrs. Brooker shows, in "grimy blankets" but "festooned" with them, as if adorned with a garland of flowers. He takes pleasure in the properties of the English language, savoring the details of vocabulary and phrase that define the English literary tradition of Shakespeare and the King James Bible, and of Orwell's favorites, Jonathan Swift and Charles Dickens.

Another, more direct, harder element of Orwell's perversity, however, is linked to the judgments he makes and our response to them. How, after all, do we tell the difference between good and bad perversity in his, or in any critic's or intellectual's, judgments? When is a writer not boldly incisive or enlightening but perverse (that is, "merely" perverse)? When, on the other hand, is a writer brave and honorable precisely because he or she is perverse, cutting against the grain of received wisdom or confronting power like Milton's Abdiel, "faithful found; / Among the faithless, faithful only he"?

Perversity can function as a heroic force in a writer's style of judgment making. One concurs with Irving Howe's assessment: "In his readiness to stand alone and take on all comers, [Orwell] was a model for every writer of our age."[30] But then again, perversity can be unthinking and lead to formulaic writing. When this happens, we grow accustomed to the perversity: the writer's sentences take their turns but exert no pressure on the reader. You know what to expect—perversity, an always contrarian angle whatever the subject. Oscar Wilde, George Bernard Shaw, H. L. Mencken: each can come to feel mannered, his thought grooved, predictable in a fondness for unpredictability, paradox, and mockery of traditional views and values.

A complication arises: we say that a writer is perverse, but is perversity really a position that someone can occupy? It isn't self-sufficient: you are perverse only in relation to something that you turn against or away from. Alfred Kazin touches on this point when he remarks of Orwell that he "conceives the beginning but cannot bear the end. . . . He knew best what he was against."[31] The risk of perverse writing and thinking is a dead end: a critic is against *this,* but, perversely, is against *that* too. No system, state, or institution will do, and this implies a perpetual dissatisfaction that has the ring of relativism. What is Orwell *for* if everything he says he is *for* is flawed? Perversity: Isn't *this* what he is for?

Capitalism, Orwell believed, is a system that no decent person wants; he declared in 1947 that it "has manifestly no future."[32] Socialism is the better way—one recalls the memorable pages on socialism in chapter 8 of *Homage to Catalonia.* But the problem for Orwell is that socialists have perversely equated their cause with the defense of Stalin's Russia and hence dwell in an echo chamber of unrealities. Who could accept the betrayal of conscience required to stand with them? Where, then, is Orwell standing?

My concern about relativism may be mistaken. Surely perversity can be classified and distinguished, this kind from that—we believe we can make distinctions about Orwell and other authors. Perversity of a bad kind means that someone is really wrong—history has confirmed it. Perversity of a good kind means that someone was or is really right, as when we say: Perverse to many in his own era because of his critique of the Left, Orwell now represents the truth that others at that time failed to see and give voice to; now, as Christopher Hitchens has argued, he is the touchstone that retrospectively exposes the perversity of others who embraced Soviet dogma uncritically.[33]

Comparisons might help my inquiry. To whom might we compare Orwell, as exemplars of bad and good perversity? When the African American intellectual W. E. B. Du Bois exalted Stalin and supported the Soviet crackdown on the Hungarians in 1956, he was being perverse in a bad way. He wrote, for example, "Joseph Stalin was a great man: few other men of the 20th century approach his stature. He was simple, calm and courageous. He seldom lost his poise; pondered his problems slowly, made his decisions clearly and firmly; never yielded to ostentation nor coyly refrained from holding his rightful place with dignity."[34] Another instance is the ill-tempered introduction that Edmund Wilson wrote in November 1961 for *Patriotic Gore* (1962), his magisterial study of Civil War literature. Aligning the Civil War with the cold war, Wilson tenders the cranky claim that virtues, values, and ideologies are irrelevant, totally delusional: ultimately, there is "at bottom the irrational instinct of an active power organism in the presence of another such organism, of a sea slug of vigorous voracity in the presence of another such sea slug."[35] Such a formidable, intellectually curious writer is Wilson, and yet this Darwinian moral equivalence is hectoring and reductive, perverse.

Examples come to mind of writers who started with good perversity and ended in bad perversity. The British literary critic F. R. Leavis preached powerfully in the 1940s and 1950s for D. H. Lawrence's achievements as a novelist and critic, but he grew so wedded to his conception of Lawrence's "supreme intelligence"[36] that other writers eventually loomed for him as defective and unhealthy. An equally notable case is the art critic Clement Greenberg, who almost alone spoke and wrote as an advocate of the abstract expressionists (above all, Jackson Pollock) in the 1940s.[37] He praised their work before anyone else and developed from it an influential understanding of modernism and color field painting. Yet Greenberg became dogmatic, ever more narrowing in his interests and sympathies. Enslaved to a formula, Greenberg later in his career was left with only three or four artists to care much about.

These points of comparison, however, dramatize for me the special interest and richness of Orwell's perversity: he is more successfully and consistently perverse than are other writers. Orwell's perversity is everywhere in his style, in his approach to an issue, in the way he attacks it and compels attention to it. His perversity is central to his poised wit, to his irony. Here is the first sentence of "Bookshop Memories" (November 1936): "When I worked in a second-hand bookshop—so easily pictured, if you don't work in one, as a kind of paradise where charming old gentlemen browse eternally among calf-bound folios—the thing that chiefly struck me was the rarity of really bookish people."[38] And this, from the first page of "The Lion and the Unicorn" (February 1941):

> Also, one must admit that the divisions between nation and nation are founded on real differences of outlook. Till recently it was thought proper to pretend that all human beings are very much alike, but in fact anyone able to use his eyes knows that the average of human behaviour differs enormously from country to country. Things that could happen in one country could not happen in another. Hitler's June purge, for instance, could not have happened in England.[39]

For me the most potent examples of Orwell's perversity occur during the period from 1945 to 1950, with the cold war shadowing and then dominating political discussion and debate, argument and analysis.[40] "Considering how likely we all are to be blown to pieces by it within the next five years," Orwell says, "the atomic bomb has not roused so much discussion as might have been expected."[41] And then in "Catastrophic Gradualism" (November 1945): "In his much-discussed essay, [Arthur] Koestler is generally assumed to have come down heavily on the side of the Yogi. Actually, if one assumes the Yogi and the Commissar to be at opposite points of the scale, Koestler is somewhat nearer to the Commissar's end."[42]

Orwell typically seizes on a topic or theme that seems settled, where a consensus of opinion resides, a feeling shared by nearly all, and then he briskly tacks the other way. He relishes this moment. "Whatever the subject," says Michael Shelden, "Orwell was always tempted to look at it from both sides. And when he considered another point of view, he did not usually do it halfheartedly. He became immersed in it and used all the powers of his imagination to identify with it."[43]

More Orwellian perversity, an eagerness to destabilize and unnerve the reader, appears in this first sentence from a book review: "If one were obliged to write a history of the world, would it be better to record the true facts, so far as one could discover them, or would it be better simply to make the whole thing up? The answer is not so self-evident as it appears."[44] We are familiar with this question and (so we tell ourselves) know the answer, which is exactly the answer that Orwell challenges in the second sentence, his hook. He is an exceptionally honest writer, but he is indeed a writer, agile and crafty; he is attuned from start to finish to the expectations and responses of readers to his sentences, and he is working with *that* every step of the way.

Perversity is also a central feature of Orwell's literary criticism, as in "Good Bad Books" (November 2, 1945), where he states that the "supreme example" is *Uncle Tom's Cabin*: "It is an unintentionally ludicrous book, full of preposterous melodramatic incidents; it is also deeply moving and essentially true; it is hard to say which quality outweighs the other."[45] And in his introduction to Jack London's *Love of Life and Other Stories* (November 1945): "On several points London was right where nearly all other prophets were wrong. . . . His best stories have the curious quality of being well told and yet not well written."[46] Then, this review of *The Prussian Officer and Other Stories* (November 16, 1945), where he observes of D. H. Lawrence: "Yet he does often seem to have an extraordinary power of knowing imaginatively something that he could not have known by observation."[47]

Perverse he may be, yet Orwell possesses a strangely adhesive literary personality—a lively, probing intelligence, stimulating and credible even when the reader is prompted to disagree with the judgments presented. Perversity in Orwell is frequently first confessional ("this is how I felt") and then a lot or a little coercive ("this is how you feel, or should"), but one is struck by how little one minds this. Some do mind it, but the fervor of their criticisms shows that Orwell has seized them: he will not let them go; they cannot let go of him.

"In a political and moral sense I am against him, so far as I understand him," states Orwell about Jonathan Swift: "Yet curiously enough he is one of the writers I admire with least reserve, and *Gulliver's Travels,* in particular, is a book which it seems impossible for me to grow tired of."[48] There's this firm pair of sentences from "Lear, Tolstoy, and the Fool" (March 1947): "One's first feeling is that in describing Shakespeare as a bad writer [Tolstoy] is saying something demonstrably untrue. But that is not the case."[49] Orwell *pushes* from the point taken for granted, turning away and turning aside.

Orwell says what he thinks, even if what he says makes him seem bizarre or outrageous or inconsistent, and because hardly anyone does that, he affects readers as perverse. He famously launches "Reflections on Gandhi" (January 1949): "Saints should always be judged guilty until they are proved innocent . . . ." There's the shock to received opinion. Yet the sentence is not done: ". . . but the tests that have to be applied to them are not, of course, the same in all cases."[50] He invokes a sense of obligation that likely was not there in us ("have to be applied"), with the phrase "of course" enforcing the enigmatic obligation and aligning itself with the equally insistent "always." The reader has been made captive.

Orwell's style "can be deceptive," Richard Rees proposes: "It is so swift and simple and unpretentious that his best arguments sometimes appear much easier and more obvious than they really are."[51] But there is another aspect to the perverse style, to which the literary critic Hugh Kenner alludes when he avers that the "plain style" practiced by Orwell is "the most disorienting form of discourse yet invented by man."[52] Few readers ever become lost amid Orwell's sentences, but they are disorienting, unbalancing, even as they give pleasure in their plainness. Few dare to write and sound like that. Though we tend to think of the plain style as the basic or foundational style, and other styles as its perversions, the reality (so Kenner, I think, implies) is the reverse: it's the plain style, pitched against other styles, that's the oddity, that's perverse.

The illusions, delusions, and folly of the attitudes that people cling to—these are among the favorite topics that Orwell rubs against the grain of his prose:

> I am always amazed when I hear people saying that sport creates goodwill between the nations, and that if only the common peoples of the world could meet one another at football or cricket, they would have no inclination to meet on the battlefield. . . . International sporting contests lead to orgies of hatred.[53]

> Every generation imagines itself to be more intelligent than the one that went before it, and wiser than the one that comes after it. This is an illusion, and one should recognise it as such, but one ought also to stick to one's own world-view, even at the price of seeming old-fashioned: for that world-view springs out of experiences that the younger generation has not had, and to abandon it is to kill one's intellectual roots.[54]

> We are all capable of believing things which we *know* to be untrue, and then, when we are finally proved wrong, impudently twisting the facts so as to show that we were right. . . . To see what is in front of one's nose needs a constant struggle.[55]

Orwell insists that much thinking is perverse. Not said, but of course intimated, is that a writer must be rare, quite perverse, to gain mastery over common and embedded perversity. It is terribly difficult to cease looking sideways and, redirected, see what is right in front of us. Someone thrust against the face makes us uncomfortable, intruding on space that does not belong to them. Would you prefer someone to stand smack in front of your nose, or to be off a ways? When we look to the side or away, there's more room to feel at ease, to invent, embellish, pretend, lie.

Orwell's political writing features the perversity I have been describing—para-doxically, the perverse look is the straight-on look—and there it is still more pronounced and morally stiffening.

> The organized lying practiced by totalitarian states is not, as is sometimes claimed, a temporary expedient of the same nature as military deception. It is something integral to totalitarianism, something that would continue even if concentration camps and secret police forces had ceased to be necessary.[56]

> Politico-literary intellectuals are not usually frightened of mass opinion. What they are frightened of is the prevailing opinion within their own group. At any given moment there is always an orthodoxy, a parrot-cry which must be repeated, and in the more active section of the Left the orthodoxy of the moment is anti-American-ism.[57]

Perversity, for Orwell himself, is a resistance to orthodoxy, and that mandates a rigorous clarity in the uses of language as he takes aim at the perversity he identifies in others. As he maintains in "The Prevention of Literature" (January 1946): "To write in plain, vigorous language one has to think fearlessly, and if one thinks fearlessly one cannot be politically orthodox."[58] Orwell locates himself in relation to orthodoxy, and once he has it defined, his style is energized: he has *that* to turn against:

> It is queer to look back and think that only a dozen years ago the abolition of the death penalty was one of those things that every enlightened person advocated as a matter of course, like divorce reform or the independence of India. Now, on the other hand, it is a mark of enlightenment not merely to approve of executions but to raise an outcry because there are not more of them.[59]

> Nearly the whole of the English Left has been driven to accept the Russian regime as "Socialist," while silently recognizing that its spirit and practice are quite alien to anything that is meant by "Socialism" in this country. Hence there has arisen a sort of schizophrenic manner of thinking, in which words like "democracy" can bear two irreconcilable meanings, and such things as concentration camps and mass deportations can be right and wrong simultaneously.[60]

Yet I must acknowledge that Orwell's perversity is sometimes too perverse, as in the conclusion he draws in the following passage about literary censorship in the USSR:

> The thing that politicians are seemingly unable to understand is that you cannot produce a vigorous literature by terrorizing everyone into conformity. A writer's inventive faculties will not work unless he is allowed to say approximately what he feels. You can destroy spontaneity and produce a literature which is orthodox but feeble, or you can let people say what they choose and take the risk that some of them will utter heresies. There is no way out of that dilemma so long as books have to be written by individuals. That is why, in a way, I feel sorrier for the persecutors than for the victims.[61]

Orwell is wrong: the persecutors do not deserve sympathy more than their victims. But, perversely, Orwell feels the need to add that twist, knowing that readers will respond to it as I have done. Irritatingly, Orwell is sharper than you or me: he bothers and jostles, making readers inhabit untried attitudes and experience uncomfortable points of view about subjects upon which it has been agreed that the truth is already known. What Orwell says in this example is surprising, but I am not surprised he says it. If I do not hurry to criticize him, his manner of thinking may do me some good.

Sometimes, as Morris Dickstein pointed out to me, Orwell seems to be constructing an orthodoxy that he can then, perversely, take issue with. True, I think, yet Orwell often implicates himself in the orthodoxies and antiorthodoxies he challenges, as in this passages from "Politics and the English Language" (November 1946): "Look back through this essay, and for certain you will find that I have again and again committed the very faults I am protesting against."[62] Orwell's point is that such faults are inevitable, but his tone implies his own willfulness—"again and again committed," as though he knew where the "faults" were and chose to leave them in.

There is also a theatrical quality to some of Orwell's perverse passages, where he leaves the reader wondering: Does he really mean this, or is it a potent ploy, a strategic joke, he means for me to see through? Consider this, from "Such, Such Were the Joys":

> You were supposed to love God, and I did not question this. Till the age of about fourteen I believed in God, and believed that the accounts given of him were true. But I was well aware that I did not love him. On the contrary, I hated him, just as I hated Jesus and the Hebrew patriarchs. If I had sympathetic feelings towards any character in the Old Testament, it was towards such people as Cain, Jezebel, Haman, Agag, Sisera; in the New Testament, my friends, if any, were Ananias, Caiaphas, Judas, and Pontius Pilate.[63]

Few writers sought truth telling and integrity as intently as did Orwell, yet here he names as his boyhood compatriots the Bible's best-known murderers, hypocrites, liars, and traitors. "What is truth?" Pilate asked (John 18:38), a question that Francis Bacon, William Cowper, William Blake, Gerard Manly Hopkins, and Aldous Huxley, among others in the English literary tradition, responded to. The sheer asking of the question, in Pilate's case, exposes his own failure of vision, for Jesus, the figure of truth, is standing before his eyes (". . . that I should bear witness to the truth. Every one that is of the truth heareth my voice" [John 18:37]). It is hard to imagine a more spectacular case of moral blindness, with the possible exception of the panoramic blindness to Soviet crime that Orwell himself called attention to and denounced. Orwell thus ends his sentence, with delicious perversity, with the name that stands in most glaring contrast to the kind of writer he became.

I asserted at the outset that Orwell is hard to get hold of, and that's where I must move now, as the final consequence of his perversity. An honest man, a plain writer: as we read and think about him, Orwell embodies these simple phrases with depth and power. Yet his irony, paradox, perversity: Can you say you know him, this resistant writer and critic? "If you state your principles clearly and stick to them," Orwell professed, "it is wonderful how people come round to you in the end."[64] What I want to know is this: Is perversity, the motivating principle that I see in Orwell, a principle that others can adopt? Is the lesson he teaches: be perverse?

Orwell's perversity was always there, in the reversal and anticonsensus thrust of his style and operations of mind. Yet it is more starkly present and disquieting in his work of the mid- to late 1940s. He makes more statements like these, which declare the perversity, as he envisioned it, of his enterprise as a writer:

> When one considers how things have gone since 1930 or thereabouts, it is not easy to believe in the survival of civilization. . . . I think one must continue the political struggle, just as a doctor must try to save the life of a patient who is probably going to die. . . . Exactly at the moment when there is, or could be, plenty of everything for everybody, nearly our whole energies have to be taken up in trying to grab territories, markets and raw materials from one another. Exactly at the moment when wealth might be so generally diffused that no government need fear serious opposition, political liberty is declared to be impossible and half the world is ruled by secret police forces. Exactly at the moment when superstition crumbles and a rational attitude towards the universe becomes feasible, the right to think one's own thoughts is denied as never before. The fact is that human beings only started fighting one another in earnest when there was no longer anything to fight about.[65]

Postwar history tends in the wrong direction, taken astray by humanity's friends and foes alike. But Orwell's deeper implication is that human beings are intrinsically perverse: *that* is what he is in contact with, and *that* is why he perceives an inner perversity in history's bad design.

"Part of our minds—in any normal person it is the dominant part—believes that man is a noble animal and life is worth living," Orwell reflects. He completes the sentence: "but there is also a sort of inner self which at least intermittently stands aghast at the horror of existence."[66] Normality is believing—in order to get through the day—in something that may not be true: the impact of this sentence is apparent if one switches its parts, with the horror first, and the doughty accommodation to it second, as the sentence's place of rest.

Here is one of Orwell's assertions: "The civilization of nineteenth-century America was capitalist civilization at its best." He continues: "Soon after the Civil War, the inevitable deterioration started."[67] Conspicuous by its absence is any mention of slavery, which Orwell either neglects or fails to see. But more noteworthy is his "inevitable," with its accent of mordant certainty that a high point never endures. What's striking is less Orwell's historical blind spot than the rhythm of his thinking in these sentences, the cadence of decline and decay.

This perverse passage has an odd but revealing relationship to another, in "Such, Such Were the Joys": "How difficult it is for a child to have any real independence of attitude could be seen in our behavior towards Flip. I think it would be true to say that every boy in the school hated and feared her. Yet we all fawned on her in the most abject way, and the top layer of our feelings towards her was a sort of guilt-stricken loyalty."[68]

"Independence of attitude": this is Orwell's distinction. Yet he emphasizes that such an attitude in a child is dreadfully hard to secure. Hate and fear are the true feelings, but the behavior in response to them, perversely, is abject fawning. In Orwell's tone is the same chord of inevitability—this, always, is how persons tend to behave. The conduct of the boys prophesies the submissiveness to authority they will display as adults.

The ultimate perversity, for Orwell, is the absurdity of the human predicament, its unchanging core. History pursues its course, and we are who we are: "From time to time a human being may dye his hair or become converted to Roman Catholicism, but he cannot change himself fundamentally."[69] The sane thing in a way would be to stop working. Why write at all? This is a question that Orwell wondered about, and for which he provides a complex, illuminating, and egregious answer:

> I give all this background information because I do not think one can assess a writer's motives without knowing something of his early development. His subject matter will be determined by the age he lives in—at least this is true in tumultuous, revolutionary ages like our own—but before he ever begins to write he will have acquired an emotional attitude from which he will never completely escape. It is his job, no doubt, to discipline his temperament and avoid getting stuck at some immature stage, or in some *perverse* mood: but if he escapes from his early influences altogether, he will have killed his impulse to write.[70]

> In a reasonable world a writer who had said his say would simply take up some other profession. In a competitive society he feels, just as a politician does, that retirement is death. So he continues long after his impulse is spent, and, as a rule, the less conscious he is of imitating himself, the more grossly he does it.[71]

There is, Orwell believes, no stopping work, even if the work is grossly imitative, because stopping would mean death. But in Orwell's case, as his biographers have recorded, he drove himself with near-suicidal intensity to complete *Nineteen Eighty-Four* amid wracking illness. His execution of this book ensured his death. Why do that? It's pointless, yet for Orwell utterly necessary.

Orwell was a writer: he kept working: he had to work. And his impact has been astounding. In the turn of his sentences and judgments, he remains brilliantly and memorably perverse.

NOTES

1. George Orwell, *The Collected Essays, Journalism and Letters,* ed. Sonia Orwell and Ian Angus (New York: Harcourt Brace Jovanovich, 1968), 4:5. (Henceforth referred to as *CEJL.*)

2. George Orwell, *Burmese Days* (New York: Harcourt Brace Jovanovich, 1962), 133.

3. Orwell, *Burmese Days,* 176.

4. George Orwell, *Nineteen Eighty-Four* (New York: Harcourt Brace Jovanovich, 1982), 10.

5. Orwell, "The English People," *CEJL,* 3:26.

6. Orwell, *CEJL,* 4:479.

7. Orwell, *CEJL,* 3:158, 3:163.

8. Lionel Trilling, "George Orwell and the Politics of Truth," in *The Opposing Self: Nine Essays in Criticism* (New York: Viking, 1955), 155.

9. Ian Slater, *Orwell: The Road to Airstrip One* (New York: W.W. Norton, 1985), 183.

10. Malcolm Muggeridge, "A Knight of the Woeful Countenance," in *Nineteen Eighty-Four to 1984: A Companion to the Classic Novel of Our Time,* ed. C. J. Kuppig (New York: Carroll and Graf, 1984), 276–77.

11. Richard Rees, *George Orwell: Fugitive from the Camp of Victory* (Carbondale: Southern Illinois University Press, 1962), 147.

12. Bernard Crick, *George Orwell: A Life* (New York: Penguin, 1982), 362.

13. Diana Trilling, "Fiction in Review," *The Nation,* June 25, 1949, 717.

14. Dwight Macdonald, "Trotsky, Orwell, and Socialism," *The New Yorker,* March 28, 1959, reprinted in *Discriminations: Essays and Afterthoughts* (New York: Da Capo, 1985), 341.

15. Louis Menand, "Honest, Decent, Wrong: The Invention of George Orwell," *The New Yorker,* January 27, 2003, 87.

16. Timothy Garton Ash, "Orwell in 1998," *The New York Review of Books,* October 22, 1998.

17. Steven Marcus, "George Orwell: Biography as Literature," *Partisan Review* (Winter 1993): 46.

18. V. S. Pritchett, "Orwell in Life," *The New York Review of Books,* December 15, 1966.

19. Christopher Hitchens, "The Power of Facing" (interview), *Atlantic Unbound* (http://www.theatlantic.com/unbound/unb_index.htm), October 23, 2002.

20. A brief digression: In his survey of biographical accounts of Orwell's "prep school" experiences, Robert Pearce concludes: "These writers, aware that Orwell did not always tell the whole truth, nevertheless insist that he did not lie: he produced an account which, to use one of his own favorite phrases, was 'essentially true.'" (Robert Pearce, "Truth and Falsehood: George Orwell's Prep School Woes," *The Review of English Studies,* new series, 43, no. 171 [August 1992]: 367–86.) This is convincing but curious, more than a little perverse if not dangerous: When does the shading of truth reach a point when the essential truth becomes discredited? Or is the idea that if you know that something is essentially true, you can take liberties that the reader may never detect?

21. Alaric Jacob, "Sharing Orwell's 'Joys'—But Not His Fears," in *Inside the Myth: Orwell: Views from the Left* (London: Lawrence and Wishart, 1984), 73.

22. Christopher Norris, "Language, Truth, and Ideology: Orwell and the Post-War Left," in *Inside the Myth,* 249–50.

23. Raymond Williams, *Politics and Letters: Interviews with the New Left Review* (London: Verso, 1979), 390.

24. Orwell, *CEJL,* 4:502.

25. Audrey Coppard and Bernard Crick, eds., *Orwell Remembered* (New York: Facts on File, 1984), 171.

26. Mary McCarthy, "The Writing on the Wall," *The New York Review of Books,* January 30, 1969.

27. Stephen Spender, "The Truth about Orwell," *The New York Review of Books,* November 16, 1972.

28. Quoted in Miriam Gross, ed., *The World of George Orwell* (New York: Simon & Schuster, 1971), 80.

29. Orwell, *The Road to Wigan Pier* (New York: Harcourt, Brace, Jovanovich, 1958), 20–21.

30. Irving Howe, "George Orwell: 'As the Bones Know,'" in *Decline of the New* (New York: Horizon, 1970), 270.

31. Alfred Kazin, "'Not One of Us,'" *The New York Review of Books,* June 14, 1984.

32. Orwell, *CEJL,* 4:375.

33. Christopher Hitchens, *Why Orwell Matters* (New York: Basic Books, 2002).

34. W. E. B. Du Bois, "On Stalin," *National Guardian,* March 16, 1953, reprinted in *Newspaper Columns,* vol. 2, 1945–1961, ed. Herbert Aptheker (White Plains, N.Y.: Kraus-Thomson, 1986), 910.

35. Edmund Wilson, *Patriotic Gore: Studies in the Literature of the American Civil War* (New York: Oxford University Press, 1962), xxxii.

36. F. R. Leavis, *D. H. Lawrence: Novelist* (New York: Simon and Schuster, 1969), 14.

37. Clement Greenberg, *The Collected Essays and Criticism,* vols. 1 and 2, ed. John O'Brian (Chicago: University of Chicago Press, 1986).

38. Orwell, *CEJL,* 1:242.

39. Orwell, *CEJL*, 2:56.

40. Volume 4 of the *Collected Essays, Journalism and Letters* reprints many of Orwell's best-known and most-admired pieces from 1945 to 1950, including "The Prevention of Literature," "Politics and the English Language," "James Burnham and the Managerial Revolution" (as well as a later piece on Burnham), "Politics vs. Literature: An Examination of *Gulliver's Travels*," "How the Poor Die," "Lear, Tolstoy, and the Fool," "Writers and Leviathan," "George Gissing," and "Reflections on Gandhi."

41. Orwell, *CEJL*, 4:6.

42. Orwell, *CEJL*, 4:17.

43. Michael Shelden, *Orwell: The Authorized Biography* (New York: HarperCollins, 1991).

44. Orwell, *CEJL*, 4:116.

45. Orwell, *CEJL*, 4:22.

46. Orwell, *CEJL*, 4:24, 4:29.

47. Orwell, *CEJL*, 4:32.

48. Orwell, *CEJL*, 4:220

49. Orwell, *CEJL*, 4:290.

50. Orwell, *CEJL*, 4:463.

51. Rees, *George Orwell*, 111.

52. Hugh Kenner, "The Politics of the Plain Style" (1984), in *Mazes: Essays* (San Francisco: North Point Press, 1989), 261–69.

53. Orwell, *CEJL*, 4:41.

54. Orwell, *CEJL*, 4:51.

55. Orwell, *CEJL*, 4:124, 4:125.

56. Orwell, *CEJL*, 4:63; see also 4:158.

57. Orwell, *CEJL*, 4:398; see also 4:409.

58. Orwell, *CEJL*, 4:66; see also 4:135.

59. Orwell, *CEJL*, 4:240.

60. Orwell, *CEJL*, 4:410.

61. Orwell, *CEJL*, 4:267.

62. Orwell, *CEJL*, 4:137.

63. Orwell, *CEJL*, 4:360.

64. Orwell, *CEJL*, 4:399–400.

65. Orwell, *CEJL*, 4:248–49.

66. Orwell, *CEJL*, 4:222.

67. Orwell, *CEJL*, 4:247.

68. Orwell, *CEJL*, 4:350.

69. Orwell, *CEJL*, 4:276.

70. Orwell, *CEJL*, 1:3.

71. Orwell, *CEJL*, 4:253.

16

Prescience and Resilience in George Orwell's Political Aesthetics

LYNETTE HUNTER

This essay attempts to work through Orwell's writing to delineate some recent developments in left-wing theory and to open out some areas that need attention. The argument will not work pragmatically within politics or sociology but with the political implications of art and knowledge, and it deals largely with rhetorical strategies.

We are all aware of the European context for the way that Orwell's writings rehearse before the event the left-wing agendas of the past fifty years. Throughout the early to mid-1930s, he was concerned with the issue of proletarian art and its production and consumption, just as this preoccupied thinkers in the 1950s to 1960s. He became obsessed with the totalitarian tendencies in authority around the end of the 1930s and developed many of the arguments about overdetermination that are also found in the work of his contemporaries Jacques Lacan and Louis Althusser writing into the 1970s. Unlike them, he moved on in the early 1940s to investigate ways of challenging authority from within, dispelling any hope for the effectiveness of anarchy, ideas that we find in the work of the later Michel Foucault or of Ernesto Leclau and Chantal Mouffe in the 1980s. And in his last works, Orwell despaired about the cynicism and passivity of political relativism in an early critique of the effects of ahistorical postmodernism so rife in the early 1990s.[1]

Orwell even leaves clues about the problems that will arise about global culture and what I have elsewhere termed the impact of Global State Apparatuses (GSAs) on the nation-state structure of liberal social contract aesthetics.[2] But although this is an important issue, it is more difficult and more helpful in the long term to look instead at what his writing is contributing to specific, materially located, political-aesthetic concepts today. Orwell's thinking doesn't just stop with postmodernism. Concurrent with his entire trajectory of political thinking that offers such an incisive critique of both neo-Marxism and hyperliberalism, he's working out practical strategies, strategies embedded in his work as a craftsperson with words.

I would like to use Orwell's writing to delineate current thinking among radical and left-wing groups concerned to develop a wider access to political, cultural, social, and scientific power. Although I know comparatively little about left-wing politics on a national or broadsheet scale in the United States, many of the groups whose work is drawn upon in this essay are based in the United States, Canada, and Latin America. They are working at the coal-face of words and arguments where you have work before going out into the street and onto the page: they are hammering out a vocabulary. Hence this analysis may well contribute to the debates raised by others in this volume, but it will come from a slightly different location. Yes, Orwell explores the impossibility of proletarian literature and proletarian power, the overdetermination of bourgeois art and liberal politics, but he doesn't leave it at that. He moves on through to a critique that bears all the hallmarks of the current philosophical interest in standpoint epistemology (the sophisticated kind), situated knowledge, the political theory of deliberative democracy, and what I term situated textuality.[3]

What all of these moves have in common is a radical critique of the three primary philosophical issues underlying the humanism of the liberal social contract from the late seventeenth century. First, the autonomous individual who is also universal man: the individual with an essential self predicated on notions of the universal/relative split. Second, rationalism: the process of arguing as quest, working in a decreasing tree structure, lopping off extraneous branches as one gets closer to the "end," that so often becomes reductive. Third, the face-off between subjective and objective knowledge: the idea that what we know is either objectively "true" for all people or subjectively relativist. The implications of these elements for verbal craft are widespread but center on the fact that within this system language is considered inadequate to the communication of reality and therefore we have to transcend it: the artist is our hero continually risking the inadequacies of communication out on the rim of reality (4:87).

Depending on their discipline, the recent moves produce critiques of the modes of production and consumption in politics, science, and sociology, but in the category of aesthetics the analysis is only thinly developed. Political philosophers such as Jürgen Habermas, Seyla Benhabib, or Nira Yuval Davis have contributed substantially to a re-thinking of the need for differentiated public spaces within which people who do not normally get access to making an impact on political power can not only learn how to do so but also begin to do so.[4] People interested in the social study of science such as Hilary Rose[5] or Sandra Harding[6] have, with a number of others, begun to draw a fascinating picture of post-Einsteinian science, what scientific knowledge might look like if we paid acute attention to the involvement of the observer in the experiment: asking, What would African science look like? What would feminist science look like? What would Native American science look like? Writers such as Doreen Massey,[7] working on human geography and sociology, or Lorraine Code,[8] working on radical philosophy, have asked about differentiated concepts of logic, time, and space that require us to jettison the concepts of universal/relativist as tied to a particular ideology that prevents attention to current democratic needs. This kind of thinking offers a radical and sound challenge to liberal social contract humanism

However, having produced critiques of the modes of production and consumption in their different disciplines, each gestures toward material practice. For example, those interested in standpoint theory or situated knowledge in the sciences gesture to the arts[9] and deliberative democratic political theory gestures on and off to "story" or "rhetoric."[10] But in effect none of them seem to grasp what Orwell grasped wholly: that the "arts," that "story," is just as liable to be compromised in the liberal social contract as, for example, scientific discourse or political debate. There is a sense that because we all tell stories we all know how they work. So I offer one proviso: none of these areas of politics, science, or knowledge can exist without communication, and what is desperately needed for advance in any of the areas under consideration is an idea of a differentiated public voice[11] or a situated textuality. What this essay proceeds to explore is how Orwell is clear about the limitations of art and has much to contribute to the area of situated textuality, which is what I have termed the kind of art that all of these investigations are calling upon, and upon the modes of production and consumption that make it possible or impossible.

POLITICS AND "ART"

Throughout the late 1930s Orwell is obsessed with countering the claims that proletarian literature can exist in a bourgeois state structure. He notes in a review of a book by Phillip Henderson that "To the Communist, good literature means 'proletarian literature.' (Mr Henderson is careful to explain, however, that this does not mean literature written by proletarians; which is just as well, because there isn't any)" (1:289). To his working-class friend Jack Common Orwell writes, "As to the great proletarian novel, I really don't see how it's to come into existence," and continues by citing the different languages people use and laying down language change as the foundation for any change in literary aesthetic (1:348). But even Common only partially manages to write in a "proletarian" manner: "much more than most writers of this kind he preserves his proletarian viewpoint" (1:371). In a slightly later 1940 essay on Dickens, Orwell notes that "If you look for the working classes in fiction, and especially English fiction, all you find is a hole" (1:455). Novelists mostly show "class" by how they treat women, for example if they are working class, women are, he notes, considered "fair game" as sexual objects (1:479).

After his experiences in Spain, Orwell turns squarely to the issue of the influence of politics on art, saying that in a time of revolution, specifically a time of conflict between fascism and socialism, all art is propagandic but not all propaganda is art (1.492). But there is the problem that party politics brings to the surface, "the struggle that always goes on between the individual and the community" (2:161). In a liberal state we have the illusion that we are autonomous, and in literature "we instinctively take the autonomous individual for granted" (2:161), asking them to be true to their feelings, to be sincere. But under totalitarian regimes (fascist or communist) the individual is forbidden to think some things and required to think others, because totalitarian states work through an all-pervading ideology. As Althusser was to delineate two decades later, Orwell describes this complete ideology as one trying "to govern your emotional life as well as setting up a code of conduct. And as far as possible it isolates you from the outside world, it shuts you up in an artificial universe in which you have no standards of comparison" (2:162). Totalitarian ideology is different from earlier structures of ideology because it sets up dogmas, or what the new Marxism of the 1960s called representations,[12] only to change them according to the needs of "power politics":

(2:163). This is all very well, but for Orwell the issue is that socialism, in getting rid of the economic autonomy of the individual, may well end up getting rid of the creative autonomy of the individual, in effect depriving them of liberal agency and ending up like totalitarianism. And in this early part of the Second World War, Orwell could not imagine any agency that was not liberal.

The conscious shaping of representation by the state is mimicked and exacerbated by advertising, and prior to the coming into being of totalitarian states, advertising is an index of the contradictory interchange between individuals and structures of power. For example, Gordon Comstock in *Keep the Aspidistra Flying* layers advertising over poetry as a form of personal control over his world. Both Marx and Freud worked on the assumption that privileged people, the citizens of nation-states, would always be able to intersect with power, while the marginalized or excluded were subjected to the whims of those with "human rights." With the consolidation of large international power structures, strategies for representation become integrated into nation-state strategies for economic power, displaying on a public level contradictions that have to be repressed by citizens because they can no longer do anything about them. Intimations of this growing sense of powerlessness in face of representation are found in Orwell's complaint that by 1944 advertisements had begun to reappear on the streets, conveying offensive social messages that implied, for example, that most people had "a secret fantasy life" (3:216) in which they like to imagine they are part of the upper classes even though they know they can't be. What is more telling is that these ads are replacing "ministry" announcements, calling attention to the cohabitation between the state and big business. Any conscious shaping of representation becomes too big for the individual, and the relation between the state and those with political rights changes. If a totalitarian state emerges, like the Leviathan predicted by Hobbes it overdetermines the representations allowed to people who count as citizens so that they, too, become subjected, become subjects.

In a system like this the concept of "rights" disappears—one is lucky to have a representation. But in the not-yet totalitarian state of the 1940s, the fact that what privileged people call human rights are in effect "special rights" that others do not possess is still an accessible concept.[13] "Rights" indicates the ability to change the representations offered by the state for the way one lives. For example, the fact that gay and lesbian individuals have been able to begin to legitimate a homosexual way of life indicates not that they should have special rights because they are different, but that they are able to make a recognized claim on general human rights. Others, such as those living in poverty, have not been successful in making this claim and are still usually "dealt with" by being apportioned so-called special rights. The poor also find it exceptionally difficult to change the representations of them on offer by the state, for example that they are usually shiftless and irresponsible.[14]

Orwell's insight into just who can and cannot affect representations, incidentally sheds light on the concept of hegemony popularized by Chantal Mouffe and Ernesto Laclau[15] by offering one explanation for the activity of participation within strong ideological power structures that the early Foucault called "discursive." The only way that people will be able to affect the ideology of a neoliberal state structure that has such strong control over representation is if they speak the language of that state. They need to use its accepted rhetorical strategies, in other words those of the bourgeois liberal, and enter the discursive realm in which representations are contested and confirmed.[16] By definition, working-class people are alienated or marginalized by the use of bourgeois strategies, hence the plethora of special interest groups that can exclude the issue of class: gender, sexuality, ethnicity, ability. Class would complicate things, and it does appear to continue to do so.

Today we rarely use the word "bourgeois," which used to be a relatively unembarrassed critical term for a defensively privileged middle class. The culture and way of life indicated by the term is now so widespread in Western nations that it is more usually called the liberal social contract. Orwell frequently notes the convergence in class aspirations especially through the mass media and the clothes people wear (1:340, 2:97, 3:44). The bourgeois way of life is a general aspiration for many people, largely driven by the condition of women because the key signifier of the bourgeois household is the leisured woman, the woman who does not have to do housework, around whom the service society is built. Orwell acknowledges this problem early in his writing, noting that without mechanical aids to housework, equality for women is neither possible nor imaginable (1:455). Later, shortly after his wife left her job to work in the home looking after their adopted son, he takes off in an "As I Please" article on housework as "uncreative and life-wasting" (3:376), for which he can find only three solutions: we simplify our lives, or we assume that "it is entirely natural for the average woman to be a broken-down drudge at the age of thirty," or we rationalize the interior of our houses with the intelligence we have spent on transport systems (3:376). He suggests that we either encourage communal dishwashing services or eat out of paper cartons, but he admits that the problem is that some people will have to become full-time dishwashers, something he would have recognized as problematic and unpleasing, having worked as a dishwasher himself.[17]

We don't use the word "bourgeois" precisely because it is a class signifier that underlines, despite general aspiration, the inequality of those who serve. Yet of course this is partly an illusion that has to do with ignoring the rest of the world. Just as Orwell pointed out consistently that the bettered condition of the working class from pre-1914 to post-1945 was built on the continued exploitation of imperial holdings, so the bettered condition of women and men in the West from pre-1950 to today has been built on the continued exploitation by global economics and transnational corporations of less-industrial nations. The signal difference between the category "woman" and that of "working class" is that the latter is by definition peripheral to economic power, whereas some women are economically privileged and therefore in a position to prosecute advance and change available representations. Trade unions were supposed to do this for the working class, but they have been systematically repressed in a manner that may be a warning to women despite the categorical differences (for example, Iran or Afghanistan when they pulled back from "westernization").

BOURGEOIS ART

In the nation-state structure of early twentieth-century England, and for the preceding two hundred and fifty years, the only individuals with the leisure and money to be able to make "art" or "literature" were those who were also classified as "citizens" within the liberal social contract.[18] This very small proportion of the population, rising to around 15 percent by the end of the nineteenth century, consisted of private people, working largely in isolation from each other according to the commentators on art and dealing with truths and feelings unique to the autonomous individual. These people produced bourgeois art, or art within nation-state ideology. They were part of the privileged group that ruled the nation, and they acted as the licensed transgressors of the representations allowed to citizens within the state. However, because they were so close to centers of power, their transgressions, although valuable in themselves, usually fell well within the boundaries of acceptability.[19] As Orwell explained, to be recognized as an artist a person had to write in this way, and increasingly since education became more accessible in the 1890s, people from other classes—he suggests D. H. Lawrence—had learned to produce bourgeois literature (2:55ff). As he notes in "Why I Joined the Independent Labour Party" (1938), "The time is coming . . . when every writer will have the choice of being silenced altogether or of producing the dope that a privileged minority demands" (1:343).

Orwell articulates this analysis in detailed commentary from 1936 to 1940, culminating in the statement from the interview "The Proletarian Writer" (1940): "I don't believe the proletariat can create an independent literature while they are not the dominant class. I believe that their literature is and must be bourgeois literature with a slightly different slant" (2:54). He also recognizes that with the franchises of 1918 and 1928 people in England were claiming rights not only to political power via representative democracy but also to cultural power. However, the way that many of them speak cannot be "heard," and what they might speak about cannot yet be "said" because there has been no previous articulation and others cannot recognize the words.[20] Orwell notes that a number of writers have managed to get into print details about the lives of the working class, and he mentions Robert Tressel's *The Ragged Trousered Philanthropist* as a key text (2:56). But he goes on to say that speaking about the kitchen sink smelling "won't last as long as the siege of Troy" (2:58). Hence working-class writers, and others trying to write outside "bourgeois art," will have to focus more on language and form to convey the alterity of their way of life and thinking.

But, Orwell also has much to say about morally responsible bourgeois writing, as well as about writing from those who have never had access to cultural power who pose a different set of issues to the question of proletarian power. In "Why I Write," an influential if conservative essay, he lays out the terms of moral responsibility for the autonomous individual (bourgeois) writer, who uses rational prose and striving for objective truth to reality. He notes that writers of this kind are often selfish, "gifted, wilful people who are determined to live their lives to the end" (1:25). They are interested in the "perception of beauty in the external world, or . . . in words and their right arrangement" (1:25), and have a desire to "see things as they are" and to push the world in "a certain direction" (1:28).

Bourgeois artists are selfish because they have to resist ideological pressure, but their isolation leaves them less able to offer alternatives (see also 2:162). They are interested in beauty and words in the right order precisely because "beauty" is a philosophical concept that only works within defined parameters; words have to be in the "right" order because we usually don't recognize something as beautiful until we have been taught to recognize it as such. These artists see things "as they are," but if the only way of seeing is rational the art becomes blinkered and narrow.

And Orwell offers elsewhere a critique of the wish to push the world in a "certain" direction when he deconstructs "certainty" as working on self-evident bases, taking things for granted with a Marxian false consciousness that argues for the absolute truth of something that it has itself defined.

Yet Orwell also has the imagination to recognize that bourgeois art and liberal humanism is only one way of doing things. If the artist in the social contract nation-state is a subject writing against or over their subjectivity, discursively shifting representations that tie people down but/and able to do so only to the extent that they are complicit in the hegemony, then the working-class writer or any newly enfranchised artist has no subjective representations to shift, only the shadows of other people's representations that they used to fill. What we have here is an analysis that is sprung from the implications of the late-nineteenth- and early-twentieth-century franchises: people throughout England suddenly gained access (technically) to political power but also to something many were aware aware of, access to cultural power.[21] What did that mean? Among other things it means access to cultural power that is controlled by those controlling the means of production and consumption, and for Orwell as a writer in the first half of the twentieth century this means printing (nonelectronic) and publishing.

ORWELL, PRINTING, AND THE MEDIA

Orwell was fascinated by the print media and by conditions of publishing. He writes extensively about issues of distribution for magazines and pamphlets (3:326), of the impact of the cost of novels, and the need for libraries, borrowers, and bookshops (3:38–39, 2:43). The essays are filled with discussions of the role of the reader and consumer of printed material, their education, the coteries they form, what they can afford to pay for, and what they want to read. Presciently commenting on the argues of the following half century dealing with state support for the arts, Orwell argues the pros and cons of patronage, whether ideologically controlled (mainly via rich sponsors) (3:265, 4:82, 4:237), commercially controlled (by market forces) (3:265), or institutionally controlled (by government) (4:82, 4:237). Often with his own writing in focus, he talks about the network of rewards and favors, the old-boy network of reviewers and editors that silently puts pressure on the writer. There is explicit and perceptive analysis of big business, of the way the printing industry and the publishers intersect with and respond to advertising and finance. And he is unusually honest about the pragmatics of writing; echoing Virginia Woolf's comments on the need for a room of one's own, he adds that it must be a warm room at that and with no interruptions (4:237)—hence within the capitalist nation-state that he lives, writing can only be accessible to the middle class.

Well before Marshall McLuhan and coincident with Herald Innis, Orwell was elaborating on print as the capitalist medium par excellence that requires all the money for an investment up front before you know if you can sell the product. He also had the wit to understand that printing and publishing was the most significant factor aiding and abetting the liberal social contract state and that it had done so since the Renaissance (4:88). It is, like the contract, based on the autonomous individual of the "author" (1:576; see also his comments on the value of an authorial "name," 2:38, 3:170), concerned to employ rational devices in its emphasis on the reality effect of realism as well as fantasy (3:257, 4:92), and aiming at objectivity or the production of the knowledge needed to maintain the representations of ideology. Because capitalism is central to his analysis, he notes that it has a similar effect on film and radio. He talks frequently and at length of the problem of commercial control (2:381) and of the monopoly over these modes of production (1:105–6, 4:82). But at the same time, just as he recognizes a moral responsibility for the bourgeois artist (as above), he recognizes the positive impact of printing and publishing (2:326) and the positive potential for film and radio to offer the media that will make alternative verbal art possible in the future (2:24, 3:38–39).

GENRES OF WRITING

Orwell's essays carry out this development of an analysis of production and consumption, what became fifteen years later "histoire du livre" and is now big business in arts departments, in terms of an exploration of the novel, of folk literature and of verse, these genres separating more and more into what he calls "prose" and what he calls "poetry."

Orwell's primary study of the novel is found in "Inside the Whale," for understanding the novel is being inside the whale. The large generic structures of post-Renaissance realism produce a genre that is too ideologically bound, too determined, too predictable, finally too open to ideological power (1:568); and it is interesting that all Orwell's fictional work is a series of generic experiments with the realistic novel. Against his late 1930s' conviction that totalitarian power is inevitable he argues, "The autonomous individual is going to be stamped out of existence" and with this destruction of liberalism goes writing, for "*as a writer* he [the creative writer] is a liberal": "The literature of liberalism is coming to an end and the literature of totalitarianism has not yet appeared and is barely imaginable" (1:576). Yet the point of this essay is not only to reiterate his thoughts on bourgeois liberalism but also to suggest that there is a choice in how one might respond to the dilemma. On the one hand he places Henry Miller, who although a good stylist simply accepts that he will live "inside the whale," cosily and passively, accepting the womb of totalitarian politics. This is the idea that we are all made up of other people's words (Beckett,[22] Barthes[23]) lying at the heart of the ahistorical aesthetic, which Orwell later accurately describes as the coming political condition for Anglo-European cultures (3:437, 4:89, 4:469–70). On the other hand he places James Joyce, who comes to stand for an alternative response to liberal aesthetics because he has dared to write something that has never been written before: "Here is a whole world of stuff you have lived with since childhood, stuff which you supposed to be of its nature incommunicable, and somebody has managed to communicate it. The effect is to break down, at any rate momentarily, the solitude in which the human being lives" (1:543). Literature is a liberal concept, only valuable within its own framework, and if you remove the framework you remove the value. Joyce's ability is to build a world "outside space and time," which is necessary if one is not to be trapped back into either the liberal bourgeois or the totalitarian. At the same time both of these writers are contrasted to the mechanistic and formulaic propaganda novels that Orwell fears will result from too much toeing of the party line. Hence the essay posits three positions: the liberal artist such as Henry Miller (who comes to represent the passive condition of the [postmodern] artist) (4:136), the alternative in James Joyce, and formulaic propaganda (see also his comments on mechanization and the formulaic structure of books [4:92ff]).

The essays also offer an acute analysis of "folk literature." The comments in "Boy's Weeklies" (1:105–6) criticize both the weeklies and women's magazines for being too ideologically bound because they are too commercial. In a later "As I Please" column he notes that women's magazines may argue the moral superiority of the poor but are, in fact, a deadly form of "escapism," "a sublimation of the class struggle" (3:230–21). In contrast are the smaller, more specifically targeted periodicals, such as *Exchange and Mart* (1:106), which, because they exist only for a specific community, are closer to their readers and reflect their needs and interests. Donald McGill's postcards may be subversively vulgar but they are founded on the institution of marriage (2:193). Kipling's books may be a challenge of "good-bad" writing, but they are basically popular because they are full of platitudes (2:229). But there is a different impulse behind the ballads, work songs, war songs, broadsheets (2:58), and jokes (see also 3:327–29) of the more localized press with smaller circulation. What Orwell's comments outline is that these forms are either un-self-consciously compromised by ideology or self-consciously and commercially so. The analysis distinguishes between folk literature and popular culture, the former being nonironic and the latter ironic, and in this it explains why popular culture fits so neatly into postmodernism while folk literature is anathema.

Neither analysis, of the novel or of folk/popular literature, helps Orwell's thinking as much as his growing understanding of verse and poetry. At first he is not that interested in what verse has to offer, which is not surprising when you look at his fairly banal Georgian efforts from the 1930s (1:148, 1933). In my opinion he would probably have made a good concrete poet, someone who still believes in the print medium but wants to radically rearrange it, like Sterne, Thackeray, Ford Madox Ford before him, and bpNichol and countless text-messagers after. But working at the BBC from 1941 to 1943, often on productions with poets and dealing first-hand with the oral medium of radio,[24] he seems to come to a completely different idea of what poetry does with words, which gives him a tool for understanding what could be different from the bourgeois art typified by realistic prose.

POETRY AND VERSE

In "The Prevention of Literature" poetry is, importantly, despised by the authorities (4:90). Therefore, in a classic standpoint argument, it is not as open to their control. The essay argues that poetry is about form rather than content, which is a crude way of saying that it works on grammar and syntax rather than genre, on the taken for granted detail of the text (see also his despairing comments that much work on language comes from a "half-conscious belief that language is a natural growth and not an instrument which we shape for our own purposes" [4:156]) rather than on the larger more commercially recognizable aspects that often define where a book is placed on a shelf. And possibly most significantly, he argues that poetry is "composed cooperatively by groups of people" (4:90).

Drawing from a series of essays from the middle of the 1940s, a sophisticated attempt to articulate the conditions of an alternative verbal practice begins to emerge. If we look first at what precisely we do when we work on words in "poetry": first, we invent new words, to deal with the parts of our experience that are practically unnameable to language (2:17); second we move beyond the chess board world of rationalism and direct reference, to dreams, that disordered stream of nameless things, so nameless they could be thoughts or feelings or images (2:18); and third, we use demotic speech rather than stilted bookish language in an upper-class accent, speech with spoken and oral rhythms and rules (3:163) (here there is an implication that the written is tied too much to print and the ideological, whereas the spoken is not and so there is more scope for difference).

To focus even further on these elements Orwell specifically sets prose up against poetics (3:164). He comments, "Prose literature as we know it is the product of rationalism, of the Protestant centuries, of the autonomous individual" (4:92). Prose writing is filled with dead metaphors, false verbal limbs, pretentious diction, and meaningless words (4:156). But through poetics these become "new words," appropriate syntax and grammar, demotic speech, and concrete reference (4:156). Poetry and poetics are there to make us attend to these elements, and here Orwell turns to Shakespeare, whose writing is "chaotic, detailed, discursive" and interested in "the actual process of life" (4:338). Orwell is insistent on *detail* being at the heart of this new kind of writing. A sample of his own early writing demonstrates the hunger: "He pushed the door open and entered the room. A yellow beam of sunlight, filtering through the muslin curtains, slanted on to the table, where a matchbox, half open, lay beside the inkpot" (1:24). The consistent love of detail is found in his early appreciation for the work of James Joyce (1:546) or his praise for the "intimate day-to-day pictures" of the Spanish revolution in *Red Spanish Notebook* by Mary Low and Juan Brear (1:321).

THE NEW POLITICS AND THE NEW "ART"

In view of the collective work that Orwell suggests, his insistence that the new writing has to be from an individual's experience can appear as a direct contradiction. The essay I am writing is not concerned to speak about the concurrent political developments in Orwell's thinking at this time. But as a direct result of the Dunkirk evacuation and the massive response by the British populace, he developed the idea of a socialism that is neither totalitarian nor capitalist, in which the individual loses economic freedom but not intellectual freedom (2:164), and reconceived the notion of the "individual." The essay "The Lion and the Unicorn" talks about the way war brings home to the individual that he is not altogether an individual (2:114). The apparent contrast between the collective action of writing and the importance of individual experience, which in the early work is called a contradiction between the individual and the community in liberal bourgeois culture (2:61), is in this new kind of socialist culture a necessity: the individual is necessarily part of a group of people—they are necessarily situated with respect to one another (3:160).

Hence the increasing praise for the "truthfulness" and "sincerity" of autobiographical elements in otherwise unremarkable writing. He praises "Good Bad Books" for "their lack of shame in writing autobiography" (4:39), reclaims Herbert Read as "memorable" when he draws on experience and uses "autobiographical writings" (4:73), rescues Leonard Merrick when he describes "*his own* adventures in Paris" (4:74), and offers cautious praise for Henry Miller's "slab of unpretentious autobiography" (4:87) in *The Cosmological Eye*—or, as in "The Prevention of Literature," he states that "literature is an attempt to influence the viewpoint of one's contemporaries by recording experience" (4:87), using the underlying autobiographical impulse that he notes in himself in "Why I Write" (1946) as a sort of "continuous 'story' about myself" (1:24). This focus on autography, that English studies has seen for the past twenty years in its reclamation of the autobiographical genre, of the journal, diary, and letter, is a key marker of a new political consciousness in aesthetics.

If this is what it is to work differently with words, there is still the issue of how we do it. Orwell's essays suggest that we write in this way in order to communicate, to speak to others about things not understood between people, to show meaning in an unmistakable form and to share its value (2:24). In effect it doesn't have value beforehand because there was no communication in which to recognize it. This is a version of the question generated by the gesture to the arts by situated knowledge and deliberative democracy: if we do not understand how to communicate the differentiated voice/space/time/logic, there can be no material basis for the development of the philosophy into action. For example, how can you have effective knowledge without communication of knowledge? Second, we work on words in a collective: words have to be recognized by others as worth being used to name; nameless feelings that come into recognition have to be those that some human beings have in common (2:25), and they have to collectively decide on the appropriateness of the sound, physical form, and gesture they take on. Words have to work across class, and "Language ought to be the joint creation of poets and manual workers" (3:46; see also the comments on the "best" nonsense poetry being produced "by communities rather than by individuals" [4:68]).

Third, this different kind of work with words may occur in a number of ways, but it has to be primarily through education (3:295). This conclusion is one reached by any serious thinker interested in social change from Plato to Erasmus, and like them Orwell links education to equality and democracy (3:46–47). Education is necessary to understand the verbal skills necessary for the new collective individual to use, in other words education is needed to understand poetic action, to acquire what Orwell calls "taste" (2:380). In contrast to Herbert Read, who believes that beauty is "absolute," Orwell counters that "one's aesthetic judgement is only fully valid between fairly well-defined dates" (4:72). "Taste" is socially learned and all people can be educated past "bad" taste in order to participate in culture (2:380). This kind of education can be learned not only at school but also through other media, and he claimed that part of the work of the periodical *The Tribune* that he edited (3:355) was to educate all classes to the importance of poetry partly because it gives us information we didn't have before and therefore makes us think, but also because it opens up new ways of thinking.

Poetry and poetics offer a concept of the writer as a collective individual who is not autonomous, a writer who is the artist in every person. This writer is someone able to deal with chaos, disorder, and dream to say things that are not-yet-said, rather than someone attempting to represent the world through realist strategies that bolster up the ideological status quo. This writer is someone speaking from personal experience that is neither objective and universal nor subjective and relativist but situated. The delineation of such a writer is effectively a delineation of a differentiated public voice—and one of the most precise to exist in philosophical thinking today—and it calls for a different kind of reader. This writer is not a solution for the proletarian writer but a change for all people under a nonliberal and nontotalitarian socialism.

If this is Orwell beginning to delineate the verbal work of the situated textuality necessary to situated knowledge, deliberative democracy, and any conceptualization outside the universal/relative dichotomies of Western philosophy, his ability to define its modes of production and consumption was more limited. He knew how to critique the modes of bourgeois art and liberal social contract capitalism, but he only gives us hints such as the few words on film and radio and the importance of the oral medium. The 1940s were arguably the cusp before the disappearance of the oral in the United Kingdom or its shift away from individual tellers and the human body into the state-controlled media. There are his observations that poetry has a small audience, which is an important recognition of the niche marketing that has begun today to develop in scale as people realize that they cannot possibly read all the books that are published and are "good." We increasingly construct our own particular reading communities; many of us do so via the Internet, a development that Orwell could not have been expected to foresee. In effect, until the twentieth century, most verbal craft valued as "art" was produced by privileged writers addressing a very small group of similarly privileged people who could afford to buy their work. What Orwell did foresee was that verbal craft could only develop democratically though responses by producers that would target smaller groups of people and construct consumption on the basis of smaller markets. At the time, publishing would have found this commercially threatening, but today a book can be produced, even by a small press, to recoup its costs with as few as fifty buyers.

Orwell also makes offhand comments in a late essay on soil erosion and pollution indicating that writerly conviction may come from a collective political stance rather than individual egoism. But by far the most substantial of his discussions on modes for production and consumption of verbal craft different to bourgeois art concerns the effects of education. The impact of education in the potential of language to construct alternative ways of living is usually cast solely in terms of the vision of *Nineteen Eighty-Four* and propagandic manipulation. However, as noted above, education can also open potential out rather than close it down. There is a consistent strain of inquiry in Orwell's later essays concerning democratic access to verbal craft that implies that if all people can be intelligent readers they can also be writers. As he notes in "A Controversy," "In a healthy society everyone would be an artist of sorts" (3:294).

This finds its most specific form in Orwell's interest in worker writing groups and in writing correspondence courses. For example there is the letter from a woman in a mining village about the pressure to write about domestic issues and not about socialism (3:290). Both she and Orwell self-consciously discard the distinction between her as a woman and her as a socialist as an egalitarian move of the kind that informed 1960s and 1970s feminism. In this Orwell was being politically correct for his time, if not when he comments that the writing instructor must have been a woman. But it is important to recognize his absolute conviction that all people should have access to education in the skills of verbal craft.

11. See Lynette Hunter, "Listening to Situated Textuality: Working on Differentiated Public Voices," *Feminist Theory,* special issue: Gendering Ethics/The Ethics of Gender, ed. Linda Hogan and Sasha Roseneil, 2:2 (August 2001): 205–18.

12. See Diane Macdonnel, *Theories of Discourse* (Oxford: Blackwell, 1986).

13. For a provocative early discussion of the interchange between special rights and human rights, see Carol Pateman, *Democracy, Freedom, and Special Rights* (Swansea: University of Wales, Swansea, 1995).

14. For an analysis of this, see Hunter, "Unruly Fugues," 233–52.

15. See Chantal Mouffe and Ernesto Laclau, *Hegemony and Socialist Strategy: Towards a Radical Democratic Politics,* trans. Winston Moore and Paul Cammack (London: Verso, 1985).

16. See Young, *Intersecting Voices.*

17. George Orwell, *Down and Out in Paris and London* (New York: Harper and Bros., 1933/75), 51ff.

18. See Hunter, *Critiques of Knowing,* chap. 6.

19. 19. See Lynette Hunter, *Literary Value and Cultural Power* (Manchester: Manchester University Press, 2001), especially chap. 7.

20. See Hunter, *Critiques of Knowing,* chaps. 1 and 6.

21. Lynette Hunter, "George Orwell's Blood and Marmalade: Nation-State Ideology in a Print Society," in *Rewriting the Thirties: Modernism and After,* ed. Keith Williams and Steven Matthews (London: Longmans, 1997), 202–16.

22. Beckett, "I'm in words, made of words, others' words," *The Unnamable* in *Molloy, Malone Dies, The Unnamable* (Paris: Olympia Press, 1959), 390.

23. Roland Barthes, "The Death of the Author," in *Literature in the Modern World,* ed. Dennis (Milton Keynes: Open University Press, 1991/1967).

24. See *Orwell, The War Commentaries,* ed. William John West (London: Duckworth, 1985).

DISCUSSION

Because the essay I am writing has addressed politics and aesthetics there
some who find it esoteric. I would argue that it is an account of a radical ap
to social policy in education: one that argues that the artist is not a special c
that anyone can produce art. It is an important blueprint for cultural powei
based on shifting the three elements at the heart of the liberal social c
drawing attention to the fact that cultural power is part of political pow
there is a need to change the political and economic control of the m
production of cultural power, and hence to shift the entire economic syste
   Orwell claimed that this shift was revolutionary, but not modeled as m
olutions are on something that has come before. He never recognized tl
exploration added up to an analysis, and he was never convinced he'd
heard any of it—this practice that I have called situated textuality. Yet he
from "In the future it is possible that a new kind of literature, not in
individual feeling or truthful observation, may arise, but no such thing is at
imaginable" (4:92), to "It is [not] too much to hope that the classless soci(
secrete a culture of its own" (4:517). Of course we don't have a classless
so we'll never know. But we are still part of bourgeois culture and C
observations on how that might diversify, if not change, are, in today's incr
ly transcultural societies, not just highly relevant but vital.

NOTES

   1. *The Collected Essays, Journalism and Letters of George Orwell,* ed. Sonia
and Ian Angus (London: Secker and Warburg, 1968), 4:136. Hereafter volume a
numbers for quotations from Orwell's work will appear in parentheses in the text.
   2. For an analysis of this, see Lynette Hunter, "Unruly Fugues," in *Interrogating
al Studies: Theory, Politics, and Practice,* ed. Paul Bowman (London: Routledge
233–53.
   3. See Lynette Hunter, *Critiques of Knowing: Situated Textualities in Science,* (
ing, and the Arts (London: Routledge, 1999), chaps. 5 and 6.
   4. See Seyla Benhabib, ed., *Democracy and Difference: Contesting the Bound*
the Political (Princeton, N.J.: Princeton University Press, 1996); see also Nira Yuva
Gender and Nation (London: Sage, 1997).
   5. Hilary Rose, *Love, Power, and Knowledge: Towards a Feminist Transformatic*
Sciences (London: Cambridge University Press, 1994).
   6. Sandra Harding, *Whose Science? Whose Knowledge? Thinking from Women*
(Milton Keynes: Open University Press, 1991).
   7. Doreen Massey, *Space, Place, and Gender* (Cambridge: Polity, 1994).
   8. For example, Lorraine Code, "How to Think Globally: Stretching the Li
Imagination," in *Decentering the Centre: Philosophy for a Multicultural, Postcolon*
Feminist World, ed. Uma Narayan and Sandra Harding (Bloomington: Indiana Ur
Press, 2000).
   9. See Hunter, *Critiques of Knowing,* chap. 5.
   10. The political philosopher Iris Young explores this issue in *Intersecting Voi(*
lemmas of Gender, Political Philosophy, and Policy (Princeton, N.J.: Princeton Ur
Press, 1997).

17

Outside/Inside: Searching for Wigan Pier

MARGERY SABIN

I start with a peculiar twist on the topic of Orwell's "enduring influence." I was searching the Internet using Google the other day for current references to Orwell's book about the unemployment conditions in the industrial north of England, *The Road to Wigan Pier.*[1] More specifically, I was trying to get a better handle on the Wigan Pier of the title, understanding only imperfectly that there was a joke in it. Briefly within the book, and still not completely in a later BBC broadcast of 1943, Orwell explained that Wigan Pier doesn't exist, and didn't exist in 1936, when he made a special journey to see it.[2] He knew the phrase, he says, from the music hall comedians who had ironically linked a tumble-down coal loading jetty going into the Leeds-Liverpool canal with more popular seaside recreational piers. Even the ruins of that dilapidated plank of wood were gone by the time Orwell got to Wigan. Orwell understood the "joke" made popular by music hall comedians to have first been a piece of grim local humor. I was hoping to find this sequence explained more exactly somewhere on the Internet.

Instead, I was astonished to find a dozen Web sites attesting to the fact that Wigan Pier now *does* exist—as a "restored and refurbished" heritage museum on an 8½-acre site, bordering a thoroughly cleaned-up canal. A central feature is a hall named "The Orwell": "the perfect venue for your wedding or private party."[3] Costumed actors in the museum "bring history to life performing short scenarios," the museum Web site explains. "At Wigan Pier, whatever your age, sex, or nationality you are sure to find something which will remind you of a special time or a favourite thing."

How nasty a joke on the question of Orwell's influence is the "restored and refurbished" Wigan Pier? It is safe to guess that Orwell would have been of at least two minds, a feature of his thought that I will say more about later. On the one hand, he would have had to give one cheer that the fame of his book had created a remarkable opportunity of postindustrial commerce for at least a portion of the community that he had seen in 1936 suffering the prospect of permanent unemployment. Any new prosperity could hardly be regretted by anyone genuinely moved, as Orwell was, by the earlier poverty and hopelessness he recorded. But the Heritage Wigan Pier museum pays tribute to Orwell by essentially erasing what his book offers. The museum's promise of universal enjoyment—every visitor reminded of "a special time or favourite thing"—erases Orwell's distinctive imaginative accomplishment in *The Road to Wigan Pier*. That book tries to draw, and succeeds in drawing, readers *away* from their own favorite thoughts and things so as to grapple with the social and historical reality of Depression suffering in the north of England, almost the opposite of the museum's promise to confirm enjoyment of the visitor's own favorite things. The irony of this contrast offers a suggestive angle into the special power of Orwell's writing to move the reader outside his own preoccupations at the same time as he insists on the ways that full access into other worlds is inevitably limited by what you cannot help but bring to them.

My purpose in this essay is to identify the qualities in Orwell's writing that differentiate it from what one Web site calls a "Museum of Memories." This approach must, however, recognize that *The Road to Wigan Pier* was in many ways a failure from the point of view of the commission it was written to fulfill. In his publisher's note and foreword to the book, Victor Gollancz describes the assignment to have been "a documentary report on conditions among the unemployed in the north of England" (vii) for the Left Book Club, a socialist group committed in its publicity to the goal of helping "in the terribly urgent struggle *for* World Peace & a better social & economic order & against Fascism, by giving (to all who are determined to play their part in this struggle) such *knowledge* as will immensely increase their efficiency" (ix). Whatever may be said on behalf of Orwell's book, "efficiency" in bringing about a new social and economic order is not high on the list. After the first 118 pages of description of social conditions, part II of the book shifts to 50 pages of autobiographical narrative, followed by 60 pages of troubled, skeptical, and inconclusive ruminations about socialism and the obstacles to overcoming class barriers in England. Orwell is not absolutely hopeless about the future, but he is not especially exuberant about any form of the future he can envision. In direct contradiction to the Left Book Club's mission, Orwell has a special animus against efficiency: "all mechanical progress is towards greater and greater efficiency; ultimately, therefore towards a world in which nothing went wrong" (193), he remarks later in the book. That Orwell should recoil from such a prospect (far-fetched as it must now seem) infuriated as well as baffled Left Book Club members in 1936, as it infuriates many readers today. Nevertheless, *The Road to Wigan Pier,* despite what might be thought of as its *inefficiencies* as a book, was Orwell's first big success with the reading public; it established his distinctive voice and advanced him to the status of a major social critic.

Some regard both the voice and the project as a continuation of *Down and Out in Paris and London* (1933), Orwell's engaging account of his four years as a kind of social dropout, working, if at all, in odd jobs like dishwashing or hop-picking, but sometimes just living on the rough, dressed in the costume of a tramp or derelict to try out the perils of survival at the social rock bottom of Europe in the late 1920s and early 1930s. Since, in England at least, Orwell did have off-stage resources of other clothes, food, and bathtubs in the flats of friends and relatives, this semitheatrical experiment has struck readers as simultaneously gallant and eccentric, shocking and amusing, but finally somewhat absurd. The adventures did produce his classic, *Down and Out in Paris and London,* but by the time of writing

The Road to Wigan Pier in 1937, Orwell himself came to ridicule his own earlier fantasy of getting right down *inside* the life of the lowest social strata through this method of what he came to call "masquerade" (150).

Orwell's reportage in *The Road to Wigan Pier* is as much a critical commentary as a continuation of his earlier experiment in downward mobility. By 1936, Orwell looked back on his tramping days with irony, if also with some nostalgia: "I was very happy," he recalls: "Here I was, among 'the lowest of the low,' at the bedrock of the Western world! The class-bar was down, or seemed to be down. And down there in the squalid and, as a matter of fact, horribly boring sub-world of the tramp I had a feeling of release, of adventure, which seems absurd when I look back, but which was sufficiently vivid at the time" (152–53).

In *The Road to Wigan Pier,* Orwell denies himself the naïve satisfaction of belief that he could breach the class-bar in England of the Depression years so easily or, even if he could, that release from his own inner demons would be his reward. If Orwell had come to discard the disguise of the tramp by 1937, he also was refusing to mask himself in a socialist party line, or even in the more neutral objectivity of the documentary reporter. Orwell's attitude toward language in the book is more personal than objective, and with more sharp turnabouts of judgment than is customary in documents of either journalism or partisan politics. The book's colloquial directness and its seemingly improvisational structure add up to an effect of the artless and the natural, so that we feel in contact with someone who is refusing disguise and masquerade. It is thus easy to forget that the writing in *The Road to Wigan Pier* is itself a style, with definable advantages and limitations. The chief advantage of its freedom from visible uniform or costume is the mobility and flexibility it allows, like ordinary well-worn clothes.

The style is better suited to skepticism than to polemic, but to a skepticism that is dynamic rather than paralyzing. It is true that he becomes *almost* paralyzed, or at least severely incapacitated, by the literal effort of experiencing from the inside the work of a coal miner. Yet the voice reporting his day following miners down into a coal pit is itself full of lively movement: "for a week afterwards your thighs are so stiff that coming downstairs is quite a difficult feat; you have to work your way down in a peculiar sidelong manner, without bending the knees. Your miner friends notice the stiffness of your walk and chaff you about it ('How'd ta like to work down pit, eh?' etc.). Yet even a miner who has been long away from work—from illness for, instance—when he comes back to the pit, suffers badly for the first few days" (28).

Orwell's account vividly conveys the unnatural physical contortions demanded by this arduous and dangerous work. Characteristically, however, Orwell makes careful distinctions between his agonies as a novice and the skilled agility of the regulars. "Certainly, it is not the same for them as it would be for you or me" (29). Orwell's skilled agility as *a writer* allows him to keep shifting angles. The miners' skill is an astonishing feat, but still not quite a natural talent, he explains, since some time off the job returns the body to normal. To do his work, the miner undergoes a trained denaturalizing of the human body. Orwell admires the Wigan miners, but from the outside also sees their learned ability to skip crouching around the low pit props to make them move "almost like dogs." The work dehumanizes the bodies of miners, but Orwell goes on to reinstate their humanity by insisting that, as human beings, they are conscious of their condition: "it is quite a mistake to think that they enjoy it" (29).

Although the employed miners are not strictly within Orwell's assignment to study the conditions of *un*employment, the famous chapter about their work has a rightful place near the beginning of the book, as Orwell's exemplum of what the reader (the "you" addressed throughout part I) as well as he himself can hardly imagine or, more to the point, ordinarily doesn't bother to imagine at all:

> More than anyone else, perhaps, the miner can stand as the type of the manual worker, not only because his work is so exaggeratedly awful, but also because it is so vitally necessary and yet so remote from our experience, so invisible, as it were, that we are capable of forgetting it as we forget the blood in our veins. In a way it is even humiliating to watch coal-miners working. It raises in you a momentary doubt about your own status as an "intellectual" and a superior person generally. For it is brought home to you, at least while you are watching, that it is only because miners sweat their guts out that superior persons can remain superior. You and I and the editor of the Times Lit. Supp., . . . and Comrade X, author of *Marxism for Infants*—all of us *really* owe the comparative decency of our lives to the poor drudges underground, blackened to the eyes, with their throats full of coal dust, driving their shovels forward with arms and belly muscles of steel. (35)

I quote this famous passage at length partly because it is one of my favorites— its sharp colloquial wit cuts through to uncomfortable if common truth, while rising and opening out at the end to an eloquence of tribute that still remains within the colloquial flow. Orwell's sharpest jabs here are directed at the general state of oblivion that characterizes even the members of the Left Book Club, an insult only slightly softened by the prominent inclusion of himself. "You," "I," "all of us," including the editors and intellectuals and reformers who write and read and prescribe while sitting by a comfortable coal fire, only rarely make any mental connection between that underlying condition of our functioning life and the "black stuff that arrives mysteriously from nowhere, in particular, except that you have to pay for it" (34). The first responsibility of social reportage, this argument implies, is to break through that ordinary oblivion, to bring such connections up from the social unconscious where lower-class realities are ordinarily consigned.

Orwell performs here as the intermediary between the miner and the reader. He is an outsider who has in physical agony, if only for a day, gone down inside the mine and submitted mind and body to the rigors of this labor, and thereby has broken through the oblivion that he had previously shared with "you" the reader. Orwell insists in this early chapter on the crucial importance of the difference between getting inside and being outside, which is also a vertical distance. Just as the elegant diners in the fancy Parisian hotel in *Down and Out in Paris and London* remain oblivious to the almost comic horrors of the kitchen in the basement, the social hierarchy of modern life ensures a literal as well as cognitive barrier between the physical reality of the workers down below and the taken-for-granted comfort of their superiors.

Orwell's sympathetic and detailed account of hardships normally invisible to those in a superior position does not now seem novel; it represents a kind of reportage that—sometimes more, sometimes less effectively—has come to dominate mainstream social journalism (partly as a result of his influence). There are also plentiful antecedents from more than a century of earlier English writing: from Jack London, D. H. Lawrence, and George Gissing, back to Friedrich Engels, Thomas Carlyle, Henry Mayhew, and Charles Dickens. It is not a belittlement of his achievement to note that Orwell is doing this writing in an established tradition of English prose.

From the perspective of social science, this literary tradition of social reportage is vulnerable to many charges: for example, of sympathy unsupported by adequate data about the social facts. Orwell quite blithely releases the term *fact* from statistical or theoretical rigor. Still, with the miners there is the example of dirt. "Middle-class people," he generalizes, "are fond of saying that the miners would not wash themselves properly even if they could, but this is nonsense, as is shown by the fact that where pit-head baths exist practically all the men use them" (38). The term *fact* here is not a matter of statistics, but works more loosely as the corrective that direct observation brings to prejudice and received opinion. The usage is respectable in ordinary speech: "As a matter of fact," he goes on to note, "it is surprising that miners wash as regularly as they do, seeing how little time they have between work and sleep" (38). Orwell's *matter of fact* is a colloquial synonym of *actually, in truth, really, the way it really is* if you go to see for yourself and then think it over intelligently.

Other examples of Orwell's idiomatic version of *fact* appear in his account of the caravan colonies, the extensive clusters of converted buses and covered wagons that had appeared after the Great War in response to supposedly temporary housing shortage but had by 1936 become quasi-permanent slum housing for about one thousand people in the area of Wigan alone. "Anyone who wants to see the effects of the housing shortage at their very worst" (61) should, Orwell suggests, go visit a caravan colony. Orwell eschews pretensions to expertise or specialized knowledge. "Go see for yourself," is the subtext of his colloquial exhortations, even though he includes some numbers and measurements. "Inside," he begins, "these places are usually about five feet wide by six high." But this form of documentation rather quickly yields to qualitative description, punctuated by disclaimers that his words can adequately substitute for the actual experience: "the dirt and congestion of these places is such that you cannot well imagine unless you have tested it with your own eyes and more particularly your nose." Although Orwell's nose has been disparaged as overfastidious, his own descriptive language more often asserts imaginative authority through visual images: "one woman's face stays by me, a worn skull-like face on which was a look of intolerable misery and degradation. I gathered that in that dreadful pigsty, struggling to keep her large brood of children clean, she felt as I should feel if I were coated all over with dung" (63).

This picture, in almost the same words, already appears in "The Road to Wigan Pier Diary," the notebook Orwell kept on his tour and used as his aid to memory and composition.[4] The diary entry for February 15, 1936, makes clearer than the later narrative that Orwell toured the caravan colony with the Northern Union of Working Men (NUWM), collectors of "facts" about housing conditions, for the purpose of what Orwell reports as repeated but up to that point futile public complaints and appeals about intolerable living conditions (177). After mentioning in the diary that he has taken some notes on these facts, Orwell proceeds in the diary also from facts to faces, first the face of misery already cited, then another, seen while passing up a "horrible squalid side-alley":

> youngish but very pale and with the usual draggled exhausted look, kneeling by the
> gutter outside a house and poking a stick up the leaden waste-pipe, which was

blocked. I thought how dreadful a destiny it was to be kneeling in the gutter in a back-alley in Wigan, in the bitter cold, prodding a stick up a blocked drain. At that moment she looked up and caught my eye, and her expression was as desolate as I have ever seen; it struck me that she was thinking just the same thing as I was. (178)

Intimate identification with expressively suffering faces produces Orwell's most intense writing in *The Road to Wigan Pier* and often occurs as the pivot of profound changes in his social perspective. In the book's later autobiographical section, he recalls the images that displaced the "outside" vision of imperialism that had led to his initial willingness to serve in the imperial Burmese police: "Seen from the outside the British rule in India appears—indeed, it *is*—benevolent and even necessary" (144). But as an ordinary person not "trained . . . to be indifferent to the expression of the human face," the particulars of imperial rule entered his imagination and conscience with intolerable haunting power: "The wretched prisoners squatting in the reeking cages of the lock-ups, the grey cowed faces of the long-term convicts . . . the women and children howling when their menfolk were led away under arrest" (146). Part II of *The Road to Wigan Pier* ascribes Orwell's flight from the Burmese police service to the intolerable burden of bad conscience stirred by such visions. As a traveling reporter in the north of England, Orwell is not of course directly administering the system of social victimization as he was in his role of policeman in Burma. But, his style repeatedly insists, if you allow yourself to *see* such faces, you *will* feel directly implicated; at the least you will be stripped of the outsider's illusion (or rationalization) that other kinds of people somehow don't mind their poverty or imprisonment, that unlike yourself, they prefer to live that way.

The line is delicate between sensitive recognition of what faces express and the false presumption of "inside" authority to interpret facial expressions. The dramatic moment of eye contact with the woman poking the stick up the blocked drainpipe in the diary may represent an illusory intimacy occurring largely in Orwell's own imagination. The impression of fiction is increased when, in the published book, Orwell moves this particular face to a more prominent place, out of the housing chapter to the end of chapter 1, where it acquires emblematic meaning as the parting vision from his train slowly moving out of Wigan at the end of his tour. Other details also change in this transposition. The dramatic eye contact disappears, replaced by a clearer argument about interpretation itself:

It struck me then that we are mistaken when we say that "It isn't the same for them as it would be for us," and that people bred in the slums can imagine nothing but the slums. For what I saw in her face was not the ignorant suffering of an animal. She knew as well as I did what was happening to her—understood as well as I did how dreadful a destiny it was to be kneeling there in the bitter cold, on the slimy stones of a slum backyard, poking a stick up a foul drain-pipe. (18)

The historian Robert Pearce, disparaging Orwell's status as an "objective" reporter in *The Road to Wigan Pier,* selects this passage to illustrate Orwell's unconvincing "mind-reading" and recommends that we should doubt Orwell's "ability to find the mind's construction in the face and to empathize with people from backgrounds very different from his own."[5] Furthermore, Pearce regards Orwell's inconsistency about whether or not the poor become accustomed to their lot as a weak ambivalence, unsupported by the data he offers in either direction. But if one accepts that the book is *not* to be assessed as the detached, objective document that historical scholarship might prefer, Orwell's ambivalences and visions can have their own value. Orwell is consistently arguing against the self-assuaging middle- and upper-class opinion that the poor are not really that conscious of their misery, a view that is, in itself, a form of mind reading (or mind denying) since, whether from distance or trained indifference, it denies consciousness to people from other backgrounds. Orwell's visions argue against that denial: the crouching miners are not dogs; the woman kneeling on the slimy stones in the cold is not *ignorant* of her suffering, like an animal. Yet the issue of how far Orwell can presume to use his own feelings and judgments in the interpretation of Wigan appearances remains an important if unresolved issue for him, and this uncertainty is a provocative feature of the book, one of its valuable enduring influences.

One deliberate example of this uncertainty pertains to diet, an item of signifi- cance especially in relation to the food allowances and sample recommended bud- gets and diets that Orwell cites from official documents. Orwell reports that the families of the unemployed relying on these allowances eat virtually none of the things recommended by the nutritionists: no fruit, hardly any vegetables. "The basis of their diet, therefore, is white bread and margarine and corned beef, sug- ared tea and potatoes—an appalling diet" (95). Orwell himself is known to have liked vegetables so much that guests to his cottage mocked his austere offerings to them.[6] In judging Wigan diets, however, Orwell subordinates his own taste in order to snub the nutritionists' failure to get inside the dietary preferences of the poor:

> A millionaire may enjoy breakfasting off orange juice and Ryvita biscuits; an unem-
> ployed man doesn't. . . . When you are unemployed, which is to say when you are
> underfed, harassed, bored, and miserable, you don't *want* to eat dull wholesome
> food. You want something a little bit "tasty." There is always some tasty, pleasant
> thing to tempt you. Let's have a three pennorth of chips! Run out and buy us a
> twopenny ice-cream! Put the kettle on an we'll all have a nice cup of tea! *That* is
> how your mind works when you are at P.A.C. level. (96)

The snippet of dialect speech is like a facial expression in signaling the feeling behind the food choice. It also marks the line between Orwell's taste and what he presents as the appetite of those reduced to public assistance. A novelist, such as Dickens, would and did develop such dialogue further. Orwell, however, quickly shifts back to his own voice and to the other side of the issue, observing the effects of poor nutrition visible from the outside. "If you use your own eyes," he insists more than once, "the physical degeneracy of modern England" (99) is a fact that must be registered. So he is "torn both ways": at once sympathetic to the feelings that promote bad nutrition and at the same time lamenting that "merely for the lack of a proper tradition, people should pour muck like tinned milk down their throats" (100).

The idea that "tradition" enters into taste and judgment strikes a fault line through Orwell's entire enterprise of getting "inside" the life of the Wigan unem- ployed. The Wigan poor force on him this self-consciousness more sharply than did the tramps and social outcasts befriended on his earlier expeditions, a differ- ence he explores in the autobiographical portion of the book by remarking that the tramps and derelicts tended to be "exceptional" beings, and in that sense more akin to the masquerading dropout that Orwell himself was at the time he selected them for his companions. "Nothing is easier than to be bosom pals with a pickpocket, if you know where to look for him; but it is very difficult to be bosom pals with a bricklayer" (154). Therefore, although the extreme conditions of industrial unemployment during the Depression had cast out large portions of the population of northern industrial England from any normal working-class life, the more "normal" the life, the more difficult did he find any real intimacy to become, as he observes in relation to the coal miners. "For some months I lived entirely in coalminers' houses. I ate my meals with the family, I washed at the kitchen sink, I shared bedrooms with the miners, drank beer with them, played darts with them, talked to them by the hour together. But though I was among them, and I hope and trust they did not find me a nuisance, I was not one of them, and they knew it even better than I did" (156).

Rather than achieving intimate contact with the working class, Orwell on his trip to the north ends up resigned to aspects of his own class identity that he had previously thought perhaps too easy to discard:

> It is easy for me to say that I want to get rid of class-distinctions, but nearly everything I think and do is a result of class-distinctions. All my notions—notions of good and evil, of pleasant and unpleasant, of funny and serious, of ugly and beautiful—are essentially *middle-class* notions; my taste in books and food and clothes, my sense of honour, my table manners, my turns of speech, my accent, even the characteristic movements of my body. (161–62)

For Orwell, acceptance of this unsheddable middle-class identity is far from the complacent self-indulgence that it might be for others, since he openly dislikes many of the features he finds himself bound to. "There is much in middle-class life that looks sickly and debilitating when you see it from a working-class angle"(116), he remarks, in the context of noting that no working-class boy of eighteen would yield to the unmanly idea that he ought to go to school "in a ridiculous uniform and even [be] caned for not doing his lessons!" (116)—a self-derisive image obviously drawn from Orwell's own humiliating Eton schooldays.

For the writer, however, the problem of costume or uniform comes down to language, where Orwell proves English to be a more flexible garment than he found in other forms of life. But the capacity to write about any *ordinary* life, regardless of class, is a difficult literary feat. "Books about ordinary people behaving in an ordinary manner are extremely rare," he remarks in a book review of 1936, "because they can only be written by someone who is capable of standing both inside and outside the ordinary man."[7]

Orwell's standard of the "ordinary" constitutes the meeting point of his sought-for subject matter and his sought-for style of writing. For Orwell, that relation was not as simply mimetic as his own plain style has sometimes been taken to demonstrate. Perhaps surprisingly, his supreme example of a talent for rendering the ordinary was James Joyce in *Ulysses*: "I think the interest of Bloom is that he is an ordinary uncultivated man described from within by someone who can also stand outside him and see him from another angle,"[8] he writes to a friend, in a very long letter about his reading of *Ulysses* in 1933. The tribute recurs in a more self-deprecatory tone in an earlier letter: "When I read a book like that and then come back to my own work, I feel like a eunuch who has taken a course in voice production and can pass himself off fairly well as a bass or a baritone, but if you listen closely you can hear the good old squeak just the same as ever."[9]

The "ordinary" voice that Orwell made his hallmark is not to be confused with what some might call a simply "natural" or artless voice. It is a composed and produced instrument to achieve flexibility and power in relation to social conditions none of which he comfortably inhabited simply from the inside. Orwell looked to "the ordinary" as a source of manly strength in style. Through ordinary language he could lower his voice, in more than one way. "The truth is," he remarks in one of the reviews already cited, "the written word loses its power if it departs too far, or rather if it stays away too long, from the ordinary world where two and two make four."[10] This seemingly assured common sense fits awkwardly with admiration for Joyce, but less so if you take the whole sentence, with its emphasis on motion, words in motion, traveling toward or away from one world or another. It is this mobile quality that enables Orwell to keep his voice dynamic in his book, at some moments venturing further inside but then quickly acknowledging the limits of his access and making of his outside position another angle of approach. Rather than faulting his lack of stable objectivity, it makes more sense to me to fault his occasional overinsistence that two plus two does always equal four in the arithmetic of social reality and social change. Orwell's style of the 1930s teaches us to approach the "ordinary" world equipped with never fewer than two minds and to add up what we see with more than ordinary circumspection.

NOTES

1. George Orwell, *The Road to Wigan Pier* (New York: Harcourt Brace Jovanovich, 1958). Page numbers for quotations from this novel will be given in parentheses in the text.

2. BBC program, "Your Questions Answered," December 2, 1943, in *An Age Like This: 1920–1940,* vol. 1 of *The Collected Essays, Journalism, and Letters of George Orwell,* ed. Sonia Orwell and Ian Angus (New York: Harcourt, Brace, and World, 1968), 264.

3. "Welcome to the Orwell at Wigan Pier," http://www.theorwell.co.uk/content/home; see also "The Wigan Pier Experience," http://www.museumsunited.org.uk/wiganpier; "The Borough of Wigan (1): http://www.manchester2002-uk.com/towns/wigan1; and "Wigan Ancient and Loyal," http://freepaes.geneology.rootsweb.com/-anderton/places/wigan.

4. *The Road to Wigan Pier* Diary, in *An Age Like This,* 170–214. Citations for quotations from the diary will henceforth appear in the text in parentheses, referring to this edition.

5. Robert Pearce, "Revisiting Orwell's Wigan Pier," *History: The Journal of the Historical Association* (July 1997), accessed online at http://www.seas.upenn.edu—allport/chestnut/wwigpier.htm.

6. Jeffrey Meyers, *Orwell: Wintry Conscience of a Generation* (New York: Norton, 2000), 124.

7. Review of recent fiction in *New English Weekly,* September 24, 1936, in *An Age Like This,* 230.

8. Letter to Brenda Salkeld (extract), Sunday [December 10?, 1933], *An Age Like This,* 128.

9. Letter to Brenda Salkeld (extract), Wed. night [early September? 1934], *An Age Like This,* 139.

10. Review in *New English Weekly,* in *An Age Like This,* 231.

18

Orwell's Satirical Vision on the Screen: The Film Versions of *Animal Farm* and *Nineteen Eighty-Four*

ERIKA GOTTLIEB

Both *Animal Farm* and *Nineteen Eighty-Four* are classics of political satire that have been turned into film; in fact, each attempt has been made twice so far. *Animal Farm* was turned into the first full-length animated film in England in 1954 by John Halas and Joy Batcheler, and in 1999, directed by John Stephenson, into a film with depressingly "real" animals and "real" human beings. Released in 1955, Michael Anderson's *Nineteen Eighty-Four* has the coherent, suspenseful plot of a political thriller in the form of a reliable black-and-white B movie. Released in 1984, the movie's title year, Michael Radford's *Nineteen Eighty-Four* is in full color, where the sophisticated special effects of a modern sci-fi movie are combined with the surrealism of a proletcult Bunuel. I believe that the two films made in the 1950s are closer to Orwell's point of view. Yet neither the earlier nor the later versions are what one could call successful translations of Orwell's most widely read works of political allegory into cinema. Is Orwell turning in his grave at the lack of respect and understanding shown his work by the screenwriters and directors? Or is it simply that a translation of political allegory, especially when it comes to highly acclaimed works of fiction, cannot be made successfully on the screen?

In order for readers to appreciate Orwell's satires, they should be able to recognize the strikingly apt analogy between the satirical vision and the detail of the historical process this vision alludes to. It is as if the author asked the reader: Isn't it marvelous that the story of Manor Farm changing into Animal Farm and then, once again, back into Manor Farm offers such a striking series of analogies with the Russian Revolution that attempted to change tsarist exploitation into an egalitarian system, only to change it back to a regime of exploitation and oppression due to the very people who claimed to be the leaders of the revolution? And isn't it exciting to discover that Orwell's England of 1984, in his last novel, replays the same process but on a much larger scale and in the time frame of eternity?

Within the framework of the genre, allegory makes the enlightened reader respond to the allusions with a smile of recognition, as if asking, Am I not exceptionally intelligent in recognizing all the parallels of history the author serves up to the reader indirectly through the fictional framework? Allegory, then, creates an extended comparison implied between a given aspect of reality and the fictional framework, but this comparison is only alluded to, never direct or explicit.

Let us take the example of the Soviet show trials in the 1930s, a series of theatricals including the stunning accusations against former Bolshevik leaders to conspiracy against the Soviet Union with the "Enemy," followed by the stunning confessions, a form of suicidal self-condemnation, of those accused. This phantasmagoria was aggravated by the fact that the series of show trials followed by mass purges also made it necessary for the Soviet Union to continuously rewrite history, to introduce the idea that Trotsky, after Lenin the most important leader of the Russian Revolution and the founder of the Red Army, was in effect far less important from the very beginning than Stalin, and in a later rewriting, that he was actually a traitor, a conspirator against the very Red Army he had set up to defend the regime.

This continuous rewriting of history in order to discredit Trotsky, the representative of all scapegoats of the Soviet regime, is one of the central targets of Orwell's satire both in *Animal Farm* and in *Nineteen Eighty-Four*—but it is barely touched upon in any of the four film versions. After his first-hand experience of the Big Lie perpetrated by Stalin through the Comintern in Spain, paralleled by the Big Lie perpetrated in the USSR by the purges, Orwell had been driven by the need to explain the significance of this strange phenomenon to the British public. Eager "to translate the most sensational Russian event of the past two years, the Trotskyist trials, into English terms,"[1] in 1938 Orwell takes it for granted that we are familiar with the actual historical events and asks his readers to imagine the following: "Mr Winston Churchill, now exile in Portugal, is plotting to overthrow the British empire and establish Communism in England. By the use of unlimited Russian money he has succeeded in building up a huge Churchillite organization which includes members of Parliament, factory managers, Roman Catholic bishops and practically the whole of the Primrose League" (1:368).

What Orwell satirizes here is the absurdity of the Soviet phantasmagoria. To accuse Trotsky of setting up a machinery to overthrow the Soviet system with British money is as ludicrous as it would be to accuse Churchill of trying to overthrow the Western capitalist system with Soviet money. How would a filmmaker today convey this satire? For Orwell's points to work at all, we should be aware of the facts that Trotsky was sent to exile by Stalin in 1928; that he was accused of conspiring with all the imaginable enemies against the USSR; of the fact that Trotsky, who had been away from the USSR for over a decade, was still held responsible for acts of sabotage, in effect, for any blunders committed by those in charge of the Soviet economy.

Orwell explains the witch trials with their incredible accusations against alleged Trotskyites in the Soviet Union by inventing a process in Great Britain that an enlightened Western public would recognize as equally incredible.

> Almost every day some dastardly act of sabotage is laid bare—sometimes a plot to blow up the House of Lords, sometimes an outbreak of foot and mouth disease in the Royal racing stables. Eighty percent of the beefeaters are discovered to be agents of the Comintern. . . . Lord Nuffield, after a seven-hour interrogation by Mr.

Norman Birkett, confesses that ever since 1920 he has been fomenting strikes in his own factories. Casual half-inch paras. in every issue of the newspapers announce that fifty more Churchillite sheep-stealers have been shot in Westmoreland or that the proprietress of a village shop in the Cotswolds had been transported to Australia for sucking the bull's eyes and putting them back in the bottle. (1:369)

In this mini-satire based on consistent reversal, Orwell suggests that we should recognize the degree of rivalry between Stalin and Trotsky as if the Churchillites "never ceased from proclaiming that it is they who are the real defenders of capitalism and that Chamberlain and his gang are no more than a set of bolsheviks in disguise" (1:369).

There is no doubt that the grotesqueness of this satirical framework will not, by itself, create a great stir among the British readers. But then Orwell raises the question: "Anyone who has followed the Russian trials knows that this is scarcely a parody. The question arises, Could anything like this happen in England? Obviously it could not" (1:369).

Yet, Orwell feels, already in 1938, that is before the outbreak of World War II, that "the truth about Stalin's regime, if we could only get hold of it, is of first importance. Is it Socialism, or is it a peculiarly vicious form of state-capitalism?" (1:368–69). Already in this review Orwell finds it important to point out that the vicious terror of Stalin's allegedly socialist regime

does not [in fact] seem to be very different from Fascism. . . . The G.P.U. [later called the KGB or NKVD] are everywhere, everyone lives in constant terror of denunciation, freedom of speech and of the press are obliterated to an extent we can hardly imagine. There are periodical waves of terror, sometimes "liquidation" of kulaks or Nepmen, sometimes some monstrous state trial at which people who have been in prison for months or years are suddenly dragged forth to make incredible confessions, while their children publish articles in newspapers saying "I repudiate my father as a Trotskyist serpent." Meanwhile the invisible Stalin is worshipped in terms that would have made Nero blush. (1:370)

Neither film version of Orwell's *Animal Farm* is able to convey the nature or the intensity of Orwell's political passion expressed in his journalism. There is no doubt that it was not only the incredible theatricals of the Big Lie created in the Soviet Union that captivated the satirist's imagination but also the simply unprecedented gullibility of the Western intelligentsia that was misled by its sympathy with the Soviet Union, accepting the "myth" that it was a country building socialism. The mini-satire comparing Churchill to Trotsky is a good indication of Orwell's struggle for a satirical vision, to find a strikingly powerful way to "translate" the irrationality of the Soviet process.

In fact the satirical vision did not develop gradually, as it were, through natural evolution, throughout Orwell's works. He spent a long and painstaking apprenticeship writing naturalistic fiction (*Burmese Days, A Clergyman's Daughter, Keep the Aspidistra Flying,* and *Coming Up for Air*) and his shockingly straightforward "documentaries" (*Down and Out in Paris and London, The Road to Wigan Pier,* and *Homage to Catalonia*). *Animal Farm* suddenly presents us with an entirely new aspect of Orwell's imagination. The satire bespeaks the intellectual and moral passion, the clear focus and conviction of great political allegory—his first work with the universality and compelling vision of a major writer.

I believe this new development has much to do with the twofold experience in the Spanish Civil War that compelled Orwell to write satire. In Barcelona in 1937, he describes his newfound commitment to socialism: "I have seen wonderful things and at last really believe in Socialism, which I never did before" (3:301). At almost exactly the same time as this newfound commitment, however, Orwell also becomes aware of the Stalinist betrayal of socialism through the Russian apparatchiks' liquidation of their leftist rivals in Spain and through the witch hunts of the outrageous show trials and purges in the USSR. The impetus for writing satire is born out of the satirist's anger that his confrere and adversary, the deceived leftist intellectual, is blissfully unaware of the Soviet myth. *Homage to Catalonia,* "Spilling the Spanish Beans," and "Looking Back at the Spanish War" criticize not only the dictator's cynical betrayal of the goals of socialism but also the Western intellectuals' unwillingness to recognize this betrayal. "The whole point," Orwell explains, "is the effect of the Russian mythos on the Socialist movement here. . . . One cannot possibly build up a healthy Socialist movement if one is obliged to condone no matter what crime when the USSR commits it" (3:443).

Yet it took Orwell several years after his return from Spain in 1937 (and five years after his mini-satire we've just mentioned) before he found the central conceit, the organizing metaphor that led to the literary realization of his twofold experience in Spain:

> On my return from Spain I thought of *exposing the Soviet myth* in a story that could be easily understood by almost everyone and which could be easily translated to other languages. However, the actual details of the story did not come to me for some time until one day (I was then living in a small village) I saw a little boy, perhaps ten years old, driving a huge cart-horse along a narrow path, *whipping it* whenever it tried to turn. It struck me that if only such animals became aware of their strength we should have no power over them, and that men *exploit* animals in much the same way as the rich exploit the proletariat. (3:458–59, my italics)

Creating a sharp contrast between the starved, overworked animals and their cruel, arrogant human master with a whip, the metaphor immediately establishes where Orwell's sympathies will lie. When the cruel human master is first overthrown by the animals, only to be supplanted by another animal, Napoleon, a pig who gradually begins to walk on his hind legs and carry a whip, this metaphor by itself could carry the full weight of "exposing the Soviet myth," that is, the myth that Stalin's USSR is a socialist country based on the principle of egalitarianism. In *Animal Farm* Orwell compels us to see that in the USSR the new ruling class has greater privileges and is even more oppressive and exploitative than the prerevolutionary ruling class was.

To what extent are the film versions of *Animal Farm* successful in re-creating the satirical vision based on allusions, driven by Orwell's particular satirical passion? The novel published in 1945 was turned into an excellent animated film by the husband-and-wife team of John Halas and Joy Batcheler in 1954. It was remade in 1999, using depressingly "real" people and "real" animals—unfortunately missing both the charm of a "fairy tale" and the coherence of political allegory. Although stylized in a way that reminds one at times too inconveniently of Orwell's bête noire, the seductive charms of Walt Disney, the animated version is clearly aiming for a faithful illustration of the novel. By contrast, the 1999 "realistic" version seems to be significantly different from the novel's plot, political target, and atmosphere.

There is no doubt that in 1954 Halas and Batcheler still could expect the audience to recognize Napoleon as Stalin, Snowball as Trotsky, Frederick as Hitler, and Pilkington as the composite representative of the Western democracies. By 1999 the filmmakers of the "realistic version" must have decided that there was not a chance the audience would recognize Orwell's political-historical context. This may be the reason for their changing the allegorical framework entirely, as if assuming that the audience simply would not remember the historical context of the mid-1940s. Yet, as John Rodden would agree, by missing the allegorical correspondences, the viewer may completely misread Orwell's target.[2] Actually, it is quite a relief to me that some of the readers on the Internet registered their disapproval of the film, objecting to the filmmakers' desire to "update" Orwell by pushing aside the satirical target in the most cavalier fashion.

This does not mean, of course, that Halas and Batcheler's animated version did not change some of Orwell's content. At the end of their film, the animals look into the old manor house where the pigs are now playing cards with human beings. To the other animals' great amazement, the pigs are walking on their hind legs, and their facial expressions have also changed to the point that they have become identical to those of the human beings, the archetype in the novel for the spirit of exploitation. No doubt Halas and Batcheler must have found Orwell's ending too dark, because in their last scene they make the shocked animals start singing the Internationale, the revolutionary song that started the entire attempt to overthrow the oppressors. In Halas and Batcheler's interpretation, the animals are getting ready for another revolution, this time against their exploitative new rulers.

This change between the novel and its 1954 film version shows that Halas and Batcheler are no longer sensitive to the subtlety of Orwell's satirical machinery. They assume, correctly, that Orwell had sympathy with the revolution. What they forget is that it was Orwell's purpose to show Western readers that the USSR was not a feasible example for the building of a truly socialist regime; Orwell's target in showing the disappointing results of the revolution is to expose the Big Lie behind the Soviet myth to the Western reader.

But the ending that would be so vital for establishing Orwell's satirical framework is even a great deal more problematic in Stephenson's 1999 film version. Here the film ends with the female narrator, Jessie the dog, going into hiding, waiting for the deaths of tyrannical Napoleon and his cohorts. It is Jessie who observes the arrival of the new masters, the undoubtedly American owners of the farm who arrive in a sleek new car to the tune of "Blueberry Hill," to advertise their political goodwill, efficiency, and clean-cut democratic values. Jessie makes it clear that she hopes the new masters will not make the mistakes both Napoleon and Mr. Jones used to make. No doubt, the filmmakers want to infuse hope regarding the future of the Soviet Union at the time of the big change from the communist regime to the ideas of free-market economy. Unfortunately, this framework plays havoc with the allegory.

There is no doubt that the even in this "realistic" version the animals' revolution failed—Napoleon's regime left the farm in ruins. However, it also seems that the animals, even those who managed to go into hiding, are simply unwilling to emerge to tackle the task of leading the animals to a regime of equality again. In Orwell's novel human beings were representatives of oppression (as is also made quite clear by Orwell's generative image of the little boy beating the large powerful horse that is unaware of its power and therefore accepts the beating). By ending their film with the triumphant and good-natured return of a new generation of human masters, do the filmmakers wish to imply that oppression and exploitation are here to stay with us indefinitely albeit in a more benevolent fashion? If so, are there any indications that the new human masters are going to be any less cruel and neglectful than Jones or Napoleon used to be? Or did the filmmakers simply overlook the connection Orwell established between the oppressed animals and the masses that act as beasts of burden, and between the human beings who act as ruthless exploiters, the connection central to Orwell's political allegory?

Of course, the entire misguided attempt at "realistic verisimilitude" makes the film fail as a political allegory. In spite of the splendid voices of actors such as Paul Scofield, Peter Ustinov, and Kelsey Grammer, the characters are not served well by their visual shape and presence. Old Major, whose ideas inspired the animals' thinking about freedom and justice, is "realistically" portrayed as an old swine with all the repellant physical features of its species, in addition to the clinically observed signs of old age. In fact, the pigs as the new and deceptive leaders of the revolution are visually far more ugly than would be necessary, as if the physical signs of repulsiveness—and the director aims at a strange sense of realism in the midst of the animal fable here—were to evoke moral and intellectual repulsiveness.

The filmmaker's attempts at a visual sense of realism flies in the face of the allegory in most instances. In a careless gesture, at the beginning Jones wants to give Jessie a piece of Old Major's carcass; when Jessie recognizes where the meat is coming from, she rejects it in horror. How would this scene fit into Orwell's allegory? Then, in a later scene we see that Napoleon keeps Old Major's skull in the house. The decaying meat of Old Major's head is hard to take as a parallel to Lenin's mummy in the Lenin Mausoleum in Moscow; once more the ugliness of death and decay have little to do with the political allegory—the parallel is neither subtle nor compelling.

In his attempt at visual "realism," the filmmaker disrupts the role of the human characters as well. Orwell's Farmer Jones represents the tsar and his autocratic policies that led his subjects to losing the Great War and to the starvation and hopeless poverty that followed. What is the point, then, of the filmmaker's invention that Jones is engaging in sexual play with Pilkington's cruel, empty-headed wife? (She is another character "invented" by the film.) It is simply ludicrous to show irrelevant details about Jones's private behavior, including his sexual life, in close up—it was his behavior as a neglectful, cruel oppressor, a master of animals indifferent to their suffering, that created the basis of Orwell's satirical vision. The parallel between the tsar and Farmer Jones shows Orwell's impeccable skill in handling the satirical potential of a fable. Any kind of realistic detail that does not relate to this parallel is confusing. The weakness of Stephenson's film relates to the filmmaker's problem with the allegorical genre, including a visionary fabric alluding to the details of historical reality.

Halas and Batcheler in their animated film are a great deal closer to Orwell's time and reveal a far deeper understanding of its context. Their *Animal Farm*

represents, unmistakably, the Soviet Union between 1917 and 1943 with the historical figures of Lenin, Stalin, Trotsky, and the hostile Western democracies and
Germany as appropriate characters. Stephenson's "realistic" version still presents
Frederick with a carefully groomed Hitler moustache, but here it would be difficult
to recognize him as a fascist dictator: he is seen as a drinking buddy of Pilkington,
going to the Red Lion repeatedly—the viewer simply fails to register that for any
reason it was Frederick who cheated the animals and blew up the windmill (an
allusion to the 1939 Russian German Non-Aggression Pact followed by Hitler's
attack of Russia in 1941). As for the windmill, built with the sweat and blood of
Boxer, representative of the long-suffering working class, in Stephenson's overly
concrete rendering it is a strange contraption built by "realistically" clumsy animals—simply inappropriate to represent the formidable heavy industry built by
force through Stalin's five-year plans.

It is also revealing to look at the role of the narrator. In the animated version of
1954, when we are listening to an omniscient narrator, we are listening to the text,
and ostensibly, the voice of Orwell. In the "realistic" 1999 version the story is
narrated by a feminine voice. The voice is that of Jessie the dog—certainly not the
central character among the animals in Orwell's story. In the film she keeps lamenting the kidnapping of her puppies, begging Napoleon to release them. Her
laments become an expression of motherly love—no longer part of Orwell's parody about the brainwashing and indoctrination of the ruthless state police. In short,
the 1999 version of *Animal Farm,* in spite of its interesting technique of anima-
tronics, is totally misleading, and readers familiar with the book recognize it as
such. By contrast, the animated film of Halas and Batcheler shows the filmmakers'
understanding of Orwell's time and the specificity of his allusions. Interestingly, it
is by the specificity of the historical allusions that they become able to talk about
the universal problems of revolution, dictatorship, and leaders' thirst for power and
privilege. The mood, however, is still slightly lighthearted; even here the filmmakers cannot quite render the richness of Orwell's tone because they fail to render a
sense of Orwell's satirical passion, the urgency of his 1945 warning addressed to
the West, to England particularly.

The growing urgency of Orwell's warning between 1945 and 1948 is probably
the major challenge for both Michael Anderson's and Michael Radford's films of
Nineteen Eighty-Four. By 1948 Orwell was concerned about the "zones of influence" that emerged after the war and feared that the atom bomb, to be manufactured only by the three superpowers, would act as a deterrent of any change in the
future. In other words, he was concerned that the dictatorial regimes within each
power bloc would remain in equilibrium and unchangeable. Also, according to
Orwell, in the 1930s and 1940s the entire world showed itself ready to accept
dictatorial, totalitarian regimes; those on the left also believed that the USSR was
a socialist nation. Orwell feared, then, that using the people's gullibility, a new
ruling class might emerge that could delude the people into condoning and emu-
lating the Soviet system. The urgency of revealing the lie behind the "Soviet myth"
was thus becoming even stronger in 1948 than it had been in 1944, when Orwell
had finished *Animal Farm.*

The difference between a film made in 1955 and one made in 1984 inevitably
reflects the changes in cinematic style, pace, and composition. Anderson's 1955
script follows the threads of the political thriller in a clear, linear narrative style.

Radford's 1984 composition is imagistic: the juxtaposition of images, textures, and snippets of dialogue suggests a domino effect, but it makes no attempt at developing a chronologically comprehensible story line or at the building of character. In contrast to the clearly rendered political plot of Anderson's film, Radford's narrative presents us with a phantasmagoria of manifold hallucination.

The differences go beyond the aesthetics of style. The two film versions significantly reflect the different bias of two major schools of Orwell criticism. The cause of the most significant aesthetic and psychological difference between the two novels is the introduction in *Nineteen Eighty-Four* of the central consciousness of Winston Smith as Everyman, a human consciousness we can readily identify with. The psychological distance between the reader and the character, appropriate to the animal fable, has been eliminated. Since we are asked to approach Oceania through the eyes of a human being, this also means that Orwell can call upon his mastery of texture, sense perception, and intimate detail, a mastery honed to perfection in his first four novels. In other words, while *Nineteen Eighty-Four* maintains the visionary power and suspense of *Animal Farm* through the powerful structure of political allegory, Orwell could also introduce in *Nineteen Eighty-Four* the other aspects of his consummate skill as a master of detailed, closely observed texture. In *Nineteen Eighty-Four* Orwell the visionary and Orwell the naturalist finally come together. No wonder critics have pondered how to read *Nineteen Eighty-Four,* a book that according to Orwell is "in a sense a fantasy, but in the form of the naturalistic novel. This is what makes it a difficult job—of course as a book of anticipations it would be comparatively simple to write" (4:378). "It is Utopia" (political allegory) "in the form of a novel" (4:536). No wonder, "the difficult job" of criticism is also split between the political and the psychological critic.

Anderson's approach coincides with that of the exclusively political critic: he deems it unnecessary to deal with any of Winston's recurring dreams and nightmares, or indeed any of Orwell's numerous flashbacks to Winston's past. As a result, although the film offers a coherent interpretation of the novel at the level of political thriller, at no point do we get a glimpse of Winston's complex inner life. This, unfortunately, also means that having missed Winston's nightmares and his breakthrough dream explaining his phobia of the rats, in Room 101 we don't have the chance to see why the confrontation with the rats is so decisive in Winston's psychological development. Anderson's Room 101 lacks the scene's indispensable psychic dimension. Ironically, it is by concentrating so single-mindedly on Orwell's political message that Anderson misses the very essence of this message: the fatal threat implied in the *political* nightmare of totalitarianism is the individual's inevitable and irrevocable *psychic* disintegration.

In contrast to Anderson, Radford makes no attempt to reproduce the intricacies and suspense of Orwell's political plot. His focus is that of the psychological critic who assumes that the character's defeat must be the result of his neurosis and, furthermore, that the character's neurosis must reflect the author's. In fact, Radford quite explicitly suggests that Winston *is* Orwell; when in the recurring dream images Winston is shown looking at the Golden Country, he is consistently shot in a way that his silhouette, posture, even his haircut become a recognizable takeoff on some well-known photographs of Orwell.

But apart from this little in-joke, how does Radford approach the dream sequence? In the novel the dream of the Golden Country appears five or six times, each time with a slight alteration, to mark a particular new stage in Winston's psychic development. Just as important, each time the Golden Country appears, it does so after a nightmare, as if, in Orwell's words, Winston had to make an effort "to wrench his head away from the pillow"; he can will himself into the Golden Country only by deliberately tearing himself away from the nightmare world of Oceania. By the end we see that he is broken because even his dream place of escape is confined to Oceania. In Radford's treatment this important sequence is simply reversed: in the film Winston's dreams begin with his wishful glimpse at the Golden Country, until the paradisiacal landscape turns into a sinister vision of hell, accompanied by the music of the Eurythmics, who—simply by doing what they are best at—produce here the painful sound effect of stress that in the cinematic shorthand happens to signal the onset of the central character's nightmare. In Radford's rendering, what starts as Winston's wish dream for an escape ends invariably with the horrible image of a young woman's injured, dead body overrun by rats.

In fact, in spite of his seemingly psychological focus, Radford shows little inclination to analyze, interpret, or understand Orwell's masterful composition of the dream sequence. It seems to me Radford decided to play deconstructionist: having found questions in the novel about Winston's psychology he could not readily answer, he must have decided that the author simply did not, could not have had an answer either. Having missed the significance of the dreams in the character's inner development, and having blithely overlooked the vital connection Orwell established between the psychological and the political dimensions of the novel, Radford simply decided to "deconstruct" the novel by turning it into a grotesque, where Oceania becomes a surreal wasteland in the midst of a historical and political vacuum. There is no doubt that Radford's cinematography is ambitious, and the skillful domino effect of images does occasionally allow for irony and a sense of grim humor that, at times, even reminds one of Orwell. Thus we observe Winston in the Ministry of Truth as he rewrites an earlier news item to the effect that the previous chocolate ration of thirty grams will be *increased* to twenty. Seeing this item on the telescreen, Parsons makes a comment typical of the piety of the true believer: "Doubleplus good, chocolate ration *increased* to twenty grams." And now, as the telescreen goes on and on about figures of overproduction, Parsons listens with a beatific smile of approval. Only at the end of the announcement does he turn to Winston to ask: "By the way, would you have any razor blades?" Of course, Parsons's obvious anxiety about obtaining such a basic necessity negates not only the boasts on the telescreen but also Parsons's recent ecstatic celebration of overproduction.

Had Radford read the novel more closely—and with greater respect for Orwell's mastery over the symbolic structure—at this point he probably would have noted that the matter of chocolate rations also happens to be central to Winston's childhood trauma—when he deprived his starving mother and sister of their chocolate rations. It is this memory of betraying the person closest to him, of willing his mother's death by starvation in order to satisfy his own gnawing hunger—in effect to succumb to behavior similar to that of starved rats, which can be driven to devour members of their own species—that Winston had repressed for thirty years. This repression produces his phobia and recurring nightmares. Without making an attempt to understand the sequence of these nightmares or the breakthrough dream that sheds light on Winston's guilt about betraying his mother, Radford simply misses the significance of the climactic scene in Room 101. When after his breakthrough dream Winston promises never to betray Julia, he claims his second—his last—chance for retaining his humanity, his chance for redeeming himself for his childhood failure. When in Room 101 he is made to scream "Do it to Julia," he is made to fail again; by betraying the person closest to him, he betrays himself and loses his selfhood irretrievably.

I believe both filmmakers miss the full impact of the novel's climactic scene in Room 101; Anderson, because his focus is so exclusively political that he is oblivious to the dimensions of depth psychology and Radford, because he simply "deconstructs" Orwell's careful rendering of Winston's dream sequence and also because he decides to place Room 101 in the midst of a political-historical vacuum.

Which of the two filmmakers came closer to capturing the impact of Orwell's novel? For different reasons, I believe, each has missed the satirical target. Anderson's black-and-white frame story does not clarify—as Goldstein's book does in the novel—that in Oceania the totalitarian system emerged from within the Western world, from the intellectuals' totalitarian mentality in the 1940s, their readiness to condone and eventually imitate totalitarian models. Oceania, as it's made clear in the novel, was never conquered from the outside: Goldstein's book describes it as existing side by side with the other two superpowers, Eurasia and Eastasia, the entire world petrified in a state of unchangeable equilibrium.

In Radford's film Goldstein's book plays no role at all—references to it have been cut almost entirely. Anderson shows the tremendous importance the book plays in Winston's life, but he cannot show its contents. Yet Orwell's dystopian satire is based on the cause-effect relationship between the two time planes of 1948 and 1984 established in Goldstein's book. However well intentioned Anderson's film is, it cannot render the complex machinery of dystopian satire. Radford, on the other hand, seems to be determined to surgically remove the satire's points of political reference. Having removed any of Orwell's allusions to totalitarian systems of Orwell's own time, Radford's film is at its best a somewhat abstract study about the methods of propaganda in general and at its worst a rather eccentric personal nightmare, or the fantasy of science fiction.

I find the critics' dismissal of Anderson's film rather unfair. In his study *Filming Literature,* Neil Sinyard suggests that except for Michael Redgrave's performance as O'Brien, Anderson's film "had all the impact of a cold pudding," and it ended up "merely a pro-American contribution to Cold-War rhetoric."[3] John Rodden is also critical of Anderson as a director, commending Radford for presenting Oceania "in grittily naturalistic terms, treating it as a satire of wartime London," rather than conjuring up "a vague fantasy world of the future."[4] However, Sinyard's approval of Radford also implies explicit criticism of Orwell: he praises the film for cutting through the novel's "pamphleteering" and making "more of the dream atmosphere in the novel: than Orwell himself did."[5] Quite openly patronizing of Orwell's achievement, filmmaker Radford is even on record as saying that "Orwell's book is a political essay with a melodrama attached and some cardboard minor characters. What I tried to do is make it real and get the actors to play it knowing that this is a world in which betrayal is the first rule to live by."[6]

One actually wonders *why* Radford deemed *Nineteen Eighty-Four* worthwhile of adaptation to film at all. (Could it have anything to do with the lucrative prospect of bringing out a film of a novel—an all-time bestseller and the center of critical attention on three continents—in the year of that novel's title?)

Radford's superior attitude explains why he felt fully justified in "vaporizing" Orwell's satirical target—he must have decided it had been misplaced in the novel to begin with. Orwell describes Winston's body carrying a "sort of protest" against the deprivations, the indignities meted out to human beings by the party; his "sort of protest" is nurtured by a conviction that the world in the past must have been better, more beautiful, more fit for human beings, and that, consequently, such a world could exist in the future as well. If we look at John Hurt (Radford's Winston), his face is like a moon crater: here is a man who had never smiled, had never engaged in a joyful game of snakes and ladders in his childhood, had never enjoyed real coffee, real chocolate, real emotions; he had never experienced his mother's real love in the past—neither is he able to enjoy the sexual-emotional "reality" of his relationship with Julia. When, in his hoarse, cracked voice John Hurt's Winston says to Julia "I want you," Julia answers "I want you too." This is all, a far cry from Orwell's description of the two lovers' first meeting in the Golden Country with the thrush singing, the sight of the bluebells, and the girl's arm throwing away her clothes in a magnificent gesture in which the whole tyrannical world of Big Brother seems annihilated. (The fact that Radford decided, once again, to call upon the stress music of the Eurythmics in this scene does not add much to creating a sense of emotional sexual fulfillment.)

I believe that Anderson's black-and-white version of *Nineteen Eighty-Four* is actually more of a labor of love, even if it is not capable of rendering the multidimensional message of Orwell's novel. Anderson's work remains, nevertheless, a well-intentioned illustration of a vital work of literature. In contrast, it seems to me that Radford quite deliberately "deconstructed" a novel he did not particularly care about and produced something more fit for the vision of Samuel Beckett rendered by Arthur C. Clark than for Orwell's dystopian satire.

Of course, the question to examine at this point is how well the genre of dystopia, a vision of the worst of all possible worlds that grows out of our own mistakes, lends itself to film. Maybe we should consider an even more general question concerning how the essentially didactic, cerebral genre of classical satire lends itself to the more sensual, dramatic, immediate appeal of cinema. In fact, I suggest there is probably an unbridgeable gap between the cinema and the genre of satire. Cinema is direct, essentially sensory rather than cerebral, offering us a sense of quick identification with the character and hence minimal chance for intellectual distance. Satire is a mode of literature that is indirect, more cerebral than sensory, where the reader is invited to decode the target through a sophisticated recognition of the satirist's allusions.

Most importantly, to decode the political satire's target, readers should be familiar with the historical reality the satirist is alluding to. Failing to understand the satire's historical context, how could we meaningfully relate the satire to our own period? Yet, if familiarity with the historical background can be barely expected from even the college-educated reader who picks up the book written more than fifty years ago, what can we expect from the even more casual film viewer? How could the filmmaker deal with this situation? Should each viewer be asked to take a mini-course in history before entering the cinema? Should the cinema develop its own machinery of footnotes? Should the filmmakers themselves be asked to read the work more carefully, possibly with the capable and quite widely available help of Orwell scholars all around us? Or maybe it is simply impossible for a film today to explore the specific target of Orwell's allusions—without which, alas, one cannot hope that the universal meaning will emerge. Maybe it is inevitable that Orwell's rich satire, together with other masterpieces of literature, will disappear in the "memory hole," vaporized by nothing more sinister than the new generation's unwillingness to read, to explore Orwell's particular "corner" of truth in history. Maybe this is the most universal threat implied in Orwell's Appendix of Newspeak—that without the appropriate words, in a short while no one would be able to articulate the search for truth and the pursuit of freedom. And, maybe, together with the filmmakers, we should all make an attempt to heed Orwell's warning: only those who understand the past can hope to influence the future.

NOTES

1. *The Collected Essays, Journalism and Letters of George Orwell,* ed. Sonia Orwell and Ian Angus (London: Penguin Books, in association with Secker and Warburg, 1970), 1:368. All quotations to Orwell's essays are taken from this edition; volume and page numbers will be provided in parentheses in the text hereafter.

2. John Rodden, *Scenes from an Afterlife: The Legacy of George Orwell* (Wilmington, Del.: ISI Books, 2003), 45.

3. Neil Sinyard, *Filming Literature: The Art of Screen Adaptations* (London: Croom Helm, 1986), 63.

4. John Rodden, *The Politics of Literary Reputation: The Making and Claiming of St. George Orwell* (New York: Oxford University Press, 1989), 286.

5. Sinyard, *Filming Literature,* 65.

6. Cited in Michael Billington, "A Director's Vision of Orwell's *1984* Draws Inspiration from 1948," *New York Times,* June 3, 1984, 19.

V

Orwell Abroad

19

George Orwell: Russia's Tocqueville

Vladimir Shlapentokh

Alexis de Tocqueville represented the rare case when an outside observer demonstrates a better understanding of a society than its insiders. With his *Democracy in America,* the French noble proved to be more shrewd than not only most Europeans in his analysis of the new social system but also most Americans as well. For this reason, *Democracy in America* is reprinted almost every year in America and is included on the syllabi of hundreds of courses.

George Orwell was another outsider who understood a society better than its insiders. With his formidable intuition, he recognized many elements of Soviet life that escaped the notice of Western observers as well as the Soviet intellectuals of the time. Orwell may in fact deserve more credit than Tocqueville, because he did not have the advantage of visiting the USSR. Indeed, the French count traveled in America for six months, while Orwell never once crossed the border of Stalin's empire. His relevant personal experiences were reduced to spending several months with his contacts among the communists in Spain.

Suggesting that Orwell is Russia's Tocqueville, I contend that Orwell's place in history is linked more to my native Russia than to any other country besides England. I may go so far as to claim that it was Russia, not Britain, that delivered Orwell to the apex of his glory. It was not his *Homage to Catalonia, Burmese Days,* or *The Road to Wigan Pier* that made Orwell famous. The majority of Orwell's wealth and fame came from *Animal Farm* and *Nineteen Eighty-Four*—both of which were influenced by the developments in Soviet Russia, as discussed by some of the book's first reviewers.[1] Only Nazi Germany could compete with Russia's monopoly of influence on *Nineteen Eighty-Four.*

The role played by Soviet Russia in *Animal Farm* is indisputable, though the Soviet influence on *Nineteen Eighty-Four* continues to be hotly debated. Several pages of *Nineteen Eighty-Four* are devoted to describing the history of the regime in Oceania, which has many similarities to the developments in Soviet Russia (see, for instance, chapter 7).

Orwell's reviewers placed Russia and the West in different positions in *Nineteen Eighty-Four.* The main critics of the book were divided into two camps: those who saw *Nineteen Eighty-Four* as an antiutopian novel, or a dystopian fable, similar to

Brave New World, and those who regarded the book as a portrait of the real totalitarian society, in its Stalinist version, as it existed in the twentieth century.

Naturally, the members of the first camp tended to ignore or downgrade the Soviet roots of the book, hated the idea of equating Stalin's Russia to Hitler's Germany (though Orwell had no problem making this comparison),[2] and saw *Nineteen Eighty-Four* as an instrument of the cold war. Those who belonged to the second camp insisted on the similarity between Oceania and the Soviet Union.

The attitudes of the first camp were evidently influenced by their positive views of the real Soviet Union. This camp comprised many Western intellectuals who did not want to blemish Moscow or its sympathizers in England and the United States. Avoiding any reference to the Soviet Union, they talked about the book's anti-utopian character and its Western roots. Those who hated the Soviet system—such as bourgeois conservatives and the anti-Stalinist Left, or Trotskyists—insisted on the novel's realistic character.

The radical difference between the two camps was demonstrated in the first reviews of *Nineteen Eighty-Four* published in 1949 (the year of the novel's publication).[3] At that time, Daniel Bell evidently represented the first camp. In his review of the book, published in the *New Leader,* he did not say a single word that linked *Nineteen Eighty-Four* to Stalin's regime. In the same year, Bell's disregard of the Soviet roots of *Nineteen Eighty-Four* was seconded by British writer Herbert Read.[4] A few years later, Isaac Deutscher, a famous socialist, also insisted that the stark images in *Nineteen Eighty-Four* reflected not the Soviet future but "the drabness and monotony of the English industrial suburbs."[5] Other authors did the same almost twenty years later in the book *Inside the Myth of Orwell: The Views from the Left,* published in 1984.[6] More recently, the same arguments were still being made.[7]

This negation (complete or partial) of the Soviet roots of *Nineteen Eighty-Four* was typical for most of Orwell's recent biographers. Michael Sheldon wrote that "for models of authoritarian power at work Orwell could look to incidents from his life," such as the Indian imperial police, Barcelona, and the BBC. Sheldon expressed only obliquely that the novel could have been influenced by Stalinist Russia.[8] Christopher Hitchens, one of Orwell's leading biographers, defined *Nineteen Eighty-Four* as "an admonitory parable or fantasy."[9] The same tendency to underestimate the realistic character of the book is seen in the work of Jeffrey Meyers, another one of Orwell's biographers, for whom, to cite one of his book's reviewers, "*1984* . . . is harrowing and weirdly realistic of Orwell's own history and psyche."[10] Those members of the first camp who could not deny that Stalin's Russia was the model for *Nineteen Eighty-Four* labeled it as a "caricature of Soviet totalitarianism," and were eager to accuse Orwell of being a Trotskyist and particularly of being influenced by the Trotskyist James Burnham's *Managerial Revolution.*[11]

In 1949, Philip Rahv took a radically different position in his article published in the *Partisan Review.* Evidently influenced by anti-Stalinist sentiments and sympathy for Trotskyism, he highlighted many of the similarities between Oceania and the Soviet Union, as did Golo Mann in his review published the same year in *Frankfurt Rundschau.*[12] In the next fifty years, several other authors, such as Robert Conquest and Walter Laqueur, had no doubt that it was Stalin's Russia that was the major blueprint for *Nineteen Eighty-Four.*[13]

Those who insisted that *Nineteen Eighty-Four* described the Soviet society accepted the fact that Orwell's "Soviet" books were addressed not to Comrade Stalin but to the Western public as a warning of what could happen to them. Tocqueville's *Democracy in America,* as a matter of fact, was also addressed not to the Americans themselves but to the European public.

Of course, almost all Russians who came in contact with *Nineteen Eighty-Four* belonged to the second camp. For them, Orwell was not talking about the distant future but about their own lives and suffering. "It was at night that they came for you, always at night,"[14] Who among those living in Stalin's Russia would not have shivered reading this simple sentence? In Stalin's times, the Russians were continually guessing who in their office or communal apartment was spying on them. They saw themselves in Winston's shoes when he believed in the beginning that Julia was an agent of the political police. It was not surprising that the Russians surpassed Westerners in their enthusiasm for *Nineteen Eighty-Four.*[15] The Russian dissident Andrei Amalrik entitled his famous book with an allusion to Orwell: *Will the Soviet Union Survive 1984?* To this end, I might also cite myself, a Russian emigrant who organized a conference in 1984 at Michigan State University on the subject of the novel *Nineteen Eighty-Four.*

In what country other than Russia did Orwell become part of the everyday thoughts of educated people? As the prominent Russian writer Benedict Sarnov wrote in his book *Our Soviet Newspeak,* in some cases people use Orwellian phrases without knowing it.[16] Orwell's *Nineteen Eighty-Four* was one of the first foreign anti-Soviet books to be published after the start of perestroika in Russia.[17]

Surpassing Solzhenitsyn's *Gulag Archipelago,* Kafka's *Trial,* Pasternak's *Doctor Zhivago,* and Huxley's *Brave New World,* Dostoevsky's *Possessed* was one of the only books that could compete with *Nineteen Eighty-Four*'s understanding of the totalitarian society. In Stalin's time, *Possessed* was treated by the authorities with the same animosity as *Nineteen Eighty-Four.* Both books were regarded as bibles by the dissidents of the Soviet regime.[18] Later, two other highly innovative books claimed the same level of admiration as *Nineteen Eighty-Four* and *Possessed*—they were Vasilii Grossman's *Life and Destiny* and Alexander Zinoviev's *Yawning Heights.*

My Road to Orwell

My road to Orwell was very different from the paths taken by the other authors whose work appears in this volume. I am not sure that any of them can remember so distinctly as I do the circumstance under which they came in contact with Orwell. For me this definitely did not occur at the local bookstore or library.

Orwell's master work existed on the shelves of the leading Soviet libraries, such as Lenin's Library. In this respect, conditions were better in Soviet society than in Oceania, which seemingly did not tolerate even the existence of "bad" books. Similar to the books by Trotsky—Goldstein/Snowball—Orwell's works were caged in "Spezkhran," the notorious special department of the library where the most dangerous books were kept. Only a few of the most trusted scholars had access to them, though none were allowed to take notes. As a Jew and a non-party member with a bad reputation, I never, even in the post-Stalin period, had a chance to take *Nineteen Eighty-Four* in my hands.

According to legend, had I been clever enough I might have gotten access to *Animal Farm* if I had asked for it from the agricultural section of Lenin's Library, where it had supposedly been hidden until the censors discovered it. However, the Russian librarians were no more ill-informed than the American editor at Dial Press who rejected the publication of *Animal Farm,* because "it was impossible to sell animal stories in the USA."[19]

The first news about *Nineteen Eighty-Four* that reached me and my late friend Isaak Kantorovich came in 1950, when our common acquaintance Rurik told us surreptitiously about a great secret he (or one of his friends) had heard on foreign radio, listening to which was a very dangerous act in itself.[20] Blending his (or somebody else's) recollection of the radio broadcast on *Nineteen Eighty-Four* with his imagination, he told us about a book that had recently been published in the West in which a hero living in a society like ours discovered in the garret of his home an old manuscript, that described the history of society in a radically different way than the official one.

The news had a great impact on us. Kantorovich and I discussed the message with excitement for several days in row. To understand our reaction I should make a few biographical remarks. Living in a real totalitarian society, I was much happier than Smith in his Oceania because, unlike me, he was absolutely alone with his initial suspicions about the official ideology. ("What certainty had he that a single human creature now living was on his side?" sadly thought Winston until he met Julia [25]). Unlike Smith, I had a close friend with whom I could discuss ideas about Stalinist Russia. No less afraid of the system than Smith, we did not permit anybody to join in our sad and hopeless reflections on a society within which we seemed doomed to live and die.

We had good grounds to be afraid of the people around us. Most of them were true believers in the Soviet system. Later I found out that in these years many prominent Russian intellectuals were great admirers of Comrade Stalin.

However, more tragic to us than the disposition of Soviet citizens were the ideas of outstanding intellectuals in the West. We learned from our childhood—and the Soviet propaganda was correct in this case—that many outstanding Western intellectuals, such as Romaine Rolland, Henri Barbusse, Sidney and Beatrice Webb, Bernard Show, Herbert Wells, Theodor Dreiser, John Priestly, and Lion Feuchtwanger praised the Soviet system and its great leader. Reading their books, we discovered reluctantly that they were of high artistic quality, which only added to our despair.

The idea of rewriting history was nothing new to us, as it was for millions of readers in the West. Even the doctoring of photographs of Soviet leaders—some of them simply disappeared from pictures after being executed—was a trivial development for us. Of course, we did not believe official statistics and knew how easy it was to manipulate them in order to demonstrate the successful fulfillment of socialist plans. The famous phrase "Those who control the past, control the future, and those who control the present control the past" (204) would not have amazed us if we had been able to read *Nineteen Eighty-Four.*

What we found more significant about Rurik's message was that somebody in the West understood what was going on in Soviet society. Our delight was almost as great as that of Winston Smith when Julia told him during their encounter on the outskirts of London that other members of the Inner Party also engaged with her in illicit sex, which challenged the party rules.

Though we were enthralled with this unnamed author, we did not understand the level of his intellectual heroism. We did not know how alone he was in the

British intellectual milieu, or that in his obituary his friend Arthur Koestler would name him "the most honest writer alive."[21]

Only much later, after experiencing life in the West, could I understand what we, with our romantic and idealized picture of Western society, made impossible. We did not comprehend what moral courage was needed for a Western intellectual who considered himself a socialist to attack so ferociously the Soviet system, as he did starting with *Animal Farm,* even during the war against Nazi Germany when in America and England "Uncle Joe" was one of the most popular figures, and the two political giants, Roosevelt and Churchill, vied with each other in commending the great Soviet leader. Only much later did I learn that in the aftermath of the war, Orwell's England was less free than in the times of Milton.[22]

All of us haters of the Soviet system—which we deemed ideologized from top to bottom in the early 1950s as well as in the post-Stalin era—naively believed that Western society had been almost completely deideologized. When we heard in the early 1970s about a book with such a title as *The End of Ideology* (unfortunately we could not actually read it, because it was also in the "Spezkhran" section of the library), we saw, from its title alone, another argument in favor of our image of the West.[23] We did not have the faintest idea about the powerful role that "passionate" (to use Bell's term) ideology—liberal or conservative—played in the West, particularly in its radical forms, even if the old battle between the Marxist revolutionary ideology and its opponents faded away. We could not see the enormous pressure ideology placed on American or British intellectuals, forcing them to ignore elementary facts that did not fit their ideological premises.

I was amazed when I came to this country in the late 1970s and found an absurd and almost unanimous praise for the Chinese Cultural Revolution, including its most despicable elements, such as the school of 7th May. No Soviet intellectual had any doubt about the heinous character of this Maoist enterprise nor about its horrible origin. In my first class at Michigan State University in 1979, I assigned a student to study publications on the Cultural Revolution in the *New York Review of Books* over a ten-year period. The student could not find even one article that condemned the atrocities of this catastrophic period in Chinese history. Having studied carefully the attitudes of the American intelligentsia toward the Cultural Revolution I found many prominent people who repeated word by word the Maoist version of this event and lauded it as a brilliant assault on bureaucracy, a great leap toward social equality, and a formidable success toward the elimination of the differences between mental and physical work and between the city and the countryside. I found not one professor or journalist who could call a spade a spade and see this development as one of the biggest disasters of the twentieth century, quite comparable to Stalinist collectivization and the Great Terror in the 1930s. There was not one intellectual figure of prominence who characterized China as Orwell described the triumphant Soviet Union in 1945 and then in 1949.

MY FIRST ENCOUNTER WITH ORWELL IN THE SOVIET CONTEXT

My first encounter with a copy of *Nineteen Eighty-Four* occurred in Academic Town in Novosibirsk in 1965, sixteen years after it was first published. We were living in a relatively liberal period in which foreign books began to penetrate the country by various means. The manuscript was given to me by a graduate student in physics, Vladimir Zakharov (a future dissident and a member of the Academy of Science). I am not certain how Zakharov acquired it. It may have been given to him by a foreign scholar or by some bold traveler to the West.

In those years, to read Orwell, to share *Nineteen Eighty-Four* with others, or even to discuss it was considered no less than "the dissemination of anti-Soviet slander." Though you would not be sentenced to a concentration camp for this felony, you might find yourself in serious trouble. You might, for instance, be ousted from your research post or teaching position.

I was given a copy of *Nineteen Eighty-Four* just before a business trip to Moscow. The iron rule among readers of samizdat and *Tamizdat* (books published "there," "tam," in the West) demanded that such books should never be brought along on trips, particularly if you planned on staying in a hotel or with strangers. However, I was unable to stop reading the book and decided to take it with me. I read it on the plane going there and coming back. After returning to Academic Town, I started to unpack my luggage and could not find the volume. For me it was evident that the KGB would need only two minutes to figure out who among the passengers of TU 134 would be reading this deeply anti-Soviet book. I envisioned myself being fired from my position at the university. However, my tribulations ended rather swiftly when I found the book in the chaos of my luggage.

Later, with the gradual relaxation of the regime, Orwell's work became more accessible, which in no way diminished his godlike status among the Soviet intelligentsia. With the private markets flourishing in Soviet society, Orwell's value could be measured in rubles. On the black market in Moscow, *Nineteen Eighty-Four* was sold for 100 rubles, about two-thirds of the average monthly salary (169 rubles in 1980), which is equivalent to about $1,800 in America today (the average salary was $2,900 per month in 2000).

WHY ORWELL SURPASSED WESTERN OUTSIDERS

My delight about *Nineteen Eighty-Four* was mostly intellectual. Of course, I felt a great deal of emotional excitement when I first read the text. I could easily put myself in Smith's shoes. But this identification was not at all the major source of my admiration of the book. Much more important for me was the meeting of a person who looked to me like a genius.

Indeed, my friends and I always believed that nobody, literally nobody, outside the country could understand the horrors of the system. All we knew about the writing of Western authors on Soviet society was that we mostly disliked it. Even Koestler's *Darkness at Noon,* which we read as a samizdat text in the 1960s, did not change our general negative attitudes toward the intellectual abilities of Western writers and scholars. Koestler's explanation of the behavior of Stalin's victims smacked of revolutionary sentimentalism and seemed extremely implausible. In fact, few other foreign books on Soviet society aroused in us more dissatisfaction. Perhaps one exception, which rehabilitated the West in our eyes, was Robert Conquest's *Great Terror.* However, even Conquest, who published his book almost fifteen years after *Nineteen Eighty-Four,* with his focus on the repressions of the Soviet system, lacked in our opinion a deep understanding of the complexities of the Soviet system, which ardent anticommunists tended to simplify.

In contrast, Orwell jolted my friends and me with his insights on the Soviet system. We could have only agreed with Czeslaw Milosz that it was amazing that "the author who never lived in Russia should have so keen a perception into its life."[24] Orwell knew the Soviet system so well that it was possible to imagine that he was born in Eastern Europe, as contended the famous Russian poet and dissident Natalia Gorbanevskaia.[25] However, Orwell's shrewdness went far beyond his understanding of terror and the spying on citizens, which were trivial observations, known to the residents of Soviet Russia almost immediately after the Great October Revolution.

My main point is that Orwell not only was the first in the West who understood the essential elements of totalitarian society but also stands up today against the thousands of researchers of totalitarian society, now fifty years after his death, and still sounds like a fresh voice. This is especially true with respect to the legion of scholars, so called revisionists, who with their open or hidden hatred of capitalism and their attempts to embellish the Soviet system, attacked the concept of totalitarianism in the 1970s and early 1980s under the specious pretext that this concept "simplifies" the complexity of the totalitarian society and ignores the social life within it. They rejected the Orwellian model, denouncing *Animal Farm* and *Nineteen Eighty-Four* as "fictions," as anticommunist propaganda, and as biased and tendentious, even if they did not go so far as the Soviet journalists who labeled Orwell "a renegade of socialism" and "an agent of reaction," whose Oceania is modeled after the imperialist West.[26]

If you read the numerous volumes of Sheila Fitzpatrick (the leader of the revisionist school) on the Soviet Union you will not find many remarks about Orwell.[27] In only one of her publications did she mention Orwell in a rather dismissive way: *Nineteen Eighty-Four* was cited along with *Darkness at Noon* as "fictions" that "set the tone mainly in a Cold War context of knowing the enemy." These books, along with scholarly works in the aftermath of World War II, were accused of being supportive of "the totalitarian model, based on the demonized conflation of Nazi Germany and Stalin's Russia."[28] In the prestigious book *Russia: A History,* prepared under the guidance of Gregory Freeze, it is possible to find the names De Maistre and Guizot, but no Orwell.[29]

It is amusing how some of the most ardent champions of the antitotalitarian model tried to reconcile their views with the facts of Orwell's vision and how, after the collapse of the Soviet Union, they could not deny the facts. One of them, Arch Getty, who completely ignored Orwell's concept of the Soviet society, vehemently denied the model of *Nineteen Eighty-Four.* Trying to save face, he lamented that "working without Moscow archives I was unable to apprehend and historicize the complicated and politicized use of language inside the system," as if Orwell, with the shrewdness of a genius, did not explain the definition of doublethink many years before.[30]

Paradoxically, even British experts on Soviet society, who are also influenced by the antitotalitarian pathos of American liberals, ignored Orwell, one of their most famous intellectuals. In the thousand-page volume of the well-known British historian Orlando Figes, *A People's Tragedy,* you will find references to the observations on Nikolai's Russia made by Marquis de Custine, as well as references to Marie-Antoinette, queen of France, who had nothing to do with Russia; however, you will find no mention of Orwell.[31] Another British author, Robert Service, in his book *A History of Twentieth-Century Russia,* a volume of almost the same size as Figes's, again found relevant to Russian history the thoughts of his compatriots Agatha Christie and John Le Carré, but not the ideas of Orwell.[32] More surprising was the total absence of Orwell in Robert Conquest's famous six-hundred-page book, *The Great Terror,* which was devoted to a subject so dear to Orwell.[33] The disregard of Orwell in this book is particularly strange when we see that Koestler was honored by numerous references.[34] Later, Robert Conquest wrote an article about Orwell that greatly praised the author.[35]

Those Western intellectuals who did not deny the totalitarian nature of Soviet society were more benign toward Orwell, although even they did not pay much attention to him and did not credit him for what he understood about Soviet society. Richard Pipes, in his magisterial work on Russia, mentioned *Nineteen Eighty-Four* only as a novel inspired by Zamiatin's *We.*[36] Another known member of the totalitarian camp, Martin Malia, is also far from recognizing Orwell's contribution to the analysis of the Soviet system. While qualifying, condescendingly, *Animal Farm* as an antiutopian novel,[37] Malia only nonchalantly mentions Orwell as the author of the first authentic description of the psychology in a totalitarian world, though he only mentions Orwell's idea of "doublethink."[38]

However, even more astounding is that Hannah Arendt ignored Orwell in her volume *The Origins of Totalitarianism.* She wrote her preface to the first edition in summer 1950 and the preface to part two (*Imperialism*) in July 1967.[39] It is simply out of the question that she did not know about Orwell's books on totalitarian society. The appearance of *Nineteen Eighty-Four* was accompanied immediately by numerous reviews.[40]

How do Soviet intellectuals differ from Western authors in their views of Orwell? The differences are indeed vast. You can find references of admiration for Orwell in almost every book written by Soviet dissidents before 1985,[41] as well as by many post-Soviet Russian authors after 1985.[42] Mikhail Heller and Alexandre Nekrich went so far as to begin their famous book *Utopia in Power* by praising Orwell as "probably the single Western author who understood the nature of the Soviet world."[43] Were these Soviet intellectuals correct in their statement? Let me enumerate briefly the aspects of Soviet society that were mostly or totally ignored even by the most shrewd Western Sovietologists.

FEARS AND HUMAN RELATIONS

Certainly, those who rejected the concept of totalitarianism either ignored the issue of fear as a major element of Soviet society[44] or restricted its significance to the families with "bad social origins" without describing it as a part of everyday Soviet life.[45] However, even the advocates of the totalitarian model were far from Orwell in their understanding of the omnipresent fear in a totalitarian society, that within such a society "no emotion was pure, because everything was mixed up with fear and hatred" (105), and where "the espionage, the betrayals, the arrests, the tortures, the executions, the disappearances will never cease" (221).

With his unbelievable acumen, fifty years prior to the publication of memoirs of the people who lived in the USSR and China and before the opening of the archive of the East German Stasi, Orwell was able to grasp many important elements of human relations under totalitarianism, that were completely ignored by foreigners and are still not incorporated in the textbooks on totalitarian society.

In *Nineteen Eighty-Four,* for instance, Orwell described it as absolutely normal that a woman's husband was "vaporized a couple of years ago" or that the names of recently executed people were assiduously deleted from various materials (38). Orwell did not know that in the years he published both of his "Soviet" books, Sergei Vavilov was diligently performing his duty as the president of the Academy of Science while his brother, a famous scholar, was dying in the gulag. He could not know that Viacheslav Molotov would continue ardently working for Stalin after his wife, Polina Zhemchuzhina, had been exiled. Orwell would hardly find these Shakespearian episodes in Soviet history amazing. He was the first in the West to realize how fears penetrated the family and how parents were afraid of their children. Orwell knew how each citizen in a totalitarian society "would implicate hundreds of others by his testimony before vanishing" (41).

THE DOMINANT AND OPPRESSED CLASSES

Orwell's acumen also manifested itself when he described the totalitarian system's social stratification. His analysis in this area was superior to that of other analysts, not only to those leftist scholars who respected Soviet or Maoist socialist systems and denied that social inequality existed in totalitarian society, but also to those who recognized it.

Indeed, if you take, for instance, a typical text that harshly criticizes communism, such as Malia's *The Soviet Tragedy,* you will find the description of the nomenklatura as a class that enjoyed various privileges.[46] But Orwell saw totalitarian society as more complex than many of its critics. Orwell was an absolutely unique thinker who understood that the Soviet proles were in some ways happier and more free than the members of the ruling class. He showed that the members of the ruling elite (the inner party) were more constrained in their behavior than ordinary people (proles). They had less freedom to choose their friends, spouses, and entertainment. There were also greater restrictions on their alcohol consumption and womanizing (as well as their contacts with the church) than on Soviet proles.

Perhaps only Arthur Koestler, besides Orwell, realized that the ruling elites in the Soviet Union despised the toiling masses.[47] Both the protagonist and antagonist in Koestler's novel *Darkness at Noon* despised the masses. In *Nineteen Eighty-Four,* when one of Winston's colleagues in the Ministry of Truth said "the proles are not human beings" (47), he conveyed exactly the point of view of all Soviet leaders—from postrevolutionary Lenin to Stalin to Brezhnev and Andropov.[48]

Orwell managed to grasp another important element of Soviet society—the existence of a class of activists (i.e., little bosses, or the members of the outer party) who did not have the same privileges as the inner party but served the regime with joy nonetheless. Their feelings of superiority over the proles and their proximity to the center of power, which diminished their fear of being "vaporized," was more than enough to stimulate their activity. I saw Winston's colleagues in droves in Soviet society, people who implemented with fervor any decision of the Kremlin without material compensation.

THE MILITARIZATION OF SOCIETY

Up until now, most Western publications on the nature of the Soviet system did not describe militarism as the most important element of Soviet society. Some authors wrote about the military-industrial complex in Russia.[49] However, some authorities on totalitarianism, such as Hannah Arendt, spoke about the aggressive policy of totalitarian states but completely ignored the subject of militarism.[50] Up to now only Orwell has been able to convey the importance of the deep militarization of totalitarian society, the orientation toward war and the psychology of the besieged fortress and the omnipresent influence of militarization on all major aspects of life in Oceania, "a nation of warriors and fanatics" (64) and evidently on its permanent rivals Eurasia and Eastasia. "Winston could not definitely remember a time when his country had not been at war" (30). Orwell realized that the military industry was the single sector of the economy that progressed in Soviet society (152–66).

POWER AND GEOPOLITICS VERSUS IDEOLOGY

Probably even more remarkable was Orwell's understanding of the relationship between ideology, power, and geopolitics. Who more than he described the role of ideology in a totalitarian society? He also understood, however, unlike many experts on totalitarian society, the instrumental value of ideology for the regime. Compare Orwell with the dozens of authors who saw Soviet ideology, with its socialist slogans, as the major mechanism that determined the conduct of the leaders, as if to believe that the leaders were concerned with the victory of the World Revolution or the construction of a communist paradise in Russia. Orwell mocked this view, which outlived him nonetheless, and was cited in many publications on Soviet society.[51] Meanwhile, as early as 1938, in his *Homage to Catalonia,* Orwell demonstrated amazing shrewdness in his understanding of the Soviet foreign and ideological policy. He wrote that "official Communism is . . . an anti-revolutionary force" and that "the whole Comintern policy is now subordinated . . . to the defense of the USSR," and not at all interested in fomenting the world revolution.[52] Even fifty years later, well-known authors regarded the Spanish Civil War as a confrontation between the fascism led by Nazi Germany and communism headed by the Soviet Union and not as a big geopolitical struggle among major powers.[53]

In fact, as Orwell showed, ideology was for the ruling elites only an instrument of power, a means by which to brainwash the population. The public ideology was addressed not to the inner party, and definitely not to Big Brother, but to the masses, a circumstance that most Sovietologists could not understand.[54]

However, even more interesting is that Orwell indeed realized that ideology had nothing to do with international relations. The best experts in the world were mesmerized by the role of communist ideology in the USSR and China and could not imagine that the two colossi would conflict with each other. Only in the late 1960s, when a war between the USSR and China seemed imminent, did some scholars begin to understand that geopolitics had little to do with ideology. Orwell, with his deep understanding of the role of geopolitical games for totalitarian states, almost exactly predicted the possibility of this confrontation.

NEGATIVE IDEOLOGY

It was Orwell who first realized fully the role of negative ideology in society as an important tool for mobilizing the masses in support of the regime. Koestler also appreciated the significance of negative ideology ("mankind could never do without scape goats"[55]), though his friend greatly surpassed him.

Orwell grasped the idea that negative ideological campaigns were more important for the regime than positive ones. He realized further that a negative ideology, as the bulwark of propaganda, demanded constant invention of new enemies. In this day and age, the concept of negative ideology is quite important. Indeed, anti-Americanism in each country of the world is used as a negative ideology that serves the various needs of elites.

Orwell pinpointed one of the most interesting phenomenons in public opinion, not only under totalitarianism but also in other types of societies. He understood the difference between the pragmatic and ideological sectors of the mind—the first deals with the concrete facts of everyday life, and can often be critical of the official ideology; the second relates only to abstract concepts that are beyond one's personal experiences, where the individual is at the mercy of the media and propaganda. In *Nineteen Eighty-Four*, Julia "only questioned the teachings of the Party when they in some way touched upon her own life. Often she was ready to accept the official mythology, simply because the difference between truth and falsehood did not seem important to her. She believed, for instance, having learnt it at school, that the Party had invented aeroplanes" (127).[56]

ORWELL'S GREATEST DISCOVERY

In the previous sections of this essay I have dared to say that many of Orwell's observations about totalitarian society were rather trivial for insiders. This, however, was not the case with Orwell's concept of love of Big Brother, which showed a great deal of insight on public opinion in totalitarian society. Here Orwell made a discovery that astounded the most perspicacious insiders. Most authors who wrote on Orwell almost totally ignored this great discovery. Even Erich Fromm— whose book *Escape from Freedom* was close to this part of Orwell's vision, and who wrote the famous afterword to *Nineteen Eighty-Four* in 1961—failed to mention the role of one's love of Big Brother in this society.[57]

Social psychologists almost totally ignored the role of the fear-love complex in hierarchical organizations, particularly in its totalitarian version.[58] Among the 93 different types of love cited in a study by Beverly Fehr and James Russel, the love of one's superior in an organization was absent, while they did mention the love of animals and food.[59]

How to Adjust to Big Brother

What made this Orwellian concept an extraordinary idea was that it explained how people adapt to their environment, particularly to adverse conditions. As a self-made psychologist, Orwell was almost obsessed with the mechanism of survival that people used in a totalitarian society. The process of adaptation was in no way reduced to a simple obeisance to the orders of the regime and ultimately to Big Brother.[60]

This process demanded not only the immediate execution of orders and the diligent performance of one's duties but also spying on other people from early childhood (from "seven years old" [50]) and hiding one's unorthodox thoughts and negative feelings. As Winston sadly reflected, after being frightened by the attention of a girl in the canteen, "It was terribly dangerous to let your thoughts wander when you were in any public place or within range of a telescreen. The smallest thing could give you away" and the most deadly danger of all was talking in your sleep (54, 56).

Orwell understood how millions of people collaborated actively with the dominant political power not merely to acquire some petty material reward but also in order to feel like part of the system. Most people worked as secret agents for the political police only in order to enhance their own security. But even this was not enough, as Winston understood while observing Syme, one of his colleagues who demonstrated the most active involvement in composing the Eleventh Edition of the Newspeak Dictionary and was destroying words because "he was too intelligent." Winston was certain that Syme would be "vaporized" (5).

Love as the Only Guarantee

It was only an uncritical form of love of Big Brother that could guarantee (though nothing was absolutely certain) that the individual would not end up in the gulag. In many respects, the love of Big Brother has been described in terms of attachment theory in social psychology, which deals with the relationship between a child and a caregiver and focuses on the child's feelings of security.[61] The famous Stockholm syndrome—the quick transformation of hostages into supporters of the terrorists—is only one version of the love of Big Brother.

The denizens of totalitarian society were not the only ones moved by the instincts of survival and therefore pushed to love Big Brother. The ruling class participated actively in promoting this love, while destroying all other possible objects of love. First of all, the totalitarian states of the twentieth century destroyed the love of God, which necessitated the persecution of religion. In Oceania, only the despicable proles were permitted to have "religious worship" (7).[62] Another major victim was sexual love. Orwell wrote that "the sex impulse was dangerous to the Party" (220) and "the Party was trying to kill the sex instinct, or, if it could not be killed, then to distort it and dirty it" (57). Here there was not a modicum of anti-Utopian exaggeration. Under Stalin, for instance, lyrical poetry was forbidden and the first movie scene in which a man and a woman talked in bed did not appear until twenty years after Stalin's death. Of course, the love between parent and child was another casualty of the love of Big Brother.

Although the totalitarian system tried to downgrade as much as possible the role of various forms of love, it ignited the love of the leader to the level of the sexual passion experienced by women toward the vozhd', fuhrer, or duce. This demonstrated that power itself is a great aphrodisiac.

People Yearn for Brainwashing

Propaganda plays an important role in the process of an individual's adaptation to giving total obeisance to the leader. With his formidable intuition, Orwell is far from describing the ideological life in Oceania as pure brainwashing, or merely as Big Brother's ideological work.

In fact, indoctrination in a totalitarian society (as well as in any organization, from a department in an American university to the army in any country) is operated not only from above but also from below. Full of fear (either fear of physical repression or of more mild forms of alienation from the dominant power in the given environment), people are eager to find, as did Winston's neighbor and his colleague at the Ministry of Truth, a rationalization for their submission. They accept with joy all the stupidities that Big Brother told them.

The Explanation of Public Opinion

Orwell was the first to understand that fear can generate love and both emotions are perfectly compatible, particularly when a good portion of the ideology is used to facilitate this process. This blend of fear and love, along with the ideology that serves this alliance, is the basis for accepting Big Brother as the key explanation of public opinion in a totalitarian society.

In any case, in the fifty years after the publication of *Nineteen Eighty-Four* only a few authors drew attention to the importance of Orwell's idea about the feelings of love toward the leader for the analysis of totalitarian society.

The real alternative to Orwell was proposed, in fact, by Theodor Adorno and his coauthors in their famous book that came out almost simultaneously with *Nineteen Eighty-Four.* If Orwell explained that the fealty and love of the leader came from fear applied from above, Adorno and his coauthors claimed that the love came from below, from "authoritarian personalities whose value system includes the blind submission to authority, strict adherence to middle class conventions, aggression toward those who violate them and a rigid mode of thinking."[63] Hannah Arendt followed the same line.[64] This concept had some empirical grounds, particularly in the times of the formation of a totalitarian state. However, as soon as such a state takes control of society, Orwell's approach is much more helpful for understanding this society than Adorno's.

Various data suggest that most people in communist countries (to some degree even in the puppet regimes in Eastern Europe) were loyal to the regimes, particularly when the level of repression was high, which was revealed in the cult of the leader. Stalin, Hitler, Mao, and the leaders in other communist countries were beloved and respected by the majority of the population.[65]

The devotion of the Soviet people to the regime reached its highest level in the times of the cult of Stalin. Established in the early 1930s, this cult was evidently supported by the majority of active Russians in the cities, much like Hitler in Nazi Germany, or Mao in Communist China. Stalin was glorified by ordinary people, even in their private communications. The cult of Stalin penetrated the heart and soul of many Russians, from apparatchiks to ordinary people.[66] The intensity with which people mourned Stalin's death on March 5, 1953, was indeed amazing. Stalin's funeral was accompanied by a stampede of thousands of people yearning to deliver their last respects. The funeral stands among the most memorable events in Soviet history. With Stalin's death and the softening of the totalitarian regime, the love of Big Brother did not disappear but was transformed into a devotion to the system and to its ideology.

Meanwhile, most Western social scientists did not understand public opinion in a totalitarian society. It is unbelievable that all of the big publications on Soviet society in the last fifty years ignored the subject of public opinion in the Soviet Union. This was true in the 1950s and 1960s when none of the most prominent authors, such as Robert Conquest or Daniel Bell, discussed the people's attitudes in the Soviet Union.[67] In the next two decades the subject continued to be ignored by critics of the totalitarian model, such as Sheila Fitzpatrick and Arch Getty as well as by conservatives such as Martin Malia. Only a few authors of the second group suggested that the masses are against the regime, though they did not support their claims with any data.[68]

The Russian authors, whatever their political sympathies, alluded to this subject as much as their Western colleagues.[69] Only a few authors, such as Vladimir Brovkin[70] and particularly the famous dissident Vladimir Bukovsky, dared to make general statements asserting, contrary to the data, that the "Soviet society lived on a volcano," and that millions of Russians were ready to join the struggle against the Kremlin if they had been encouraged by the West and the Russian intelligentsia.[71]

It is easy to understand why most Sovietologists of all political colors ignored Soviet public opinion. Those scholars who held benign views of the Soviet system were reluctant to acknowledge that the popular consensus was based considerably on the fear of the socialist regime. For the anticommunists, the advocates of the totalitarian model, it was impossible to recognize that the masses loved the ruler.

WHAT ORWELL DID NOT UNDERSTAND

Orwell's model of the attitudes of the masses in totalitarian society toward the leader has one major flaw. With his tendency to share the anarchistic vision—he hated inequality, but also hated the state as an institution—he did not take into account that Big Brother is a guarantor of order in society. In part, this circumstance accounts for the love of Big Brother. Living in such a nice country as England, where the police did not have to fire their weapons, and with Hobbes's world lost in the distant past, Orwell could not grasp how important order was for the Russians after the civil war, for the Germans after the chaos of the Weimar Republic, or for the Chinese after the war between warlords in the 1920s and 1930s. He did not see how the cost of repression looked small compared to the benefits of order.

In this respect, Orwell neglected the importance of order just as most Western social scientists did in the second half of the twentieth century. Many social scientists insisted that the intensive use of coercion erodes the legitimacy of the state.[72] Another sociologist talked about the "taming of the state," describing the state as "a constant threat to its citizens."[73] Michel Foucault and his legion of followers played a special role in the Western literature that detracted from the state as an institution.[74]

The attitudes of the masses toward Leviathan are quite different from those of most liberals. Part of the love of Big Brother should be attributed to the yearning of the masses for order and stability. For the same reason, many post-totalitarian societies have experienced nostalgia for the old leaders and the old systems. This can be seen not only in post-Soviet Russia, where the respect for Stalin has increased enormously in the last years,[75] but also in many other countries, including eastern Germany. What is more, it would be easy to predict the same tendency in Iraq.

In view of Orwell's disregard of the importance of social order, it would be wrong to use the idea of Big Brother (as leftists often do) to attack the attempt of the state to protect people from crime or international terror.[76] I can even imagine that if Orwell, who was known as an implacable foe of colonialism, had watched the developments in Africa and Asia, where millions of people suffer from disorder and chaos in the postcolonial period, he would have reconsidered to some degree his views on the empire and may have agreed in many respects with Niall Ferguson's book *Empire,* in which he described several positive elements of the British empire.[77]

Conclusion: A Rebuttal to Louis Menand

There are two schools of thought on the issue of whether personal information about a writer or artist is necessary for understanding his or her work. The first school believes that one must study the details of the lives of Hegel, Tolstoy, or Chopin to understand their masterpieces. The second school supposes that such a study is unnecessary and perhaps even detrimental to understanding a work. Arthur Koestler was among those who mocked the advocates of the first approach. I myself gravitate toward the second school. To understand *A Christmas Carol,* must we know that Charles Dickens hated his wife and neglected his children? Is it important for us to know about the number of Tocqueville's mistresses when we read *Democracy in America*?

To appreciate *Nineteen Eighty-Four,* is it important for us to know that Orwell liked "slurping his tea," or that he was "obsessed with body odor"? These were primary concerns for Louis Menand, whose essay in *The New Yorker* suggested that "Orwell as a personality was invented." Let us accept this diagnosis but not forget that such an accusation can be lodged against any biography of any person, including Menand's essay on Orwell. However, *Nineteen Eighty-Four* has an objective value as the greatest piece of work in political philosophy. I have only pity for Menand, who mocked this book as a collection of platitudes and "conversion stoppers."[78]

Turning the table on Menand, it would be in his own spirit to contend that he could not understand the greatness of this book, because he never lived in a totalitarian society and did not study it as an outsider. For this reason, I agree with British author Timothy Ash (also an expert on totalitarian society with first-hand experience), who recently characterized Orwell as "the most influential political writer of the twentieth century," placing Orwell higher than such novelists as Alexander Solzhenitsyn and Albert Camus, playwrights such as Bertolt Brecht, and philosophers Karl Popper, Friedrich von Hayek, and Hannah Arendt, or even Jean-Paul Sartre, who was active in many genres.[79] I accept Ash's verdict on Orwell.

Notes

The author wishes to thank Joshua Woods for his editorial contribution to this essay.

1. See, for instance, Diana Trilling's review in the *The Nation*, June 25, 1949, reprinted in Jeffrey Meyers, ed., *George Orwell: Critical Heritage* (London: Routledge, 1975), 4.

2. See Orwell's review of Franz Borkenau's *The Totalitarian Enemy* (1940), cited in Stuart Hall, "Conjuring Leviathan: Orwell on the State," in *Inside the Myth: Orwell: The Views from the Left,* ed. Christopher Norris (London: Lawrence and Wishart, 1984), 228.

3. See these reviews in Meyers, *George Orwell,* 247–94.

4. Meyers, *George Orwell,* 283–85.

5. Isaac Deutscher, *Heretics and Renegades* (London: H. Hamilton, 1955), 43.

6. Andy Croft, "World without End Foisted upon the Future," in *Inside the Myth of Orwell,* ed. Christopher Norris, 198–216.

7. Some authors downgraded the influence of the Soviet experience on *Nineteen Eighty-Four.* They ignored the fact that this novel was a direct continuation of *Animal Farm,* which certainly has Russian roots (see, for instance, Jeffrey Meyers, *Orwell: Wintry Conscience of a Generation* [New York: Norton, 2000], 280–81).

8. Michael Sheldon, *Orwell: The Authorized Biography* (New York: Harper, 1991), 513–14.

9. Christopher Hitchens, *Why Orwell Matters* (New York: Basic Books, 2002), 83.

10. See Meyers, *George Orwell,* 280–81; and Alexander Kafka, "The Wintry Orwell," *The American Prospect* 11, no. 22 (October 23, 2000), available online at http://www.prospect.org/print/V11/22/.

11. See Stuart Hall, "Conjuring Leviathan: Orwell on the State," in *Inside the Myth of Orwell,* ed. Christopher Norris, 220.

12. See Meyers, *George Orwell,* 276.

13. See Robert Conquest, "In Celia's Office," *Hoover Digest,* no. 2 (1999), available online at http://www-hoover.stanford.edu/publications/digest/992/conquest.html, and Walter Laqueur, *The Dream That Failed* (New York: Oxford University Press, 1994), 85, 87, and 93.

14. George Orwell, *Nineteen Eighty-Four* (New York: Signet Classic, 1961), 8. Henceforth page references for quotations from the novel will be given in parentheses in the text.

15. It is also remarkable that as soon they acquired freedom of speech, Soviet intellectuals immediately adopted the totalitarianists' evaluation of Soviet society and rejected the approach of "revisionists" (see David Remnick, "Getting Russia Right," *New York Review of Books,* September 22, 1994, available online at http://www.nybooks.com/articles/article-preview?article_id=2146). They distinguished the likes of Richard Pipes and Robert Conquest as their intellectual heroes.

16. Benedict Sarnov, *Nash Sovietskii novoiaz* (Moscow: Materik, 2002), 6.

17. Hedrick Smith, *The New Russians* (New York: Random House, 1990), 101.

18. François Furet's admiration of Orwell matched that of the Soviet intellectuals. He praised Orwell as the most honest and rebellious writer in postwar Europe who fought the defenders of totalitarianism (François Furet, *La passe d'une illusion* [Paris: Laffont, 1995], 441).

19. See Meyers, *George Orwell,* 20.

20. It may have been a play broadcast by the BBC in 1949 that Golo Mann wrote about in his essay on Orwell (see Meyers, *George Orwell,* 277).

21. See Meyers, *George Orwell,* 296.

22. George Orwell, "The Prevention of Literature," in *Shooting an Elephant and Other Essays* (New York: Harcourt, 1950), 207.

23. Daniel Bell, *The End of Ideology* (Cambridge, Mass.: Harvard University Press, 1960).

24. Czeslaw Milosz, *The Captive Mind,* transl. Jane Zielonko (New York: Knopf, 1953).

25. Timothy Garton Ash, "Orwell for Our Times," *The Guardian,* May 5, 2001, available online at http://www.guardian.co.uk/saturday_review/story/0,3605,485972,00.html.

26. See Melord Sturua, "1984 i 1984," *Izvestia,* January 14, 1984, 5. Today Sturua is living in America, where perhaps for the sake of continuity he joined the anti-Orwellian camp and

praised John Reed's "Snowball's Chance." He savored the accusation against Orwell that he reported on his colleagues to the British authorities during the war ("Vzorvat Oruella," *Izvestia,* January 11, 2003). See the convincing rebuttal to Orwell's contemporary detractors in Christopher Hitchens, "Orwell's List," *The New York Review of Books,* September 26, 2002, available online at http://www.nybooks.com/articles/article-preview?article_id=15679.

27. See her *Stalin's Peasants* (New York: Oxford University Press, 1994); *Everyday Stalinism* (New York: Oxford University Press, 1999); *The Cultural Front: Power and Culture in Revolutionary Russia* (New York: Cornell University Press, 1992), and a volume that she edited, *Cultural Revolution in Russia 1928–1931* (Bloomington: Indiana University Press, 1984). It is impossible to find references to Orwell in any publication belonging to other members of the revisionist school (see, for instance, the works of Jerry Hough and Moshe Lewin).

28. Sheila Fitzpatrick, *The Russian Revolution* (New York: Oxford University Press: 1982/1994), 6.

29. Gregory Freeze, ed., *Russia: A History* (New York: Oxford University Press, 1997).

30. See the preface by Arch Getty, in Arch Getty and Oleg Naumov, *The Road to Terror* (New Haven, Conn.: Yale University Press, 1999), xii.

31. Orlando Figes, *A People's Tragedy* (New York: Penguin Books, 1996).

32. Robert Service, *A History of Twentieth-Century Russia* (Cambridge, Mass.: Harvard University Press, 1998).

33. Robert Conquest, *The Great Terror: Stalin's Purge of the Thirties* (London: Macmillan, 1968).

34. In his *Harvest Sorrow* (New York: Oxford University Press, 1986), Conquest made one reference to Orwell, though not to one of his numerous insights on the nature of the society that was responsible for the terrible famine in the Ukraine in the 1930s but to Orwell's rather casual remark about the disregard of this tragedy by English Russophiles (321).

35. Conquest, "In Celia's Office."

36. Richard Pipes, *Russia under the Bolshevik Regime* (New York: Knopf, 1993), 302. Pipes, who was never critical of Orwell, was, however, not very appreciative of Orwell in his book *Survival Is Not Enough* (New York: Simon and Schuster, 1984), 80.

37. In fact, *Animal Farm* is a satirical historical novel, quite similar to Anatole France's *L'ile de Penguines,* which no one placed in the genre of antiutopian literature.

38. Martin Malia, *The Soviet Tragedy: A History of Socialism in Russia, 1917–1991* (New York: The Free Press, 1994), 269; *Russia under Western Eyes* (Cambridge, Mass.: Harvard University Press, 1999), 365.

39. Hannah Arendt, *The Origins of Totalitarianism* (New York: Harcourt, 1976).

40. See some of these reviews in Meyers, *George Orwell,* 247–87.

41. See, for instance, Vladimir Bukovsky, *Jugement à Moscou* (Paris: Laffont, 1995), 70, 335, 560.

42. See, for instance, Mikhail Kapustin, *Konez utopii* (Moscow: Novosti, 1990), 12.

43. Mikhail Heller and Alexandre Nekrich, *Utopia in Power: The History of the Soviet Union from 1917 to the Present* (New York: Summit Books, 1986), 8.

44. See, for instance, Lewis Siegelbaum, "Building Stalinism, 1929–1942," in *Russia: A History,* ed. Gregory Freeze, 291–319.

45. Fitzpatrick, *Everyday Stalinism.*

46. Malia, *The Soviet Tragedy,* 349, 351.

47. See Arthur Koestler, *Darkness at Noon* (New York: Bantam, 1968).

48. Concerning the image of ordinary people in the mentality of the Soviet leaders, see Vladimir Shlapentokh, *The Politics of Sociology in the Soviet Union* (Boulder: Westview Press, 1987).

49. See, for instance, Malia, *The Soviet Tragedy.*

50. Hannah Arendt, *The Origins of Totalitarianism,* 305–483.

51. See, for instance, Malia, *The Soviet Tragedy,* 1994),142, 288, 295; Robert Conquest, "Red to Go," *Times Literary Supplement,* July 9, 1993; available online at http://www.thetls.co.uk/archive/; George Kennan, *Russia and the West under Lenin and Stalin* (Boston: Little, Brown, 1993), 389; Adam Ulam, "The Myth of Leninism," *Times Literary Supplement,* November 6, 1992, 344.

52. Orwell, *Homage to Catalonia* (San Diego: Harvest Books, 1952), 56.

53. See, for instance, Malia, *Russia under Western Eyes,* 316.

54. In my works on Soviet society, I made the distinction between the open ideology addressed to the masses and the closed ideology addressed to the ruling class. By analyzing the Soviet media and various printed materials, one can easily separate the ideologies from each other, even if there are areas where they overlap; see Vladimir Shlapentokh, *Soviet Public Opinion and Ideology: Mythology and Pragmatism in Interaction* (New York: Praeger, 1986); and *A Normal Totalitarian Society: How the Soviet Union Functioned and How It Collapsed* (Armonk, N.Y.: M. E. Sharpe, 2001).

55. Koestler, *Darkness at Noon,* 183.

56. For more about this phenomenon, see Vladimir Shlapentokh, "Two Levels of Public Opinion: The Soviet Case," *Public Opinion Quarterly,* vol. 49 (Winter 1985): 443–59.

57. Erich Fromm, afterword, in George Orwell, *1984* (New York: Signet Classic, 1961), 257–67.

58. The various identification theories that in some cases discuss the relationship between the individual and the leader are not fully applicable to totalitarian society, because they tend to disregard the idea of direct coercion or fear of coercion as a major generator of the identification with the leader. They ascribe the identification process to different motives of "free individuals," such as the enhancement of one's own importance and the maintenance of self-esteem (see Marilynn Brewer and Rupert Brown, "Intergroup Relations," in *The Handbook of Social Psychology,* 4th ed., ed. Daniel T. Gilbert, Susan T. Fiske, and Gardner Lindzey (Boston: McGraw-Hill, 1998), 2:561–65.

59. Beverly Fehr and James Russel, "The Concept of Love Viewed from a Protype Perspective," *Journal of Personality and Social Psychology* 60 (1991): 424–38.

60. Meeting one his zealous colleagues in the canteen, Winston divined that this ardent servant of the regime was doomed: "There was something subtly wrong with Syme. There was something that he lacked: discretion, aloofness, a sort of saving stupidity. You could not say that he was unorthodox. He believed in the principles of Ingsoc, he venerated Big Brother, he rejoiced over victories, he hated heretics, not merely with sincerity but with a sort of restless zeal, an up-to-dateness of information, which the ordinary Party member did not approach. Yet a faint air of disreputability always clung to him. He said things that would have been better unsaid, he had read too many books, he frequented the Chestnut Tree Café, haunt of painters and musicians" (48–49).

61. See John Bowlby, *A Secure Base* (New York: Basic, 1988).

62. The attitudes of the rulers toward religion was different in the monarchies in which the king or tsar was also the supreme religious leader, or considered to be anointed by God.

63. Theodor W. Adorno, Else Frenkel-Brunswik, Daniel J. Levinson, and R. Nevitt Sanford, *The Authoritarian Personality* (New York: Harper, 1950).

64. Hannah Arendt, *The Origins of Totalitarianism,* 352–53, 382.

65. About the attitudes of the Soviet masses to the regime, see Vladimir Shlapentokh, *A Normal Totalitarian Society*; and Boris Grushin, *Chetyre zhizni Rossii v zerkale oprosov obshchestvennogo mnenia* (Moscow: Progress Traditsia, 2001).

66. According to his diary, Vladimir Stavsky, an official writer of the 1930s, was overwhelmed with his feelings toward a woman, apparently his mistress. He used the most passionate words, remembering with rapture their trysts. In the eulogy of his carnal love, he enmeshed the name of Stalin as a god who protected their love: "I want to love, together with the epoch, together with Stalin, together with you, my beloved, my darling" (Veronique

Garros, Natalia Korenevskaya, and Thomas Lahusen, eds., *Intimacy and Terror: Soviet Diaries of the 1930s* [New York: New Press, 1995], 24).

67. Bell, *The End of Ideology,* 315–52; Robert Conquest, *Common Sense about Russia* (New York: Macmillan, 1961); Conquest, *Power and Policy in the U.S.S.R.: The Study of Soviet Dynastics* (New York: St. Martin's Press, 1961); Conquest, *The Great Terror: Stalin's Purge of the Thirties*; and Conquest, *The Great Terror: A Reassessment,* (New York: Oxford University Press, 1990).

68. Pipes suggested that Russians "pretended to conform while holding their private and often strong opinion to themselves." To say that they were dominated by official ideology "is grossly unfair" (Richard Pipes, "East Is East," *New Republic,* April 26, 1999, 100–108). However, reflecting on the longevity of the Soviet system in the end of his big book on the Bolshevik regime, Pipes melancholically noted that the regime "had the support of its own people" (Richard Pipes, *Russia under the Bolshevik Regime,* 511).

69. Irina Pavlova and Sergei Kuleshov were among the few authors who included in their books on Soviet history short special sections on public opinion. Irina Pavlova, *Stanovlenie mechanizma vlasti* (Novosibirsk, Russia: Sibirskii Khronograf, 1993); and Sergei Kuleshov, ed., *Nashe otechestvo* (Moscow: Terra, 1990), 267.

70. Vladimir Brovkin, *Russia after Lenin: Politics, Culture and Society, 1921–1929* (New York: Routledge, 1998).

71. Bukovsky, *Jugement à Moscou,* 133–34.

72. Robert Jackman, *Power without Force: The Political Capacity of Nation-States* (Ann Arbor: University of Michigan Press, 1993), 8, 10–11.

73. Rodney Stark, *Sociology: An Internet Edition* (Belmont, Calif.: Wadsworth, 2001), 438–39.

74. Michel Foucault, *Discipline and Punish: The Birth of the Prison,* trans. Alan Sheridan (New York: Vintage Books, 1979).

75. Boris Dubin, "Stalin i drugie," *Monitoring obshchestvennogo mnenia,* no.1 (January-February 2003): 13–25.

76. See, for instance, Eric Lichtblau and Adam Liptak, "On Terror, Spying and Guns, Ashcroft Expands Reach," *New York Times,* March 15, 2003, A1.

77. Niall Ferguson, *Empire: The Rise and Demise of the British World Order and the Lessons for Global Power* (New York: Basic Books, 2003).

78. Louis Menand, "Honest, Decent, Wrong," *The New Yorker,* January 27, 2003, available online at http://www.newyorker.com/critics/atlarge/?030127crat_atlarge.

79. Timothy Garton Ash, "Orwell for Our Times," *The Guardian,* May 5, 2001, available online at http://www.guardian.co.uk/saturday_review/story/0,3605,485972,00.html.

20

May Days in Barcelona: Orwell, Langdon-Davies, and the Cultural Memory of War

Miquel Berga

On May 3, 1937, the streets of Barcelona witnessed the bloody clash between the forces of the communist-dominated Republican authorities and the anarchist militants of the CNT (the anarcho-syndicalists of the Confederación Nacional del Trabajo) backed by the tiny anti-Stalinist Marxist POUM (Partido Obrero de Unificación Marxista). After four days of street fighting, the outcome was four hundred antifascists dead and around one thousand wounded. Politically, the so-called Events of May came to represent the great divide inside the Popular Front. There and then, in spite of having Franco, Hitler, and Mussolini at their doors, the old fight between libertarians and authoritarians was, once again, being staged. That deep cleft in political principles sparked, indeed, a civil war inside the civil war. The differences on how to conduct the war and on the nature of social revolution, which had been latent on the Republican side right from the outbreak of the war, came out in the open. The ideological confrontation turned into street warfare, which Orwell witnessed from the roof of the Poliorama Theatre on the Rambles.

It was by accident that Orwell found himself in the middle of this crucial episode in the Spanish Civil War but, having served in the POUM militia, he was doomed to be on the losing side as is now clear from evidence found in the State Military Archive in Moscow.[1] What he saw there became a kind of political epiphany and, to put it in his own words, "thereafter I knew where I stood."[2] If Orwell's capacities as a fighter had had a very minor impact on the outcome of the war, his abilities as a skilled writer played, in the long run, a most important role in shaping our cultural memory of that war. Orwell's first impulse was to write an impassioned vindication of the POUM with the moral authority of the eyewitness. He certainly had "a lie [he wanted] to expose" and "a fact to which [he wanted] to draw attention," but when he wrote *Homage to Catalonia* he did it "without violating [his] literary instincts" and his main concern was "to get a hearing."[3] In other words, he understood how important it was to mold documentary on the narrative strategies of prose fiction. Knowing full well that the *tale* is only listened to if there is an efficient command of the art of *telling,* he produced a narrative that has become ingrained in our memory of the Spanish Civil War not only because of its central truth but also because it rested on the carefully planned stylistic fabric of his text.[4] Orwell's enormous influence in political speculation is crucially indebted "to his awareness of the complexity of literary and linguistic strategy." The will for a style was there from the beginning and the measure of his success is directly related to his "search for a valid voice with which to persuade others and express opinion," as Lynette Hunter demonstrated in her perceptive and groundbreaking approach to Orwell's works way back in 1984.[5] In my view, the writing of *Homage to Catalonia* has to be seen as Orwell's first big test for his writing powers in the light of those aspirations. The soldier managed to survive the bullets in the Aragon Front and in the Catalan barricades. Likewise, the writer managed to come clean, to the present day, from the ideological and textual battles of the thirties that made the Spanish Civil War, in MacNeice's famous line, "the whetstone of our aspirations."[6]

Drawing from some unpublished writings by the English author and journalist John Langdon-Davies,[7] I would like to contribute in this essay a discussion on some aspects of "the gathering storm" prior to the Events of May and the main lines of the polemic, contrasting Langdon-Davies's account with Orwell's and commenting on some of its literary consequences from, as it were, a Catalan angle.

What ignited the mounting tension on the Republican side was the seizing of the telephone exchange on the morning of May 3, 1937, by the Commissioner of Public Order of the Catalan Autonomous Government. The anarchist CNT ran the building and it became clear that Joan Comorera, leader of the PSUC (the Catalan Communist Party) and a minister in the Catalan government, had instigated the daring move. It was the last straw in the "latent" fratricidal struggle to determine the most appropriate strategy for winning the war against Franco that had opposed anarcho-syndicalists, on one side, and bourgeois republicans and communists on the other, practically from the brave days of July 1936 when the military coup was neutralized in the streets of Barcelona by a popular uprising.

In order to oppose the military, the Republic had availed itself of the revolutionary fervor of the workers, who insisted on the creation of an army made up of popular militias. This initial reaction brought about the formulation of the objectives of the war in terms of social revolution rather than strictly in terms of the defense of a Republican legality conforming to the model of the so-called bourgeois democracies. After some months of virtual stalemate in the military conflict, while the European democracies maintained a timid, if not cynical, attitude toward aiding the Spanish Republic, strength was being gained by those who argued for less revolutionary fervor and for more pragmatism. This meant acknowledging that their only real support was coming from Stalin's Russia and from the International Brigades (an operation clearly communist in inspiration and design). It also meant acknowledging the consequent necessity of following the strategy openly advocated by the party, that is to say, the transformation of the militias into a regular, hierarchically structured army and the adoption of the policy of first winning the war and only then undertaking social revolution.

The emergent Communist Party (the PSUC), in these circumstances thus became, paradoxically, the party of law and order in Catalonia. The anarcho-syndicalists of the CNT and the Federación Anarquista Ibérica (FAI) or revolutionary

Marxist parties like the POUM, whose paper *La Batalla* had already been denouncing the Moscow show trials of 1936, detected or intuited in this situation the long arm of Stalinist totalitarianism, and they opposed the change in strategy from the conviction that without binding a new revolutionary social order to the war effort the necessary energies would not be found to resist the fascist onslaught. These were the issues that were settled by gunfire and between barricades on the streets of Barcelona during the first week of May 1937. Our two English writers had already been in the city for some days.

John Langdon-Davies is following events as a journalist for the liberal *News Chronicle*. George Orwell is in the city as a militiaman of the POUM detailed for the Aragon Front, preparing to enjoy a short period of leave with his wife, who is also in Barcelona. Curiously enough, he is also using his furlough to get discharge papers from the militia in order to join the communist-controlled International Brigades in Albacete.[8] The two writers do not know one another and their individual relationships with Catalonia are quite different, but both of them will immediately appreciate the seriousness of the situation. Langdon-Davies begins to make notes for his reports sitting in the Rugby Bar at 11:00 on the night of May 3. What begins as a letter to his wife ends up as a three-day draft report of the events, which captures the strange atmosphere of the embattled city.[9] Orwell begins to ponder upon the situation from the roof of what is now the Poliorama Theatre, on the Rambles, where he has been sent to keep guard and protect the POUM headquarters located in a building directly opposite. Langdon-Davies is able to use his Catalan contacts. The author of two successful books about Catalonia, *Dancing Catalans* (1929) and his best-selling *Behind the Spanish Barricades* (1936) dealing with the first months of the civil war, he follows events aided by personal acquaintance with many of the protagonists and is able to speak fluent Catalan. Orwell spends three sleepless nights up on the flat roof of the Poliorama Theatre, reading Penguin paperbacks in the company of other English volunteers.

Both writers had arrived in the city at the end of April (one on the 25th, the other on the 26th) and they were thus able to observe the subtle changes in the atmosphere of the rear guard, which denoted a new "state of play," compared with how things were at the outbreak of war. Orwell notes that "the revolutionary atmosphere had vanished" and he describes numerous details that he sees as typical of a bourgeois city. The great change, according to Orwell, is the result of two new phenomena: "One was that the people—the civil population—had lost much of their interest in the war; the other was that the normal division of society into rich and poor, upper class and lower class, was reasserting itself."[10]

Langdon-Davies makes a similar point in the preface to the third edition of his *Behind the Spanish Barricades,* where he remarks that the "modest and petty bourgeois dare once more to go out wearing hat and tie."[11] What Orwell describes as a backward movement in the situation is, however, viewed by Langdon-Davies as a positive symptom of normality. Langdon-Davies has moved from his initial fascination with Catalan anarchism to an ever-closer siding with the theses of the communists, and for much of the war he acts, quite consciously, as a "fellow-traveler" of the party. The steady changes in his political position can be traced in the war diary of his friend, the Catalan poet Marià Manent. Some of his entries make it clear that the Englishman is someone with clear insight into the likely course of events. As early as February 9, 1937, Manent writes: "Yesterday, with our friend Langdon-Davies, there was also conversation about Russia. . . . He also told me that he sees as inevitable, eventually, a violent clash between the CNT and the POUM, on one side, and the Generalitat [the official Catalan government] with the UGT on the other. The Trotskyites, he says, are counter-revolutionaries, despite claims they might make to being pure revolutionaries."[12]

The divergences between the two writers become sharper as the anticipated May Day celebrations approach. Both of them see the murder of Roldán Cortada, a trade-unionist secretary of the communist minister of labor in the Catalan government, Rafael Vidiella, as something likely to ignite the tension simmering on the streets. Cortada was struck down by gunfire from rogue elements in the anarchist FAI, and his interment on the afternoon of April 27 brought the latent tension to the surface. Langdon-Davies watched the funeral procession from the balcony of a bank in the Paseo de Gracia, Orwell from a window in the Hotel Continental down on the Rambles. What they saw was captured by the camera of Catalan photographer Agustí Centelles: Cortada's coffin, carried by militants from the Carlos Marx House, the communist headquarters, presided over an impressive parade of dignitaries and thousands of soldiers of the new Popular Army. The message inscribed in the scarlet banner carried by uniformed troops, brought from the front line to Barcelona for the occasion, made the message clear: "The Combatants at the Front are not Disposed to Tolerate Any Longer the Impunity of Assassins and Bandits Who Can Only Show Courage in the Rear Guard."

Remembering that parade, Orwell, with the benefit of hindsight, reflects as follows:

> At the end of April, just after I got to Barcelona, Roldán Cortada, a prominent member of the UGT, was murdered, presumably by someone in the CNT. The Government ordered all shops to close and staged an enormous funeral procession, largely of Popular Army troops, which took two hours to pass a given point. From the hotel window I watched without enthusiasm. It was obvious that the so-called funeral was merely a display of strength; a little more of this kind of thing and there might be bloodshed.[13]

Langdon-Davies, it goes without saying, makes a more enthusiastic appraisal and interprets that same parade from a very different perspective:

> The challenge of anarcho-syndicalism had been accepted. For the first time the non-anarchist workers and petty-bourgeoisie of Barcelona were standing up against a social revolution whose only offspring was chaos heading to defeat. In face of murder, robbery, threats, discrimination, the UGT policy had been to retire and wait. And here in this vast procession, felt the UGT, was the tangible proof that only through socialism can revolutions be successful. . . . Marching rank on rank in perfect military formation, perfectly uniformed, obviously disciplined, came thousands of the new People's Army, the Army which the socialists and communists along with the republicans had strained every effort to build up out of early reckless brave militiamen.[14]

What we get in this last paragraph is a sort of prose version of some of the central metaphors in Auden's "Spain," which have often been misread as being simply antifascist metaphors. When Auden writes "To-day the struggle," states that "Madrid is the heart," or mentions "the People's army," he is embedding in his famous poem the communist orthodoxy before the Events of May. That is, Madrid is the priority and not the anarchist- and POUM-dominated Aragon Front; the People's Army is the regular army the central government wishes to create in order to do away with, once and for all, the reckless revolutionary militias controlled by the CNT and the POUM. And the resounding "To-day the struggle"—counterposed to "Tomorrow"—is an echo of the communist slogan in Spain: "Today victory in the war. Tomorrow we can discuss revolution." It is this kind of "taking sides" (which included the notorious reference to "necessay murder") that was later to embarrass Auden and cow him into accepting Orwell's ferocious critique of his poem. It was the private knowledge that he had used this kind of rhetoric as a tool for what became increasingly the tool of a repressive Soviet foreign policy that made Auden disown, eventually, the whole poem. In this regard, his answer to an American scholar when asked to recall his Spanish experiences is most significant: "I did not wish to talk about Spain when I returned because I was upset by many things I saw or heard about. Some of them were described better than I could ever had done by George Orwell, in *Homage to Catalonia*."[15]

But not everybody watching the big funeral parade in the streets of Barcelona held the same views, of course. As I have remarked, Langdon-Davies is very familiar with Catalan society of the time and despite his expressions of enthusiasm he glimpses the contradictions and the potential conflict in the situation. Thus he hastens to advise his readers about the existence of different political sensibilities:

> You might have thought that anti-fascist Barcelona would have viewed the coming of this new Army with unmixed delight. But if you could have talked to certain members of the crowd, and with some of the people who stayed away, you would have found a host of contradictory reasons for its unpopularity. Consider this: here is Barcelona turning out by the hundred thousand to demonstrate for socialist order against anarchist disorder. But this is the same Barcelona that turned out a few months ago at Durruti's funeral to honor anarchism. And the same Barcelona that has turned out time and again at funerals to honor Catalan nationalism in its struggle against a central Spanish Madrid Government. That is what makes the situation so complicated. You have three main currents of political emotion, each used to express by means of public demonstration at which hundred of thousands attend.

Langdon-Davies identifies the three main currents as the anarchist, the socialist-communist, and the Catalan nationalist. These are his concluding remarks:

> And so we can say that the crowd looking on, or staying away, think as follows of Roldán Cortada's funeral: The anarcho-syndicalist: "They are using this murder as an excuse to rattle the sabre of authoritarianism. Every state is devilish and here we have the Stalinists threatening to enslave the worker in a communist state." The Esquerra Catalana bourgeois: "Thank goodness here is a force which will bring order to the rearguard and keep the Murcian FAI anarchists in its proper place. But of course if this force tries to impose Valencia on Catalunya we will oppose it to the length of joining up with the anarchists." Such was the state of *anti-fascist* unity in Barcelona when May 1st 1937 came round.[16]

It is obvious that Langdon-Davies is abreast of the situation and well informed. Yet when trouble begins on May 3 he writes a long report about the situation in Barcelona for *The News Chronicle* in which the fellow-traveler's vision overrides investigative journalism and comes out with the official party line: it is all down to a frustrated putsch started by the POUM (a party he describes, inaccurately, as *Trotskyite*), which has taken the government forces by surprise. Langdon-Davies could not have been aware of the consequences of his—and many others in the communist press—reporting the official party line. They were certainly used by the party in creating a state of opinion favorable to the effort under way, determined by the Stalinist strategy, to declare the POUM illegal. This was the necessary first step that led to a show trial against its leaders, put its militants into jail, and proceeded with the abduction of its main figure, Andreu Nin, who after "unsuccessful" torture was, to put it in Newspeak, turned into an "Unperson." It is worth noticing that although Langdon-Davies's published report focuses on the role supposedly played by the POUM, there is not even a single mention of that party in the notes he took while the trouble lasted.

Several pages of *Homage to Catalonia* are devoted to a lengthy, patient and detailed refutation of Langdon-Davies's version of events published in *The News Chronicle*. But Langdon-Davies is soon provided with a perfect opportunity to reply in defense of his own position when *The Daily Worker*, the official organ of the British Communist Party, commissions from him a review of Orwell's book and others on Spain. Langdon-Davies chooses to ignore the allusions to himself. Instead, he dismisses Orwell's book with a couple of sentences directly inspired by the communist orthodoxy of the moment:

> Better than these [two books on Catalonia by the scholar Allison Peers] are some books produced by individualists who have splashed their eyes for a few months with Spanish blood. Typical is Orwell's Homage to Catalonia. The Road to Wigan Pier leads on to Barcelona and the POUM. The value of the book is that it gives an honest picture of the sort of mentality that toys with revolutionary romanticism but shies violently at revolutionary discipline. It should be read as a warning.[17]

If any of the communist daily's readers actually read *Homage to Catalonia*, their minds must have been put at rest by this assessment. Orwell is a misguided devil who is incapable of accepting revolutionary discipline, meaning, naturally, that the tiresome *purists* fail to understand that the end justifies the means, however squalid these might be. Just note the implication of the sentence "The Road to Wigan Pier leads on to Barcelona and the POUM." Langdon-Davies clearly has in mind the controversial second part of Orwell's *The Road to Wigan Pier*, where he was critical of the attitude of certain socialist militants. The implication is, then, that one begins to get used to raising objections to the working of a particular organization (the Third International in this case) and one ends up joining the POUM, initials which, for *The Daily Worker* and at that moment, signify a nest of dangerous counterrevolutionaries.

It must be said that, after the German-Soviet pact of August 1939, Langdon-Davies's political stand is that of a fervent anti-Stalinist and he will go on to denounce the perversions of the system.[18] Despite this, he never undertakes any self-criticism in relation to his biased attitude toward *Homage to Catalonia*, and in an unpublished manuscript from the 1960s about the civil war, there are still echoes of the old dispute: "An excellent writer, George Orwell, has written about it all, but unfortunately he was impelled by a hatred of Stalinism almost as powerful as his love of Spain and liberty and apt to blind him; and what he wrote is most tendentious."[19]

This particular controversy offers many opportunities for reflection. Had Orwell not become universally famous for his *Animal Farm* and *Nineteen Eighty-Four,* would his *Homage to Catalonia*—with its poor sales at the time of publication—now be as forgotten as Langdon-Davies's best seller, *Behind the Spanish Barricades*? To what extent are literary skills essential in making readers accept eyewitness narratives that intend to set historical records right? What processes of verification need to operate in making the autobiographical mode a reliable source in our perceptions of the past? Or, to put it à la Oscar Wilde, how does one get away with truth? That is why I would like to conclude with some references to the author of the photos taken in Barcelona in 1937.

As it happens, Agustí Centelles, the Catalan Robert Kappa of the Spanish Civil War, is also the author of the famous picture showing Orwell with head and shoulders above the POUM militia in the Lenin barracks, an *ekphrastic* moment depicting the first sentence of *Homage to Catalonia.* That photo is important not only as an eloquent silent rebuttal of Claude Simon's notorious debunking of *Homage to Catalonia* but also because its own history is most significant. In 1939, Centelles, with thousands of other Spaniards on the Republican side, went into exile and like most of them ended up in French camps where the horrendous hardship was to be followed by trying to survive as left-wing refugees in Nazi-occupied France. The interesting thing is that Centelles had left Catalonia with his basic personal belongings, which crucially included a suitcase with all his Leica negatives. He knew that, had those negatives been left in Spain and found by the Francoist police, they would have become incriminating evidence for hundreds of antifascists. Centelles managed to keep his box of negatives, and when he left the concentration camp of Bram in southern France the suitcases were still with him. He stayed on a farm near Carcassone until late 1944, when the hope of an imminent Allied victory in the war made many exiles try a clandestine return to Spain. Before leaving, he cautiously entrusted the box of negatives to the farmers in Carcassone thinking he was soon going to recover them. But despite Hitler's final defeat, Franco and his regime survived for almost forty years with the complacency of the victorious democracies. Centelles had to occupy himself as a discreet commercial photographer (shooting weddings and so forth) in Francoist Barcelona. Only after Franco's death was he able to obtain a passport and in August 1976 he went back to the farm in Carcassone where the negatives had, indeed, been kept. Thirty-two years had elapsed, but that was, clearly, the first day of the second life of Agustí Centelles.

Orwell's photo at the Lenin barracks only surfaced in 1979 when, while helping Professor Bernard Crick in the first full Orwell biography, I went through Centelles's negatives searching for visual evidence of "Orwell in Catalonia." Centelles had no idea he had actually photographed the, by then, famous writer. So when I pointed out the tall Englishman in the POUM parade he was full of wonder and delight. In a way, this photo captures and preserves traces of the past, as all photos do, but it seems to me that it also epitomizes a kind of reemergence of the work of two artists—Orwell and Centelles—whose testimony was silenced by political oppression coming from opposite sides. Marching along the long and winding road of history, they managed to be respected eyewitnesses of the past, and their works bear witness to the potential of certain texts to challenge the common idea that history is simply what gets written in books by life's winners.

Let me conclude by stating that those Barcelona May Days of 1937, so crucial for Orwell's artistic and ideological development, stayed on in his mind until the very end. In a couple of letters written in bed just a few months before his death (but not included in the *Complete Works* edited by Peter Davison), Orwell writes to one of his Catalan POUM comrades, then exiled in Paris, offering his nominal support to the *Federación Española de Internados y Deportados*: "If you wish to use my name, you are at liberty to do so," he says, and he asks for instructions as to how to contribute some money for their plight. In some sadly premonitory words, he adds, "I imagine that I shall not even be allowed to leave my bed for some months to come."[20] Too many years later, in 1998, Catalonia paid Orwell back for having converted its name into a mythical *topos* for many readers in the world. The socialist mayor of Barcelona unveiled a plaque naming a square in the old town after the author of *Homage to Catalonia*. Christopher Hitchens holds that "that small, informal investiture and naming in Barcelona summarized much of the moral grandeur of the Left."[21] I wonder if he knows that, in a surprising move, the municipal authorities chose Plaza Orwell—of all the squares in Barcelona—to install some inconspicuous cameras in a pilot scheme for surveillance of public thoroughfares. The square, in an admittedly fine Orwellian paradox, is still endowed with those Big Brotherish eyes watching over the passersby. The persistent appeal of Orwell's life and work is closely related to the insistence of present-day power politics in proving his suspicions still plausible.

NOTES

An earlier version of this essay was given as the Annual Joan Gili Memorial Lecture at the University of Wales (Cardiff), on November 16, 2002.

1. See Ronald Radosh, Mary R. Habeck, and Grigory Sevastianov, *Spain Betrayed: The Soviet Union in the Spanish Civil War* (New Haven, Conn.: Yale University Press, 2001).

2. "Why I Write," in *The Complete Works of George Orwell,* ed. Peter Davison (London: Secker and Warburg, 2000), 18:316–21.

3. Orwell, "Why I Write," 18:319.

4. On Orwell's textual strategies in *Homage to Catalonia,* see Lynette Hunter, *George Orwell: The Search for a Voice* (Milton Keynes, U.K.: Open University Press, 1984); Valentine Cunningham, "*Homage to Catalonia* Revisited: Remembering and Misremembering the Spanish Civil War," in *Actes du Colloque: La Guerre Civile d'Espagne—Histoire et Culture* (Brussels: Université Libre de Bruxelles, 1986), 501–14; Richard Filloy, "Orwell's Political Persuasion: A Rhetoric of Personality" in *George Orwell,* ed. Graham Holderness, Brian Loughrey, and Nahem Yousef, New Casebook Series (London: Macmillan, 1998), 47–63; Miquel Berga, "Orwell's Catalonia: Textual Strategies and the Eyewitness Account" in *The Road from George Orwell,* ed. Alberto Lázaro (Bern: Peter Lang, 2001), 53–70.

5. Lynette Hunter, *George Orwell: The Search for a Voice,* 1.

6. Louis MacNeice, "Autumn Journal" in *Poetry of the Thirties,* ed. Robin Skelton (Harmondsworth, U.K.: Penguin Books, 1964), 163.

7. These materials were published in Catalan in Miquel Berga, ed., *John Langdon-Davies: La setmana tràgica de 1937* (Barcelona: Edicions 62, 1987) and amply discussed in Miquel Berga, *John Langdon-Davies: Una biografía anglo-catalana, 1897–1971* (Barcelona: Portic, 1991).

8. See letter by Eileen Blair in *The Complete Works of George Orwell,* 9:367. For a detailed summary of Orwell's contradictory motives concerning this issue and a critical

view of his political stand concerning the Spanish Civil War, see Robert Stradling, *History and Legend: Writing the International Brigades* (Cardiff: University of Wales Press, 2003).

9. See a Catalan translation in Berga, *John Langdon-Davies: La setmana tràgica de 1937,* 155–62.

10. Orwell, *Homage to Catalonia* (London: Penguin Books, 1989), 90. But there might be here some a posteriori construction of his own impressions since Orwell got to Barcelona when the war had gone on for more than five months and, for better or worse, the "revolutionary atmosphere" of the first weeks was no longer in the air. See Stradling, *History and Legend,* 57–58.

11. John Langdon-Davies, *Behind the Spanish Barricades,* 3rd ed. (London: Secker and Warburg, 1937). The book was first published in November 1936 and the third edition appeared in April 1937.

12. Marià Manent, *El vel de Maria* (Barcelona: Destino, 1975), 27.

13. Orwell, *Homage to Catalonia,* 99.

14. Langdon-Davies, "The Tragic Week," ms., Patricia Langdon-Davies Archive. Published in Catalan translation in Berga, *John Langdon-Davies: La setmana tràgica de 1937.*

15. For readings of "Spain" along these lines see Nicholas Jenkins, "Auden in Spain," in *W. H. Auden: The Map of all my Youth,* ed. Katherine Bucknell and Nicholas Jenkins (Oxford: Clarendon Press, 1990), 88–93, and Stradling, *History and Legend,* 85–87.

16. Langdon-Davies, "The Tragic Week," 130.

17. *Daily Worker,* Special Supplement on Spain, May 21, 1938, 6.

18. Langdon-Davies is the author of vigorous denunciations of Soviet policy: *Finland, The First Total War* (London: Routledge, 1940) and *Russia Puts the Clock Back* (London: Gollancz, 1949).

19. "The Spanish Civil War: Reporting," ms., Patricia Langdon-Davies Archive.

20. Letters to Jordi Arquer, June 22, 1949, and July 28, 1949, Arquer Archive, Centre d'Estudis Històrics Internacionals (CEHI), Barcelona.

21. Christopher Hitchens, *Why Orwell Matters* (New York: Basic Books, 2002), 78.

21

From Ingsoc to Capsoc:
Perceptions of Orwell in France

GILBERT BONIFAS

Orwell's death did not pass totally unnoticed in France,[1] and most of his books had been translated by 1960 (with the notable exceptions of *The Road to Wigan Pier* and most of the essays), but one cannot say that he was by then well known and widely read outside academic circles.[2] Although *Down and Out in Paris and London* had been translated as early as 1935, the print run of 5,500 copies had not yet sold out twenty years later; *Animal Farm* scarcely created a ripple when it appeared in 1947, possibly for political reasons;[3] *Nineteen Eighty-Four* was published in paperback only in 1964,[4] ten years after the first Penguin edition, and most significant of all, the prestigious Gallimard publishing house, which in the mid-1960s held the rights for *Keep the Aspidistra Flying, Homage to Catalonia, Animal Farm,* and *Nineteen Eighty-Four,* gradually lost interest: in 1981–1982 all Gallimard titles passed to a new publisher, Les Editions Champ Libre.[5] The only exception was *Nineteen Eighty-Four,* which remained in Gallimard's fold; this leaves little doubt that Gallimard got rid of the other titles because they did not sell well enough.

Thus it took Orwell a long time to become part of the French intellectual landscape. In a way it was Bernard Crick's bibliography that did it. Its press coverage was surprisingly good, even before publication of the French translation in 1982.[6] It was as if critics and journalists who only knew *Animal Farm* and *Nineteen Eighty-Four* were astounded and fascinated by what they learned in the Crick book and they decided that at last it was time to rescue Orwell from the anonymity wherein they were convinced he still remained with the general public who hardly read beyond *Nineteen Eighty-Four.*[7] In late 1983 and early 1984 two books[8] and several articles were written about Orwell, clearly aimed at a reading public supposedly still little informed about his oeuvre. Many of them were hardly more than able overviews of his life and work, too often tending to the hagiographic.[9] Inevitably the lion's share of the critique was reserved for *Nineteen Eighty-Four,* with many commentators trying to work out the exact relationship between the novel and the past and present situation in the Soviet Union. To a few, like the French philosopher André Glucksmann, *Nineteen Eighty-Four* was of in-

terest in 1984 solely to the historian of ideas. The whole Russian population was
so stupefied by vodka and ignorance that it had not even retained a glimmer of
intelligence and reflection. There was no need to keep rewriting the past, to devise
a Newspeak. Dictatorship in the real world had become much simpler than in
Oceania. As a result the only value of the novel was that it revealed how "people
perceived classical totalitarianism in the industrial age."[10] To many, on the other
hand, Orwell had foreseen the postwar developments of the communist regimes
and their *nomenklaturas*. The world of Oceania was increasingly that of Vietnam,
of China, of Russia, of Poland, of Czechoslovakia.[11] It was the world we lived in;
the novel remained a warning to the West to stay vigilant. The totalitarian, aka
communist, peril had not yet gone away and even remained, in the words of a
critic of Orwell as early as 1981, "the finite horizon of our political thinking."[12] In
fact much of what was then published on Orwell was written in the shadow of
events that seemed to prove that totalitarianism was not only alive and well but
also still bent on conquering Western Europe.

What gave so much topicality to Orwell's book was the considerable protest in
many European countries in 1982–1983 over the deployment of U.S. Pershing
missiles, even though the Soviet Union was refusing to withdraw the 240 SS20s
that had been pointed at Western European targets since 1976. To many of Orwell's commentators this showed that there were still people in the West who had
not yet understood what communist totalitarianism was, nor the reality of its
menace, since they chanted that they preferred to be "red rather than dead," preferred, that is, surviving at the biological level of the proles in *Nineteen Eighty-
Four* to fighting for what alone could keep them free and human.[13]

The novel had thus an immediate didactic value. The 1983 crisis had been "the
last warning"[14] and *Nineteen Eighty-Four* and other aspects of Orwell's life and
work, notably his rallying to the war against Hitler in 1939,[15] were the antidote to
pacifism and the temptation of appeasement. Without Orwell's novel, it seemed,
the democratic will to resist might well be sapped and snap. In his *Orwell ou
l'horreur de la politique,* Simon Leys's conclusion was that from a strictly literary
point of view posterity would never have remembered Orwell, whom he ranked on
a par with Somerset Maugham. If Orwell had become "the major prophet of our
century," it was because he had denounced with great courage and clarity of vision
"the unprecedented totalitarian threat that hangs over mankind today."[16] The last
two lines of Leys's text were: "I do not think there is a single writer whose work
could be of more practical, more urgent, more immediate use for us."[17] In the
1980s, therefore, it was the overpowering presence of the Soviet Union in international politics that first and foremost determined the status and role of Orwell in
French intellectual life. He was primarily perceived as a fighter for liberty, an
essential figure to stem the advance of communism in the minds of Westerners.[18]

That said, French intellectuals being by nature left-leaning, they were not willing to follow in Norman Podhoretz's footsteps. His being against communism,
they were sure, could not have turned Orwell, had he stayed alive, into a supporter
of an American-type neoconservatism. There was enough evidence in Orwell's
essays and letters to consider that at least since his visit to Wigan he had been a
socialist first and an antitotalitarian second. How could he have been, therefore, in
favor of a system in which justice and liberty were often in considerable disagree-
ment, Leys asked?[19] To many of his critics it was clearly essential that Orwell's

reputation as an antitotalitarian should not be allowed to eclipse his reputation as a socialist. One must not forget that the French Socialists in office since 1981 were still hopeful that they could oppose a more humane countermodel to Reaganomics and Thatcherism then in full swing. It was, therefore, a matter of ideological importance that Orwell, who by now was beginning to be commonly perceived as a "virtuous man,"[20] the advocate of a "civilised society," should be seen as a member of the self-styled camp of progress and not as conniving at cutthroat capitalism. Unsurprisingly, when *Le Monde,* which by then had long assigned to itself the mission of leading France and quite possibly mankind to a world of sweetness and light, chose to publish a passage of Leys's book, it was the one dealing with the permanency of Orwell's socialism that was selected, the initial sentence being: "Orwell's anti-totalitarian struggle was but the corollary of his socialist conviction . . . that only the defeat of totalitarianism could render the victory of socialism certain."[21]

Would Orwell have remained a socialist? Would he have become a liberal? For all the heat of the moment these questions soon lost their importance as the French socialist government, after three disastrous years, rediscovered and, discreetly but very earnestly, set about practicing most of the virtues of liberal capitalism. Besides, asked Jean-François Revel, an influential political pundit, were they really apposite? The central issue was not what Orwell himself would have become but what his novel demonstrated, namely that for there being liberals and socialists, a Right and a Left, there must be democratic pluralism. The dividing line did not run between the democratic Right and the democratic Left but between democracy and dictatorship.

By 1984, then, Orwell may still have been comparatively unknown to the general public,[22] but for French intellectuals and the reasonably educated classes he had become firmly established as one of the icons of mainstream political thinking, a democratic socialist or simply a democrat but certainly not somebody likely to take one into uncharted ideological country, well beyond the conventional boundaries of the political and social debate. It was the fall of the Berlin Wall, spelling the end of the cold war, that was going to change and radicalize the nature of Orwell's contribution to intellectual life in France.

Hardly anything to speak of was published about Orwell in the ten years that followed 1984. There was however a revival of interest in the media from the mid-1990s, when the publication of *The Collected Essays, Journalism and Letters* at last got under way, followed in 2000 and 2001 by the republication of many of Orwell's other books.[23] They received far from full coverage either in the national press or in the literary magazines, but what reviews there were, however, were appreciative, concluding unanimously that Orwell became one of the luminaries of the twentieth century by pointing out essential lies and crucial truths to his contemporaries. Obviously Orwell's late-1990s commentators were seduced by what Lionel Trilling once called Orwell's peculiar "quality of mind": "It is difficult to be always in agreement with him," *La Quinzaine littéraire* wrote, "but how can one not be impressed by his clear-thinking and by his uprightness when . . . he shows what a free thought, a straight look, a pointed sentence can do to unravel modern confusion."[24] Moreover Orwell's iconoclasm was of the right (or is it left?) type, of the sort that made him agreeable to all sincere liberals and staunch progressives since it left no doubt that he was the friend of humanity. After all, *Le*

Monde declared, he was an enemy of the politically correct principally when it consisted in saying that the USSR was the land of freedom.[25] Otherwise he disliked the American way of life and the tyranny of the market,[26] and though he lambasted the socialist intelligentsia, he did the same to Kipling, Lawrence, Wells.[27] Throughout his work he was visibly on the side of exploited workers, homeless people, the classless society, justice, equality, and democracy. The Right tried to "annex" him said *L'Evénement du Jeudi,* but that made absolutely no sense. Orwell was simply "a progressive who could not tolerate the lies issuing from Moscow."[28]

It was still his exposure of the Soviet Union and Soviet communism, therefore, that made Orwell, if not a saint, at least a martyr. To the left-wing *Nouvel Observateur,* the mental, moral, and literary strain of political writing in defense of truth literally killed him.[29] For the liberal *Commentaire,* there was no doubt that the denunciation of Marxism was Orwell's chief merit and that *Animal Farm* was one of the ten most important books of the twentieth century.[30] But now Orwell was no longer perceived merely as a paladin of the free world but as Saint George killing the dragon of communism. *Le Nouvel Observateur* had no hesitation in asserting that he was a major contributor to the collapse of the Berlin Wall and "the debacle of the great dealers in State falsehoods."[31]

After 1989, then, could Orwell become anything but a past master? It was the view that he had tried to make the world safe from totalitarianism that had made him famous. Now that the geopolitical bipolarization which so concerned him was gone, possibly thanks to him, was there a place for him elsewhere than in the history of ideas? To these questions *Commentaire* replied that Orwell's role as a model and guide was certainly not yet over, for what was crucial was that even when he was close to the far left he never stopped believing in the essentiality of democracy, in its centrality even in revolutionary times.[32] Democracy had become, in the discourse of the Great and the Good of this world, the global panacea for all types of economic, social, and political evils, and Orwell seemingly still had all the required credentials to remain recommended reading and play a major part in current debates—on the side of the mainstream—as the need arose. Except that while these reassuring noises were being made, somebody came in and snatched the icon.

The body snatcher was Jean-Claude Michéa, who teaches philosophy in the old university town of Montpellier in the south of France.[33] Convinced that Orwell's critics had not succeeded in "apprehending the true meaning of [his] theoretical works,"[34] Michéa set himself the task of radicalizing him in three books written since 1995: one focused on Orwell's writings (*Orwell, anarchiste tory,* 2000) and two in which Orwell is repeatedly referred to in order to provide political guidance and ideological anchorage (*L'Enseignement de l'ignorance et ses conditions modernes,* 1999; *Impasse Adam Smith,* 2002[35]).

Michéa's fundamental belief is that under the impact of what he calls the capitalist modernization of life, the world will sooner or later be "ecologically unsustainable and anthropologically impossible."[36] Through laissez-faire and free trade, global capitalism has destroyed old, established communities and social relations, the traditions, customs, and values that still obstructed it. With the collaboration of "the new world elites"[37] of politics and the media, capitalism has spawned a mass culture of low entertainments, cheap thrills, and omnipresent advertising that have turned man into a voracious consumer, a pathetic pleasure seeker whose bondage to dictated lifestyles grows by the day.

Things have come to such a pass because the Left never was a serious enemy of capitalism. Michéa draws a distinction between "socialism"—working class, egalitarian, antimechanistic, antimodern—and the "Left," merely the positivist side of the liberalism born of the Enlightenment. With Adam Smith and the classical economists, capitalism set itself up as the historical agent of that progress and emancipation wished for by liberalism. According to Michéa, the Left had entertained the same ideals since the days of Saint-Simon, but it claimed to be able to carry out the political, technical, and moral modernization of society in a less messy way than liberal capitalism, and so for quite a while the Left had the working classes on its side. But with the obvious failure of the Soviet system it became difficult to run capitalism down. There did not seem to be any valid alternative, especially after the last attempt at a state-controlled economy lamentably failed in France between 1981 and 1983.

Meanwhile capitalism had realized that it could hugely increase its profits if a certain number of bourgeois value with which it had traditionally cohabited— thrift, morality, self-denial—were thrown overboard and man became a mere desiring machine. Osmosis could thus become effective between a "second Left" devoid of any economic project of its own, incapable of any radical criticism of capitalism, turned libertarian and permissive in the aftermath of May 1968, and latter-day capitalism,[38] which was itself doing its damnedest to promote hedonism. So long as the Left could persuade itself that each act of hedonism was a blow against a stuffy, stultifying, bourgeois, reactionary order—in actual fact defunct, but perpetually referred to as a menace—the liberal-libertarian axis could expand and become the dominant ideology. It is this ideology, born of the "merger" of capitalism and socialism, that in the past twenty years or so has atomized, decivilized, and Disneyfied society. Recently one of the most perceptive observers of contemporary intellectual life, Pascal Bruckner, has coined for it the Orwellian-sounding name of Capsoc.[39] It is what was waiting in ambush for mankind at the further end of "the Adam Smith cul-de-sac" from which one can only escape by moving in reverse.[40]

In Michéa's dissection of the capitalist project and in his working out of a radical alternative, two fundamental influences are at work: those of Christopher Lasch and Orwell.[41] There are many convergences between Michéa and Lasch (the villains and the alternatives are very similar), whose best-known works Michéa has had translated and published in France.[42] However it is Orwell whom he openly claims as his mentor.[43] He focuses mainly on the 1968 version of *The Collected Essays, Journalism and Letters of George Orwell,* and his book on Orwell is basically a reading of these in conjunction with *Nineteen Eighty-Four;* only in the second edition (2000) does Michéa refer to *Homage to Catalonia* and *The Road to Wigan Pier,* and with the exception of *Nineteen Eighty-Four* the novels are ignored, even those that are most Laschian in their denunciation of the shoddiness of modern civilization. Michéa never mentions *Keep the Aspidistra Flying* and devotes only one brief footnote to *Coming Up for Air,* even though he sees it as "one of the most interesting and most neglected of Orwell's novels."[44] Thus Michéa's Orwell is very much a truncated Orwell. His ambition, however, is not to write a critique of Orwell's oeuvre, but to represent him as the thinker of "the New Resistance."[45]

What Michéa likes about Orwell is first of all his refusal of the materialist utopia, his suspicion that the conditions of life in a fully mechanized universe somehow make for an impoverished and dehumanized existence.[46] This opinion that the consumer society may be dysgenic was bound to appeal to Michéa, whose writings are clearly underpinned by an immense detestation of life in the modern world. On two occasions he reminds his readers that Orwell regarded the mountain Berbers of Morocco, for all their primitive way of life, as healthier and happier than their English contemporaries,[47] proof that he had succeeded in uncoupling socialism from the worship of efficiency and mechanization, glass and concrete. Reading Orwell, one learns that socialism is not merely another name for "the complete and unlimited modernisation of the world"; one learns how to look at the world not "ideologically" but "exactly," which is crucial in not becoming an ally of consumer capitalism.[48]

To be convinced that today is not necessarily better than yesterday and worse than tomorrow is to cease to believe that a transformation of the world unavoidably implies a total break with the past; it is to become aware, like Winston Smith in Mr. Charrington's antique shop[49] that no decent future society[50] will be built if certain ethical and social values from the past are not recovered. That is the vital meaning of Winston's revolt, which is a "conservative revolt"[51]: "Not only are conservative leanings compatible with the revolutionary spirit, but History shows that they are generally its sine qua non, and that the initial desire to merely retain ancient things often results in the most radical transformations."[52]

Using Orwell's essay on Dickens, "Raffles and Miss Blandish," and his 1938 review of Jack Common's *The Freedom of the Streets,* Michéa tries to demonstrate that, according to Orwell, these conservative defenses were to be found in the common people alone, that there existed "a moral dignity peculiar to the exploited working-class." These considerations inevitably direct Michéa to the concept of "common decency," which runs through all his books as the ultimate touchstone for intellectual and political honesty and for which he provides a definition on several occasions, seeing it as "that common sense that warns us that certain things are not done,"[53] an inability to dominate and exploit one's fellow men, a natural disposition toward kindness, solidarity, and uprightness which alone can foster a true sense of community and make a decent society sustainable.[54] In the days of Orwell these qualities made "ordinary people" deaf to the sirens of totalitarianism. Now, Michéa believes, common decency is the key not only to a last-ditch resistance to the "economic horror"[55] engendered by transnational capitalism[56] but to a counterattack that still has a slim chance of ushering in a new social organization which will be "truly human, that is to say free, equal and decent."[57]

The struggle is almost desperate, for "capitalist modernity" creates both a world that is unbearable and individuals that can bear with it,[58] but there is a little time left and there is evidence that the moral code of the common people survives in places and can resurface at times.[59] If men could be reawoken to "their vast anthropological and moral legacy,"[60] then, perhaps, their minds would be "decolonized," a radical critique of the economic representation of the world as it emerged from the Enlightenment would become possible,[61] and a cultural revolution could take place that might bring the great wall erected by "bourgeois political economy"[62] crashing down like the Berlin Wall.[63] Humanity would then travel back from atomization to association. For this delicate maneuver Orwell, with his Tory anarchism,[64] supplies according to Michéa both the tactics—not a return to but a detour via the past—and the aims—the precedence of humanity over technology and profit making, the blessings of a simpler life.[65]

Orwell becomes once again, therefore, a Giant Killer.[66] After contributing to the collapse of the actual Berlin Wall by his writings against totalitarianism, he becomes in Michéa's books the moral and intellectual dynamiter of that capitalism that leads both to redundancies and the swinishness of "overmodernity."[67] Thus a new role for Orwell in the early twenty-first century takes form: the undermining of that "axiomatics of self-interest"[68] that has underpinned political economy since Adam Smith and the promotion of an antiutilitarian society that will put an end to "ultra-liberal desocialisation," will have "giving" as one of its core values and will thus reassert the primacy of bonding over owning.[69] These, according to Michéa, are the characteristics of a decent rather than a good, that is, affluent, society. The choice of the former, however, was fraught with political dangers until Orwell came along and changed the perspective.

Past thinkers, from Harrington to Rousseau,[70] convinced that man was fundamentally selfish, could only imagine a victory of rectitude over the corruption necessarily engendered by commerce and the thirst for riches through a superhuman act of will that often meant in history a despotism of virtue exercised by those capable of such an act over the less heroic mass of their fellow men—and in modern times this despotism often assumed the darker form of totalitarianism, thus supplying liberalism with the best alibi for its self-proclaimed supremacy over all other polities.[71] But Orwell has the answer to this other cul-de-sac because he does not see virtue, or common decency, as the result of a heroic effort to overcome one's instinct for self-seeking but as a quality that is not only within reach of ordinary people but indeed already part of their nature and palpable in their daily behavior "in normal times,"[72] that is, when capitalist modernity does not rule the earth.[73] In other words, by thinking laterally,[74] Orwell blazed a new trail for mankind: "Thus Orwell swept away all prior approaches at a stroke, and gained a sufficient philosophical footing to equally dismiss both the republican (and later, totalitarian) worship of the virtuous State, and the liberal worship of selfish calculation."[75]

Orwell is thus eminently "subversive"[76] and that is why, Michéa thinks, as in the case of many other "incorrect" books, the translation of Orwell's essays came very late and, even more revealingly, passed largely unnoticed. The aim was to keep the French reading public as much as possible in the dark about what Michéa calls "Orwell's critique of the current state of things." And should some people be curious enough to go and see for themselves, there will always be "official critics," those whose job is to present the "mercantile modernization of the world" as in keeping with God's will, to launch a smear campaign as they already did in 1996 when Orwell's so-called black list was published.[77]

As in England, the black list affair was in France a storm in a teacup: a few sensationalist headlines followed by very tame articles that were quite reassuring as to Orwell's intentions and integrity.[78] Yet it enraged a number of people[79] who, like Michéa, were beginning to look on Orwell as an essential ally in their struggle against Capsoc. They saw it all[80] as a setup intended to deflect people from asking embarrassing questions about Orwell's importance today, notably: "Would not Orwell's analysis of totalitarianism have some validity in the global society in which we live?"[81]—a question that takes us a step further into Orwell's contemporary relevance. Not only are his writings indispensable to arm us with moral and social guidelines to reconstruct society as Michéa suggests; more immediately they are essential to grasp the true political nature of the prevailing Capsoc regime.

Michéa may have been the first in France to argue that because of the philosophical origins of the collusion between capitalism and the would-be party of progress it has now become impossible to outflank the former on its left, but he certainly has not been the only one these last few years to highlight the rapprochement between the "modernizing Left" and the liberal Right. A growing number of better-known intellectuals now consider Capsoc to be a reality,[82] and to deplore the deepening rift between ordinary people and the ruling elites has almost become a banality. Most of these people, however, are not yet inclined to reach the conclusion that neoliberal regimes are totalitarian,[83] and even less so that they must not be reformed but terminated.

Others have no such qualms, perhaps because they have read Orwell (whom their more prestigious counterparts seldom quote) and have concluded that between Oceania and modern western society there is a difference in form and degree but not in essence. This is a view that underlies a book on *Nineteen Eighty-Four* written in 2000 by François Brune titled *Under Big Brother's Sun,* with the revealing subtitle *A Handbook on 1984 for the Use of the Twenty-first Century.*[84] Brune makes his case about the contemporaneity of Orwell by comparing practices in the world of Big Brother with current realities and finding striking parallels. Far from being of purely historical interest as an anticommunist tract, *Nineteen Eighty-Four* now provides a good benchmarch against which the "acts of oppression" of liberal capitalism can be measured.[85]

In the eyes of a smallish group of writers, essayists, and journalists, such acts are already sufficiently numerous and consistent to form a pattern that leaves no doubt that market democracies are societies whose totalitarianism is very real but stealthy and hard to detect—were it not for the yardsticks provided by Orwell. These people do not form a school,[86] but to all of them the customary right/left cleavage has become meaningless and ideological fissures run differently across the political terrain: they separate the supporters of Capsoc from those Michéa calls "the dissenters from modernity." These may be defined in varying proportions as holist, antiutilitarian, antiliberal, hostile to globalization and cosmopolitan democracy, preoccupied with the destruction of cultural identities and historical communities, and sickened by what European civilization has become. There is, of course, a strong dose of populism in their politics and inevitably they are antiestablishment.

The hard core of their literature can be read in two rather heretical cultural reviews, *Immédiatement* and *Eléments.*[87] The central argument, clearly inspired by Lasch,[88] is grounded on the certainty that in Western societies liberal democracy is gradually sinking into oligarchy because it has been confiscated by a "New Class," "Hyperclass," "Establishment," or "Ascendancy,"[89] the functionaries and profiteers of the media age and of transnational capitalism. Their aim is certainly the completion of the kind of "hedonistic utopia" portrayed by Orwell in his "Pleasure Spots" essay,[90] a more vulgar version of Huxley's dystopia. But for the time being History has not yet deserted our societies, and the New Class cannot but be aware of the ravages of globalization. Revolt born of hardship or cultural resistance is not yet an impossibility; it may even remain a permanent menace if, as many anti-Capsoc authors believe, free trade does not deliver the dream of evergrowing prosperity but the nightmare of a Hobbesian world.[91] To the New Class, Oceanian methods of social control remain indispensable to stifle all discontent.

As a consequence, contemporary society becomes, like Oceania, a world of propaganda, slogans, and untruths. It is a society that, like that of *Nineteen Eighty-Four,* prevents its citizens from breaking ranks by claiming both great victories and the permanence of great perils: Michéa's *Impasse Adam Smith* begins with a passage in which the "telescreens of the modern world" in the same breath inform the population of yet another great economic leap forward and of the need, given the state of global competion, to work harder and retire older.[92] Thus, by the carrot of consumerism and the stick of mass unemployment, but also by the old stratagem of bread and circuses, by plunging youth into a parallel cyber universe, by television and advertising, by dumbing down, freedom has become slavery and ignorance strength.[93] The goal is to stop all serious indictment of the liberal system. After the fall of the Berlin Wall and the demise of communism, liberalism began to behave like any other ideology. It too could now afford to claim it embodied absolute principles and display a Manichean vision of the world, a messianic will to reshape society according to its dogmas. Inevitably liberalism started to exhibit distrust and intolerance of all those who did not exactly toe the line,[94] hence the increasing surveillance under which we all live. Every one of our acts is, or will soon be, recorded, computerized, combined, or compared with others in one gigantic database. The ultimate consequences have been fictionalized by Jérôme Leroy[95] in a short novel entitled in French *Big Sister,* in which an ultraliberal panoptic society (in fact, the European Union) is effectively ruled by a computer,[96] Big Sister, whose main concern is to draw up hit lists[97] of all those who might prove a danger to the system.

At present, when means of control are not yet so sophisticated, the methods of the neoliberal oligarchs look even more reminiscent of those of the masters of Oceania, and Goldstein-type scapegoats play a crucial part in the preservation of the regime. The anti-Capsoc intellectuals are convinced that the people are kept in line by the periodic invention, and intense media coverage of, objectively nonexistent neofascist perils: a clever ploy to frighten people out of their wits with dangers belonging to the past, while politicians and big business carry on with their destructive policies and by contrast can even pass themselves off as good democrats, honest citizens, and reasonable men. In an *Immédiatement* article, "Jörg Haider, a post-Orwellian hero," Sébastien Lapaque found no other explanation for the demonization of Haider,[98] nor indeed for the hysterical campaign, not unlike the hate sessions of *Nineteen Eighty-Four,* staged against the radical Right candidate who by no stretch of the imagination could be supposed to obtain more than 25 percent of the votes[99] between the first and the second rounds of the French presidential election in the spring of 2002. It persuaded most of those who had originally voted against the right-of-center representative of the system to reelect him triumphantly,[100] in practice adding to the legitimacy of neoliberalism:[101]

Democracies in which public opinion cannot be discounted wish to be judged on their opponents, not on their results. The Manichean vision of the world of their leaders ceaselessly brings forth new Enemies of the People, new vessels of Hate whose function it is to unhinge the minds of the citizens, to make them forget their free will and love the power that presides over their destinies. Consequently antifascism now comes before fascism.[102]

It is certainly intellectually risky to undertake an Orwellian critique of the modern world with arguments Orwell used in an altogether different historical and political context long ago.[103] However, if one is satisfied that despite its dated plot *Nineteen Eighty-Four* remains fully pertinent because Orwell had guessed that the defeat of Nazism or communism would not necessarily signify the end of totalitarianism,[104] and presumably would have carried on fighting it just as he would have continued to denounce the meretriciousness of modern society,[105] then it is possible to consider that in his works he pointed out certain ominous features of our modernity, certain disturbing trends at work in our world.[106] Whether he would have followed Michéa in trying the "only unexplored way"[107] out of the Adam Smith cul-de-sac, whether he would have had no problem equating market democracy with totalitarianism, is another matter, but at least it means that he ceases to be a past master and becomes once again our contemporary, a decipherer of "these dark times,"[108] to some an emancipator.[109]

NOTES

1. *Le Monde* produced a short obituary ("Mort de George Orwell," January 24, 1950, 2) presenting Orwell as the author of *Animal Farm* and *Nineteen Eighty-Four* (no other titles were mentioned), a man "whose work will leave its stamp on contemporary Anglo-Saxon literature." But see also Jean Plumyène, "Mort d'Orwell: RAS," *Le Magazine littéraire,* December 1983, 4. The communist press ignored both his death and the publication of his last novel in France. Unlike Arthur Koestler, Orwell had not even become the butt of Marxist abuse.

2. Orwell, and more generally British literature and culture between the wars, became popular subjects for doctoral research in France in the 1960s. They went out of fashion in the mid-1980s. It is a measure of Orwell's current standing in French academic circles today that there was no Orwell conference planned in France for 2003.

3. Maurice Nadeau, "Relisons Orwell," *La Quinzaine littéraire,* May 16, 1981, 16; Nicolas Weill, "Quand Orwell dénonçait au Foreign Office les 'cryptocommunistes,'" *Le Monde,* July 13, 1996, 26; Orwell, *The Collected Essays, Journalism and Letters of George Orwell* (Harmondsworth: Penguin Books, 1970), iv, 101, 112, 170–71 (hereafter referred to as *CEJL*).

4. The novel, however, first came out on June 30, 1950, and a longish review by Marcel Brion appeared in *Le Monde* on July 20 ("Un roman de George Orwell: 1984," 7). Brion, considering the way the world was going, saw the novel as a far more plausible prognosis than Huxley's *Ape and Essence,* published the year before in France, and aptly summed it up as a terrifying love story in which men were eventually taken to pieces and remade so that they might love the very principle of evil. A rather more misleading review of the English version had been published in *Le Monde* on December 3, 1949 (Robert Escarpit, "Cauchemars et utopies," 3). Confusingly, the world of Oceania was described as "stern and inhuman," but the novel as "an amusing but facile caricature of the soviet regime," the conclusion being that the message of the book was that the future belonged to the proles because they were still able to enjoy their pint at the corner pub while Winston was too much obsessed with the past.

5. Les Editions Champ Libre sometimes commissioned new and better translations. They also translated for the first time *The Road to Wigan Pier.* But *Burmese Days* was not

republished, and to this day *A Clergyman's Daughter* has left every French publisher indifferent.

6. There was a dossier devoted to Orwell as early as May 16, 1981, in *La Quinzaine littéraire.*

7. "It's about time to discover Orwell's essays, novels, reportage," Robert Louit concluded in "1984, hier et demain," *Le Magazine littéraire,* December 1983, 18. Or Simon Leys in *Orwell ou l'horreur de la politique* (Paris: Herman, 1984), 1–2: "In France he remains, if not unknown, at least widely misunderstood. . . . When French people read Orwell, it is usually from an angle worthy of *The Reader's Digest*: his work is then scaled down to the format of an anti-communist war-machine." It is significant, too, that *La Quinzaine littéraire*'s May 1981 dossier was for a large part taken up with mere abstracts of all the books by Orwell that had been translated into French.

8. Jean-Daniel Jurgensen, *Orwell ou la route de 1984* (Paris: Robert Laffont, 1983); and Simon Leys, *Orwell ou l'horreur de la politique.* Academics, of course, read or published a number of papers on Orwell in their own conferences or little magazines. As before, very little of this activity seeped into the quality newspapers or even the literary magazines targeting the cultured public. Throughout the 1984 celebrations the press made no reference whatsoever to Orwellian research in France.

9. Thus on several occasions Orwell became the most significant writer of the twentieth century.

10. André Glucksmann, "Camarade Big Brother," *Le Magazine littéraire,* December 1983, 28–29.

11. See, for instance, Pierre Daix, "Un diagnostic de la grande maladie du siècle," *Le Quotidien de Paris,* September 28, 1982, 29, and Michel Heller, "Le novlangue, langue officielle d'un tiers de l'humanité," *Le Monde,* December 30, 1983, 10–11.

12. Jean Gattegno, "Du bon usage de l'anticommunisme primaire," *La Quinzaine littéraire,* May 16, 1981, 16.

13. A point made by Anthony Burgess in "*1984* au rendez-vous de 1984," *Le Point,* January 2, 1984, 65, and by Jeanyves Guérin in "Pour Orwell," *Esprit,* January 1984, 15. Allusions to *Nineteen Eighty-Four* were also useful to many to make their point that should Yuri Andropov invade France, he would have no difficulty in finding among communists the necessary personnel to distort truth and rewrite history (see *L'Express,* February 3, 1984, 99 (unsigned): "*L'Huma* persiste et signe" about a book entitled *Le Ministère de la vérité* that exposed the communist *L'Humanité* newspaper's changes of line over Cambodia and the Khmer Rouge according to what was coming from Moscow).

14. Jurgensen, *Orwell ou la route de 1984,* 26.

15. Jurgensen, *Orwell ou la route de 1984,* 89–104; also Simon Leys, *Orwell ou l'horreur de la politique,* 49–50.

16. Leys, *Orwell ou l'horreur de la politique,* 55.

17. Leys, *Orwell ou l'horreur de la politique,* 56. See also Jurgensen, *Orwell ou la route de 1984,* 40, for the same idea.

18. Orwell's political usefulness to the free world certainly accounted for the virulence with which some articles trying to uncouple *Nineteen Eighty-Four* from the contemporary context were received. Thus "one Professor Stansky" was taken severely to task for refusing to see, in an article published in *The Herald Tribune* for December 28, 1983, that the society of *Nineteen Eighty-Four* was the archetypal "communist society," and for claiming that Orwell's prophecies had not come true since many of his fears had not materialized in the democratic world (Jean-François Revel, "Est-il trop clair?", *Le Point,* February 6, 1984, 109).

19. Leys, *Orwell ou l'horreur de la politique,* 47–52.

20. Gil Delannoi, "La logique de la lucidité," *Esprit,* January 1984, 22: "A virtuous man, actuated by a deep concern for probity and moral behavior."

21. Simon Leys, "L'horreur de la politique," *Le Monde,* December 30, 1983, 9, 11. See also Jurgensen, *Orwell ou la route de 1984,* 66 and Gil Delannoi, "La logique de la lucidité,"

23. Delannoi concludes that Orwell would not have liked his name to be attached solely to the antitotalitarian struggle. He sought all his life for "positive values" and certainly was not a man to be satisfied with the triumph of "the lesser evil." *The Lion and the Unicorn* was also much quoted, never being seen as an occasional piece but as an essay that reflected Orwell's deep social and political convictions so much that he was not likely to disown its content even ten years and a world war later (see Leys, *Orwell ou l'horreur de la politique,* 49–50). No less significantly *Le Magazine littéraire* (December 1983, 39–40) chose to translate "Literature and Totalitarianism," in which Orwell considered that "the period of free capitalism is coming to an end" and that the challenge for societies in the West would be "to evolve a form of socialism which is not totalitarian."

22. Until late April 1984, the weekly charts of best-selling books showed *Nineteen Eighty-Four* to be in the ten most sold novels (at least among paperbacks) most weeks. None of the other titles, however, ever appeared. The film adaptation of *Nineteen Eighty-Four* was released in November and got a good, if not enthusiastic, press review, but its reception by the public was lukewarm and it was not shown for very long. In the Paris area, it ran for fifteen weeks and 235,834 people went and saw it, a very average figure; in its first week, in November, it was in competition with eight other new films and was only fourth in terms of spectators (see *Le Film français,* no. 2011, November 16, 1984, 2, and no. 2027, March 8, 1985, 72). The Orwell Conference organized in early April at Strasbourg under the aegis of the Council of Europe caused very little stir (however, see *Le Figaro:* "1984: les vérités d'Orwell," April 2, 1984, 29, and "Le colloque 'Orwell 1984' à Strasbourg: protéger l'Europe des totalitarismes," April 6, 1984, 23). The principal conference of the year, however, was probably the venue at Cérisy-la-Salle, a small village in Normandy, August 6–16, on "George Orwell's *1984* and the Modern Anti-Utopia." Several excellent papers were read, but significantly the proceedings were never published. No publisher was ready to risk his money on Orwell, even in 1984.

23. The first volume of the *Collected Essays* was published in late 1995, followed by the other three in the summer of 1996, September 1998, and late 2001. *Keep the Aspidistra Flying, Homage to Catalonia,* and *Coming Up for Air* were republished in early 2000, and *Down and Out in Paris and London* and *The Road to Wigan Pier* were published in early 2001.

24. Pierre Pachet, "Le combat de George Orwell," *La Quinzaine littéraire,* July 3, 1996, 15.

25. Alain Frachon, "Quand Orwell fustigeait le 'politiquement correct,'" *Le Monde,* January 27, 1999, 30 (on Orwell's preface to *Animal Farm*).

26. Eric Conan, "Orwell, gêneur et rebelle," *L'Express,* January 10, 2001, 47.

27. Philippe Dagen, "Descente aux enfers de la misère," *Le Monde,* April 6, 2001 (*Le Monde des Poches* Supplement, p. iv).

28. Eric Dior, "Non, Orwell n'était pas une balance!" *L'Evénement du Jeudi,* August 8, 1996, 61.

29. Claude Roy, "Orwell est de retour," *Le Nouvel Observateur,* November 9, 1995, 110. See also Jean Chesneaux, "Orwell, un écrivant," *La Quinzaine littéraire,* December 15, 1995, 7.

30. "'Selon les règles admises de l'antique liberté': Préface inédite à Animal Farm," *Commentaire,* vol. 21 (Winter 1998–99): 957. *Commentaire,* however, did not dismiss *Nineteen Eighty-Four* as irrelevant. Two issues later, it included a text entitled "How Communism Lost Power," which was an excerpt from Goldstein's Black Book on the "four ways in which a ruling group can fall from power" (*Commentaire,* vol. 22 [Summer 1999]: 326).

31. Roy, "Orwell est de retour," 110.

32. Charles Jacquier, "George Orwell ou l'impossible neutralité," *Commentaire,* vol. 21 (Autumn 1998): 859.

33. On Michéa's background see an interesting interview of him in a little Montpellier sheet, *La Gazette,* no. 595, September 10, 1999. It can be found on the Internet at <perso.club-

internet.fr/sergbelh/jcmichea.html>. Also, Elisabeth Lévy, "Jean-Claude Michéa, l'intello qui nous veut du bien," *Marianne,* January 20, 2003, 66–67.

34. Jean-Claude Michéa, *Orwell, anarchiste tory* (Castelnau-le-Lez: Editions Climats, 2000), 65.

35. *The Teaching of Ignorance and Its Modern Context; The Adam Smith Cul-de-sac.*

36. Michéa, *L'Enseignement de l'ignorance et ses conditions modernes* (Castelnau-le-Lez: Editions Climats, 1999), 79.

37. Michéa, *L'Enseignement de l'ignorance,* 32.

38. "Terminal capitalism," in the words of Michéa, like terminal disease.

39. Bruckner coined the term in an essay on the various guises of anticapitalism (and the excesses of consumerism), *Misère de la prospérité: La religion marchande et ses ennemis* (Paris: Grasset, 2002), 179.

40. The full title of Michéa's latest book is *Impasse Adam Smith: Brèves remarques sur l'impossibilité de dépasser le capitalisme sur sa gauche* (Castelnau-le-Lez: Editions Climats, 2002). The subtitle translates as "short remarks about the impossibility of outflanking capitalism on its left."

41. Although, going by Michéa's own brief references, one should not neglect either Adorno and his theory that a critique of the Enlightenment is a necessary prerequisite to a critique of capitalism or the situationist Guy Debord and his "society of the spectacle" in which men are no more than the manipulated consumers of ersatz existences.

42. *La Révolte des élites et la trahison de la démocratie* [The Revolt of the Elites and the Betrayal of Democracy] in 1996, *La Culture du narcissisme* [The Culture of Narcissism] in 2000, *Culture de masse ou culture populaire* [Mass Culture Reconsidered] in 2001, *Le seul et vrai paradis* [The True and Only Heaven: Progress and Its Critics] in 2002, were all published by Climats, the small publishing house of which Michéa is one of the pillars. The substantial prefaces to Lasch's books were all written by Michéa who regards Lasch as "one of the most penetrating minds of this century" (*L'Enseignement de l'ignorance,* 11).

43. Early in *Impasse Adam Smith* Michéa quotes at length from the passage in *The Road to Wigan Pier* in which Orwell observes that at a time when everyone should be a socialist, more and more people desert socialism because of its worship of progress and modernity; Michéa concludes: "The short essay that follows has no other purpose but to expand these few remarks as methodically as possible" (*Impasse Adam Smith,* 14).

44. Michéa, *Orwell, anarchiste tory,* 132.

45. Michéa, *Orwell, anarchiste tory,* 142.

46. Michéa, *Orwell, anarchiste tory,* 88–89.

47. Michéa, *Orwell, anarchiste tory,* 81; *Impasse Adam Smith,* 86.

48. Michéa, *Orwell, anarchiste tory,* 85–86, 140–41.

49. Michéa, *Orwell, anarchiste tory,* 94. Michéa also quotes another revealing view of Orwell's on this from a 1948 review of Osbert Sitwell's memoirs (90).

50. Interestingly, Climats published the French translation of Avishai Margalit's *The Decent Society* in a series whose editor is Michéa. Margalit himself considers that the best source of inspiration for his decent society was Orwell's socialism (A. Margalit, *La société décente* [Castelnau-le-Lez: Editions Climats, 1999], 17; see 5–6 in the Harvard University Press edition of 1996).

51. Michéa, *Orwell, anarchiste tory,* 136.

52. Michéa, *Impasse Adam Smith,* 121. See also, *Orwell, anarchiste tory,* 134.

53. Michéa, *Orwell, anarchiste tory,* 29.

54. Michéa, *L'Enseignement de l'ignorance,* 28; *Impasse Adam Smith,* 96.

55. This is a convenient phrase. It formed the title of a best-selling book that, however, lost much credibility by equating liberal globalization with genocide. Michéa never cites it (Vivianne Forrester, *L'Horreur économique* [Paris: Fayard, 1995]).

56. Michéa, *L'Enseignement de l'ignorance,* 111–12.

57. Michéa, *Impasse Adam Smith,* 12.

58. Michéa, *Impasse Adam Smith,* 54.

59. Michéa perceives a manifestation of this moral code in the results of the first round of the French presidential election in April 2002, when nearly two-thirds of those who went to the polls unexpectedly gave their votes to lesser candidates (see *Impasse Adam Smith,* 80–81).

60. Michéa, *Orwell, anarchiste tory,* 134.

61. Michéa, *Impasse Adam Smith,* 53.

62. Michéa, *Orwell, anarchiste tory,* 138.

63. Michéa, *Impasse Adam Smith,* 52–55, 97, 105.

64. Michéa regards Orwell as a Tory due to his refusal to reject the past and his resorting to traditional values to prepare a better future and as an anarchist because he does not believe that salvation will come from the state, nor from any kind of economic mechanism, but from a set of moral and social values applied to life in society (see *Impasse Adam Smith,* 93).

65. Michéa finds this idea of a simpler life well illustrated by Orwell's description of life in Barcelona and his 1946 essay on "Pleasure Spots."

66. And thus, in Orwell's own view, a perfect symbol of the Western world's moral tradition. See Orwell's reference to Jack the Giant Killer in "Raffles and Miss Blandish" (*CEJL,* 3:258).

67. Michéa, *Orwell, anarchiste tory,* 92 ("surmodernité") and 111 ("surmodernisation").

68. Michéa, *L'Enseignement de l'ignorance,* 89.

69. Michéa, *L'Enseignement de l'ignorance,* 135.

70. On this point Michéa relies on Quentin Skinner's *Liberty Before Liberalism.*

71. Michéa, *Impasse Adam Smith,* 98–101.

72. Michéa, *Impasse Adam Smith,* 101.

73. This total identification of Orwell with the values and conduct of ordinary people leads to the one serious error of interpretation in Michéa's books. In his analysis of *Nineteen Eighty-Four* he totally dissociates Orwell from Winston Smith and refuses to consider that Winston's political conduct is fully conditioned by Orwell's gloomy apprehensions when he was writing his novel. On the contrary, Michéa believes that through Winston's failed rebellion Orwell wished to show what must not be done. Instead of joining hands with the people, even though he sees salvation only through them, Winston prefers to join the Brotherhood, another clique, another party whose values, as they show through the inhuman deeds required of Winston and Julia, do not partake of common decency. Refusing to go by what he intellectually perceives, that the only hope lies in the moral code, in the "socialism," of the proles, Winston is bound to fail. But this is clearly contradicted by the text. Nowhere does Orwell allow his readers, or Winston himself, to believe that there are true revolutionary potentialities in the proles as they are described or that they embody the "democratic socialism" Orwell claimed to have been his main inspiration since 1936 (see "Why I Write," *CEJL,* 1:28). Yet this is what Michéa concludes (*Orwell, anarchiste tory,* 61–62), evidently taking liberties with Orwell's text and thought. But for the sake of his demonstration, he must have an Orwell pinning all his hopes on the common people, especially in his best-known and last book.

74. "One of the major attractions of Orwell's thought is that it starts off almost without fail from where most traditional analyses have to give up" (*Impasse Adam Smith,* 91)

75. Michéa, *Impasse Adam Smith,* 101–2.

76. Michéa, *L'Enseignement de l'ignorance,* 95.

77. Michéa, *Orwell, anarchiste tory,* 7–9. According to Michéa, this also explains the little success of Lasch's books in France. They are simply ignored.

78. See Nicolas Weill, "Quand Orwell dénonçait au Foreign Office les 'cryptocommunistes,'" *Le Monde,* July 13, 1996, 26; Eric Dior, "Orwell en mouchard anticommuniste," *Libération,* July 15, 1996, 33; Dior, "Non, Orwell n'était pas une balance," 60–61; J.M.M., "Brother Orwell." *L'Histoire,* no. 203 (October 1996): 11. Only the last-mentioned was truly

venomous. In 1998, when the matter of "Orwell's shopping list," as *The Daily Telegraph* put it in its leaders of June 22 (p.19), was raised again the response in France was feeble: a brief item of news in *Le Monde des Livres* of June 26, 1998, viii ("Grande-Bretagne: Orwell en Big Brother"), a passing reference in *Le Monde diplomatique* of September 1998 (Nicolas Truong, "La résistance de George Orwell," 32), and an indignant look back on the 1996 episode as it was presented by the French press in *Commentaire*'s Autumn 1998 issue (Charles Jacquier, "George Orwell ou l'impossible neutralité," 857).

79. More than the newspaper articles, it was a ninety-five-minute radio program that rather incomprehensibly raised passions. The host certainly did his best to get his guests to speak of "Orwell and the police" (his own words to me) but failed except for a few moments at the end, when one of the participants maladroitly repeated what the press had said ("Une vie, une oeuvre: George Orwell, 1903–1950," February 6, 1997, on France Culture radio station).

80. Especially in a furious pamphlet: *George Orwell devant ses calomniateurs: Quelques observations* (Paris: Editions Ivréa/Editions de l'Encyclopédie des Nuisances, 1997). It was Les Editions Ivréa and Les Editions de l'Encyclopédie des Nuisances that had jointly undertaken the publication in French of *The Collected Essays, Journalism and Letters*.

81. *George Orwell devant ses calomniateurs,* 27. A related explanation was belatedly supplied by Eric Conan in "Orwell, gêneur et rebelle," 47: that Orwell might be an "anticommunist snitch" was a rumor started by former "sixty-eighters" who, in order to feel less lonely in their betrayal, would like a world without heroes and full of renegades. The allusion was to those anarchists and libertarians of the May 1968 uprising in France, many of whom have become upholders and even practitioners of ultraliberal global capitalism.

82. Pierre-André Taguieff considers France to be run by "a great liberal, libertarian, social-democratic club" ("Une entreprise d'épuration du champ intellectuel," *Marianne,* November 11, 2002, 68) the left-wing members of which, according to Marcel Gauchet, are "emancipated bankers and switched-on technocrats" ("Les Robespierristes de la bien-pensance ont perdu," *Marianne,* December 2, 2002, 20).

83. Even though there is growing annoyance at the ever more numerous constraints, legal or otherwise, on freedom of expression in France and at the spread of political correctness. See in particular Elisabeth Lévy, *Les maîtres censeurs* (Paris: Lattès, 2002) and Emmanuelle Duverger and Robert Ménard, *La censure des bien-pensants* (Paris: Albin Michel, 2002). In "Les Robespierristes de la bien-pensance ont perdu," Marcel Gauchet thinks that what one witnesses now in France is the rise of a "democratic fundamentalism" (21).

84. François Brune, *Sous le soleil de Big Brother: Précis sur 1984 à l'usage des années 2000* (Paris: L'Harmattan, 2000). This was Brune's second book on Orwell. The first was more academic: *1984 ou le règne de l'ambivalence* (Paris: Minard, 1983).

85. Brune, *Sous le soleil de Big Brother,* 165. See also Stéphane Mandard, "Trois questions à François Brune," *Le Monde,* Supplément *Le Monde interactif,* November 1, 2000, iii.

86. Some come from the radical Right, many from the far Left, and others are orphans of Gaullism or even of royalism. Besides they are far from seeing eye to eye on every issue.

87. The former is an organ of the "national republicans" or *souverainistes* who see only perdition outside and beyond the historic nation-states. On its Web site it claims to take its inspiration from "Georges Bernanos, George Orwell, Pierre Boutang, Dominique de Roux, Simone Weil, Hannah Arendt" (see www.immediatement.com). The latter is the journal of the French "nouvelle droite" (no affinity with the Anglo-Saxon New Right), whose approach to many issues is possibly best described for brevity's sake as Nietzschean and antiuniversalist. Anti-Capsoc recusants, however, constitute a more complex galaxy that on its fringes merges into other forms of dissidence. On Orwell, the following articles have been published in *Eléments* and *Immédiatement*: Pierre Bérard, "Jean-Claude Michéa: un anarchiste conservateur?" *Eléments,* no. 101 (May 2001): 23; Emmanuel Lévy, "George Orwell, libertaire et rebelle," *Eléments,* no. 104 (March 2002): 52–56; Emmanuel Lévy, "George Orwell

et l'autre totalitarisme," *Eléments,* no. 105 (June 2002): 51–53; Falk van Gaver, "Catalunya heroica," *Immédiatement,* no. 13 (February 2000): 40; Luc Richard, "Il n'aimait pas Big Brother," *Immédiatement,* no. 16 (December 2000): 7–8; Jean-Claude Michéa, "La Dauche c'est la Groite," *Immédiatement* no. 16 (December 2000): 9–11; Jérôme Leroy, "Winston, Joseph, Bernard et les autres," *Immédiatement,* no. 16 (December 2000): 12–13; Philippe Cohen, "La vérité n'est pas ailleurs," *Immédiatement,* no. 16 (December 2000): 14–15; Xavier Perez, "George Orwell, socialiste français," *Immédiatement,* no. 16 (December 2000): 16–17; Véronique Hallereau, "Portrait d'Orwell en intellectual," *Immédiatement,* no. 16 (December 2000): 18–19; Marc Crapez, "Le pari de l'intelligence," *Immédiatement,* no. 16 (December 2000): 20–22; Sébastien Lapaque, "Jörg Haider, héros post-orwellien," *Immédiatement,* no. 16 (December 2000): 23; Véronique Hallereau, "Animal politique," *Immédiatement,* no. 22 (September 2002): 43.

88. See, for instance, Luc Richard, "Le monde selon Lasch," *Immédiatement,* no. 15 (September 2000): 17–18; Véronique Hallereau, "La révolution petty bourgeoise," *Immédiatement,* no. 23 (February 2003): 58–59; Charles Champetier, "Le peuple contre la Nouvelle Classe," *Eléments,* no. 85 (June 1996): 5–10; Norbert Kanchelkis, "Sortir de l'impasse Adam Smith avec Christopher Lasch," *Eléments,* no. 108 (April 2003): 50–53; Sébastien Lapaque, "Lasch: feu sur la subversion autorisée," *Le Figaro littéraire,* 26 April 2001, 7 (Lapaque, a young novelist and literary critic is one of the archenemy of Capsoc).

89. In French, *La Nouvelle Classe, L'Hyperclasse, L'Etablissement, La Domination.* This last is the term preferred by one of the translators of Orwell's *Essays,* Jaime Semprun, in his own very anti-Capsoc antimodern *L'abîme se repeuple* (Paris: Editions de l'Encyclopédie des Nuisances, 1997).

90. *CEJL,* 4:102–8. "Pleasure Spots" is cited by Michéa in *Orwell, anarchiste tory,* 85–86.

91. In a recent novel that is indebted to Fritz Lang, Poe, and Orwell (the proles, called here, in the French text, "the outers," are the "semislaves" of *Nineteen Eighty-Four*), Jérôme Leroy, a novelist who often contributes to *Immédiatement,* writes: "That (European) Federation that everybody presented as the end of History, the ultimate hedonistic Eden, had turned out to be the battlefield of the war of all against all" (*Bref rapport sur une très fugitive beauté* [Paris: Les Belles Lettres, 2002], 27). The novel is the vision of a world in which a small class of enormously wealthy capitalists and their well-paid managers let the workers, to whom they had promised paradise under laissez-faire, rot in their slums. But the end is nigh. . . .

92. Michéa, *Impasse Adam Smith,* 9–11.

93. See Eric Werner, *L'Après-démocratie* (Lausanne: L'Age d'Homme, 2001), 26–27. Werner is a Swiss political scientist close to the *Eléments* group. Postdemocracy is the present-day political system running capitalist societies. Sometimes Werner calls it, less cautiously, "Western neo-totalitarianism" (23). Also, Philippe Cohen, "La vérité n'est pas ailleurs," 14–15, trying to demonstrate that "1984 is not behind but in front of us"; Michéa, *Impasse Adam Smith,* 9–11, *Orwell, anarchiste tory,* 82–83; Jean-Paul Duarte, "Salauds de riches," *Immédiatement,* no. 21 (May 2002): 44.

94. Although they can be found in much of the anti-Capsoc literature, these ideas are perhaps best synthesised in Werner's *L'Après-démocratie.* The influence of Alexander Zinoviev has been considerable here. His judgment on the totalitarian future of Western societies is often cited approvingly.

95. Jérôme Leroy has been defined, together with Sébastien Lapaque and a few others, as one of those young authors who have turned antiliberalism into an aesthetics (Philippe Lacoche, review of *Les idées heureuses* by Sébastien Lapaque, in *Le Magazine littéraire,* no. 380 [October 1999]: 88).

96. The Big Sister project is said to have taken its inspiration from the American Echelon program (Jérôme Leroy, *Big Sister* [Paris: Librio, 2001], 60).

97. Via a satellite called *Miniamour,* in other words Minilove (Leroy, *Big Sister,* 63).

98. Sébastien Lapaque, "Jörg Haider, héros post-orwellien," 23.

99. According to Christian Authier ("Le fascisme ne repassera pas," *Immédiatement, no.* 22 [September 2002]: 12) it was a period when "Orwellian gramophone minds" had a field day.

100. In the second round the president of the French Republic was reelected with more than 80 percent of the votes cast, although he had scored hardly more than 20 percent in the first round.

101. Sébastien Lapaque, "Sous le regard de Big Brother: les élections à la lumière d'Orwell," *Le Figaro,* May 10, 2002, 12, and "Philippe Meyer: règlements de comptes de campagne," *Le Figaro,* September 12, 2002, 8.

102. Sébastien Lapaque, "Jörg Haider, héros post-orwellien," 23.

103. Indeed one has sometimes the feeling that Michéa, for one, reads too much into Orwell and wrenches some of the things he says out of context.

104. See Emmanuel Lévy, "George Orwell et l'autre totalitarisme," 51. The evidence is said to lie in a passage of the originally unpublished preface to *Animal Farm* in which Orwell wrote, "For all I know, by the time this book is published my view of the Soviet regime may be the generally accepted one, but what use would that be in itself? To exchange one orthodoxy for another is not necessarily an advance" ("The Freedom of the Press. By George Orwell," *The Times Literary Supplement,* September 15, 1972, 1039). A sentence which Jaime Semprun regards as a premonition of the advent of political correctness and intellectual intolerance in liberal democracies (*L'Abîme se repeuple,* 13–14).

105. See the conclusion of Xavier Perez, "George Orwell, socialiste français," 17.

106. The conclusion of Emmanuel Lévy, "George Orwell, libertaire et rebelle," 56.

107. Michéa, *Impasse Adam Smith,* 18.

108. "Le temps obscur où nous sommes," *Immédiatement,* no. 16 (December 2000): 5.

109. A few months after this essay was written Michéa published another little book on Orwell entitled *Orwell éducateur* [Orwell as Teacher] (Castelnau-le-Lez: Editions Climats, 2003) in which he again has recourse to Orwell's "political philosophy" to evaluate "the present course of events and where it is taking us" (12) and to supply us with an intellectual "tool kit" (11) that we might use to free ourselves from the various "theologies that compose our Modernity" (20).

About the Contributors

Miquel Berga is Professor of English Literature at the Universitat Pompeu Fabra in Barcelona where he is currently Dean of the Humanities Faculty. His principal publications are *Entre la ploma i el fusell* (1981), a study of British writers who died in the Spanish Civil War; *Mil nou-cents vuitanta-quatre: radiografia d'un malson* (1984), on the Catalan influence in George Orwell's last novel; and *John Langdon-Davies: una biografía anglo-catalana* (1991). Berga has also edited various works by Langdon-Davies. A selection of his journalistic writing has been collected in the book *Amants i altres estranys* (2000) and he has recently edited the anthology *Cinco mujeres locas: cuentos góticos de la literatura norteamericana.* Berga has translated works by various contemporary British and American playwrights, the latest being Harold Pinter's *Betrayal (Engany)* (2001). Berga chairs APAC, the Association of Teachers of English in Catalonia.

Gilbert Bonifas is Professor of English History and Civilization at the University of Nice in France. He has published *George Orwell: L'Engagement* (1984) and written several articles on Orwell and his time. Bonifas is coauthor of *Pouvoir, classes et nation en Grande-Bretagne au XIXe siècle* (1993) and has recently selected and edited the French socialist Louis Blanc's letters on England (*Louis Blanc: Lettres d'Angleterre, 1861–1865* [2001]). When his chairmanship of the Department of English and American Studies at Nice allows, he currently researches ultra- and radical Tory thought in the nineteenth century.

William E. Cain is Mary Jewett Gaiser Professor of English and American Studies at Wellesley College. The author of *The Crisis in Criticism* (1984) and *F. O. Matthiessen and the Politics of Criticism* (1988), he has edited many books, including *William Lloyd Garrison and the Fight against Slavery: Selections from The Liberator* (1995), *The Blithedale Romance: A Cultural and Critical Edition* (1996), and *A Historical Guide to Henry David Thoreau* (2000). Cain is also the author of a study of American literary and cultural criticism from 1900 to 1950 that is included in *The Cambridge History of American Literature,* vol. 5.

Thomas Cushman is Professor of Sociology at Wellesley College and the founder and editor of *Journal of Human Rights.* He is the author of several books and numerous articles in the sociology of culture, human rights, genocide, and the war in Bosnia-Herzegovina. His recent books include *A Matter of Morality: Humanitarian Arguments for the War in Iraq* (editor, 2005) and *The Human Rights Case for the War in Iraq* (2005).

Morris Dickstein is Distinguished Professor of English at the Graduate Center of the City University of New York, where he teaches courses in literature, film, and American cultural history. He is a senior fellow of the Center for the Humanities, which he founded in 1993. His books include a study of the 1960s, *Gates of Eden* (1977), which was nominated for the National Book Critics Circle Award in criticism; *Double Agent: The Critic and Society* (1992); and *Leopards in the Temple,* a social history of postwar American fiction published in 2002 by the Harvard University Press. Dickstein's recent essays and reviews have appeared in the *New York Times Book Review,* the *Times Literary Supplement* (London), the *Washington Post, The American Scholar, The Nation,* the *Chronicle of Higher Education,* and *Partisan Review,* where he was a contributing editor from 1972 to 2003.

Todd Gitlin is the author of ten books, most recently *Letters to a Young Activist* and *Media Unlimited: How the Torrent of Image and Sound Overwhelms Our Lives.* His previous books include *The Twilight of Common Dreams: Why America Is Wracked by Culture Wars; The Sixties: Years of Hope, Days of Rage; Inside Prime Time; The Whole World Is Watching*; and two novels, *The Murder of Albert Einstein* and *Sacrifice.* He is Professor of Journalism and Sociology at Columbia University.

Erika Gottlieb is the author of *Dystopian Fiction East and West: Universe of Terror and Trial* (2001); *The Orwell Conundrum: A Cry of Despair or Faith in the Spirit of Man?* (1992); and *Lost Angels of a Ruined Paradise: Themes of Cosmic Strife in Romantic Tragedy* (1982). Her essays are published in *Contemporary Literary Criticism, Shakespearean Criticism,* and *Utopian Studies.* Gottlieb has taught at McGill and Concordia Universities in Montreal; at the Faculty of English in Budapest's ELTE University; and in Toronto at Seneca College and Ryerson Polytechnic University.

Christopher Hitchens is a Visiting Professor of Liberal Studies at New School University and a columnist for *Vanity Fair.* His book *Why Orwell Matters* was published in 2002.

Lynette Hunter is Professor of the History of Rhetoric at the University of Leeds and Professor of the History of Rhetoric and Performance at the University of California–Davis. She has written extensively on postmedieval literary criticism and book history, and her research interests are now moving toward explorations of democratic modes of access in the verbal arts within various kinds of contemporary democracies. Her two most recent books, *Critiques of Knowing* (2000) and *Literary Value/Cultural Power* (2002), have addressed the challenges posed by rhetorics of situated textuality and situated knowledge to the hegemonic rhetorics of discourse and cultural studies. Her book *George Orwell: The Search for a Voice* (1984) continues to be a primary study in the understanding of Orwell's rhetorical strategies.

Jonathan B. Imber is Class of 1949 Professor in Ethics and Professor of Sociology at Wellesley College. He has been Editor-in-chief of *Society* since 1997 and is the author and editor of seven books, including, most recently, *Therapeutic Culture: Triumph and Defeat.*

Daphne Patai was born in Jerusalem and emigrated to the United States as a child. She is Professor of Brazilian Literature at the University of Massachusetts Amherst, where she also teaches literary theory and utopian fiction. Among other books, she has written *Heterophobia: Sexual Harassment and the Future of Feminism* (1998); *Professing Feminism: Education and Indoctrination in Women's Studies* (coauthored with Noretta Koertge; new, enlarged edition, 2003); *Brazilian Women Speak: Contemporary Life Stories* (1988); and *The Orwell Mystique: A Study in Male Ideology* (1984). She is also coeditor of *Rediscovering Forgotten Radicals: British Women Writers 1889–1939* (1993) and *Women's Words: The Feminist Practice of Oral History* (1991). Her book *"What Price Utopia?" and Other Essays on Life and Literature* is forthcoming (2005). Together with Will H. Corral, she is currently editing a volume entitled *Theory's Empire: An Anthology of Dissent,* forthcoming (2005).

John Rodden is the author of *George Orwell: The Politics of Literary Reputation* (1989, 2002) and *Scenes from an Afterlife: The Legacy of George Orwell* (2003), among other books. He has also edited *Understanding Orwell: Animal Farm in Historical Context* (1999).

Jonathan Rose is Professor of History at Drew University. His most recent book, *The Intellectual Life of the British Working Classes* (2001), won the Jacques Barzun Prize in Cultural History, the Longman-History Today Historical Book of the Year Prize, and the British Council Prize. He edited *The Holocaust and the Book: Destruction and Preservation* (2001) and *The Revised Orwell* (1992). Currently he is writing a literary biography of Winston Churchill.

Lawrence Rosenwald is Anne Pierce Rogers Professor of English at Wellesley College. He has written extensively on American diaries, translation, and the relations between words and music; he has also published translations from Latin, French, German, and Yiddish. Rosenwald's current projects include a book on how American literature, both in English and in other languages, represents language contact, and a series of essays on various aspects of nonviolence.

Margery Sabin is Lorraine Chiu Wang Professor of English at Wellesley College. Her most recent book is *Dissenters and Mavericks: Writings about India in English, 1765–2000* (2002). She is also the author of *The Dialect of the Tribe: Speech and Community in Modern Fiction* (1987), *English Romanticism and the French Tradition* (1976), and numerous essays on topics in modern British and postcolonial literature, culture, and criticism.

Vladimir Shlapentokh is Professor of Sociology at Michigan State University. Before immigrating to the United States in 1979, he belonged to a group of the most distinguished Soviet sociologists. He conducted the first national polls in the Soviet Union in the 1960s and 1970s. In the United States, he has published more than a dozen scholarly books. One of Shlapentokh's latest academic works is *A Normal Totalitarian Society* (2001), which offers a new perspective on Soviet society. In addition to the publication of books and articles (some published in the *New York Times,* the *Washington Post,* the *Christian Science Monitor,* and the *Los Angeles Times*), he has recently published in Russian his memoir *Fear and Friendship in Our Totalitarian Past.*

Jim Sleeper, a journalist and writer on American national identity and political culture, was a political columnist for the *New York Daily News* in the mid-1990s and is a lecturer in political science at Yale. He is the author of *The Closest of Strangers: Liberalism and the Politics of Race* in New York (1990) and *Liberal Racism* (1997, 2003).

Peter Stansky teaches modern British history at Stanford University. With William Abrahams he wrote *The Unknown Orwell* (1972) and *Orwell: The Transformation* (1979). He edited a collection of essays about Orwell in 1984 and is at present at work on an anthology of pieces by and about Orwell.

Anthony Stewart is Assistant Professor of English literature at Dalhousie University in Halifax, Nova Scotia. He recently published *Orwell, Doubleness, and the Value of Decency* (2003). His recent article, "Penn and Teller Magic: Self, Racial Devaluation, and the Canadian Academy," appears *in Racism Eh? A Critical Inter-Disciplinary Anthology on Race in the Canadian Context* (2004). Stewart's current project examines how the fiction of Ralph Ellison, Hanif Kureishi, and Percival Everett critiques the commodification of otherness.

Ronald F. Thiemann is Professor of Theology and of Religion and Society at Harvard Divinity School and a Faculty Fellow of the Center for Public Leadership and the Hauser Center for Non-Profit Organizations at Harvard's Kennedy School of Government. For the past five years he has served on the steering committee of the Hauser Center's Intellectual Foundations project, and he has contributed essays to two volumes on faith-based institutions, *Who Will Provide: The Changing Role of Religion in American Social Welfare* (2000) and *Taking Religion Seriously* (2004). From 1986 to 1998 Thiemann served as Dean of the Divinity School and was also the founding director of Harvard's Center for the Study of Values in Public Life. A specialist on the role of religion in public life, Thiemann is the author of *Revelation and Theology: The Gospel as Narrated Promise* (1985), *Constructing a Public Theology: The Church in a Pluralistic Culture* (1991), and *Religion in Public Life: A Dilemma for Democracy* (1996). He is currently completing a book-length manuscript entitled "Prisoners of Conscience: Public Intellectuals in a Time of Crisis," which will include substantial material on George Orwell as public intellectual. Before coming to Harvard, Thiemann taught for ten years at Haverford College, where he also served as Acting Provost and Acting President. Among his many honors and awards are fellowships from the Lilly Endowment, the Mellon Foundation, and the DuBois Institute as well as honorary degrees from Wabash College and Trinity Seminary.

Ian Williams's first book, *The Alms Trade,* was published in 1989 and his second, *The UN for Beginners,* was published in 1995. *The Deserter: Bush's War on Military Families, Veterans and His Past* was published by Nation Books in July 2004. In 2004 he will have chapters published in *Why Kosovo Matters: The Debate on the Left Revisited,* edited by Danny Postel, and in *Irving Howe,* edited by John Rodden, and in 2005 he will have a chapter published in *The Iraq War,* edited by Rick Fawn and Raymond Hinnebusch. A prolific journalist, Williams is a regular columnist for George Orwell's old newspaper, *Tribune.* Born in Liverpool in 1949, he graduated from Liverpool University, despite several years' suspension for protests against its investments in South Africa. Consequently, he had a variegated career path, which included a drinking competition with Chinese Premier Chou En-lai and an argument on English literature with Chiang Ching, aka Mme Mao, and a spell as speech writer for British Labour leader Neil Kinnock in 1987. He now lives in New York.

Dennis Wrong is Professor Emeritus of Sociology at New York University. He is the author of many influential books in sociology and political theory, including *The Problem of Order: What Unites and Divides Society; Power: Its Forms, Bases, and Uses;* and *The Modern Condition: Essays at Century's End.*